Myths & Legends

Babylonia & Assyria

Assyrian Type of Gilgamesh

Contents: Babylonia & Assyria in History & Legend; Babylonian Cosmogony; Early Babylonian Religion; Gilgamesh Epic; Later Pantheon of Babylonia; Great God Merodach & His Cult; Pantheon of Assyria; Babylonia Star-Worship; Priesthood, Cult, & Temples; Magic & Demonology of Babylonia & Assyria; Mythological Monsters & Animals of Chaldea; Tales of the Babylonian & Assyrian Kings; Comparative Value of the Babylonian & Assyrian Religions; Modern Excavation in Babylonia & Assyria; Twilight of the Goods; Glossary & Index.

Lewis Spence

ISBN 1-56459-500-5

Request our FREE CATALOG of over 1,000
Rare Esoteric Books
Unavailable Elsewhere

Alchemy, Ancient Wisdom, Astronomy, Baconian, Eastern-Thought, Egyptology, Esoteric, Freemasonry, Gnosticism, Hermetic, Magic, Metaphysics, Mysticism, Mystery Schools, Mythology, Occult, Philosophy, Psychology, Pyramids, Qabalah, Religions, Rosicrucian, Science, Spiritual, Symbolism, Tarot, Theosophy, *and many more!*

Kessinger Publishing Company
Montana, U.S.A.

Sacrificing to Bel
Evelyn Paul

PREFACE

THE purpose of this book is to provide not only a popular account of the religion and mythology of ancient Babylonia and Assyria, but to extract and present to the reader the treasures of romance latent in the subject, the peculiar richness of which has been recognized since the early days of archæological effort in Chaldea. Unfortunately, with few exceptions, writers who have made the field a special study have rarely been able to triumph over the limitations which so often obtrude in works of scholarship and research. It is true that the pages of Rawlinson, Smith, Layard, and Sayce are enlivened at intervals with pictures of Assyrian splendour and Babylonian glory—gleams which escape as the curtains which veil the wondrous past are partially lifted—but such glimpses are only interludes in lengthy disquisitions which too often must be tedious for the general reader.

It was such a consideration which prompted the preparation of this volume. Might not a book be written which should contain the pure gold of Babylonian romance freed from the darker ore of antiquarian research? So far, so good. But gold in the pure state is notoriously unserviceable, and an alloy which renders it of greater utility may detract nothing from its brilliance. Romance or no romance, in these days it will not do to furnish stories of the gods without attempting some definition of their nature and origin. For more than ever before romance and knowledge are a necessary blend in the making of a satisfactory book on mythology.

Nevertheless, it is anticipated that it will be to the modern reader who loves the romance of antiquity that

MYTHS OF BABYLONIA AND ASSYRIA

this book will especially appeal. It is claimed that the greater part of Chaldean romance clusters around the wonderful mythology and religion of that land; it is therefore of these departments of Chaldean lore that this volume chiefly treats. But the history of Babylonia and Assyria has not been neglected. The great names in its records will be found to recur constantly in these pages, in most instances accompanied by a tale or legend which will illuminate the circumstances of their careers and serve to retain these in the mind of the reader. Nor has the Biblical connexion with Chaldea been forgotten; the reader will find as he proceeds frequent references to the pages of the most picturesque Book in the world.

L. S.

PREFACE

THE purpose of this book is to provide not only a popular account of the religion and mythology of ancient Babylonia and Assyria, but to extract and present to the reader the treasures of romance latent in the subject, the peculiar richness of which has been recognized since the early days of archæological effort in Chaldea. Unfortunately, with few exceptions, writers who have made the field a special study have rarely been able to triumph over the limitations which so often obtrude in works of scholarship and research. It is true that the pages of Rawlinson, Smith, Layard, and Sayce are enlivened at intervals with pictures of Assyrian splendour and Babylonian glory—gleams which escape as the curtains which veil the wondrous past are partially lifted—but such glimpses are only interludes in lengthy disquisitions which too often must be tedious for the general reader.

It was such a consideration which prompted the preparation of this volume. Might not a book be written which should contain the pure gold of Babylonian romance freed from the darker ore of antiquarian research? So far, so good. But gold in the pure state is notoriously unserviceable, and an alloy which renders it of greater utility may detract nothing from its brilliance. Romance or no romance, in these days it will not do to furnish stories of the gods without attempting some definition of their nature and origin. For more than ever before romance and knowledge are a necessary blend in the making of a satisfactory book on mythology.

Nevertheless, it is anticipated that it will be to the modern reader who loves the romance of antiquity that

MYTHS OF BABYLONIA AND ASSYRIA

this book will especially appeal. It is claimed that the greater part of Chaldean romance clusters around the wonderful mythology and religion of that land; it is therefore of these departments of Chaldean lore that this volume chiefly treats. But the history of Babylonia and Assyria has not been neglected. The great names in its records will be found to recur constantly in these pages, in most instances accompanied by a tale or legend which will illuminate the circumstances of their careers and serve to retain these in the mind of the reader. Nor has the Biblical connexion with Chaldea been forgotten; the reader will find as he proceeds frequent references to the pages of the most picturesque Book in the world.

L. S.

CONTENTS

CHAPTER		PAGE
I.	BABYLONIA AND ASSYRIA IN HISTORY AND LEGEND	11
II.	BABYLONIAN COSMOGONY	70
III.	EARLY BABYLONIAN RELIGION	88
IV.	THE GILGAMESH EPIC	154
V.	THE LATER PANTHEON OF BABYLONIA	184
VI.	THE GREAT GOD MERODACH AND HIS CULT	199
VII.	THE PANTHEON OF ASSYRIA	203
VIII.	BABYLONIAN STAR-WORSHIP	231
IX.	THE PRIESTHOOD, CULT, AND TEMPLES	239
X.	THE MAGIC AND DEMONOLOGY OF BABYLONIA AND ASSYRIA	257
XI.	THE MYTHOLOGICAL MONSTERS AND ANIMALS OF CHALDEA	289
XII.	TALES OF THE BABYLONIAN AND ASSYRIAN KINGS	299
XIII.	THE COMPARATIVE VALUE OF THE BABYLONIAN AND ASSYRIAN RELIGIONS	313
XIV.	MODERN EXCAVATION IN BABYLONIA AND ASSYRIA	339
XV.	THE TWILIGHT OF THE GODS	377
	GLOSSARY AND INDEX	381

LIST OF ILLUSTRATIONS

	PAGE
Sacrificing to Bel (*Evelyn Paul*) *Frontispiece*	
Assault on a City	16
Basalt Stele engraved with the Text of Khammurabi's Code of Laws	20
Sennacherib receiving Tribute	30
The Death of Sardanapalus (*L. Chalon*)	32
The Library of King Assur-bani-pal at Nineveh (*Fernand L. Quesne*)	36
Daniel interprets the Dream of Nebuchadrezzar (*Evelyn Paul*)	38
Grant of Privileges to Ritti-Marduk by Nebuchadrezzar I	40
Birs Nimrûd, the Tower of Babel	48
The Murder of Setapo (*Evelyn Paul*)	58
The Seven Tablets of Creation	70
" Mighty was he to look upon " (*Evelyn Paul*)	76
Conflict between Merodach and Tiawath	80
Types of En-lil, the Chief God of Nippur, and of his Consort Nin-lil	94
Ishtar, as (1) Mother-goddess, (2) Goddess of War, (3) Goddess of Love	124
The Mother-goddess Ishtar (*Evelyn Paul*)	136
Assyrian Rock Sculpture	148
Assyrian Type of Gilgamesh	162
Ut-Napishtim makes Offering to the Gods (*Allan Stewart*)	176
Nebo	184
Hall in Assyrian Palace (*Sir Henry Layard*)	196
Tiglath-Pileser I directed by Ninib (*Evelyn Paul*)	216

MYTHS OF BABYLONIA AND ASSYRIA

	PAGE
Assur-nazir-pal attended by a Winged Mythological Being	222
Zikkurats of the Anu-Adad at Ashur	242
Stage-tower at Samarra	242
Excavated Ruins of the Temple of E-Sagila	250
Exorcising Demons of Disease	262
Clay Object resembling a Sheep's Liver	282
Eagle-headed Mythological Being	296
Capture of Sarrapanu by Tiglath-Pileser II (*Evelyn Paul*)	300
The Fatal Eclipse (*M. Dovaston, R.B.A.*)	306
Shalmaneser I pouring out the Dust of a Conquered City (*Ambrose Dudley*)	308
The Marriage Market (*Edwin Long, R.A.*)	310
A Royal Hunt	318
Elijah prevailing over the Priests of Baal (*Evelyn Paul*)	326
The 'Black Obelisk' of Shalmaneser II	342
Outline of the Mounds at Nimrûd (*Sir Henry Layard*)	346
The Palaces of Nimrûd (*James Ferguson*)	348
Work of the Excavators in Babylon	354
Ruins of Babylon	366
The Hanging Gardens of Babylon (*M. Dovaston, R.B.A.*)	370

CHAPTER I: BABYLONIA AND ASSYRIA IN HISTORY AND LEGEND

TO our fathers until well-nigh a century ago Babylon was no more than a mighty name—a gigantic skeleton whose ribs protruded here and there from the sands of Syria in colossal ruin of tower and temple. But now the grey shroud which hid from view the remains of the glow and glitter of her ancient splendour has to some extent been withdrawn, and through the labours of a band of scholars and explorers whose lives and work must be classed as among the most romantic passages in the history of human effort we are now enabled to view the wondrous panorama of human civilization as it evolved in the valleys of the Tigris and Euphrates.

The name 'Babylon' carries with it the sound of a deep, mysterious spell, such a conjuration as might be uttered in the recesses of secret temples. It awakens a thousand echoes in the imagination. It holds a music richer than that of Egypt. Babylon, Babylon—the sonorous charm of the word is as a line from some great epic. It falls on the ear of the historian like distant thunder. Behind the grandeur of Rome and the beauty of Greece it looms as a great and thick darkness over which flash at intervals streams of uncertain light as half-forgotten kings and priests, conquerors and tyrants, demigods and mighty builders pass through the gloom from obscurity to obscurity—sometimes in the full glare of historical recognition, but more often in the half-light and partially relieved dusk of uncertainty. Other shapes, again, move like ghosts in complete and utter darkness, and these are by far the most numerous of all.

But the spirit of Babylon is no soft and alluring thing eloquent of Oriental wonders or charged with the delicious fascination of the East. Rather is it a thing stark and strong, informed with fate and epical in its intense recognition of destiny. In Babylonian history there are but two figures of moment—the soldier and the priest. We are dealing with a race austere and stern, a race of rigorous religious devotees and conquerors, the Romans of the East—but not an unimaginative race, for the Babylonians and Assyrians came of that stock which gave to the world its greatest religions, Judaism, Christianity, and Mohammedanism, a race not without the sense of mystery and science, for Babylon was the mother of astrology and magic, and established the beginnings of the study of the stars; and, lastly, of commerce, for the first true financial operations and the first houses of exchange were founded in the shadows of her temples and palaces.

The boundaries of the land where the races of Babylonia and Assyria evolved one of the most remarkable and original civilizations in the world's history are the two mighty rivers of Western Asia, the Tigris and Euphrates, Assyria being identical with the more northerly and mountainous portion, and Babylonia with the southerly part, which inclined to be flat and marshy. Both tracts of country were inhabited by people of the same race, save that the Assyrians had acquired the characteristics of a population dwelling in a hilly country and had become to some extent intermingled with Hittite and Amorite elements. But both were branches

THE AKKADIANS

of an ancient Semitic stock, the epoch of whose entrance into the land it is impossible to fix. In the oldest inscriptions discovered we find those Semitic immigrants at strife with the indigenous people of the country, the Akkadians, with whom they were subsequently to mingle and whose beliefs and magical and occult conceptions especially they were afterward to incorporate with their own.

The Akkadians

Who, then, were the Akkadians whom the Babylonian Semites came to displace but with whom they finally mingled? Great and bitter has been the controversy which has raged around the racial affinities of this people. Some have held that they were themselves of Semitic stock, others that they were of a race more nearly approaching the Mongol, the Lapp, and the Basque. In such a book as this, the object of which is to present an account of the Babylonian mythology, it is unnecessary to follow the protagonists of either theory into the dark recesses whither the conflict has led them. But the probability is that the Akkadians, who are usually represented upon their monuments as a beardless people with oblique eyes, were connected with that great Mongolian family which has thrown out tentacles from its original home in central Asia to the frozen regions of the Arctic, the north of Europe, the Turkish Empire, aye, and perhaps to America itself! Akkadian in its linguistic features and especially in its grammatical structure shows a resemblance to the Ural-Altaic group of languages which embraces Turkish and Finnish, and this is in itself good evidence that the people who spoke it belonged to that ethnic division. But the question is a thorny one, and pages, nay, volumes might be occupied in presenting the arguments for and against such a belief.

It was from the Akkadians, however, that the Babylonian Semites received the germs of their culture; indeed it may be avowed that this aboriginal people carried them well on the way toward civilization. Not only did they instruct the Semitic newcomers in the arts of writing and reading, but they strongly biased their religious beliefs, and so inspired them with the idea of the sanctity of their own faith that the later Babylonian priesthood preserved the old Akkadian tongue among them as a sacred language, just as the Roman priesthood has retained the use of the dead Latin speech. Indeed, the proper pronunciation of Akkadian was an absolute necessity to the successful performance of religious ritual, and it is passing strange to observe that the Babylonian priests composed new religious texts in a species of dog-Akkadian, just as the monks of the Middle Ages composed their writings in dog-Latin! —with such zeal have the religious in all ages clung to the cult of the ancient, the mystic and half-forgotten thing unknown to the vulgar.

When we first encounter Babylonian civilization we find it grouped round about two nuclei, Nippur in the North and Eridu in the South. The first had grown up around a sanctuary of the god En-lil, who held sway over the ghostly animistic spirits which at his bidding might pose as the friends or enemies of men. A more 'civilized' deity held sway at Eridu, which was the home of Ea, or Oannes, the god of light and wisdom, who exercised his knowledge of the healing art for the benefit of his votaries. From the waters of the Persian Gulf, whence he rose each morning, he brought knowledge of all manner of crafts and trades, arts and industries, for the behoof of his infant city, even the mystic and difficult art of impressing written characters on clay. It is a beautiful picture which we have from the old legend of this sea-born wisdom daily enlightening the life of the little white city near the waters. The Semites possessed a deep and almost instinctive love of wisdom. In the writings attributed to Solomon and in the rich and wondrous Psalms of David—those deep mines of song and sagacity—we find the glories of wisdom again and again extolled. Even yet there are few peoples among whom the love of scholarship, erudition, and religious wisdom is more cultivated for its own sake than with the Jews.

These rather different cultures of the North and South, working toward a common centre, met and fused at a period prior to the commencement of history, and we even find the city of Ur, whence Abram came, a near neighbour of Eridu, colonized by Nippur! The culture of Eridu prevailed nevertheless, and its mightiest offshoot was the ultimate centre of Euphratean civilization—Babylon itself. The first founders of the city were undoubtedly of Sumerian stock—the expression 'Sumerian' being that in vogue among modern scholars for the older 'Akkadian,' and therefore interchangeable with it.

The Semite Conquerors

It was probably about the time of the juncture of the civilizations of Eridu and Nippur that the Semites entered the country. There are indications which lead to the belief that, as in the case of the

MYTHS OF BABYLONIA AND ASSYRIA

Semitic immigrants in Egypt, they came originally from Arabia. The Semite readily accepted the Sumerian civilization which he found flourishing in the valley of the Euphrates, and adapted the Sumerian system of writing to his own language, in what manner will be indicated later. But the Sumerians themselves were not above borrowing from the rich Semitic tongue, and many of the earliest Sumerian texts we encounter are strongly Semitized. But although the Semites appear to have filtered into Sumerian territory by way of Eridu and Ur, the first definite notices we have of their presence within it are in the monuments of the more northern portion of that territory, in what is known as Akkad, in the neighbourhood of Bagdad, where they founded a small kingdom in much the same manner as the Jutes founded the kingdom of Kent. The earliest monuments, however, come from Lagash, the modern Tel-lo, some thirty miles north of Ur, and recount the dealings of the high-priest of that place with other neighbouring dignitaries. The priests of Lagash became kings, and their conquests extended beyond the confines of Babylonia to Elam on the east, and southward to the Persian Gulf.

A Babylonian Conqueror

But the first great Semitic empire in Babylonia was that founded by the famous Sargon of Akkad. As is the case with many popular heroes and monarchs whose deeds are remembered in song and story—for example, Perseus, Œdipus, Cyrus, Romulus, and our own King Arthur—the early years of Sargon were passed in obscurity. Sargon is, in fact, one of the 'fatal children.' He was, legend stated, born in concealment and sent adrift, like Moses, in an ark

Assault on a City
From a bas-relief representing the Campaigns of Sennacherib
Photo W. A. Mansell and Co.

of bulrushes on the waters of the Euphrates, whence he was rescued and brought up by one Akki, a husbandman. But the time of his recognition at length arrived, and he received the crown of Babylonia. His foreign conquests were extensive. On four successive occasions he invaded Syria and Palestine, which he succeeded in welding into a single empire with Babylonia. Pressing his victories to the margin of the Mediterranean, he erected upon its shores statues of himself as an earnest of his conquests. He also overcame Elam and northern Mesopotamia and quelled a rebellion of some magnitude in his own dominions. His son, Naram-Sin, claimed for himself the title of "King of the Four Zones," and enlarged the empire left him by his father, penetrating even into Arabia. A monument unearthed by J. de Morgan at Susa depicts him triumphing over the conquered Elamites. He is seen passing his spear through the prostrate body of a warrior whose hands are upraised as if pleading for quarter. His head-dress is ornamented with the horns emblematic of divinity, for the early Babylonian kings were the direct vicegerents of the gods on earth.

Even at this comparatively early time (*c.* 3800 B.C.) the resources of the country had been well exploited by its Semitic conquerors, and their absorption of the Sumerian civilization had permitted them to make very considerable progress in the enlightened arts. Some of their work in bas-relief, and even in the lesser if equally difficult craft of gem-cutting, is among the finest efforts of Babylonian art. Nor were they deficient in more utilitarian fields. They constructed roads through the most important portions of the empire, along which a service of posts carried messages at stated intervals, the letters conveyed by these being stamped or franked by clay seals, bearing the name of Sargon.

The First Library in Babylonia

Sargon is also famous as the first founder of a Babylonian library. This library appears to have contained works of a most surprising nature, having regard to the period at which it was instituted. One of these was entitled *The Observations of Bel*, and consisted of no less than seventy-two books dealing with astronomical matters of considerable complexity; it registered and described the appearances of comets, conjunctions of the sun and moon, and the phases of the planet Venus, besides recording many eclipses. This wonderful book was long afterward translated into Greek by the Babylonian historian Berossus, and it demonstrates the great antiquity of Babylonian astronomical science even at this very early epoch. Another famous work contained in the library of Sargon dealt with omens, the manner of casting them, and their interpretation—a very important side-issue of Babylonian magico-religious practice.

Among the conquests of this great monarch, whose splendour shines through the shadows of antiquity like the distant flash of arms on a misty day, was the fair island of Cyprus. Even imagination reels at the well-authenticated assertion that five thousand seven hundred years ago the keels of a Babylonian conqueror cut the waves of the Mediterranean and landed upon the shores of flowery Cyprus stern Semitic warriors, who, loading themselves with loot, erected statues of their royal leader and returned with their booty. In a Cyprian temple De Cesnola discovered, down in the lowest vaults, a hæmatite cylinder which described its owner as a servant of Naram-Sin, the son of Sargon, so that a certain degree of communication must have been kept up between Babylonia and the distant island, just as early Egypt and Crete were bound to each other by ties of culture and commerce.

Gudea

But the empire which Sargon had founded was doomed to precipitate ruin. The seat of power was diverted southward to Ur. In the reign of Dungi, one of the monarchs who ruled from this southern sphere, a great vassal of the throne, Gudea, stands out as one of the most remarkable characters in early Babylonian antiquity. This Gudea (*c.* 2700 B.C.) was high-priest of Lagash, a city perhaps thirty miles north of Ur, and was famous as a patron of the architectural and allied arts. He ransacked western Asia for building materials. Arabia supplied him with copper for ornamentation, the Amames mountains with cedar-wood, the quarries of Lebanon with stone, while the deserts adjacent to Palestine furnished him with rich stones of all kinds for use in decorative work, and districts on the shores of the Persian Gulf with timber for ordinary building purposes. His architectural ability is vouched for by a plan of his palace, measured to scale, which is carved upon the lap of one of his statues in the Louvre.

There is no intention in this sketch to follow minutely the events in the history of Babylonia and Assyria. The purpose is to depict and describe the circumstances, deeds, and times of its most outstanding figures, its most typical and characteristic rulers. By following this plan we hope to be better able to present the reader with a more faithful and genuine picture of the civilization the myths of which we are about to peruse, than if we squandered space and time in the description of the reigns of kings during whose tenure of the throne no event of importance is recorded.

Khammurabi the Great

Like that which preceded it, the dynasty of Ur fell, and Arabian or Canaanite invaders usurped the royal power in much the same manner as the Shepherd Kings seized the sovereignty of Egypt. A subsequent foreign yoke, that of Elam, was thrown off by Khammurabi, perhaps the most celebrated and most popularly famous name in Babylonian history. This brilliant, wise, and politic monarch did not content himself with merely expelling the hated Elamites, but advanced to further conquest with such success that in the thirty-second year of his reign (2338 B.C.) he had formed Babylonia into a single monarchy with the capital at Babylon itself. Under the fostering care of Khammurabi, Babylonian art and literature unfolded and blossomed with a luxuriance surprising to contemplate at this distance of time. It is astonishing, too, to note how completely he succeeded in welding into one homogeneous whole the various elements of the empire he carved out for himself. So surely did he unify his conquests that the Babylonian power as he left it survived undivided for nearly fifteen hundred years. The welfare of his subjects of all races was constantly his care. No one satisfied of the justice of his cause feared to approach him. The legal code which he formulated and which remains as his greatest claim to the

Basalt Stele engraved with the Text of Khammurabi's Code of Laws

The scene represents the King receiving the Laws from Shamash, the Sun-god

Photo W. A. Mansell and Co.

KHAMMURABI THE GREAT

applause of posterity is a monument of wisdom and equity. If Sargon is to be regarded as the Arthur of Babylonian history surely Khammurabi is its Alfred. The circumstances of the lives of the two monarchs present a decidedly similar picture. Both had in their early years to free their country from a foreign yoke, both instituted a legal code, were patrons of letters and assiduous in their attention to the wants of their subjects.

If a great people has frequently evolved a legal code of sterling merit there are cases on record where such an institution has served to make a people great, and it is probably no injustice to the Semites of Babylonia to say of them that the code of Khammurabi made them what they were. A copy of this world-famous code was found at Susa by J. de Morgan, and is now in the Louvre.

What the Babylonian chronologists called 'the First Dynasty of Babylon' fell in its turn, and it is claimed that a Sumerian line of eleven kings took its place. Their sway lasted for 368 years—a statement which is obviously open to question. These were themselves overthrown and a Kassite dynasty from the mountains of Elam was founded by Kandis (c. 1780 B.C.) which lasted for nearly six centuries. These alien monarchs failed to retain their hold on much of the Asiatic and Syrian territory which had paid tribute to Babylon and the suzerainty of Palestine was likewise lost to them. It was at this epoch, too, that the high-priests of Asshur in the north took the title of king, but they appear to have been subservient to Babylon in some degree. Assyria grew gradually in power. Its people were hardier and more warlike than the art-loving and religious folk of Babylon, and little by little they encroached upon the weakness of the southern kingdom until at length an affair of tragic proportions entitled them to direct interference in Babylonian politics.

A Court Murder

The circumstances which necessitated this intervention are not unlike those of the assassination of King Alexander of Serbia and Draga, his Queen, that happened 3000 years later. The Kassite king of Babylonia had married the daughter of Assur-yuballidh of Assyria. But the match did not meet with the approval of the Kassite faction at court, which murdered the bridegroom-king. This atrocious act met with swift vengeance at the hands of Assur-yuballidh of Assyria, the bride's father, a monarch of active and statesmanlike qualities, the author of the celebrated series of letters to Amen-hetep IV of Egypt, unearthed at Tel-el-Amarna. He led a punitive army into Babylonia, hurled from the throne the pretender placed there by the Kassite faction, and replaced him with a scion of the legitimate royal stock. This king, Burna-buryas, reigned for over twenty years, and upon his decease the Assyrians, still nominally the vassals of the Babylonian Crown, declared themselves independent of it. Not content with such a revolutionary measure, under Shalmaneser I (1300 B.C.) they laid claim to the suzerainty of the Tigris-Euphrates region, and extended their conquests even to the boundaries of far Cappadocia, the Hittites and numerous other confederacies submitting to their yoke. Shalmaneser's son, Tukulti-in-Aristi, took the city of Babylon, slew its king, Bitilyasu, and thus completely shattered the claim of the older state to supremacy. He had reigned in Babylon for some

TIGLATH-PILESER

seven years when he was faced by a popular revolt, which seems to have been headed by his own son, Assur-nazir-pal, who slew him and placed Hadad-nadin-akhi on the throne. This king conquered and killed the Assyrian monarch of his time, Bel-kudur-uzur, the last of the old Assyrian royal line, whose death necessitated the institution of a new dynasty, the fifth monarch of which was the famous Tiglath-pileser I.

Tiglath-Pileser

Tiglath-pileser, or Tukulti-pal-E-sana, to confer on him his full Assyrian title, came to the throne about 1120 B.C., and soon commenced the career of active conquest which was to render his name one of the most famous in the warlike annals of Assyria. Campaigns in the Upper Euphrates against alien immigrants who had settled there were followed by the conquest of the Hittites of Subarti, in Assyrian territory. Pressing northward toward Lake Van in the Kurdish country he subsequently turned his arms westward and overran Malatia. Cappadocia and the Aramæans of Northern Syria next felt the force of his arms, and he penetrated on this occasion even to the sources of the Tigris. He left behind him the character of a great warrior, a great hunter, and a great builder, restoring the semi-ruinous temples of Asshur and Hadad or Rimmon in the city of Asshur.

It is not until the reign of Assur-nazir-pal III (*c.* 883 B.C.) that we are once more enabled to take up the thread of Assyrian history with any degree of certainty. In this reign artistic development appears to have proceeded apace; but it cannot be said of Assur-nazir-pal that in him culture went hand in hand with humanity, the records of his cruelties being long and revolting. His successor, Shalmaneser II, possessed an insatiable thirst for military glory, and during his reign of thirty-five years overthrew a great confederacy of Syrian chiefs which included Ahab, King of Israel. He was disturbed during the latter part of his reign by the rebellion of his eldest son. But his second son, Samsi-Rammon, came to his father's assistance, and his faithful adherence secured him the succession to the throne in 824 B.C.

Semiramis the Great

It was probably in the reign of this monarch that the queen known in legend as Semiramis lived. It would have been wonderful indeed had the magic of her name not been connected with romance by the Oriental imagination. Semiramis! The name sparkles and scintillates with gems of legend and song. Myth, magic, and music encircle it and sweep round it as fairy seas surround some island paradise. It is a central rose in the chaplet of legend, it has been enshrined in music perhaps the most divine and melodious which the songful soul of Italy has ever conceived—yet not more beauteous than itself. Let us introduce into the iron chain of Assyrian history the golden link of the legend of this Helen of the East, and having heard the fictions of her greatness let us attempt to remove the veils which hide her real personality from view and look upon her as she was—Sammuramat the Babylonian, queen and favourite of Samsi-Rammon, who crushed the assembled armies of Media and Chaldea, and whose glories are engraved upon a column which, setting forth the tale of her conquests, describes her in all simplicity as "A woman of the palace of Samsi-Rammon, King of the World."

Legend says that Ninus, King of Assyria, having conquered the Babylonians, proceeded toward Armenia with the object of reducing the people of that country. But its politic king, Barsanes, unable to meet him by armed force, made a voluntary submission, accompanied by presents of such magnificence that Ninus was placated. But, insatiable in his desire for conquest, he turned his eyes to Media, which he speedily subdued. His next ambition was to bring under his rule the territory between the Tanais and the Nile. This great task occupied him for no less than seventeen years, by which time all Asia had submitted to him, with the single exception of Bactria, which still maintained its independence. Having laid the foundations of the city of Nineveh, he resolved to proceed against the Bactrians. His army was of dimensions truly mythical, for he was said to be accompanied by 7,000,000 of infantrymen, 2,000,000 of horse-soldiers, with the addition of 200,000 chariots equipped with scythes.

It was during this campaign, says Diodorus Siculus, that Ninus first beheld Semiramis. Her precise legendary or mythical origin is obscure. Some writers aver that she was the daughter of the fish-goddess Ataryatis, or Derketo, and Oannes, the Babylonian god of wisdom, who has already been alluded to. Ataryatis was a goddess of Ascalon in Syria, and after birth her daughter Semiramis was miraculously fed by doves until she was found by one Simmas, the royal shepherd, who brought her up and married her to Onnes, or Menon, one of Ninus's generals. He fell by his own hand, and Ninus thereupon took Semiramis to wife, having profoundly admired her ever since her conduct at the capture of Bactria, where she had greatly distinguished herself. Not long afterward Ninus died, leaving a son called Ninyas. During her son's minority Semiramis assumed the regency, and the first great work she undertook was the interment of her husband, whom she buried with great splendour, and raised over him a mound of earth no less than a mile and a quarter high and proportionally wide, after which she built Babylon. This city being finished, she made an expedition into Media; and wherever she went left memorials of her power and munificence. She erected vast structures, forming lakes and laying out gardens of great extent, particularly in Chaonia and Ecbatana. In short, she levelled hills, and raised mounds of an immense height, which retained her name for ages. After this she invaded Egypt and conquered Ethiopia, with the greater part of Libya; and having accomplished her wish, and there being no enemy to cope with her, excepting the kingdom of India, she resolved to direct her forces toward that quarter. She had an army of 3,000,000 foot, 500,000 horse, and 100,000 chariots. For the passing of rivers and engaging the enemy by water she had procured 2000 ships, to be so constructed as to be taken to pieces for the advantage of carriage: which ships were built in Bactria by men from Phœnicia, Syria, and Cyprus. With these she fought a naval engagement with Strabrobates, King of India, and at the first encounter sunk a thousand of his ships. After this she built a bridge over the river Indus, and penetrated into the heart of the country. Here Strabrobates engaged her. Being deceived by the numerous appearance of her elephants, he at first gave way, for being deficient in those animals she had procured the hides of 3000 black oxen, which, being properly sewn and stuffed with straw, presented the appearance of so many elephants. All this was done so naturally that even the real elephants of the Indian king were deceived. But the stratagem was at last discovered, and Semiramis was obliged to retreat, after having lost a great part of her army. Soon after this she resigned the government to her son Ninyas, and died. According to some writers, she was slain by his hand.

It was through the researches of Professor Lehmann-Haupt of Berlin that the true personal significance of Semiramis was recovered. Until the year 1910 the legends of Diodorus and others were held to have been completely disproved and Semiramis was regarded as a purely mythical figure. Old Bryant in his *Antient Mythology*, published at the beginning of last century, proves the legendary status of Semiramis to his own satisfaction. He says: " It must be confessed that the generality of historians have represented Semiramis as a woman, and they describe her as a great princess who reigned in Babylon; but there are writers who from their situation had opportunities of better intelligence, and by those she is mentioned as a deity. The Syrians, says Athenagoras, worshipped Semiramis, and adds that she was esteemed the daughter of Dercatus and the same as the Suria Dea. . . . Semiramis was said to have been born at Ascalon because Atargatus was there worshipped under the name of Dagon, and the same memorials were preserved there as at Hierapolis and Babylon. These memorials related to a history of which the dove was the principal type. It was upon the same account that she was said to have been changed to a dove because they found her always depicted and worshipped under that form.... From the above I think it is plain that Semiramis was an emblem and that the name was a compound of Sama-ramas, or ramis, and it signified 'the divine token,' a type of providence, and as a military ensign, (for as such it was used) it may with some latitude be interpreted 'the standard of the most High.' It consisted of the figure of a dove, which was probably encircled with the iris, as those two emblems were often represented together. All who went under that standard, or who paid any deference to that emblem, were styled Semarim or Samorim. It was a title conferred upon all who had this device for their national insigne." There is much more of this sort of thing, typical of the mythic science of the eighteenth and early nineteenth centuries. It is easy to see how myth became busy with the name of the Assyrian Queen, whose exploits undoubtedly aroused the enthusiasm not only of the Assyrians themselves but of the peoples surrounding them. Just as any great work in ancient Britain was ascribed to the agency of Merlin or Arthur, so such monuments as could not otherwise be accounted for were attributed to Semiramis. Western Asia is monumentally eloquent of her name, and even the Behistun inscriptions of Darius have been placed to her credit. Herodotus states that one of the gates of Babylon was called after her, and that she raised the artificial banks that confined the river Euphrates. Her fame lasted until well into the Middle Ages, and the Armenians called the district round Lake Van, Shamiramagerd.

There is very little doubt that her fame became mingled with that of the goddess Ishtar: she possesses the same Venus-like attributes, the dove is her emblem, and her story became so inextricably intertwined with that of the Babylonian goddess that she ultimately became a variant of her. The story of Semiramis is a triumphant vindication of the manner in which by certain mythical processes a human being can attain the rank of a god or goddess, for Semiramis was originally very real indeed. A column discovered in 1909 describes her as " a woman of the palace of Samsi-rammon, King of the World, King of Assyria, King of the Four Quarters of the World." This dedication indicates that Semiramis, or, to give her her Assyrian title, Sammuramat, evidently possessed an immense influence over her husband, Samsi-rammon, and that perhaps as queen-mother that influence lasted for more than one reign, so that the legend that after a regency of forty-two years she delivered up the kingdom to her son, Ninyas, may have some foundation in fact. She seems to have made war against the Medes and Chaldeans. The story that on relinquishing her power she turned into a dove and disappeared may mean that her name, Sammuramat, was easily connected with the Assyrian *summat*, the word for 'dove'; and for a person of her subsequent legendary fame the mythical connexion with Ishtar is easily accounted for.

The Second Assyrian Empire

What is known as the Second Assyrian Empire commenced with the reign of Tiglath-pileser III, who organized a great scheme of provincial government. This plan appears to have been the first forecast of the feudal system, for each province paid a fixed tribute and provided a military contingent.

Great efforts were made to render the army as

irresistible as possible with the object of imposing an Assyrian supremacy upon the entire known world. Tiglath overran Armenia, defeated the Medes and Hittites, seized the seaports of Phœnicia and the trade routes connecting them with the centres of Assyrian commerce, and finally conquered Babylon, where in 729 B.C. he was invested with the sovereignty of 'Asia.' Two years later he died, but his successor, Shalmaneser IV, carried on the policy he had initiated. He had, however, only five years of life in which to do so, for at the end of that period the usurping general Sargon, who laid claim to be a descendant of Sargon the Great of Akkad, seized the royal power of Babylon. He was murdered in 705 B.C., and his son Sennacherib, of Biblical fame, appears to have been unable to carry on affairs with the prudence or ability of his father. He outraged the religious feelings of the people by razing to the ground the city of Babylon, because of the revolt of the citizens. The campaign he made against Hezekiah, King of Judah, was marked by a complete failure. Hezekiah had allied himself with the Philistine princes of Ascalon and Ekron, but when he saw his Egyptian allies beaten at the battle of Eltekeh he endeavoured to buy off the invaders by numerous presents, though without success. The wonderful deliverance of Jerusalem from the forces of Sennacherib, recorded in Scripture, and sung by Byron in his *Hebrew Melodies*, appears to have a good foundation in fact. It seems that the Assyrian army was attacked and almost decimated by plague, which obliged Sennacherib to return to Nineveh, but it is not likely that the phenomenon occurred in the watch of a night. Sennacherib was eventually murdered by his two sons, who, the deed accomplished, fled to

Sennacherib receiving Tribute
From the Palace at Nineveh
Photo W. A. Mansell and Co.

SARDANAPALUS THE SPLENDID

Armenia. Of all the Assyrian monarchs he was perhaps the most pompous and the least fitted to rule. The great palace at Nineveh and the great wall of that city, eight miles in circumference, were built at his command.

His son and successor, Esar-haddon, initiated his reign by sending back the sacred image of Merodach to its shrine at Babylon, which city he restored. He was solemnly declared king in the restored temple of Merodach, and during his reign both Babylonia and Assyria enjoyed quiet and contentment. War with Egypt broke out in 670 B.C., and the Egyptians were thrice defeated with heavy loss. The Assyrians entered Memphis and instituted a protectorate over part of the country. Two years later Egypt revolted, and while marching to quell the outbreak Esar-haddon died on the road—his fate resembling that of Edward I, who died while on his way to overcome the Scottish people, then in rebellion against his usurpation.

Sardanapalus the Splendid

Esar-haddon was succeeded by Assur-bani-pal, known to Greek legend as Sardanapalus. How far the legendary description of him squares with the historical it is difficult to say. The former states that he was the last king of Assyria, and the thirtieth in succession from Ninyas. Effeminate and corrupt, he seems to have been a perfect example of the *roi fainéant*. The populace of the conquered provinces, disgusted with his extravagances, revolted, and an army led by Arbaces, satrap of Medea, and Belesys, a Babylonian priest, surrounded him in Nineveh and threatened his life. Sardanapalus, however, throwing off his sloth, made such a vigorous defence that for two years the issue was in doubt. The river Tigris at this juncture overflowed and undermined part of the city wall, thus permitting ingress to the hostile army. Sardanapalus, seeing that resistance was hopeless, collected his wives and treasures in his palace and then set it on fire, so that all perished.

It is a strange coincidence that the fate which legend ascribes to Sardanapalus was probably that which really overtook the brother of Assur-bani-pal, Samas-sum-yukin. It is likely that the self-immolation of Sardanapalus is merely a legendary statement of a rite well known to Semitic religion, which was practised at Tarsus down to the time of Dio Chrysostom, and the memory of which survives in other Greek legends, especially those of Heracles-Melcarth and Queen Dido. At Tarsus an annual festival was held and a pyre erected upon which the local Heracles or Baal was burned in effigy. This annual commemoration of the death of the god in fire probably had its origin in the older rite in which an actual man or sacred animal was burned as representing the deity. *The Golden Bough*[1] contains an instructive passage concerning the myth of Sardanapalus. Sir James Frazer writes: " There seems to be no doubt that the name Sardanapalus is only the Greek way of representing Ashurbanapal, the name of the greatest and nearly the last King of Assyria. But the records of the real monarch which have come to light within recent years give little support to the fables that attached to his name in classical tradition. For they prove that, far from being the effeminate weakling he seemed to the Greeks of a later age, he was a warlike and enlightened

[1] Vol. iii, p. 167. Second Edition. (By kind permission of Messrs Macmillan and Co.)

The Death of Sardanapalus
L. Chalon
Copyright, Braun and Co.

SARDANAPALUS THE SPLENDID

monarch, who carried the arms of Assyria to distant lands and fostered at home the growth of science and letters. Still, though the historical reality of King Ashurbanapal is as well attested as that of Alexander or Charlemagne, it would be no wonder if myths gathered, like clouds, around the great figure that loomed large in the stormy sunset of Assyrian glory. Now the two features that stand out most prominently in the legends of Sardanapalus are his extravagant debauchery and his violent death in the flames of a great pyre, on which he burned himself and his concubines to save them from falling into the hands of his victorious enemies. It is said that the womanish king, with painted face and arrayed in female attire, passed his days in the seclusion of the harem, spinning purple wool among his concubines and wallowing in sensual delights; and that in the epitaph which he caused to be carved on his tomb he recorded that all the days of his life he ate and drank and toyed, remembering that life is short and full of trouble, that fortune is uncertain, and that others would soon enjoy the good things which he must leave behind. These traits bear little resemblance to the portrait of Ashurbanapal either in life or death; for after a brilliant career of conquest the Assyrian king died in old age, at the height of human ambition, with peace at home and triumph abroad, the admiration of his subjects and the terror of his foes. But if the traditional characteristics of Sardanapalus harmonize but ill with what we know of the real monarch of that name, they fit well enough with all that we know or can conjecture of the mock kings who led a short life and a merry during the revelry of the Sacæa, the Asiatic equivalent of the Saturnalia. We can hardly doubt that for the most part such men, with death staring them in the face at the end of a few days, sought to drown care and deaden fear by plunging madly into all the fleeting joys that still offered themselves under the sun. When their brief pleasures and sharp sufferings were over, and their bones or ashes mingled with the dust, what more natural that on their tomb—those mounds in which the people saw, not untruly, the graves of the lovers of Semiramis—there should be carved some such lines as those which tradition placed in the mouth of the great Assyrian king, to remind the heedless passer-by of the shortness and vanity of life?"

According to Sir James Frazer, then, the real Sardanapalus may have been one of those mock kings who led a short but merry existence before a sacrifice ended their convivial career. We have analogous instances in the sacrifice of Sandan at Tarsus and that of the representative of the Mexican god, Tezcatlipoca. The legend of Sardanapalus is thus a distorted reminiscence of the death of a magnificent king sacrificed in name of a god.

When the real Assur-bani-pal succeeded Esarhaddon as King of Assyria, his brother Samas-sum-yukin was created Viceroy of Babylonia, but shortly after he claimed the kingship itself, revived the old Sumerian language as the official tongue of the Babylonian court, and initiated a revolt which shook the Assyrian empire from one end to the other. A great struggle ensued between the northern and southern powers, and at last Babylon was forced to surrender through starvation, and Samus-sum-yukin was put to death.

Assur-bani-pal, like Sardanapalus, his legendary

counterpart, found himself surrounded by enemies. Having conquered Elam as well as Babylonia, he had to face the inroads of hordes of Scythians, who poured over his frontiers. He succeeded in defeating and slaying one of their chiefs, Dugdamme, whom in an inscription he calls a "limb of Satan," but shortly after this he died himself. His empire was already in a state of decay, and had not long to stand.

The First Great Library

But if Assur-bani-pal was effeminate and lax in government, he was the first great patron of literature. It is to his magnificent library at Nineveh that we owe practically all that we have preserved of the literature that was produced in Babylonia. He saw that the southern part of his empire was far more intellectual and cultured than Assyria, and he despatched numerous scribes to the temple schools of the south, where they copied extensively from their archives every description of literary curiosity—hymns, legends, medical prescriptions, myths and rituals were all included in the great library at Nineveh. These through the labours of Layard and Rassam have been restored to us. It is a most extraordinary instance of antiquarian zeal in an epoch which we regard as not far distant from the beginnings of verifiable history. Nearly twenty thousand fragments of brick, bearing the results of Assur-bani-pal's researches, are housed in the British Museum, and this probably represents only a portion of his entire collection. Political motives have been attributed to Assur-bani-pal in thus bringing together such a great library. It has been argued that he desired to make Assyria the centre of the religious influence of the empire. This would derogate greatly from the view that sees in him a king solely fired with the idea of preserving and retaining all that was best in ancient Babylonian literature in the north as well as in the south, and having beside him for his own personal use those records which many circumstances prove he was extremely desirous of obtaining. Thus we find him sending officials on special missions to obtain copies of certain works. It is also significant that Assur-bani-pal placed his collection in a library and not in a temple—a fact which discounts the theory that his collection of literature had a religious-political basis.

The Last Kings of Assyria

After the death of Assur-bani-pal the Scythians succeeded in penetrating into Assyria, through which they pushed their way as far as the borders of Egypt, and the remains of the Assyrian army took refuge in Nineveh. The end was now near at hand. The last King of Assyria was probably Sin-sar-iskin, the Sarakos of the Greeks, who reigned for some years and who even tells us through the medium of inscriptions that he intended to restore the ruined temples of his land. War broke out with Babylonia, however, and Cyaxares, the Scythian King of Ecbatana, came to the assistance of the Babylonians. Nineveh was captured by the Scythians, sacked and destroyed, and the Assyrian empire was at an end.

Nebuchadrezzar

But strangely enough the older seat of power, Babylon, still flourished to some extent. By superhuman exertions, Nebuchadrezzar II (or Nebuchadnezzar), who reigned for forty-three years, sent the

The Library of King Assur-bani-pal at Nineveh
Fernand Le Quesne
By permission of Messrs Hutchinson and Co.

NEBUCHADREZZAR

standard of Babylonia far and wide through the known world. In 567 B.C. he invaded Egypt. In one of his campaigns he marched against Jerusalem and put its king, Jehoiakim, to death, but the king whom the Babylonian monarch set up in his place was deposed and the royal power vested in Zedekiah. Zedekiah revolted in 558 B.C. and once more Jerusalem was taken and destroyed, the principal inhabitants were carried captive to Babylon, and the city was reduced to a condition of insignificance. This, the first exile of the Jews, lasted for seventy years. The story of this captivity and of Nebuchadrezzar's treatment of the Jewish exiles is graphically told in the Book of Daniel, whom the Babylonians called Belteshazzar. Daniel refused to eat the meat of the Babylonians, probably because it was not prepared according to Jewish rite. He and his companions ate pulse and drank water, and fared upon it better than the Babylonians on strong meats and wines. The King, hearing of this circumstance, sent for them and found them much better informed than all his magicians and astrologers. Nebuchadrezzar dreamed dreams, and informed the Babylonian astrologers that if they were unable to interpret them they would be cut to pieces and their houses destroyed, whereas did they interpret the visions they would be held in high esteem. They answered that if the King would tell them his dream they would show the interpretation thereof; but the King said that if they were wise men in truth they would know the dream without requiring to be told it, and upon some of the astrologers of the court replying that the request was unreasonable, he was greatly incensed and ordered all of them to be slain. But in a vision of the night the secret was revealed to Daniel, who begged that the wise men of Babylon be not destroyed, and going to a court official he offered to interpret the dream. He told the King that in his dream he had beheld a great image, whose brightness and form were terrible. The head of this image was of fine gold, the breast and arms of silver, and the other parts of brass, excepting the legs which were of iron, and the feet which were partly of that metal and partly of clay. But a stone was cast at it which smote the image upon its feet and it brake into pieces and the wind swept away the remnants. The stone that had smitten it became a great mountain and filled the whole earth.

Then Daniel proceeded to the interpretation. The King, he said, represented the golden head of the image; the silver an inferior kingdom which would rise after Nebuchadrezzar's death; and a third of brass which should bear rule over all the earth. The fourth dynasty from Nebuchadrezzar would be as strong as iron, but since the toes of the image's feet were partly of iron and partly of clay, so should that kingdom be partly strong and partly broken. Nebuchadrezzar was so awed with the interpretation that he fell upon his face and worshipped Daniel, telling him how greatly he honoured the God who could have revealed such secrets to him; and he set him as ruler over the whole province of Babylon, and made him chief of the governors over all the wise men of that kingdom.

But Daniel's three companions—Shadrach, Meshach, and Abednego—refused to worship a golden image which the King had set up, and he commanded that they should be cast into a fiery furnace, through which they passed unharmed.

This circumstance still more turned the heart.

Daniel interprets the Dream of Nebuchadrezzar
Evelyn Paul

NEBUCHADREZZAR

of Nebuchadrezzar in the direction of the God of Israel. A second dream which he had, he begged Daniel to interpret. He said he had seen a tree in the midst of the earth of more than natural height, which flourished and was exceedingly strong, so that it reached to heaven. So abundant was the fruit of this tree that it provided meat for the whole earth, and so ample its foliage that the beasts of the field had shadow under it, and the fowls of the air dwelt in its midst. A spirit descended from heaven and called aloud, demanding that the tree should be cut down and its leaves and fruit scattered, but that its roots should be left in the earth surrounded by a band of iron and brass. Then, ordering that the tree should be treated as if it were a man, the voice of the spirit continued to ask that it should be wet with the dew of heaven, and that its portion should be with the beasts in the grass of the earth. " Let his heart be changed from a man's," said the voice, " and let a beast's heart be given him; and let seven times pass over him."

Then was Daniel greatly troubled. He kept silence for a space until the King begged him to take heart and speak. The tree, he announced, represented Nebuchadrezzar himself, and what had happened to it in the vision would come to pass regarding the great King of Babylon. He would be driven from among men and his dwelling would be with the beasts of the field. He would be made to eat grass as oxen and be wet with the dew of heaven, and seven times would pass over him, till he knew and recognized that the Most High ruled in the kingdom of man and gave it to whomsoever he desired.

Twelve months after this Nebuchadrezzar was in the midst of his palace at Babylon, boasting of what he had accomplished during his reign, when a voice from heaven spake, saying: "O King Nebuchadrezzar, to thee it is spoken, the kingdom is departed from thee," and straightway was Nebuchadrezzar driven from man and he did eat grass as an ox and his body was wet with the dew of heaven, till his hair was grown like eagle's feathers and his nails like bird's claws.

At the termination of his time of trial Nebuchadrezzar lifted his eyes to heaven, and praising the Most High admitted his domination over the whole earth. Thus was the punishment of the boaster completed.

It has been stated with some show of probability that the judgment upon Nebuchadrezzar was connected with that weird disease known as lycanthropy, from the Greek words *lukos*, a wolf, and *anthropos*, a man. It develops as a kind of hysteria and is characterized by a belief on the part of the victim that he has become an animal. There are, too, cravings for strange food, and the afflicted person runs about on all fours. Among primitive peoples such a seizure is ascribed to supernatural agency, and garlic or onion—the common scourge of vampires—is held to the nostrils.

The Last of the Babylonian Kings

Nabonidus (555-539 B.C.) was the last of the Babylonian kings—a man of a very religious disposition and of antiquarian tastes. He desired to restore the temple of the moon-god at Harran and to restore such of the images of the gods as had been removed to the ancient shrines. But first he

Grant of Privileges to Ritti-Marduk, a famous Babylonian Captain, by Nebuchadrezzar I

Photo W. A. Mansell and Co.

THE LAST OF THE BABYLONIAN KINGS

desired to find out whether this procedure would meet with the approval of the god Merodach. To this end he consulted the augurs, who opened the liver of a sheep and drew thence favourable omens. But on another occasion he aroused the hostility of the god and incidentally of the priests of E-Sagila by preferring the sun-god to the great Bel of Babylon. He tells us in an inscription that when restoring the temple of Shamash at Sippar he had great difficulty in unearthing the old foundation-stone, and that, when at last it was unearthed, he trembled with awe as he read thereon the name of Naram-sin, who, he says, ruled 3200 years before him. But destiny lay in wait for him, for Cyrus the Persian invaded Babylonia in 538 B.C., and after defeating the native army at Opis he pressed on to Babylon, which he entered without striking a blow. Nabonidus was in hiding, but his place of concealment was discovered. Cyrus, pretending to be the avenger of Bel-Merodach for the slights the unhappy Nabonidus had put upon the god, had won over the people, who were exceedingly wroth with their monarch for attempting to remove many images of the gods from the provinces to the capital. Cyrus placed himself upon the throne of Babylon and about a year before his death (529 B.C.) transferred the regal power to his son, Cambyses. Assyrian-Babylonian history here ceases and is merged into Persian. Babylonia recovered its independence after the death of Darius. A king styling himself Nebuchadrezzar III arose, who reigned for about a year (521-520 B.C.), at the end of which time the Persians once more returned as conquerors. A second revolt in 514 B.C. caused the partial destruction of the walls, and finally the great city of Babylon became little better than a quarry out of which the newer city of Seleucia and other towns were built.

The History of Berossus

It will be of interest to examine at least one of the ancient authorities upon Babylonian history. Berossus, a priest of Bel at Babylon, who lived about 250 B.C., compiled from native documents a history of his country, which he published in Greek. His writings have perished, but extracts from them have been preserved by Josephus and Eusebius. There is a good deal of myth in Berossus' work, especially when he deals with the question of cosmology, the story of the deluge, and so forth; also the 'facts' which he places before us as history cannot be reconciled with those inscribed on the monuments. He seems indeed to have arranged his history so that it should exactly fill the assumed period of 36,000 years, beginning with the creation of man and ending with the conquest of Babylon by Alexander the Great. Berossus tells of a certain Sisuthrus,[1] whose history will be recounted in full in another chapter. He then relates a legend of the advent of the fish-man or fish-god, Oannes, from the waters of the Persian Gulf. Indeed he alludes to three beings of this type, who, one after another, appeared to instruct the Babylonians in arts and letters.

Berossus' Account of the Deluge

More important is his account of the deluge. There is more than one Babylonian version of the deluge: that which is to be found in the *Gilgamesh Epic* is given in the chapter dealing with that poem.

[1] Ut-Napishtim.

BEROSSUS' ACCOUNT OF THE DELUGE

As Berossus' account is quite as important, we shall give it in his own words before commenting upon it: "After the death of Ardates, his son (Sisuthrus) succeeded and reigned eighteen sari. In his time happened the great deluge; the history of which is given in this manner. The Deity, Cronus, appeared to him in a vision; and gave him notice, that upon the fifteenth day of the month Dæsius there would be a flood, by which mankind would be destroyed. He therefore enjoined him to commit to writing a history of the beginning, procedure, and final conclusion of all things, down to the present term; and to bury these accounts securely in the City of the Sun at Sippara. He then ordered Sisuthrus to build a vessel, and to take with him into it his friends and relations; and trust himself to the deep. The latter implicitly obeyed: and having conveyed on board every thing necessary to sustain life, he took in also all species of animals, that either fly, or rove upon the surface of the earth. Having asked the Deity whither he was to go, he was answered, To the gods: upon which he offered up a prayer for the good of mankind. Thus he obeyed the divine admonition: and the vessel, which he built, was five stadia in length, and in breadth two. Into this he put every thing which he had got ready; and last of all conveyed into it his wife, children, and friends. After the flood had been upon the earth, and was in time abated, Sisuthrus sent out some birds from the vessel; which not finding any food, nor any place to rest their feet, returned to him again. After an interval of some days; he sent them forth a second time: and they now returned with their feet tinged with mud. He made trial a third time with these birds: but they returned to him no more: from whence he formed a judgment, that the surface of the earth was now above the waters. Having therefore made an opening in the vessel, and finding upon looking out, that the vessel was driven to the side of a mountain, he immediately quitted it, being attended with his wife, children, and the pilot. Sisuthrus immediately paid his adoration to the earth: and having constructed an altar, offered sacrifices to the gods. These things being duly performed, both Sisuthrus, and those who came out of the vessel with him, disappeared. They, who remained in the vessel, finding that the others did not return, came out with many lamentations and called continually on the name of Sisuthrus. Him they saw no more; but they could distinguish his voice in the air, and could hear him admonish them to pay due regard to the gods; and likewise inform them, that it was upon account of his piety that he was translated to live with the gods; that his wife and children, with the pilot, had obtained the same honour. To this he added, that he would have them make the best of their way to Babylonia, and search for the writings at Sippara, which were to be made known to all mankind. The place where these things happened was in Armenia. The remainder having heard these words, offered sacrifices to the gods; and, taking a circuit, journeyed towards Babylonia." Berossus adds, that the remains of the vessel were to be seen in his time upon one of the Corcyrean mountains in Armenia; and that people used to scrape off the bitumen, with which it had been outwardly coated, and made use of it by way of an antidote for poison or amulet. In this manner they returned to Babylon; and having found the writings at Sippara, they set about building cities and erecting temples; and Babylon was thus inhabited again.

Analogies with the Flood Myth

It is interesting to note that Sisuthrus, the hero of this deluge story, was also the tenth Babylonian king, just as Noah was the tenth patriarch. The birds sent out by Sisuthrus strongly recall the raven and dove despatched by Noah; but there are several American myths which introduce this conception.

Birds and beasts in many cosmologies provide the nucleus of the new world which emerges from the waters which have engulfed the old. Perhaps it is the beaver or the musk-rat which dives into the abyss and brings up a piece of mud, which gradually grows into a spacious continent; but sometimes birds carry this nucleus in their beaks. In the myth under consideration they return with mud on their feet, which is obviously expressive of the same idea. Attempts have been made to show that a great difference exists between the Babylonian and Hebrew story. Undoubtedly the two stories have a common origin.

The first Babylonian version of the myth dates from about 2000 B.C. and its text is evidently derived from a still older tablet. It seems likely that this was in turn indebted to a still more archaic version, which probably recounted the earliest type of the myth. This perhaps related how the earth and its inhabitants were not to the liking of the Creator, and how he resolved to recreate the whole. The great ocean-dragon was therefore called in to submerge the world, after which the Creator re-moulded it and set the survivor and his family upon it as the

MYTHS OF BABYLONIA AND ASSYRIA

ancestors of a new human race. It is possible also that the great sea-dragon, or serpent, which was slain by the Creator, may have flooded the earth with his blood as he expired: there is an Algonquin Indian myth to this effect. In an old cuneiform text, in fact, the year of the deluge is alluded to as "the year of the raging serpent." The wise man who takes refuge in the ship or ark is warned by a dream of the forthcoming deluge. In some North American Indian myths he is warned by friendly animals. The mountain, too, as a place of refuge for the ark, is fairly common in myth.

We have dealt in Chapter II with the creation myth found in Berossus, and with this ends the part of his history which is of any importance.

Babylonian Archæology

Until about the middle of the nineteenth century our knowledge of the history and antiquities of Babylonia and Assyria was extremely scanty. The deeply interesting series of excavations which unrolled the circumstances of these ancient civilizations before the almost incredulous eyes of learned Europe are described at length towards the close of this volume. Here we may say shortly that the labours of Layard and Botta at Nineveh convinced antiquaries that the remains of a great civilization awaited discovery. Layard's excavation of the library of Assur-bani-pal was the first great step toward reconstructing the ancient life of the two kingdoms. He was followed by Oppert and Loftus, but the systematic excavation of the country was yet to be undertaken. This, as we shall see, was commenced by George Smith of the British Museum, but unfortunately he died on his way home from the East. His work at Nineveh was taken up by Mr Hormuzd Rassam, who succeeded in unearthing inscribed tables and bronze gates in bas-relief. A few years afterward Mr Rassam discovered the site of the temple of the sun-god of Sippara at Abu-habba to the south-west of Bagdad. An important find by de Sarzec was that of the diorite statues of Gudea, the Patesi or Ruler of Lagash, about 2700 B.C., the stone of which, according to the inscriptions upon them, had been brought from the Sinaitic peninsula. The university of Pennsylvania sent Mr J. H. Haynes in 1889 to excavate at Nippur, where he unearthed the remains of the great temple of En-lil, in the heart of which is a mound of bricks stamped with the names of Sargon of Akkad and his son, Naram-sin. The German expedition of 1899 explored the ruins of Babylon, the palace of Nebuchadrezzar, and the site of Asshur.

The Tower of Babel

Many attempts have been made to attach the legend of the confusion of tongues to certain ruined towers in Babylonia, especially to that of E-Sagila, the great temple of Merodach, and some remarks upon this most interesting tale may not be out of place at this point. The myth is not found in Babylonia itself, and in its best form may be discovered in Scripture. In the Bible story we are told that every region was of one tongue and mode of speech. As men journeyed westward from their original home in the East, they encountered a plain in the land of Shinar where they settled. In this region they commenced building operations, constructed a city, and laid the foundations of a tower, the summit of which they hoped would reach to heaven itself. It would appear that this edifice was constructed with the object of serving as a great landmark to the people so that they should not be scattered over the face of the earth, and the Lord came down to view the city and the tower, and he considered that as they were all of one language this gave them undue power, and that what they imagined to themselves under such conditions they would be able to achieve. So the Lord scattered them abroad from thence over the face of every region, and the building of the tower ceased and the name of it was called 'Babel,' because at that place the single language of the people was confounded. Of course it is merely the native name of Babylon, which translated means 'gate of the god,' and has no such etymology as the Scriptures pretend,—the Hebrews confusing their verb *balal*, 'to confuse or confound,' with the word *babel*. The story was no doubt suggested by one of the temple towers of Babylon. Over and over again we find in connexion with the Jewish religion that anything which savours of presumption or unnatural aspiration is strongly condemned. The ambitious effort of the Tower of Babel would thus seem abhorrent to the Hebrews of old. The strange thing is that these ancient towers or *zikkurats*, as the Babylonians called them, were intended to serve as a link between heaven and earth, just as does the minaret of the Mahommedan mosque.

The legend of the confusion of tongues is to be traced in other folk-lores than that of Babylon. It is found in Central America, where the story runs that Xelhua, one of the seven giants rescued from the deluge, built the great pyramid of Cholula in order to besiege heaven. The structure was, how-

Birs Nimrûd, the Tower of Babel

From *Nippur, or Exploration and Adventure on the Euphrates*, by J. P. Peters
By permission of Messrs G. P. Putnam's Sons

ever, destroyed by the gods, who cast down fire upon it and confounded the language of its builders. Livingstone found some such myth among the African tribes around Lake Ngami, and certain Australian and Mongolian peoples possess a similar tradition.

Nimrod, the Mighty Hunter

It is strange that the dispersion of tribes at Babel should be connected with the name of Nimrod, who figures in Biblical as well as Babylonian tradition as a mighty hunter. Epiphanius states that from the very foundation of this city (Babylon) there commenced an immediate scene of conspiracy, sedition, and tyranny, which was carried on by Nimrod, the son of Chus the Æthiop. Around this dim legendary figure a great deal of learned controversy has raged. Before we examine his legendary and mythological significance, let us see what legend and Scripture say of him. In the Book of Genesis (chap. x, 8, *ff.*) he is mentioned as "a mighty hunter before Yahweh: wherefore it is said, Even as Nimrod the mighty hunter before the Lord." He was also the ruler of a great kingdom. "The beginning of his kingdom was Babel, and Erech, and Accad, and Calneh in the land of Shinar. Out of that land went forth Asshur" (that is, by compulsion of Nimrod) "and builded Nineveh," and other great cities. In the Scriptures Nimrod is mentioned as a descendant of Ham, but this may arise from the reading of his father's name as *Cush*, which in the Scriptures indicates a coloured race. The name may possibly be *Cash* and should relate to the Cassites.

It appears then that the sons of Cush or Chus, the Cassites, according to legend, did not partake of the general division of the human race after the fall of Babel, but under the leadership of Nimrod himself remained where they were. After the dispersion, Nimrod built Babylon and fortified the territory around it. It is also said that he built Nineveh and trespassed upon the land of Asshur, so that at last he forced Asshur to quit that territory.[1] The Greeks gave him the name of Nebrod or Nebros, and preserved or invented many tales concerning him and his apostasy, and concerning the tower which he is supposed to have erected. He is described as a gigantic person of mighty bearing, and a contemner of everything divine; his followers are represented as being equally presumptuous and overbearing. In fact he seems to have appeared to the Greeks very much like one of their own Titans.

Nimrod has been identified both with Merodach, the tutelar god of Babylon, and with Gilgamesh, the hero of the epic of that name, with Orion, and with others. The name, according to Petrie, has even been found in Egyptian documents of the XXII Dynasty as 'Nemart.'

Nimrod seems to be one of those giants who rage against the gods, as do the Titans of Greek myth and the Jotunn of Scandinavian story. All are in fact earth-gods, the disorderly forces of nature, who were defeated by the deities who stood for law and order. The derivation of the name Nimrod may mean 'rebel.' In all his later legends, for instance, those of them that are related by Philo in his *De Gigantibus* (a title which proves that Nimrod was connected with the giant race by tradition),

---

[1] This passage has, however, been interpreted by some Biblical scholars to mean that "Nimrod went out of this land into Asshur" (or Assyria) "and built Nineveh." See Bryant, *Antient Mythology*, vol. vi, pp. 191–2–3.

ABRAM AND NIMROD

he appears as treacherous and untrustworthy. The theory that he is Merodach has no real foundation either in scholarship or probability. As a matter of fact the Nimrod legend seems to be very much more archaic than any piece of tradition connected with Merodach, who indeed is a god of no very great antiquity.

Abram and Nimrod

Many Jewish legends bring Abram into relationship with Nimrod, the mythical King of Babylon. According to legend Abram was originally an idolater, and many stories are preserved respecting his conversion. Jewish legend states that the Father of the Faithful originally followed his father Terah's occupation, which was that of making and selling images of clay; and that, when very young, he advised his father "to leave his pernicious trade of idolatry by which he imposed on the world."

The Jewish Rabbins relate that on one occasion, his father Terah having undertaken a considerable journey, the sale of the images devolved on him, and it happened that a man who pretended to be a purchaser asked him how old he was. "Fifty years," answered the Patriarch. "Wretch that thou art," said the man, "for adoring at that age a thing which is only one day old!" Abram was astonished; and the exclamation of the old man had such an effect upon him, that when a woman soon after brought some flour, as an offering to one of the idols, he took an axe and broke them to pieces, preserving only the largest one, into the hand of which he put the axe. Terah returned home and inquired what this havoc meant. Abram replied that the deities had quarrelled about an offering which a woman had brought, upon which the larger one had seized an axe and destroyed the others. Terah replied that he must be in jest, as it was impossible that inanimate statues could so act; and Abram immediately retorted on his father his own words, showing him the absurdity of worshipping false deities. But Terah, who does not appear to have been convinced, delivered Abram to Nimrod, who then dwelt in the Plain of Shinar, where Babylon was built. Nimrod, having in vain exhorted Abram to worship fire, ordered him to be thrown into a burning furnace, exclaiming—" Let your God come and take you out." As soon as Haran, Abram's youngest brother, saw the fate of the Patriarch, he resolved to conform to Nimrod's religion; but when he saw his brother come out of the fire unhurt, he declared for the " God of Abram," which caused him to be thrown in turn into the furnace, and he was consumed. A certain writer, however, narrates a different version of Haran's death. He says that he endeavoured to snatch Terah's idols from the flames, into which they had been thrown by Abram, and was burnt to death in consequence.

A Persian Version

The Persian Mussulmans allege that the Patriarch, who was born in Chaldea, after God had manifested himself to him, proceeded to Mecca, and built the celebrated Kaaba or temple there. When he returned home he publicly declared himself the Prophet of God, and specially announced it to Nimrod, King of Chaldea, who was a worshipper of fire. Abram met Nimrod at a town in Mesopotamia, called Urga, afterwards Caramit, and now Diarbekr, in which was a large temple consecrated

A PERSIAN VERSION

to fire, and publicly entreated the King to renounce his idolatry and worship the true God. Nimrod consulted his wise men and inquired what punishment such a blasphemer deserved, and they advised that he should be consigned to the flames. A pile of wood was ordered to be prepared and Abram was placed upon it, but to their astonishment it would not kindle. Nimrod asked the priests the cause of this phenomenon, and they replied that an angel was constantly flying about the pile and preventing the wood from burning. The King asked how the angel could be driven away, and they replied that it could only be done by some dreadful rite. Their advice was followed, but the angel still persisted, and Nimrod at length banished Abram from his dominions.

The Mussulmans also relate that the King made war against the Patriarch, and when he was marching against him, he sent a person to him with this message—"O Abram! it is now time to fight; where is thy army?" Abram answered, "It will come immediately;" and immediately there appeared an immense sun-darkening cloud of gnats, which devoured Nimrod's soldiers to the very bones.

Another tradition is preserved in the East, specially referring to the casting of Abram into a fiery furnace at Babylon by order of Nimrod, which seems to be a corrupted story of the deliverance of the three Hebrews recorded by Daniel—Nimrod merely substituted for Nebuchadrezzar, as no evidence exists that Abram ever was at Babylon. "Nimrod," it is said, "in a dream saw a star rising above the horizon, the light of which eclipsed that of the sun. The soothsayers who were consulted foretold that a child was to be born in Babylon who shortly would become a great prince, and that he (Nimrod) had reason to fear him. Terrified at this answer, Nimrod gave orders to search for such an infant. Notwithstanding this precaution, however, Adna, the wife of Azar, one of Nimrod's guards, hid her child in a cave, the mouth of which she diligently closed, and when she returned she told her husband that it had perished.

Adna, in the meantime, proceeded regularly to the cave to nurse the infant, but she always found him suckling the ends of his fingers, one of which furnished him milk and the other honey. This miracle surprised her, and as her anxiety for the child's welfare was thus greatly relieved, and as she saw that Heaven had undertaken the care, she merely satisfied herself with visiting him from time to time. She soon perceived that he grew as much in three days as common children do in a month, so that fifteen moons had scarcely passed before he appeared as if he were fifteen years of age. Adna now told her husband, Azar, that the son of whom she had been delivered, and whom she had reported dead, was living, and that God had provided miraculously for his subsistence. Azar went immediately to the cave, where he found his son, and desired his mother to convey him to the city, as he was resolved to present him to Nimrod and place him about the court.

In the evening Adna brought him forth out of his den, and conducted him to a meadow where herds of cattle were feeding. This was a sight entirely new to the young Abram, who was inquisitive to learn their nature, and was informed by his mother of their names, uses, and qualities. Abram continued his inquiries and desired to know who

A PERSIAN VERSION

produced the animals. Adna told him that all things had their Lord and Creator. "Who, then," said he, "brought me into the world?" "I," replied Adna. "And who is your Lord?" asked Abram. She answered, "Azar." "Who is Azar's Lord?" She told him, Nimrod. He showed an inclination to carry his inquiries farther, but she checked him, telling him that it was not convenient to search into other matters because of danger. At last he came to the city, the inhabitants of which he perceived deeply engaged in superstition and idolatry. After this he returned to his grotto.

One evening, as he was going to Babylon, he saw the stars shining, and among others Venus, which was adored by many. He said within himself—"Perhaps this is the God and Creator of the world;" but observing some time after that this star was set, he said—"This certainly cannot be the Maker of the universe, for it is not possible he should be subject to such a change." Soon after he noticed the moon at full, and thought that this might possibly be the Author of all things; but when he perceived this planet also sink beneath the horizon his opinion of it was the same as in the case of Venus. At length, near the city he saw a multitude adoring the rising sun, and he was tempted to follow their example, but having seen this luminary decline like the rest, he concluded that it was not his Creator, his Lord, and his God. Azar presented his son Abram to Nimrod, who was seated on a lofty throne, with a number of beautiful slaves of both sexes in attendance. Abram asked his father who was the person so much exalted above the rest. Azar answered—"The King Nimrod, whom these people acknowledge as their God." "It is impossible," replied Abram, "that he should be their God, since he is not so beautiful, and consequently not so perfect, as the generality of those about him."

Abram now took an opportunity of conversing with his father about the unity of God, which afterwards drew him into great contests with the principal men of Nimrod's court, who would by no means acquiesce in the truths he declared. Nimrod, informed of these disputes, commanded him, as we have already mentioned, to be thrown into a burning furnace, out of which he came without receiving the least hurt.

The 'Babylonica'

Fragments of Babylonian history, or rather historical romance, occur in the writings of early authors other than Berossus. One of these is to be found in the *Babylonica* of Iamblichus, a work embracing no less than sixteen books, by a native of Chalchis in Cœle-Syria, who was much enamoured of the mysterious ancient life of Babylonia and Assyria, and who died about A.D. 333. All that remains of what is palpably a romance, which may have been founded upon historical probability, is an epitome of the *Babylonica* by Photius, which, still further condensed, is as follows:

Attracted by her beauty and relying on his own great power, Garmus, King of Babylon, decided to marry Sinonis, a maiden of surpassing beauty. She, however, was already in love with another, Rhodanes, and discouraged Garmus' every advance. Her attachment became known to the King, but did not alter his determination, and to prevent the possibility of any attempt at flight on the part

THE BABYLONICA

of the lovers, he appointed two eunuchs, Damas and Saca, to watch their movements. The penalty for negligence was loss of ears and nose, and that penalty the eunuchs suffered. In spite of their close vigilance the lovers escaped. Damas and Saca were, however, placed at the head of troops and despatched to recapture the fugitives. Their relentless search was not the lovers' only anxiety, for in seeking refuge with some shepherds in a meadow, they encountered a demon—a satyr, which in the shape of a goat haunted that part of the country. This demon, to Sinonis' horror, began to pay her all sorts of weird, fantastic attentions, and finally compelled her and Rhodanes to abandon the protection of the shepherds for the concealment offered by a cavern. Here they were discovered by Damas and his forces, and must have been captured but for the opportune arrival and attack of a swarm of poisonous bees which routed the eunuchs. When the runaways were alone again they tasted and ate some of the bees' honey, and almost immediately lost consciousness. Later Damas again attacked the cavern, but finding the lovers still unconscious he and his troops left them there for dead.

In time, however, they recovered and continued their flight into the country. A man, who afterward poisoned his brother and accused them of the crime, offered them sanctuary. Only the suicide of this man saved them from serious trouble and probably recapture, and from his house they wandered into the company of a robber. Here again the troops of Damas came upon them and burned their dwelling to the ground. In desperation the fugitives masqueraded as the ghosts of the people the robber had murdered in his house. Their ruse succeeded and once again their pursuers were thrown off the scent. They next encountered the funeral of a young girl, and witnessed her apparent return to life almost at the door of the sepulchre. In this sepulchre Sinonis and Rhodanes slept that night, and once more were believed to be dead by Damas and his soldiers. Later, however, Sinonis tried to dispose of their grave clothes and was arrested in the act. Soracchus, the magistrate of the district, decided to send her to Babylon. In despair she and Rhodanes took some poison with which they had provided themselves against such an emergency. This had been anticipated by their guards, however, with the result that a sleeping draught had been substituted for the poison, and some time later the lovers to their amazement awoke to find themselves in the vicinity of Babylon. Overcome by such a succession of misfortunes, Sinonis stabbed herself, though not fatally. Soracchus, on learning this, was moved to compassion, and consented to the escape of his prisoners.

After this the lovers embarked on a new series of adventures even more thrilling than those which had gone before. The Temple of Venus (Ishtar), situated on an island of the Euphrates, was their first destination after escaping from the captivity of Soracchus. Here Sinonis' wound was healed, and afterward they sought refuge with a cottager, whose daughter consented to dispose of some trinkets belonging to Sinonis. In doing so the girl was mistaken for Sinonis, and news that Sinonis had been seen in the neighbourhood was sent at once to Garmus. While selling the trinkets the cottage girl had become so alarmed by the suspicious questions and manner of the purchasers that she hurried

The Murder of Setapo
Evelyn Paul

THE BABYLONICA

home with all possible speed. On her way back her curiosity was excited by sounds of a great disturbance issuing from a house hard by, and on entering she was appalled to discover a man in the very act of taking his life after murdering his mistress. Terrified and sprinkled with blood she sped back to her father's house. On hearing the girl's story, Sinonis realised that the safety of herself and Rhodanes lay only in flight. They prepared at once to go, but before starting Rhodanes kissed the peasant girl. Sinonis, discovering what he had done by the blood on his lips, became furious with jealousy. In a transport of rage she tried to stab the girl, and on being prevented rushed to the house of Setapo, a wealthy Babylonian of evil repute. Setapo welcomed her only too cordially. At first Sinonis pretended to meet his mood, but as time went by she relented of her treatment of Rhodanes and began to cast about for some means of escape. As the evening wore on she plied Setapo with wine until he was intoxicated, then during the night she murdered him, and in the first early dawn left the house. The slaves of Setapo pursued and overtook her, however, and committed her to custody to answer for her crime.

All Babylon rejoiced with its king over the news of Sinonis' discovery. So great was Garmus' delight that he commanded that all the prisoners throughout his dominions should be released, and in this general boon Sinonis shared. Meanwhile the dog of Rhodanes had scented out the house in which the peasant girl had witnessed the suicide of the lover who had murdered his mistress, and while the animal was devouring the remains of the woman the father of Sinonis arrived at the same house. Thinking the mutilated body was that of his daughter he buried it, and on the tomb he placed the inscription: " Here lies the beautiful Sinonis." Some days later Rhodanes passed that way, and on reading the inscription added to it, " And also the beautiful Rhodanes." In his grief he would have stabbed himself had not the peasant girl who had been the cause of Sinonis' jealousy prevented him by telling him who in reality was buried there.

During these adventures Soracchus had been imprisoned for allowing the lovers to escape, and this, added to the threat of further punishment, induced him to help the Babylonian officers to trace Rhodanes. So in a short time Rhodanes was prisoner once again, and by the command of Garmus was nailed to a cross. In sight of him the King danced delirious with revengeful joy, and while he was so engaged a messenger arrived with the news that Sinonis was about to be espoused by the King of Syria, into whose dominions she had escaped. Rhodanes was taken down from the cross and put in command of the Babylonian army. This seeming change of fortune was really dictated by the treachery of Garmus, as certain inferior officers were commanded by Garmus to slay Rhodanes should he defeat the Syrians, and to bring Sinonis alive to Babylon. Rhodanes won a sweeping victory and also regained the affection and trust of Sinonis. The officers of Garmus, instead of obeying his command, proclaimed the victor king, and all ended auspiciously for the lovers.

Cuneiform Writing

The manner in which the ancient cuneiform writing of Babylonia and Assyria was deciphered and restored to the world of science and letters may be regarded as a great triumph of human reason. The name 'cuneiform' is most appropriate, for each character or sign is composed of a wedge or combination of wedges. It is written, as most Oriental languages from left to right. The cuneiform script was first noticed by a European at such a relatively early period as the year A.D. 1470, when Josaphat Barbaro, a Venetian traveller, observed it cut on the platform of Rachmet in Persia. Another Italian, Pietro della Valle, passing that way in 1621, copied a few of the signs, which he sent back to Italy, and Sir John Chardin accurately reproduced an inscription found at Persepolis in 1711. It was obvious that three separate languages were written in this script, and these have since been found to be Persian, Babylonian, and Susian. In 1765 Niebuhr visited Persepolis, and in less than a month copied all the texts there, which were then ready for decipherment. Returning to Denmark he occupied himself with studying what he had set down at Persepolis, and divided the smaller inscriptions into three classes, which he described as Classes I, II, and III instead of into three languages. Discovering that Class I embraced only forty-two signs, he set these in order, and but little subsequent addition has had to be made to them. Deciding that the language of the signs was written in alphabetic characters, he found himself obliged to call a halt. But two other scholars were more fortunate than he. Tychsen hit upon a certain diagonal sign as that employed to separate words, and correctly identified the alphabetic signs for 'a,' 'd,' 'u,' and 's.' Münter of Copenhagen was more careful to verify his historical data than Tychsen had been, and was able to identify distinctly the authors of the inscriptions before him. He, too, independently identified the oblique wedge as a separative of words, and hit upon the significance of the sign for the letter 'b.' But after these achievements it seemed as if little more could be done. It must be remembered that up to this time no such assistance was vouchsafed the searchers as in the case of the Egyptian hieroglyphs, where a Greek inscription had been found side by side with an Egyptian one.

Grotefend

But a man of the greatest natural ingenuity was resolved to combat the difficulty presented by the cuneiform script. Georg Grotefend took up the task in the early years of the nineteenth century. Beginning with the assumption that the inscriptions represented three languages, and that one of these was ancient Persian, he took two of the inscriptions which he understood to be Persian, and placing them side by side found that certain signs were of frequent recurrence. This indicated to him the possibility that their contents were similar. A certain word appeared very frequently in the inscriptions, but it seemed to have two forms, a longer and a shorter, and this Grotefend, adopting a suggestion of Münter's, took to mean 'king' in the short form and 'kings' in the longer, the juxtaposition of the two signs thus being taken to signify 'king of kings.' In both the inscriptions studied by Grotefend he found that this expression 'king of kings' was followed by the same word, which he took to mean 'great.' But there were no definite facts to support these hypotheses. Turning to certain Sassanian inscriptions which had recently been deciphered, he found that

GROTEFEND

the expression 'great king, king of kings' inevitably occurred, and this strengthened his opinion that it was present in the inscriptions he studied. If this was so, thought he, the two texts under his observation must have been set up by two different kings, for the names were not the same at the beginning. Moreover the name with which text No. I began appears in the third line of text No. II, following the word supposed to be 'king,' and another which might mean 'son.' Grotefend thus concluded that in the two inscriptions he had the names of a triad of rulers, son, father, and grandfather. Applying to the list of the Achænenian dynasty in the attempt to find three names which would suit the conditions, he selected those of Xerxes, Darius, and Hystaspes. Supposing the name at the beginning of inscription I to be Darius, he thus considered himself to be justified in translating text I as "Darius, great king, king of kings, son of Hystaspes," and text II as "Xerxes, great king, king of kings, son of Darius." Considering that the Persian spelling of Darius would be Darheush, he applied the letters of that name to the letters of the cuneiform script. Subsequent investigation has shown that the name should have been read Daryavush, but Grotefend at least succeeded in discovering the letters for 'd,' 'a,' 'r,' and 'sh.'

But this was practically the end of Grotefend's discoveries. Burnouf, by a careful study of Persian geographical names, managed to decipher a large number of the characters of the Persian alphabet, and Professor Lassen of Bonn, by similar means, achieved a like end. These two independent achievements raised a fierce controversy as to priority of discovery, but Lassen's system was the more perfect, as he found out that the ancient Persian signs were not entirely alphabetic but were partially syllabic—that is, that certain signs represented syllables instead of letters. This meant that Grotefend's system, which had been almost vowelless, was now to a great extent filled in with the necessary vowels.

Rawlinson

At this juncture a certain Major Henry Rawlinson, a servant of the East India Company, with a good knowledge of Persian, went to Persia for the purpose of assisting to organize the native army there. He was far away from books, and when he began to copy certain cuneiform texts it was because of deep personal interest. He was quite unaware of the strenuous toil which had been lavished upon them in Europe and worked quite independently of all assistance. The strange thing is that he laboured almost on the same lines as Grotefend had done. He saw almost at once that he had three languages to deal with, and being a man of great natural gifts he soon grouped the signs in a correct manner. Strangely enough he applied the very same names—those of Hystaspes, Darius, and Xerxes—to the texts as Grotefend had done, and found them answer in the same manner. Turning his attention to the inscription of Darius at Behistun, high up in the face of the living wall of rock there, Rawlinson succeeded in copying part of it at great personal risk. In 1838 he forwarded his translation of the first two paragraphs of the Persian text, containing the genealogy of Darius, to the Royal Asiatic Society of London. The feat made a tremendous sensation, and he was supplied with all the principal works on the subject and much correspondence from European scholars. He was, however, patience personified, and would not publish a work he had written on the subject because he thought it better to wait until he had verified his conclusions and perhaps made fresh discoveries. But in 1840 he was despatched to Afghanistan on a political mission and did not return to Bagdad for three years, and it was not until 1846 that he published a series of memoirs in the *Journal* of the Royal Asiatic Society, in which he gave to the world a translation of the Persian text at Behistun. It was a marvellous achievement, for, unlike those who had been labouring on the subject in Europe, he was ignorant of the languages allied to Persian, yet he had surpassed all other scholars in his results.

But the deciphering of the second and third languages had yet to be attacked. In 1844 Westergaard, working on the lines of Grotefend, attacked the second language. He selected the names of Darius, Hystaspes, and Xerxes, and compared them with their equivalents in the Persian texts. By this means he discovered a number of signs and by their aid attempted to spell out the syllables or words. Judging the writing to be partly alphabetic and partly syllabic, he gave the name Median to the language. Morris, who had Rawlinson's copy of the second transcription of the Behistun text to work upon, deciphered nearly all of it. Shortly after this the language was named Susian. The deciphering of the third of the three languages found at Persepolis was attacked by Löwenstern, and by the Rev. Edward Hinks, an Irish clergyman. This language was Assyrian purely. Hinks was fearful of making blunders, and whilst he was engaged in assuring himself that every step he took was not a false one,

MYTHS OF BABYLONIA AND ASSYRIA

Longpriéer published in 1847 a translation of the entire text. He was only able to read it by analogy with the other texts; he could not provide the forms of the Assyrian words themselves. But Rawlinson once more came to the aid of the study, and it was shown that a large number of signs were ideographic. This paved the way for a band of others who by their united efforts succeeded in unravelling the complicated script.

Origin of Cuneiform

This peculiar system of writing originated in Babylonia, its inventors being the Sumerian or non-Semitic people who inhabited that country before its settlement by the Babylonians. It was developed from picture-writing, and indeed some of the more highly significant of the pictorial signs can still be faintly traced in their cuneiform equivalents. This early picture-writing was inscribed on stone, but eventually soft clay was adopted as a medium for the script, and it was found that straight lines impressed upon this medium tended to the shape of a wedge. The pictures therefore lost their original character and came to be mere conventional groups of wedges. The plural was represented by doubling the sign, and a term might be intensified by the addition of a certain stroke: thus the sign for 'house,' if four small strokes were added to it, would mean 'great house,' and so forth. The script was badly suited to the Assyrian language, as it had not been originally designed for a Semitic tongue. It consists of simple syllables made up of a vowel by itself or a vowel and a consonant, ideograms or signs which express an entire word, and closed syllables such as *bit* or *bal*. Again, many of the signs have more than one syllabic value, and they may be used as ideograms as well as phonetically. As in the Egyptian script, determinatives are employed to indicate the class to which the word belongs: thus, a certain sign is placed before the names of persons, another before territorial names, and a third before the names of gods and sacred beings. The date of the epoch in which this writing first began to be used was probably about 4500 B.C. and it persisted until the first century B.C. The Assyrians employed it from about 1500 B.C. until about the beginning of the sixth century B.C. This ancient form of writing was thus used first by the Sumerians, then by their Babylonian and Assyrian conquerors, then by those Persians who finally overthrew the Babylonian and Assyrian empire.

The Sacred Literature of Babylonia

The literature which this peculiar and individual script has brought down to us is chiefly religious, magical, epical, and legendary. The last three categories are dealt with elsewhere, so that it only falls here to consider the first class, the religious writings. These are usually composed in Semitic Babylonian without any trace of Akkadian influence, and it cannot be said that they display any especial natural eloquence or literary distinction. In an address to the sun-god, which begins nobly enough with a high apostrophe to the golden luminary of day, we find ourselves descending gradually into an atmosphere of almost ludicrous dullness. The person praying desires the sun-god to free him from the commonplace cares of family and domestic annoyances, enumerating spells against all of his relatives in order that they may not place their 'ban' upon him. In another, written in Akkadian, the penitent addresses Gubarra, Merodach, and other gods, desiring that they direct their eyes kindly upon him and that his supplication may reach them. Strangely enough the prayer fervently pleads that its utterance may *do good to the gods!* that it may let their hearts rest, their livers be quieted, and gladden them like a father and a mother who have begotten children. This is not so strange when we come to consider the nature of these hymns, many of which come perilously near the border-line of pure magic—that is, they closely resemble spells. We find, too, that those which invoke the older deities such as Gibi the fire-god, are more magical in their trend than those addressed to the later gods when a higher sense of religious feeling had probably been evolved. Indeed, it does not seem too much to say that some of these early hymns may have served the purpose of later incantations. Most of those ' magical ' hymns appear to have emanated from that extremely ancient seat of religion, Eridu, and are probably relics of the time when as yet magic and religion were scarcely differentiated in the priestly or the popular mind.

Hymn to Adar

A fine hymn to Adar describes the rumbling of the storm in the abyss, the ' voice ' of the god :

> The terror of the splendour of Anu in the midst of heaven.

The gods, it is said, urge Adar on, he descends like the deluge, the champion of the gods swoops down upon the hostile land. Nusku, the messenger of Mul-lil, receives Adar in the temple and addresses words of praise to him :

HYMN TO ADAR

Thy chariot is as a voice of thunder.
To the lifting of thy hands is the shadow turned.
The spirits of the earth, the great gods, return to the winds.

Many of the hymns assist us to a better understanding of the precise nature of the gods, defining as they do their duties and offices and even occasionally describing their appearance. Thus in a hymn to Nebo we note that he is alluded to as "the supreme messenger who binds all things together," "the scribe of all that has a name," "the lifter up of the stylus supreme," "director of the world," "possessor of the reed of augury," "traverser of strange lands," "opener of wells," "fructifier of the corn," and "the god without whom the irrigated land and the canal are unwatered." It is from such texts that the mythologist is enabled to piece together the true significance of many of the deities of ancient peoples.

A hymn to Nusku in his character of fire-god is also descriptive and picturesque. He is alluded to as "wise prince, the flame of heaven," "he who hurls down terror, whose clothing is splendour," "the forceful fire-god," "the exalter of the mountain peaks," and "the uplifter of the torch, the enlightener of darkness."

Such descriptive hymns are the most valuable assets possible in the hands of the judicious student of myth or comparative religion.

CHAPTER II: BABYLONIAN COSMOGONY

The Babylonian Myth of Creation

FEW creation myths are more replete with interest than those which have literary sanction. These are few in number, as, for example, the creation story in Genesis, those to be found in Egyptian papyri, and that contained in the *Popol Vuh* of the Maya of Central America. In such an account we can trace the creation story from the first dim conception of world-shaping to the polished and final effort of a priestly caste to give a theological interpretation to the intentions of the creative deity; and this is perhaps more the case with the creation myth which had its rise among the old Akkadian population of Babylonia than with any other known to mythic science. In the account in Genesis of the framing of the world it has been discovered that two different versions have been fused to form a single story; the creation tale of the *Popol Vuh* is certainly a composite myth; and similar suspicions may rest upon the analogous myths of Scandinavia and Japan. But in the case of Babylonia we may be convinced that no other influences except those of the races who inhabited Babylonian territory could have been brought to bear upon this ancient story, and that although critical examination has proved it to consist of materials which have been drawn from more than one source, yet these sources are not foreign, and they have not undergone sophistication at the hands of any alien mythographer or interpolator.

It would seem that this Babylonian cosmogony was drawn from various sources, but it appears to be con-

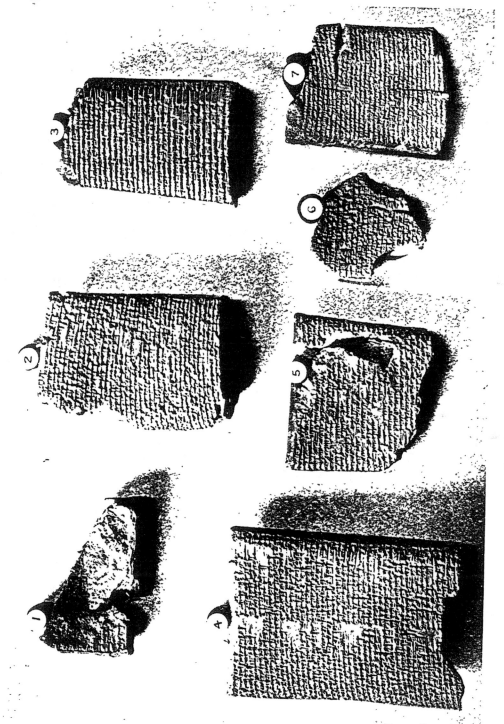

The Seven Tablets of Creation
Photo W. A. Mansell and Co.

THE BIRTH OF THE GODS

tained in its final form in what are known as the Seven Tablets of Creation, brought from the library of Assur-bani-pal at Nineveh and now in the British Museum. These have from time to time been supplemented by later finds, but we may take it that in this record we have the final official development of Babylonian belief, due to the priests of Babylon, after that city had become the metropolis of the empire. The primary object of the Seven Tablets was to record a terrific fight between Bel and the Dragon, and the account of the creation is inserted by way of introduction. It is undoubtedly the most important find dealing with Babylonian religion that has as yet come to light. Before we advance any critical speculations respecting it, let us set forth the story which it has to tell.

As in so many creation myths, we find chaotic darkness brooding over a waste of waters; heaven and earth were not as yet. Naught existed save the primeval ocean, Mommu Tiawath,[1] from whose fertile depths came every living thing. Nor were the waters distributed, as in the days of man, into sea, river, or lake, but all were confined together in one vast and bottomless abyss. Neither did god or man exist: their names were unknown and their destinies undetermined. The future was as dark as the gloom which lay over the mighty gulf of chaos. Nothing had been designed or debated concerning it.

The Birth of the Gods

But there came a stirring in the darkness and the great gods arose. First came Lahmu and Lahame; and many epochs later, Ansar and Kisar, component parts of whose names signify 'Host of Heaven'

[1] Another spelling is Tiamat.

and 'Host of Earth.' These latter names we may perhaps accept as symbolical of the spirits of heaven and of earth respectively. Many days afterward came forth their son Anu, god of the heavens.

At this point it should be explained that the name Tiawath affords a parallel to the expression *T'hom* or 'deep' of the Old Testament. Practically the same word is used in Assyrian in the form *Tamtu*, to signify the 'deep sea.'[1] The reader will recall that it was upon the face of the deep that the spirit of God brooded, according to the first chapter of Genesis. The word and the idea which it contains are equally Semitic, but strangely enough it has an Akkadian origin. For the conception that the watery abyss was the source of all things originated with the worshippers of the sea-god Ea at Eridu. They termed the deep *apsu*, or a 'house of knowledge' wherein their tutelar god was supposed to have his dwelling, and this word was of Akkadian descent. This *apsu*, or 'abyss,' in virtue of the animistic ideas prevailing in early Akkadian times, had become personalized as a female who was regarded as the mother of Ea. She was known by another name as well as that of Apsu, for she was also entitled Zigarun, the 'heaven,' or the 'mother that has begotten heaven and earth'; and indeed she seems to have had a form or variant in which she was an earth-goddess as well. But it was not the existing earth or heaven that she represented in either of her forms, but the primeval abyss, out of which both of these were fashioned.

At this point the narrative exhibits numerous defects, and for a continuation of it we must apply to Damascius, the last of the Neoplatonists, who was

[1] Sayce, *Hibbert Lectures*, p. 374.

THE BIRTH OF THE GODS

born in Damascus about A.D. 480, and who is regarded by most Assyriologists as having had access to valuable written or traditional material. He was the author of a work entitled *Doubts and Solutions of the First Principles*, in which he states that Anu was followed by Bel (we retain the Babylonian form of the names rather than Damascius' Greek titles), and Ea the god of Eridu. " From Ea and Dawkina," he writes, "was born a son called Belos or Bel-Merodach, whom the Babylonians regarded as the creator of the world." From Damascius we can learn nothing further, and the defective character of the tablet does not permit us to proceed with any degree of certainty until we arrive at the name of Nudimmud, which appears to be simply a variant of the name of Ea. From obscure passages it may be generally gleaned that Tiawath and Apsu, once one, or rather originally representing the Babylonian and Akkadian forms of the deep, are now regarded as mates—Tiawath being the female and Apsu, once female, in this case the male. These have a son, Moumis or Mummu, a name which at one time seems to have been given to Tiawath, so that in these changes we may be able to trace the hand of the later mythographer, who, with less skill and greater levity than is to be found in most myths, has taken upon himself the responsibility of manufacturing three deities out of one. It may be that the scribe in question was well aware that his literary effort must square with and placate popular belief or popular prejudice, and in no era and at no time has priestly ingenuity been unequal to such a task, as is well evidenced by many myths which exhibit traces of late alteration. But in dwelling for a moment on this question, it is only just to the priesthood to admit that such changes did not always emanate from them, but were the work of poets and philosophers who, for æsthetic or rational reasons, took it upon themselves to recast the myths of their race according to the dictates of a nicer taste, or in the interests of 'reason.'

A Darksome Trinity

These three, then, Tiawath, Apsu, and Mummu, appear to have formed a trinity, which bore no good-will to the 'higher gods.'[1] They themselves, as deities of a primeval epoch, were doubtless regarded by the theological opinion of a later day as dark, dubious, and unsatisfactory. It is notorious that in many lands the early, elemental gods came into bad odour in later times; and it may be that the Akkadian descent of this trio did not conduce to their popularity with the Babylonian people. Be that as it may, alien and aboriginal gods have in all times been looked upon by an invading and conquering race with distrust as the workers of magic and the sowers of evil, and even although a Babylonian name had been accorded one of them, it may not have been employed in a complimentary sense. Whereas the high gods regarded those of the abyss with distrust, the darker deities of chaos took up an attitude towards the divinities of light which can only be compared to the sarcastic tone which Milton's Satan adopts against the Power which thrust him into outer darkness. Apsu was the most ironical of all. There was no peace for him, he declared, so long as the new-comers dwelt on high: their way was not his way, neither was it that of Tiawath, who, if Apsu represented sarcasm deified, exhibited a fierce truculence much more overpowering than

[1] Of whom we now hear for the first time.

A DARKSOME TRINITY

the irony of her mate. The trio discussed how they might rid themselves of those beings who desired a reign of light and happiness, and in these deliberations Mummu, the son, was the prime mover. Here again the Tablets fails us somewhat, but we learn sufficient further on to assure us that Mummu's project was one of open war against the gods of heaven.

In connexion with this campaign, Tiawath made the most elaborate preparations along with her companions. She laboured without ceasing. From the waters of the great abyss over which she presided she called forth the most fearful monsters, who remind us strongly of those against which Horus, the Egyptian god of light, had to strive in his wars with Set. From the deep came gigantic serpents armed with stings, dripping with the most deadly poison; dragons of vast shape reared their heads above the flood, their huge jaws armed with row upon row of formidable teeth; giant dogs of indescribable savagery; men fashioned partly like scorpions; fish-men, and countless other horrible beings, were created and formed into battalions under the command of a god named Kingu, to whom Tiawath referred as her 'only husband' and to whom she promised the rule of heaven and of fate when once the detested gods of light are removed by his mighty arm.

The introduction of this being as the husband of Tiawath seems to point either to a fusion of legends or to the interpolation of some passage popular in Babylonian lore. At this juncture Apsu disappears, as does Mummu. Can it be that at this point a scribe or mythographer took up the tale who did not agree with his predecessor in describing Tiawath,

Apsu, and Mummu, originally one, as three separate deities? This would explain the divergence, but the point is an obscure one, and hasty conclusions on slight evidence are usually doomed to failure. To resume our narrative, Tiawath, whoever her coadjutors, was resolved to retain in her own hands the source of all living things, that great deep over which she presided.

But the gods of heaven were by no means lulled into peaceful security, for they were aware of the ill-will which Tiawath bore them. They learned of her plot, and great was their wrath. Ea, the god of water, was the first to hear of it, and related it to Ansar, his father, who filled heaven with his cries of anger. Ansar betook himself to his other son, Anu, god of the sky. "Speak to the great dragon," he urged him; "speak to her, my son, and her anger will be assuaged and her wrath vanish." Duly obedient, Anu betook himself to the realm of Tiawath to reason with her, but the monster snarled at him so fiercely that in dread he turned his back upon her and departed. Next came Nudimmud to her, but with no better success. At length the gods decided that one of their number, called Merodach, should undertake the task of combating Tiawath the terrible. Merodach asked that it might be written that he should be victorious, and this was granted him. He was then given rule over the entire universe, and to test whether or not the greatest power had passed to him a garment was placed in the midst of the gods and Merodach spoke words commanding that it should disappear. Straightway it vanished and was not. Once more spake the god, and the garment re-appeared before the eyes of the dwellers in heaven. The portion of the epic which describes

"Mighty was he to look upon"
Evelyn Paul

A DARKSOME TRINITY

the newly acquired glories of Merodach is exceedingly eloquent. We are told that none among the gods can now surpass him in power, that the place of their gathering has become his home, that they have given him the supreme sovereignty, and they even beg that to them who put their trust in him he will be gracious. They pray[1] that he may pour out the soul of the keeper of evil, and finally they place in his hands a marvellous weapon with which to cut off the life of Tiawath. "Let the winds carry her blood to secret places," they exclaimed in their desire that the waters of this fountain of wickedness should be scattered far and wide. Mighty was he to look upon when he set forth for the combat. His great bow he bore upon his back; he swung his massive club triumphantly. He set the lightning before him; he filled his body with swiftness; and he framed a great net to enclose the dragon of the sea. Then with a word he created terrible winds and tempests, whirlwinds, storms, seven in all, for the confounding of Tiawath. The hurricane was his weapon, and he rode in the chariot of destiny. His helm blazed with terror and awful was his aspect. The steeds which were yoked to his chariot rushed rapidly towards the abyss, their mouths frothing with venomous foam. Followed by all the good wishes of the gods, Merodach fared forth that day.

Soon he came to Tiawath's retreat, but at sight of the monster he halted, and with reason, for there crouched the great dragon, her scaly body still

---

[1] In many mythologies we find the gods praying and sacrificing to one another, and even to deities presumably higher than themselves and unknown to man or only guessed at by him. Thus the Vedic gods are constantly sacrificing one to the other, and there are many American instances of this worship of god by god.

gleaming with the waters of the abyss, flame darting from her eyes and nostrils, and such terrific sounds issuing from her widely open mouth as would have terrified any but the bravest of the gods. Merodach reproached Tiawath for her rebellion and ended by challenging her to combat. Like the dragons of all time, Tiawath appears to have been versed in magic and hurled the most potent incantations against her adversary. She cast many a spell. But Merodach, unawed by this, threw over her his great net, and caused an evil wind which he had sent on before him to blow on her, so that she might not close her mouth. The tempest rushed between her jaws and held them open; it entered her body and racked her frame. Merodach swung his club on high, and with a mighty blow shattered her great flank and slew her. Down he cast her corpse and stood upon it; then he cut out her evil heart. Finally he overthrew the host of monsters which had followed her, so that at length they trembled, turned, and fled in headlong rout. These also he caught in his net and " kept them in bondage." Kingu he bound and took from him the tablets of destiny which had been granted to him by the slain Tiawath, which obviously means that the god of a later generation wrenches the power of fate from an earlier hierarchy, just as one earthly dynasty may overthrow and replace another. The north wind bore Tiawath's blood away to secret places, and at the sight Ea, sitting high in the heavens, rejoiced exceedingly. Then Merodach took rest and nourishment, and as he rested a plan arose in his mind. Rising, he flayed Tiawath of her scaly skin and cut her asunder. We have already seen that the north wind bore her blood away, which probably symbolises the distribution of rivers over

A DARKSOME TRINITY

the earth.[1] Then did Merodach take the two parts of her vast body, and with one of them he framed a covering for the heavens. Merodach next divided the upper from the lower waters, made dwellings for the gods, set lights in the heaven, and ordained their regular courses.

As the tablet poetically puts it, " he lit up the sky establishing the upper firmament, and caused Anu, Bel, and Ea to inhabit it." He then founded the constellations as stations for the great gods, and instituted the year, setting three constellations for each month, and placing his own star, Nibiru, as the chief light in the firmament. Then he caused the new moon, Nannaru, to shine forth and gave him the rulership of the night, granting him a day of rest in the middle of the month. There is another mutilation at this point, and we gather that the net of Merodach, with which he had snared Tiawath, was placed in the heavens as a constellation along with his bow. The winds also appear to have been bound or tamed and placed in the several points of the compass; but the whole passage is very obscure, and doubtless information of surpassing interest has been lost through the mutilation of the tablet.

We shall probably not be far in error if we regard the myth of the combat between Merodach and Tiawath as an explanation of the primal strife between light and darkness. Among the most primitive peoples, the solar hero has at one stage of his career to encounter a grisly dragon or serpent, who threatens his very existence. In many cases this monster guards a treasure which mythologists of a generation ago almost invariably explained as that gold which is spread over the sky at the hour of sunset. The

[1] See Pinches, *The Religion of Babylonia and Assyria*, p. 39.

assigning of solar characteristics to all slayers of dragons and their kind was a weakness of the older school of mythology, akin to its deductions based on philological grounds; but such criticism as has been directed against the solar theory—and it has been extensive—has not always been pertinent, and in many cases has been merely futile. In fact the solar theory suffered because of the philological arguments with which it was bound up, and neither critics nor readers appeared to discriminate between these. But we should constantly bear in mind that to attempt to elucidate or explain myths by any one system, or by one hard and fast hypothesis, is futile. On the other hand nearly all systems which have yet attempted to elucidate or disentangle the terms of myth are capable of application to certain types of myth. The dragon story is all but universal: in China it is the monster which temporarily swallows the sun during eclipse; in Egypt it was the great serpent Apep, which battled with Ra and Horus, both solar heroes; in India it is the serpent Vritra, or Ahi, who is vanquished by Indra; in Australia and in some parts of North America a great frog takes the place of the dragon. In the story of Beowulf the last exploit of the hero is the slaying of a terrible fire-breathing dragon which guards a hidden treasure-hoard; and Beowulf receives a mortal wound in the encounter. In the Volsung Saga the covetous Faffnir is turned into a dragon and is slain by Sigurd. These must not be confounded with the monsters which cause drought and pestilence. It is a sun-swallowing monster with which we have here to deal.

The tablets here allude to the creation of man; the gods, it is stated, so admired the handiwork of Merodach, that they desired to see him execute

Conflict between Merodach and Tiawath
Photo W. A. Mansell and Co.

still further marvels. Now the gods had none to worship them or pay them homage, and Merodach suggested to his father, Ea, the creation of man out of his divine blood. Here once more the tablets fail us, and we must turn to the narrative of the Chaldean writer Berossus, as preserved by no less than three authors of the classical age. Berossus states that a certain woman Thalatth (that is, Tiawath) had many strange creatures at her bidding. Belus (that is, Bel-Merodach) attacked and cut her in twain, forming the earth out of one half and the heavens out of the other, and destroying all the creatures over which she ruled. Then did Merodach decapitate himself, and as his blood flowed forth the other gods mingled it with the earth and formed man from it. From this circumstance mankind is rational, and has a spark of the divine in it. Then did Merodach divide the darkness, separate the heavens from the earth, and order the details of the entire universe. But those animals which he had created were not able to bear the light, and died. A passage then occurs which states that the stars, the sun and moon, and the five planets were created, and it would seem from the repetition that there were two creations, that the first was a failure, in which Merodach had, as it were, essayed a first attempt, perfecting the process in the second creation. Of course it may be conjectured that Berossus may have drawn from two conflicting accounts, or that those who quote him have inserted the second passage.

The Sumerian incantation, which is provided with a Semitic translation, adds somewhat to our knowledge of this cosmogony. It states that in the beginning nothing as yet existed, none of the great cities of Babylonia had yet been built, indeed there was no land, nothing but sea. It was not until the veins of Tiawath had been cut through that paradise and the abyss appear to have been separated and the gods created by Merodach. Also did he create *annunaki* or gods of the earth, and established a wondrous city as a place in which they might dwell. Then men were formed with the aid of the goddess Aruru, and finally vegetation, trees, and animals. Then did Merodach raise the great temples of Erech and Nippur. From this account we see that instead of Merodach being alluded to as the son of the gods, he is regarded as their creator. In the library of Nineveh was also discovered a copy of a tablet written for the great temple of Nergal at Cuthah. Nergal himself is supposed to make the statement which it contains. He tells us how the hosts of chaos and confusion came into being. At first, as in the other accounts, nothingness reigned supreme, then did the great gods create warriors with the bodies of birds, and men with the faces of ravens. They founded them a city in the ground, and Tiawath, the great dragon, did suckle them. They were fostered in the midst of the mountains, and under the care of the 'mistress of the gods' they greatly increased and became heroes of might. Seven kings had they, who ruled over six thousand people. Their father was the god Benani, and their mother the queen, Melili. These beings, who might almost be called tame gods of evil, Nergal states that he destroyed.[1]

[1] This account has been claimed as a weak version of that part of the creation story which deals with the creation of the host of the abyss. The fact that Nergal states that he destroyed these monsters might justify us in believing that the myth was on this occasion so edited as to provide the monarch with an opportunity for boasting.

A DARKSOME TRINITY

Thus all accounts agree concerning the original chaotic condition of the universe. They also agree that the powers of chaos and darkness were destroyed by a god of light.

The creation tablets are written in Semitic and allude to the great circle of the gods as already fully developed and having its full complement. Even the later deities are mentioned in them. This means that it must be assigned to a comparatively late date, but it possesses elements which go to show that it is a late edition of a much earlier composition—indeed the fundamental elements in it appear, as has been said, to be purely Akkadian in origin, and that would throw back the date of its original form to a very primitive period indeed. It has, as will readily be seen, a very involved cosmogony. Its characteristics show it to have been originally local, and of course Babylonian, in its secondary origin, but from time to time it was added to, so that such gods as were at a later date adopted into the Babylonian pantheon might be explained and accounted for by it; but the legend of the creation arising in the city of Babylon, the local folk-tale known and understood by the people, was never entirely shelved by the more consequential and polished epic, which was perhaps only known and appreciated in literary and æsthetic circles, and bore the same relation to the humbler folk-story that Milton's *Paradise Lost* bears to the medieval legends of the casting out of Satan from heaven.

Although it is quite easy to distinguish influences of extreme antiquity in the Babylonian creation myth, it is clear that in the shape in which it has come down to us it has been altered in such a manner as to make Merodach reap the entire credit of Tiawath's defeat instead of En-lil, or the deity who was his predecessor as monarch of the gods. Jastrow holds that the entire cosmological tale has been constructed from an account of a conflict with a primeval monster and a story of a rebellion against Ea; that these two tales have become fused, and that the first is again divisible into three versions, originating one at Uruk and the other two at Nippur at different epochs. The first celebrates the conquest of Anu over Tiawath, the second exalts Ninib as the conqueror, and the third replaces him by En-lil. We thus see how it was possible for the god of a conquering or popular dynasty to have a complete myth made over to him, and how at last it was competent for the mighty Merodach of Babylon to replace an entire line of deities as the central figure of a myth which must have been popular with untold generations of Akkadian and Babylonian people.

Type of Babylonian Cosmology

We must now consider the precise nature of the Babylonian cosmology and its place among other creation myths. Like the cosmological efforts of most primitive or barbarian peoples it does not partake of the character of a creation myth so much as an account of an evolution from chaos and the establishment of physical laws. The primitive mind cannot grasp the idea of the creation of something out of nothing, and the Babylonians and Akkadians did not differ in this respect from other races in the same stage of development. In whatever direction we look when examining the cosmologies of barbarian or semi-civilized peoples, we find a total inability to get behind and beyond the idea that the matter of creation lay already to the hand of the creative

TYPE OF BABYLONIAN COSMOLOGY

agency, and that in order to shape a world it had but to draw the material therefor from the teeming deep or the slain body of a hostile monster. Not only does the idea of creating land and water out of nothingness seem absurd to the primitive mind, but man as well must be framed from dust, mud, clay, or the blood of the creative god himself. Yet Merodach was able to bring a garment out of nothingness and to return it thither by merely speaking a word! Why, then, did not the theology which admitted the possibility of such a phenomenon carry out its own conception to a logical conclusion and own the likelihood of the god's ability to create an entire universe in the self-same manner? Perhaps the step was too bold for an individual to take in the face of an entire theological college, and in any case what would seem a perfectly feasible act of magic to the theologians of Babylon when applied to a garment might not serve for application to the making of the earth and all that is therein. The cosmology of Babylon is therefore on a par with those of Scandinavia, China, and many North American Indian tribes, nor does it reach so high an imaginative level as those of ancient Egypt, India, or the Maya of Central America, in some of which the vocal command of a god is sufficient to bring about the creation of the earth and the waters surrounding it.

The making of the sun, the moon, and the other heavenly bodies is, as will be more fully shown later, of great importance in Babylonian myth. The stars appear to have been attached to the firmament of heaven as to a cloth. Across this the sun passed daily, his function being to inspect the movements of the other heavenly bodies. The moon, likewise, had her fixed course, and certain stars were also supposed to move across the picture of the night with greater or less regularity. The heavens were guarded at either end by a great gateway, and through one of these the sun passed after rising from the ocean, whilst in setting he quitted the heavens by the opposite portal.

The terrestrial world was imagined as a great hollow structure resting on the 'deep.' Indeed, it would seem to have been regarded as an island floating on an abyss of waters. This conception of the world of earth was by no means peculiar to the Babylonians, but was shared by them with many of the nations of antiquity.

As emanating from the blood of Merodach himself, man was looked upon as directly of heavenly origin. An older tradition existed to the effect that Merodach had been assisted in the creation of mankind by the goddess Aruru, who figures in the Gilgamesh epic as the creatress of Eabani out of a piece of clay. We also find an ancient belief current that humanity owed its origin to the god Ea, but when Merodach displaced this god politically, he would, of course, 'take over' his entire record and creative deeds as well as his powers and sovereignties. At Nippur Bel was looked up to as the originator of man. But these beliefs probably obtained in remoter times, and would finally be quenched by the advance to full and unquestioned power of the great god Merodach.

Connexion with the Jonah Legend

Some mythologists see in the story of Jonah a hidden allusion to the circumstances of Babylonian cosmology. Jonah, as we remember, was summoned to Nineveh to prophesy against it, but proceeding instead to Joppa (the scene of the later myth of

CONNEXION WITH THE JONAH LEGEND

Perseus and Andromeda) the ship in which he set sail was storm-tossed, and he himself advised the sailors to cast him overboard. They did so, and "a great fish" swallowed him. This 'fish,' it has been claimed, is merely a marine form of Tiawath, the dragon of chaos, and the three days and nights which Jonah remains inside it are "the winter months."[1] This does not seem very clear. Hercules in like manner descended into the belly of a fish and emerged again after three days, according to the Phœnicians. The name of Jonah may be compared with that of Oannes or Ea. The love-god, in the Hindu *Vishnu Purana*, thrown into the sea, is swallowed by a fish, like the ring of Gyges. Was there a local sea-monster at Joppa, a variant of Tiawath, and is it the same in the Jonah myth as that in the tale of Perseus? A tawny fountain at Joppa was thought to derive its colour from the blood of the sea-monster slain by Perseus, says Pausanias. Was then the monster who lay in wait off Joppa, Tiawath the goddess of darkness, and was Jonah none other than Ea or Oannes, her mortal foe, the god of light, whom she would mythologically swallow during the sere months of winter?

[1] *Bible Folk Lore*, London, 1884. Anonymous.

CHAPTER III: EARLY BABYLONIAN RELIGION

The Beginnings of Babylonian Religion

THE true beginning of a religion is that epoch in its history when it succeeds, by reason of local or national circumstances and environment and by racial genius, in raising itself from those purely animistic influences which are characteristic of early faith and from which all great religions have emerged, if they have not been able entirely to free themselves from associations which by reason of their antiquity and the hold they achieve on the mind of humanity are particularly difficult to cast off. Thus a sense of nationality and the attainment of a high standard of righteousness assisted in shaping Jewish religion. The necessity for military efficiency and therefore of sacrifice to the gods was moulding a real if terrible religion in ancient Mexico when the invading Spaniards ended the hideous masque of tragedy. Insight and meditation lent an air of ethical exaltation to the Vedic religion of India. Thus in a manner peculiarly its own, and according to the trend of its particular genius, did each race evolve a suitable religion from an original animistic basis.

If we are to discover the foundations of any system or cult, however, if we are to excavate the soil religious as we would the soil archæological in the hope of coming upon the basis of any particular faith, we must undertake the work in a manner as thorough as that of the antiquary who, pick in hand, delves his way to the lowest foundations of palace or temple. The earliest Babylonian religious ideas—that is, subsequent to the entrance of that people

SPIRITS AND GODS

into the country watered by the Tigris and Euphrates—were undoubtedly coloured by those of the non-Semitic Sumerians whom they found in the country. They adopted the alphabet of that race, and this affords strong presumptive evidence that the immigrant Semites, as an unlettered people, would naturally accept much if not all of the religion of the more cultured folk whom they found in possession of the soil.

There is no necessity in this place to outline the nature of animistic belief at any length. This has been done in so many other volumes of this series and in such detail that it is sufficient to state here succinctly that animism is a condition of thought or belief in which man considers everything in the universe along with himself to be the possessor of 'soul,' 'spirit,' or at least volition. Thus, the wind, water, animals, the heavenly bodies, all live, move, and have their being, and because of his fear of or admiration for them, man placates or adores them until at length he almost unconsciously exalts them into a condition of godhead. Have we any reason to think that the ancient Semites of Babylonia regarded the universe as peopled by gods or godlings of such a type? The proofs that they did so are not a few.

Spirits and Gods

Spirits swarmed in ancient Babylonia, as the reader will observe when he comes to peruse the chapter dealing with the magical ideas of the race. And here it is important to note that the determinative or symbolic written sign for 'spirit' is the same as that for 'god.' Thus the god and the spirit must in Babylonia have had a common descent. The manner in which we can distinguish between a god and a spirit, however, is simple. Lists of the 'official' gods are provided in the historical texts, whereas spirits and demons are not included therein. But this is not to say that no attempt had been made to systematize the belief in spirits in Babylonia, for just as the great gods of the universe were apportioned their several offices, so were the spirits allotted almost exactly similar powers. Thus the *Annunaki* were perhaps regarded as the spirits of earth and the *Igigi* as spirits of heaven. So, at least, are they designated in an inscription of Rammannirari I. The grouping evidently survived from animistic times, when perhaps the spirits which are embraced in these two classes were the only 'gods' of the Babylonians or Sumerians, and from whose ranks some of the great gods of future times may have been evolved. In any case they belong to a very early period in the Babylonian religion and play no unimportant part in it almost to the end. The god Anu, the most ancient of the Babylonian deities, was regarded as the father of both companies, but other gods make use of their services. They do not appear to be well disposed to humanity. The Assyrian kings were wont to invoke them when they desired to inculcate a fear of their majesty in the people, and from this it may be inferred that they were objects of peculiar fear to the lower orders of the population—for the people often cling to the elder cults and the elder pantheons despite the innovations of ecclesiastical politicians, or the religious eccentricities of kings. There can, however, be no doubt as to the truly animistic character of early Babylonian religion. Thus in the early inscriptions one reads of the spirits of various kinds of diseases, the spirit of the south wind, the spirits of the mist, and so forth. The *bit-ili* or sacred stones marking the residence of a god were probably a link between the fetish and the idol, remaining even after the fully developed idol had been evolved.

Was Babylonian Religion Semitic in Type?

It has already been stated that the religion of ancient Babylon was probably greatly influenced by those non-Semitic people whom the Semitic Babylonians found occupying the country when they entered it. The question then arises (and it is one of high importance), how far did the religion of ancient Babylonia and Assyria partake of the character of that group of religions which has been called 'Semitic.' The classical pronouncement upon this phase of the subject is probably that of the late Professor Robertson Smith, who in his *Religion of the Semites* (p. 13) says[1]: " The preponderating opinion of Assyriologists is to the effect that the civilization of Assyria and Babylonia was not purely Semitic, and that the ancient population of these parts contained a large pre-Semitic element, whose influence is especially to be recognized in religion and in the sacred literature of the cuneiform records. If this be so, it is plain that the cuneiform material must be used with caution in our enquiry into the type of traditional religion characteristic of the ancient Semites. That Babylonia is the best starting-point for a comparative study of the sacred beliefs and practices of the Semitic peoples, is an idea which has lately had some vogue, and which at first sight appears plausible on account of the great antiquity of the monumental evidence. But, in matters of this sort, ancient and primitive are not

[1] The passage is quoted by kind permission of Messrs A. & C. Black.

synonymous terms; and we must not look for the most primitive form of Semitic faith in a region where society was not primitive. In Babylonia, it would seem, society and religion alike were based on a fusion of two races, and so were not primitive but complex. Moreover, the official system of Babylonian and Assyrian religion, as it is known to us from priestly texts and public inscriptions, bears clear marks of being something more than a popular traditional faith; it has been artificially moulded by priestcraft and statecraft in much the same way as the official religion of Egypt; that is to say, it is in great measure an artificial combination, for imperial purposes, of elements drawn from a number of local worships. In all probability the actual religion of the masses was always much simpler than the official system; and in later times it would seem that, both in religion and in race, Assyria was little different from the adjacent Aramæan countries. These remarks are not meant to throw doubt on the great importance of cuneiform studies for the history of Semitic religion; the monumental data are valuable for comparison with what we know of the faith and worship of other Semitic peoples, and peculiarly valuable because, in religion as in other matters, the civilization of the Euphrates-Tigris valley exercised a great historical influence on a large part of the Semitic field."

Totemism in Babylonian Religion

Signs of totemism are not wanting in the Babylonian as in other religious systems. Many of the gods are pictured as riding upon the backs of certain animals, an almost certain indication that at one time they had themselves possessed the form of the

THE GREAT GODS

animal they bestrode. Religious conservatism would probably not tolerate the immediate abolition of the totem-shape, so this means was taken of gradually 'shelving' it. But some gods retained animal form until comparatively late times. Thus the sun-god of Kis had the form of an eagle, and we find that Ishtar took as lovers a horse, an eagle, and a lion—surely gods who were represented in equine, aquiline, and leonine forms. The fish-form of Oannes, the god of wisdom, is certainly a relic of totemism. Some of the old ideographic representations of the names of the gods are eloquent of a totemic connexion. Thus the name of Ea, the god of the deep, is expressed by an ideograph which signifies 'antelope.' Ea is spoken of as 'the antelope of the deep,' 'the lusty antelope,' and so forth. He was also, as a water-god, connected with the serpent, a universal symbol of the flowing stream. The strange god Uz, probably an Akkadian survival, was worshipped under the form of a goat. The sun-god of Nippur, Adar, was connected with the pig, and was called 'lord of the swine.' Merodach may have been a bull-god. In early astronomical literature we find him alluded to as 'the bull of light.' The storm-god Zu, as is seen by his myth, retained his birdlike form. Another name of the storm-bird was Lugal-banda, patron god of the city of Marad, near Sippara. Like Prometheus—also once a bird-god, as is proved by many analogous myths—he stole the sacred fire from heaven for the service and mental illumination of man.

The Great Gods

In the phase in which it becomes first known to us, Babylonian religion is neither Semitic nor Akkadian, but Semitic-Akkadian: that is, the elements of both religious forms are so intermingled in it that they cannot be distinguished one from another; but very little that is trustworthy can be advanced concerning this shadowy time. Each petty state (and these were numerous in early Babylonia) possessed its own tutelar deity, and he again had command over a number of lesser gods. When all those pantheons were added together, as was the case in later days, they afforded the spectacle of perhaps the largest assembly of gods known to any religion. The most outstanding of these tribal divinities, as they might justly be called, were Merodach, who was worshipped at Babylon; Shamash, who was adored at Sippar; Sin, the moon-god, who ruled at Ur; Anu, who held sway over Erech and Der; Ea, the Oannes of legend, whose city was Eridu; Bel, who ruled at Nippur, or Niffur; Nergal of Cuthah; and Ishtar, who was goddess of Nineveh. The peoples of the several provinces identified their prominent gods one with another, and indeed when Assyria rose to rivalry with Babylonia, its chief divinity, Asshur, was naturally identified with Merodach.

In the chapter on cosmology we have seen how Merodach gained the lordship of heaven. It has been shown that the rise of this god to power was comparatively recent. Prior to the days of Khammurabi a rather different pantheon from that described in later inscriptions held sway. In those more primitive days the principal gods appear to have been Bel or En-lil, Belit or Nin-lil his queen, Ningirsu, Ea, Nergal, Shamash, Sin, Anu, and other lesser divinities. There is indeed a sharp distinction between the pre- and post-Khammurabic types of religion. Attempts had been made to form a pan-

Types of En-lil, the Chief God of Nippur, and of his Consort, Nin-lil

From *Religious Belief and Practice in Babylonia and Assyria*, by Professor Morris Jastrow

By permission of Messrs G. P. Putnam's Sons

BEL

theon before Khammurabi's day, but his exaltation of Merodach, the patron of Babylon, to the head of the Babylonian pantheon was destined to destroy these. A glance at the condition of the great gods before the days of Khammurabi will assist us to understand their later developments.

Bel

Bel, or, to give him his earlier name, En-lil, is spoken of in very early inscriptions, especially in those of Nippur, of which city he was the tutelar deity. He was described as the 'lord of the lower world,' and much effort seems to have been made to reach a definite conception of his position and attributes. His name had also been translated 'lord of mist.' The title 'Bel' had been given to Merodach by Tiglath-pileser I about 1200 B.C., after which he was referred to as 'the older Bel.' The chief seat of his worship was at Nippur, where the name of his temple, E-Kur or 'mountain-house,' came to be applied to a sanctuary all over Babylonia. He was also addressed as the 'lord of the storm' and as the 'great mountain,' and his consort Nin-lil is also alluded to as 'lady of the mountain.' Jastrow rightly concludes that "there are substantial reasons for assuming that his original city was on the top of some mountain, as is so generally the case of storm-deities. . . . There being no mountains in the Euphrates valley, however, the conclusion is warranted that En-lil was the god of a people whose home was in a mountainous region and who brought their god with them when they came to the Euphrates valley."[1]

En-lil is undoubtedly of the class of tempest-

[1] *Religious Belief in Babylonia and Assyria*, p. 69.

deities who dwell on mountain peaks. No text appears to have been found which alludes to him as of a red colour. The flashing of the lightning through the clouds which veil the mountain summits usually generates a belief in the mind of primitive man that the god who is concealed by the screen of vapour is red in hue and quick in movement. The second tablet of a text known as the 'crying storm' alludes to En-lil as a storm-god. Addressing him it says: "Spirit that overcomes no evildoing, spirit that has no mother, spirit that has no wife, spirit that has no sister, spirit that has no brother, that knows no abiding place, the evil-slaying spirit that devastates the fold, that wrecks the stall, that sweeps away son and mother like a reed. As a huge deluge it tears away dwellings, consumes the provisions of the home, smites mankind everywhere, and wickedly drowns the harvests of the land. Devoted temples it devastates, devoted men it afflicts, him that clothes himself in a robe of majesty the spirit lays low with cold, him of wide pasture lands with hunger it lays low. When En-lil, the lord of lands, cries out at sunset the dreadful word goes forth unto the spacious shrine, 'Destroy.'"

Nippur, the city of En-lil, was of Sumerian origin, so we must connect the earliest cult of En-lil with the Sumerian aborigines. Many of his lesser names point to such a conclusion. But he greatly outgrew all local circumstances, and among other things he appears to have been a god who fostered vegetation. Some authorities appear to be of opinion that because En-lil was regarded as a god of vegetation the change was owing to his removal from a mountainous region to a more level neighbourhood. The truth is, it would be difficult to discover a god who wielded the powers of the wind and rain who was not a patron of agriculture, but as he sends beneficent rains, so also may he destroy and devastate, as we have seen from the foregoing text. The noise of the storm was spoken of as his 'word.' Probably, too, because he was a very old god he was regarded in some localities as a creator of the world. The great winged bull of Assyrian art may well often represent En-lil: no symbol could better typify the tempest which the Babylonians regarded as rushing and rioting unrestrained over country and city, overturning even tower and temple with its violence, and tumbling the wretched reed huts of the lower caste into the dust.

The word *lil* which occurs in the name En-lil, signifies a 'demon,' and En-lil may therefore mean the 'chief-demon.' This shows the very early, animistic nature of the god. There appear to be other traditions of him as a war-god, but these are so obscure as scarcely to be worth notice. In the trinity which consisted of Bel, Ea, and Anu, he is regarded as the 'god of the earth,' that is, the earth is his sphere, and he is at times addressed as 'Bel, the lord of the lands.'

We find the 'word' of the wind or storm-god alluded to in the *Popol Vuh* of the Kiches of Central America, where Hurakan (the deity from whose name we probably get our word 'hurricane') sweeps over the face of the primeval deep, voicing his commands.

Bel and the Dragon

The picturesque legend of Bel and the Dragon which appears in the Apocrypha, and which was at one time appended to the Book of Daniel, shows us the manner in which Bel was worshipped at Babylon, and how he was supposed to take human shape, devour food, and behave very much as a man might. The legend states that the Babylonians lavished every day upon the idol of Bel twelve great measures of fine flour, and forty sheep, and six vessels of wine. King Cyrus of Persia, who had overthrown the Babylonian kingdom, went daily to worship Bel, and asked Daniel why he did not do likewise. The prophet replied that his religion did not permit him to worship idols, but rather the living God who had created the heavens and the earth.

"Then said Cyrus: 'Thinkest thou not that Bel is the living God? Seest thou not how much he eateth and drinketh every day?'

"Then Daniel smiled and said, 'O King, be not deceived, for he is but clay within and brass without, and can never eat or drink anything.'

"Cyrus was exceeding wroth, and calling for his priests said to them, 'If ye tell me not who this is that devoureth these expenses ye shall die, but if ye can show me that Bel devours them Daniel shall die, for he hath spoken blasphemy against Bel;'" and to this Daniel cheerfully agreed.

It would have been surprising had not the provisions vanished, because we are told that the priests of Bel were threescore and ten in number and had numerous wives and children. So Cyrus and Daniel betook themselves to the temple of Bel, and the priests asked them to bless the meat and wine before Bel, and to shut the door fast and seal it with the King's own signet, stating that if they came on the morrow they would find that Bel had eaten up all of the provisions.

BEL AND THE DRAGON

But they had taken good care to protect themselves, for they had made a secret entrance underneath the great table in the temple which they used constantly, so that they might consume the good things that were set before the idol.

And Cyrus did as the priests asked, setting the meat and wine before the statue of Bel, but Daniel commanded his servants to bring ashes, which they strewed throughout the temple in the presence of the King; then they went out and shut the door and sealed it with the King's signet.

And in the night time the priests with their wives and families entered the temple by the secret way and speedily consumed the provisions.

In the morning Cyrus and Daniel betook themselves to the temple, and the King broke the seals and opened the door, and when he perceived that all the provisions had vanished he called out with a loud voice, " Great art thou, O Bel, and with thee is no deceit at all.'

But Daniel laughed, and barring the King's way into the temple requested him to look at the pavement and mark well whose footsteps he saw there.

And Cyrus replied, " I see the footsteps of men, women, and children."

He at once called the priests, who when they saw that their stratagem had been discovered showed him the secret way into the temple; and in his rage Cyrus slew them and delivered Bel into Daniel's power. The prophet speedily destroyed the idol and the temple which sheltered it.

Now in that temple was a great dragon worshipped by the people of Babylon, and the King said to Daniel: " Wilt thou also say that this is of brass, for behold! he liveth, he eateth and drinketh, therefore shouldest thou worship him!"

But Daniel shook his head and said to Cyrus: "Give me leave, O King, and I will slay this dragon without sword or staff."

Then Daniel took pitch and fat and hair and boiled them all together, and shaped them into great pieces. These he placed in the dragon's mouth, and shortly the dragon burst asunder.

Now the people of Babylon became greatly incensed at these doings and clamoured to Cyrus, asking him to deliver Daniel up to them, or else they would destroy him and all belonging to him. And, continues the legend, Cyrus being afraid for his crown delivered Daniel to the people, who cast him into a lions' den where he remained for six days. Seven lions were in the den and their food was removed from them so that they might be the fiercer, and the Apocrypha story, which differs considerably from that given in the sixth chapter of the Book of Daniel, states that the angel of the Lord took up a certain prophet called Habbacuc, who was about to carry a mess of pottage to certain reapers, and taking him by the hair of the head, conveyed him all the way from Palestine to Babylon along with the food, which he set at Daniel's feet. Daniel partook of the meal, and Habbacuc was conveyed back to Palestine in the same manner as that in which he had come.

And on the seventh day Cyrus came to the den to mourn for Daniel, and when he looked in Daniel was there. So impressed was Cyrus with the power of Daniel's God that he resolved to worship Him in future, and seizing those who had been instrumental in casting the Hebrew prophet into the den,

THE TEMPLE OF BEL

he thrust them before the lions, and they were devoured in a moment.

Beltis

Beltis, or Nin-lil, the wife of En-lil, shared his authority over Nippur, where she had a temple which went back in antiquity to the First Dynasty of Ur. As has been said, she was also called the 'lady of the mountain,' and as such she had a sanctuary at Girsu, a quarter of Lagash. In certain inscriptions she is described as 'the mother of the gods.' The name Beltis meant 'lady,' and as such was accorded to her as being 'the' lady, but it was afterwards given to many other goddesses.

The Temple of Bel

In 1876 Mr George Smith discovered a Babylonian text giving a remarkable account of the temple of Bel at Babylon. This temple, the wonder of Babylon, was founded while that city was still a place of no very great importance, but its fabric lasted until the days of Herodotus and Strabo, who have furnished us with accounts of it. The former states that it consisted of eight stages or towers one above another, forming a pyramid, the holy of holies being placed upon the highest stage of all, the height of the entire building being about 600 feet—a very questionable dimension.

In the cuneiform tablet the measurements of the outer court are given as 1156 feet in length and 900 feet in breadth. An adjoining court, that of Ishtar and Zamama, was 1056 feet by 450 feet, and had six gates which admitted worshippers to the temple—the grand gate, the gate of the rising sun looking eastward, the great gate, the gate of the Colossi, flanked by enormous figures, the canal gate, and the gate of the tower-view.

A walled space, platform or *birut*, orientated so as to face the four cardinal points, is next described. Inside this stood a building the name of which is indecipherable. It was connected in some manner with the Ziggurat or great tower, around the base of which were ranged the temples of the principal gods, all of which faced one or other of the four chief points of the compass.

On the eastern side of the group stood a large temple 117 feet by 67 feet broad, containing no less than sixteen shrines, the principal of which were sacred to Nebo, the son of Bel, and his wife Tashmit. To the north were temples to Ea and Nusku, the first 142 feet long by 50 feet broad and the second a square 58 feet either way. To the south was a shrine to Bel and Anu 117 feet by 50 feet.

The purpose of the buildings on the western side of the great tower is only to be conjectured. It is known, however, that the couch of Bel and his throne of gold alluded to by Herodotus were housed in one or other of the buildings on this side. The couch is said to have measured 15 feet by 6 feet 8 inches.

In the centre towered the great Ziggurat, rising stage upon stage, its sides facing the cardinal points. The first stage was 300 feet square and 110 feet high and was ornamented with buttresses. The second was 260 feet square and 60 feet high, the third 200 feet square and 20 feet high up to the seventh stage, which was 80 feet long, 70 feet broad, and 50 feet high. The entire height of the Ziggurat was thus 300 feet, exactly equal to the breadth of the

THE TEMPLE OF BEL

base, or only half the height attributed to it by Herodotus.

Regarding the possible site of this temple Mr Smith says: "The only ruin now existing at or near Babylon which can be supposed to represent the temple of Belus is the mound and enclosure of Bâbil, the ruins corresponding fairly with the account of these structures in the Greek authors and in the inscription. The sides of the building face the cardinal points, like those in the inscription; the remains of the two sides of the enclosure now existing indicate a circumference about equal to the Greek measurement, and slightly in excess of that in the inscription; but it must be remembered that the exact length of the Babylonian measures is not known, and there are different opinions even as to the length of the Greek stade, while the present remains of the wall require careful measurement to determine more exactly their length and the dimensions they indicate. On the other side of the Euphrates stands a ruin, Birs Nimrûd, also consisting of an enclosure, various temples, and a temple-tower; but this represents the site of the temple of Nebo at Borsippa, and its angles, instead of its sides, face the cardinal points, while not a single one of its known dimensions agrees with the corresponding point in the inscription. The mound of Bâbil, which is already identified by the best authorities with the temple of Belus, consists now of the lower stage of the tower and the ruins of the buildings round it."[1]

Yet Herodotus' account of the temple of Bel was not wholly false. He says: " It had gates of brass, and was two stadia every way, being quadrangular; in the middle of the temple a solid tower

[1] *Athenæum*, Feb. 12, 1876.

was built, a stadium in height and breadth, and on this tower was placed another, and another still on this, to the number of eight towers in all. The ascent was on the outside, and was made by a winding passage round all the towers; and about half up the ascent there is a landing and seats for rest, where those ascending may repose; and in the highest tower there is a large temple, and in the temple a large bed well furnished, and beside it a golden table; but there is no statue erected in it; and by night no one lodges in it, except a single woman of the country, whom the god has selected from the rest, as say the Chaldæans, who are the priests of this god."

An inscription was discovered and translated by Sir H. C. Rawlinson, in which King Nebuchadrezzar boasts of having repaired and completed this tower in honour of his god Merodach. "Behold now the building named 'The Stages of the Seven Spheres,' which was the wonder of Borsippa, had been built by a former king. He had completed forty-two ammas (of the height), but he did not finish its head. From the lapse of time it had become ruined; they had not taken care of the exits of the waters, so the rain and wet had penetrated into the brickwork; the casing of burnt brick had bulged out, and the terraces of crude brick lay scattered in heaps. Then Merodach, my great lord, inclined my heart to repair the building. I did not change its site, nor did I destroy the foundation platform; but in a fortunate month, and on an auspicious day, I undertook the rebuilding of the crude brick terraces and the burnt brick casing (of the temple). I strengthened its foundations, and I placed a titular record in the parts that I had rebuilt. I set my hand to build it up, and to finish

NERGAL

its summit. As it had been in former days, thus I exalted its head."

Nergal

Nergal was the patron god of Cuthah, eastward from Babylon. He was a god of extremely ancient origin, and indeed the first inscription which alludes to him is dated about 2700 B.C. He is mentioned in the Old Testament (2 Kings xvii 30) as an idol whom the Babylonians who re-peopled Israel brought with them. He seems to have had a close connexion with the nether world, indeed he is practically the head of its pantheon. He appears to have been a god of gloom and death, and his name may signify 'the lord of the great dwelling place,' that is, the grave. His city, Cuthah, may possibly have been renowned as a burial-place. We find him associated with pestilence and famine, but he has also a solar significance. He is indeed the sun in its malevolent form, fierce and destroying, for in myth the sun can be evil as well as good. We thus find the solar power depicted as a fierce warrior slaying his thousands and tens of thousands. Again it is quite possible for a solar deity to have an underworld connexion, seeing that the sun is supposed to travel through that gloomy region during the night. We thus see how Nergal could combine so many seemingly conflicting attributes. As god of the dead he has a host of demons at his command, and it may be these who do his behests in spreading pestilence and war. Where he goes violent death follows in his wake. At times he is called the 'god of fire,' the 'raging king,' 'he who burns,' and the 'violent one,' and he is identified with the fierceness of flame. In this respect he is not at all unlike the Scandinavian Loki who typifies the malevolence of fire.

Dibarra

Dibarra was probably a variant of Nergal, in his guise as solar destroyer. Concerning him a strange myth is recounted as follows:

"The sons of Babylon were as birds and thou their falconer. In a net thou didst catch them, enclose them, and destroy them, O warrior Dibarra. Leaving the city, thou didst pass to the outside, taking on the form of a lion, thou didst enter the palace. The people saw thee and drew their weapons."

So spoke Ishum, the faithful attendant of Dibarra, by way of beginning an account of the havoc wrought in the valley of Euphrates by the war- and plague-god. "Spare no one," is the gist of his commands to his satellites. "Have neither fear nor pity. Kill the young as well as the old and rob Babylon of all its treasures."

Accordingly against the first city a large army was dispatched to carry out these instructions, and the battle with bow and sword was begun, a strife which ended so disastrously for the soldiers and inhabitants that their blood flowed "like torrents of water through the city's highways." This defeat the great lord Merodach was compelled to witness, powerless to help or avert it. Enraged at his helplessness and overcome with fury, he cursed his enemies until he is said to have lost consciousness because of his grief.

From this scene of devastation Dibarra turned his attention to Erech, appointing others of his host to mete out to this city the fate of Babylon. Ishtar, goddess of Erech, saw her devoted city exposed to plunder, pillage, and bloodshed, and had to endure the agony of inactivity experienced by Merodach. Nothing she could do or say would stay the violence of Dibarra's vengeance.

"O warrior Dibarra, thou dost dispatch the just, thou dost dispatch the unjust; who sins against thee thou dost dispatch, and the one who does not sin against thee thou dost dispatch."

These words were used by Ishum, Dibarra's servant, in a subsequent address to the god of war. He knew his lord's craving for battle and bloodshed was still unappeased, and he himself was planning a war more terrible than any he had yet conducted, a conflict not only world-wide but which was to embrace heaven itself. So in order to gain Dibarra's consent to the hideous destruction he anticipated, he continued to pander to his war-like tendencies.

Said he: "The brightness of Shul-panddu I will destroy, the root of the tree I will tear out that it no longer blossom. Against the dwelling of the king of gods I will proceed."

To all of which the warrior-god listened with growing pleasure, until fired by his myrmidon's words he cried out in sudden fierce resolve—"Sea-coast against sea-coast, Subartu against Subartu, Assyrian against Assyrian, Elamite against Elamite, Cassite against Cassite, Sutaean against Sutaean, Kuthean against Kuthean, Lullubite against Lullubite, country against country, house against house, man against man. Brother is to show no mercy towards brother; they shall kill one another."

"Go, Ishum," he added later, "carry out the word thou hast spoken in accordance with thy desire."

And with alacrity Ishum obeyed, "directing his countenance to the mountain of Khi-khi. This, with the help of the god Sibi, a warrior unequalled, he attacked and destroyed all the vineyards in the forest of Khashur, and finally the city of Inmarmaon. These last atrocious acts roused Ea, the god of humanity, and filled him with wrath," though what attitude he adopted towards Dibarra is not known.

"Listen all of you to my words, because of sin did I formerly plan evil, my heart was enraged and I swept peoples away."

This was Dibarra's defence when eventually he was propitiated and all the gods were gathered together in council with him. Ishum at this point changing his tactics urged on Dibarra the necessity for pacifying the gods he had incensed.

"Appease," said he, "the gods of the land who are angry. May fruits and corn flourish, may mountains and seas bring their produce."

As he had listened to Ishum before, Dibarra listened again, and the council of the gods was closed by his promising prosperity and protection to those who would fittingly honour him.

"He who glorifies my name will rule the world. Who proclaims the glory of my power will be without rival. The singer who sings of my deeds will not die through pestilence, to kings and nobles his words will be pleasing. The writer who preserves them will escape from the grasp of the enemy, in the temple where the people proclaim my name, I will open his ear. In the house where this tablet is set up, though war may rage and the god Sibi work havoc, sword and pestilence will not touch him —he will dwell in safety. Let this song resound for ever and endure for eternity. Let all lands hear

SHAMASH

it and proclaim my power. Let the inhabitants of all places learn to glorify my name."

Shamash

Shamash, god of the sun, was one of the most popular deities of the Babylonian and Assyrian pantheon. We find him mentioned first in the reign of E-Anna-Tum, or about 4200 B.C. He is called the son of Sin, the moon-god, which perhaps has reference to the fact that the solar calendar succeeded the lunar in Babylonia as in practically all civilizations of any advancement. The inscriptions give due prominence to his status as a great lord of light, and in them he is called the 'illuminator of the regions,' 'lord of living creatures,' 'gracious one of the lands,' and so forth. He is supposed to throw open the gates of the morning and raise his head over the horizon, lighting up the heaven and earth with his beams. The knowledge of justice and injustice and the virtue of righteousness were attributed to him, and he was regarded as a judge between good and evil, for as the light of the sun penetrates everywhere, and nothing can be hidden from its beams, it is not strange that it should stand as the symbol for justice. Shamash appears at the head of the inscription which bears the laws of Khammurabi, and here he stands as the symbol for justice. The towns at which he was principally worshipped were Sippar and Larsa, where his sanctuary was known as E-Babbara, or the 'shining house.' Larsa was probably the older of the two centres, but from the times of Sargon, Sippar became the more important, and in the days of Khammurabi ranked immediately after Babylon. In fact it appears to have threatened the supremacy of the capital to some extent, and Nabonidus, the last King of Babylon, as we shall remember, offended Merodach and his priests by his too eager notice of Shamash. During the whole course of Babylonian history, however, Shamash retained his popularity, and was perhaps the only sun-god who was not absorbed by Merodach. One finds the same phenomenon in ancient Mexico, where various solar deities did not succeed in displacing or absorbing Totec, the ancient god of the sun *par excellence*. But Shamash succeeded in absorbing many small local sun-gods, and indeed we find his name used as that of the sun throughout Semitic lands. There were several solar deities, such as Nergal, and Ninib, whom Shamash did not absorb, probably for the reason that they typify various phases of the sun. There is reason to believe that in ancient times even Shamash was not an entirely beneficent solar deity, but, like Nergal, could figure as a warrior on occasion. But in later times he was regarded as the god who brings light and life upon all created things, and upon whom depends everything in nature from man to vegetable. His consort was Aa, who was worshipped at Sippar along with him. Her cult seems to have been one of great antiquity, but she does not appear to have any distinctive character of her own. She was supposed to receive the sun upon his setting, and from this circumstance it has been argued she perhaps represents the 'double sun,' from the magnified disk which he presents at sunset; but this explanation is perhaps rather too much on allegorical lines. Jastrow thinks that she may have been evolved from the sun-god of a city on the other side of the Euphrates from Sippar. "Such an amalgamation of two originally male deities into a combination of male and female, strange as it may seem to us," he says, "is in keeping with the lack of sharp distinction between male and female in the oldest forms of Semitic religions. In the old cuneiform writing the same sign is used to indicate 'lord' or 'lady' when attached to deities. Ishtar appears amongst the Semites both as male and female. Sex was primarily a question of strength; the stronger god was viewed as masculine, the weaker as feminine."

Ea

Ea was the third of the great Babylonian triad of gods, which consisted of Anu, En-lil, and himself. He was a god of the waters, and like Anu is called the 'father of the gods.' As a god of the abyss he appears to have been also a deity of wisdom and occult power, thus allegorically associated with the idea of depth or profundity. He was the father of Merodach, who consulted him on the most important matters connected with his kingship of the gods. Indeed he was consulted by individuals of all classes who desired light to be thrown upon their crafts or businesses. Thus he was the god of artisans in general—blacksmiths, stone-cutters, sailors, and artificers of every kind. He was also the patron of prophets and seers. As the abyss is the place where the seeds of everything were supposed to fructify, so he appears to have fostered reproduction of every description. He was supposed to dwell beside Anu, who inhabited the pole of the ecliptic. The site of his chief temple was at Eridu, which at one time stood, before the waters receded, upon the shore of the Persian Gulf. We have seen already that Ea, under his Greek name of Oannes, was supposed to bring knowledge and culture to the people of Eridu.

MYTHS OF BABYLONIA AND ASSYRIA

There are many confusing myths connected with him, and he seems in some measure to enter into the Babylonian myth of the deluge. Alexander Polyhistor, Apollodorus, and Eusebius, copying from Berossus, state that he rose from the sea upon his civilizing mission, and Abydenus says that in the time of Daon, the shepherd king of the city of Pantibiblon (meaning the 'city where books were gathered together'), "Annedatus appeared again from the Eruthrean sea, in the same form as those who had showed themselves before, having the shape of a fish blended with that of a man. Then reigned Aedorachus of Pantibiblon for the term of eighteen sari. In his days there appeared another personage from the sea of Eruthra, like those above, having the same complicated form between fish and man: his name was Odacon." From remarks by Apollodorus it would seem that these beings were messengers from Oannes, but the whole passages are very obscure. The chief extract from the fragments of Berossus concerning Oannes states that : " In the first year there made its appearance from a part of the Eruthrean sea, which bordered upon Babylonia, an animal endowed with reason, who was called Oannes. According to the accounts of Apollodorus the whole body of the animal was like that of a fish ; and had under a fish's head another head, and also feet below, similar to those of a man, subjoined to the fish's tail. His speech, too, was articulate and human ; and there was a representation of him to be seen in the time of Berossus. This Being in the day-time used to converse with men ; but took no food at that season ; and he gave them an insight into letters and science, and every kind of art. He taught them to construct houses, to found temples, to compile laws, and explained to them the principles of geometrical knowledge. He made them distinguish the seeds of the earth, and showed them how to collect fruits; in short, he instructed them in everything which could tend to soften manners and humanize mankind. From that time, so universal were his instructions, nothing material has been added by way of improvement. When the sun set, it was the custom of this Being to plunge again into the sea, and abide all the night in the deep." After this there appeared other creatures like Oannes, of which Berossus promises to give an account when he comes to the history of the kings.

The Writings of Oannes

"Moreover," says Polyhistor, "Oannes wrote concerning the generation of mankind; of their different ways of life, and of civil polity; and the following is the purport of what he said: "'There was nothing but darkness, and an abyss of water, wherein resided most hideous beings, which were produced of a twofold principle. Men appeared with two wings, some with four, and with two faces. They had one body, but two heads; the one of a man, the other of a woman. They were likewise in their several organs both male and female. Other human figures were to be seen with the legs and horns of goats. Some had horses' feet: others had the limbs of a horse behind; but before were fashioned like men, resembling hippocentaurs. Bulls likewise bred there with the heads of men; and dogs with fourfold bodies, and the tails of fishes. Also horses with the heads of dogs: men too, and other animals, with the heads and bodies of horses, and the tails of fishes. In short, there were creatures with the limbs of every species of animals. Add to these, fishes, reptiles, serpents, with other wonderful animals; which assumed each other's shape and countenance. Of all these were preserved delineations in the temple of Belus at Babylon. The person, who was supposed to have presided over them, had the name of Omorca. This in the Chaldaic language is Thalath; which the Greeks express *thalassa*, the sea: but according to the most probable theory, it is equivalent to *selene*, the moon. All things being in this situation, Belus came, and cut the woman-creature asunder: and out of one half of her he formed the earth, and of the other half the heavens. At the same time he destroyed the animals in the abyss. All this, Berossus said,[1] was an allegorical description of nature. For the whole universe consisting of moisture, and, animals being continually generated therein, the Deity (Belus) above-mentioned cut off his own head, upon which the other gods mixed the blood, as it gushed out, with the earth, and from this men were formed. On this account it is, that they are rational, and partake of divine knowledge. This Belus, whom men call Dis, divided the darkness, and separated the heavens from the earth; and reduced the universe to order. But the animals so lately created, not being able to bear the prevalence of light, died. Belus upon this, seeing a vast space quite uninhabited, though by nature very fruitful, ordered one of the gods to take off his head; and when it was taken off, they were to mix the blood with the soil of the earth; and from thence to form other men and animals, which should be capable

---

[1] Polyhistor is still speaking. The passage is somewhat obscure, and of course relates to the myth of Merodach and Tiawath—Bel representing Merodach, and "the woman-creature" Tiawath.

of bearing the light. Belus also formed the stars, and the sun, and moon, together with the five planets.'"

This myth, related by Ea or Oannes regarding the creation of the world, bears a very close relation to that of Merodach and Tiawath, told in Chapter II. It is not often that one finds a fish-god acting as a culture hero, although we find in Mexican myth a certain deity alluded to as the " old fish-god of our flesh." Allegorical mythology would have seen in Ea a hero arriving from another clime in a wave-tossed vessel, who had landed on the shores of the Persian Gulf, and had instructed the rude inhabitants thereof in the culture of a higher civilization. There is very little doubt that Ea has a close connexion in some manner with the Noah legend of the deluge. For example, a Sumerian text exists in which it would seem as if the ship of Ea was described, as the timbers of which its various parts were constructed are mentioned, and the refugees it saved consisted of Ea himself, Dawkina his wife, Merodach, and Inesh, the pilot of Eridu, along with Nin-igi-nagir-sir.

Of course it would seem natural to the Babylonians to regard the Persian Gulf as the great abyss whence all things emanated. As Jastrow very justly remarks : " In the word of Ea, of a character more spiritual than that of En-lil, he commands, and what he plans comes into existence—a wholly beneficent power he blesses the fields and heals mankind. His most striking trait is his love of humanity. In conflicts between the gods and mankind, he is invariably on the side of the latter. When the gods, at the instance of En-lil as the 'god of storms,' decide to bring on a deluge to sweep away mankind, it is Ea who reveals the secret to his favourite, Ut-Napishtim (Noah), who saves himself, his family, and his belongings on a ship that he is instructed to build."[1] The waters personified by him are not those of the turbulent and treacherous ocean, but those of irrigating streams and commerce-carrying canals. He is thus very different from the god En-lil, the 'lord of heaven' who possesses so many attributes of destruction. Ea in his benevolent way thwarts the purpose of the riotous god of tempest, which greatly enrages En-lil, and it has been thought that this myth suggests the rivalry which perhaps at one time existed between the two religious centres of Eridu and Nippur, cities of Ea and En-lil respectively. In an eloquent manner Ea implores En-lil not to precipitate another deluge, and begs that instead of such wholesale destruction man may be punished by sending lions and jackals, or by famines or pestilences. En-lil hearkens to his speech, his heart is touched, and he blesses Utnapishtim and his wife. If this myth is a piece of priestcraft, it argues better relations between the ecclesiastical authorities at Eridu and Nippur. Ea had many other names, the chief of which, Nin-a-gal, meaning 'god of great strength,' alluded to his patronage of the smith's art. He was also called En-ki, which describes him as 'lord of the earth' through which his waters meandered. In such a country as Babylonia earth and water are closely associated, as under that soil water is always to be found at a distance of a few feet: thus the interior of the earth is the domain of Ea.

The Story of Adapa and the South Wind

Here is the story of Adapa, the son of Ea, who, but for his obedience to his father's command, might have attained deification and immortality.

[1] *Religious Belief in Babylonia and Assyria*, p. 88.

STORY OF ADAPA AND THE SOUTH WIND

One day when Adapa was out in his boat fishing the South Wind blew with sudden and malicious violence, upsetting the boat and flinging the fisherman into the sea. When he succeeded in reaching the shore Adapa vowed vengeance against the South Wind, which had used him so cruelly.

"Shutu, thou demon," he cried, "I will stretch forth my hand and break thy wings. Thou shalt not go unpunished for this outrage!"

The hideous monster laughed as she soared in the air above him, flapping her huge wings about her ungainly body. Adapa in his fury leapt at her, seized her wings, and broke them, so that she was no longer able to fly over the broad earth. Then he went his way, and related to his father what he had done.

Seven days passed by, and Anu, the lord of heaven, waited for the coming of the South Wind. But Shutu came not; the rains and the floods were delayed, and Anu grew impatient. He summoned to him his minister Ilabrat.

"Wherefore doth Shutu neglect her duty?" he asked. "What hath chanced that she travels not afield?"

Ilabrat bowed low as he made answer: "Listen, O Anu, and I will tell thee why Shutu flieth not abroad. Ea, lord of the deep and creator of all things, hath a son named Adapa, who hath crushed and broken the wings of thy servant Shutu, so that she is no more able to fly."

"If this be true," said Anu, "summon the youth before me, and let him answer for his crime."

"Be it so, O Anu!"

When Adapa received the summons to appear in heaven he trembled greatly. It was no light thing to answer to the great gods for the ill-usage of their servant, the demon Shutu. Nevertheless he began to make preparations for his journey, and ere he set out his father Ea instructed him as to how he should comport himself in the assembly of the gods.

"Wrap thyself not in a vesture of gold, O my son, but clothe thee in the garments of the dead. At the gates of heaven thou wilt find Tammuz and Gishzida guarding the way. Salute the twain with due respect, I charge thee, baring thy head and showing all deference to them. If thou dost find favour in their eyes they will speak well of thee before Anu. And when thou standest within the precincts of heaven, don the garment that is given thee to wear, and anoint thy head with the oil that is brought thee. But when the gods offer thee food and drink, touch them not; for the food will be the 'Meat of Death,' and the drink the 'Water of Death'; let neither pass within thy lips. Go now, my son, and remember these my instructions. Bear thyself with humility, and all will be well."

Adapa bade his father farewell and set out on his journey to heaven. He found all as his father had predicted; Tammuz and Gishzida received him at the portals of the divine dwelling, and so humble was Adapa's attitude that they were moved with compassion towards him. They led him into the presence of Anu, and he bowed low before the great god.

"I am come in answer to thy summons," said he. "Have mercy upon me, O thou Most High!"

Anu frowned upon him.

"It is said of thee," he made answer, "that thou hast broken the wings of Shutu, the South Wind.

STORY OF ADAPA AND THE SOUTH WIND

What manner of man art thou, who darest destroy Shutu in thy wrath? Knowest thou not that the people suffer for lack of nourishment; that the herb droopeth, and the cattle lie parched on the scorching ground? Tell me why hast thou done this thing?"

"I was out on the sea fishing," said Adapa, "and the South Wind blew violently, upsetting my boat and casting me into the water. Therefore I seized her wings and broke them. And lo! I am come to seek thy pardon."

Then Tammuz and Gishzida, the deities whose favour Adapa had won at the gates of heaven, stepped forth and knelt at the feet of their king.

"Be merciful, O Anu! Adapa hath been sorely tried, and now is he truly humble and repentant. Let his treatment of Shutu be forgotten."

Anu listened to the words of Tammuz and Gishzida, and his wrath was turned away.

"Rise, Adapa," he said kindly; "thy looks please me well. Thou hast seen the interior of this our kingdom, and now must thou remain in heaven for ever, and we will make thee a god like unto us. What sayest thou, son of Ea?"

Adapa bowed low before the king of the gods and thanked him for his pardon and for his promise of godhead.

Anu therefore commanded that a feast be made, and that the 'Meat of Life' and the 'Water of Life' be placed before Adapa, for only by eating and drinking of these could he attain immortality.

But when the feast was spread Adapa refused to partake of the repast, for he remembered his father's injunctions on this point. So he sat in silence at the table of the gods, whereupon Anu exclaimed:

"What now, Adapa? Why dost thou not eat or drink? Except thou taste of the food and water set before thee thou canst not hope to live for ever."

Adapa perceived that he had offended his divine host, so he hastened to explain. "Be not wroth, most mighty Anu. It is because my lord Ea hath so commanded that I break not bread nor drink water at thy table. Turn not thy countenance from me, I beseech thee."

Anu frowned. "Is it that Ea feared I should seek thy life by offering thee deadly food? Truly he that knoweth so much, and hath schooled thee in so many different arts, is for once put to shame!"

Adapa would have spoken, but the lord of heaven silenced him.

"Peace!" he said; then to his attendants—"Bring forth a garment that he may clothe himself, and oil bring also to anoint his head."

When the King's command had been carried out Adapa robed himself in the heavenly garment and anointed his head with the oil. Then he addressed Anu thus:

"O Anu, I salute thee! The privilege of godhead must I indeed forego, but never shall I forget the honour that thou wouldst have conferred upon me. Ever in my heart shall I keep the words thou hast spoken, and the memory of thy kindness shall I ever retain. Blame me not exceedingly, I pray thee. My lord Ea awaiteth my return."

"Truly," said Anu, "I censure not thy decision. Be it even as thou wilt. Go, my son, and peace go with thee!"

And thus Adapa returned to the abode of Ea,

lord of the dead, and there for many years he lived in peace and happiness.

Anu

Along with En-lil and Ea, Anu makes up the universal triad. He is called the 'father of the gods,' but appears to be descended from still older deities. His name is seldom discovered in the inscriptions prior to the time of Khammurabi, but such notices as occur of him seem to have already fixed his position as a ruler of the sky. His cult was specially associated with the city of Erech. It is probable that in the earliest days he had been the original Sumerian sky-father, as his name is merely a form of the Sumerian word for 'heaven.' This idea is assisted by the manner in which his name is originally written in the inscriptions, as the symbol signifying it is usually that employed for 'heaven.' It is plain, therefore, that Anu was once regarded as the expanse of heaven itself, just as are the 'sky-fathers' of numerous primitive peoples. Several writers who deal with Anu appear to be of the opinion that a god of the heavens is an 'abstraction.' "Popular fancy," says Jastrow, "deals with realities and with personified powers whose workings are seen and felt. It would as little, therefore, have evolved the idea that there was a power to be identified with the heavens as a whole, of which the azure sky is a symbol, as it would personify the earth as a whole, or the bodies of waters as a whole. It is only necessary to state the implications involved to recognize that the conception of a triad of gods corresponding to three theoretical divisions of the universe is a bit of learned speculation. It smacks of the school. The conception of a god of heaven fits in moreover with the comparatively advanced period when the seats of the gods were placed in the skies and the gods identified with the stars."[1] A merely superficial acquaintance with the nature of animism and the sky-myths of primitive and barbarian peoples would lead us to the conclusion that the opposite is the case. In Egyptian, Polynesian, and North American Indian myth the sky itself is directly personalized. Egyptian mythological illustration depicts the sky in female form, for in Egyptian myth the sky is the mother and the earth the father of everything. Lang has shown that the sky-father is frequently personalized as a " magnified non-natural man " among races which possess no theological schools. We do not say that the arrangement of Anu, Ea, and En-lil into a triad is not " a bit of learned speculation," but to state that early animism did not first personalize the sky and the earth and the sea is rash in the extreme. When Deucalion and Pyrrha in the Greek myth asked the gods how they might best replenish the earth with the human race, they were instructed to cast " the bones of their mother " behind them, and these bones they interpreted as the stones and rocks and acted accordingly. So would primitive man all the world over have interpreted this advice, for universally he believes the very soil upon which he walks to be the great mother which produced his ancestors, out of whose dust or clay they were formed, and who still nourishes and preserves him.

Jastrow proceeds to state that " Anu was originally the personification of some definite power of nature, and everything points to this power having been the sun in the heavens. Starting from this

[1] *Religious Belief in Babylonia and Assyria*, p. 81.

point of view we quite understand how the great illuminer of heaven should have been identified with the heavens in an artificially devised theological system, just as En-lil became in this system the designation of the earth and of the region above the earth viewed as a whole."[1] The very fact that in the earliest times Anu was identified with the expanse of the sky itself, and that the symbol used to denote him meant 'heaven,' is against this supposition. Again, the theory suffers from lack of analogy. In what other mythology is there to be found a sky-god who at one time possessed a solar significance? The converse might be the case. Some sky-gods have attained the solar connexion because of their rule over the entire expanse of the heavens, just as they have attained the power of wielding lightning and the wind. But we are at a loss to recall any deity originally of distinctive solar attributes who later took the position of a sky-god.

Anu was regarded as head of the triad and the father of En-lil. We are told that the goddess Aruru first shaped man in the image of Anu, who must thus have attained an anthropomorphic condition. He appears also to have been regarded as the conqueror of primeval chaos. His consort was Anatu, probably a later feminine form of himself.

Ishtar

Ishtar was undoubtedly a goddess of Semitic origin and symbolized the fertility of the earth. She was the 'great mother' who fostered all vegetation and agriculture. It is probable that her cult originated at Erech, and in the course of centuries and under many nominal changes dispersed itself

[1] *Religious Belief in Babylonia and Assyria*, p. 82.

throughout the length and breadth of western Asia and even into Greece and Egypt. It is probable that a number of lesser goddesses, such as Nanâ and Anunit, may have become merged in the conception of this divinity, and that lesser local deities of the same character as herself may have taken her name and assisted to swell her reputation. She is frequently addressed as 'mother of the gods,' and indeed the name 'Ishtar' became a generic designation for 'goddess.' But these were later honours. When her cult centred at Erech, it appears to have speedily blossomed out in many directions, and, as has been said, lesser cults probably eagerly identified themselves with that of the great earth-mother, so that in time her worship became more than a Babylonian cult. Indeed, wherever people of Semitic speech were to be found, there was the worship of Ishtar. As Ashteroth, or Astarte, she was known to Canaanites, Phœnicians, and Greeks, and there is some likelihood that the cult of Aphrodite had also its beginnings in that of Ishtar. We shall enquire later whether she can be the Esther of the Scriptures. Astrologically she was identified with the planet Venus, but so numerous were the attributes surrounding her taken from other goddesses with which she had become identified that they threatened to overshadow her real character, which was that of the great and fertile mother. More especially did her identification with Nin-lil, the consort of En-lil, the storm-god, threaten to alter her real nature, as in this guise she was regarded as a goddess of war. It is seldom that a goddess of fertility or love achieves such a distinction. Gods possessing an agricultural significance are nearly always war-gods, but that is because they bring the fertilizing

1. Ishtar, the Mother-goddess
2. Ishtar as the Goddess of War
3. Ishtar, the Goddess of Love

From *Religious Belief and Practice in Babylonia and Assyria*, by Professor Morris Jastrow
By permission of Messrs G. P. Putnam's Sons

THE DESCENT OF ISHTAR INTO HADES

thunder-clouds and therefore possess the lightning arrow or spear. But Ishtar is specifically a goddess of the class of Persephone or Isis, and her identification with battle must be regarded as purely accidental. In later times in Assyria she was conceived as the consort of Asshur, head of the Assyrian pantheon, in days when a god or goddess who did not breathe war was of little use to a people like the Assyrians, who were constantly employed in hostilities, and this circumstance naturally heightened her reputation as a warlike divinity. But it is at present her original character with which we are occupied, indeed in some texts we find that, so far from being able to protect herself, Ishtar and her property are made the prey of the savage En-lil, the storm-god. "His word sent me forth," she complains; "as often as it comes to me it casts me prostrate upon my face. The unconsecrated foe entered my courts, placed his unwashed hands upon me, and caused me to tremble. Putting forth his hand he smote me with fear. He tore away my robe and clothed his wife therein: he stripped off my jewels and placed them upon his daughter. Like a quivering dove upon a beam I sat. Like a fleeing bird from my cranny swiftly I passed. From my temple like a bird they caused me to fly." Such is the plaint of Ishtar, who in this case appears to be quite helpless before the enemy.

The myth which best illustrates her character is that which speaks of her journey to Aralu, the underworld.

The Descent of Ishtar into Hades

The poem, which in its existing form consists of 137 lines in cuneiform characters, appears to be incomplete. We are not told therein what was the purpose of the goddess in journeying to the 'House of No-return,' but we gather from various legends and from the concluding portion of the poem itself that she went thither in search of her bridegroom Tammuz, the sun-god of Eridu. The importance of the myth of Ishtar and Tammuz lies partly in the fact that, travelling westwards to Greece by way of Phœnicia, it furnished a groundwork for classic myths of the Adonis-Attis type, which still provide mythologists with matter for endless speculation. The mythological significance of the poem and the persons it mentions will be dealt with later; the theories concerning the primitive status of Tammuz and Ishtar are numerous and distinct, more than one of them being sufficiently plausible to call for a careful scrutiny. Consideration of the myth may therefore be deferred till we have glanced at the Babylonian story itself and some of its principal variants and analogues.

Tammuz and Ishtar

The myth of Tammuz is one of high antiquity, dating possibly from 4000 B.C. or even earlier. Both Tammuz and Ishtar were originally non-Semitic, the name of the former deity being derived from the Akkadian Dumu-zi, 'son of life,' or 'the only son,' perhaps a contraction of Dumu-zi-apsu, 'offspring of the spirit of the deep,' as Professor Sayce indicates. The 'spirit of the deep' is, of course, the water-god Ea, and Tammuz apparently typifies the sun, though he is not, as will presently be seen, a simple solar deity, but a god who unites in himself the attributes of various departmental divinities. An ancient Akkadian hymn addresses Tammuz as " Shep-

TAMMUZ AND ISHTAR

herd and lord, husband of Ishtar the lady of heaven, lord of the under-world, lord of the shepherd's seat;" as grain which lies unwatered in the meadow, which beareth no green blade; as a sapling planted in a waterless place; as a sapling torn out by the root. Professor Sayce identifies him with that Daonus, or Daos, whom Berossus states to have been the sixth king of Babylonia during the mythical period. Tammuz is the shepherd of the sky, and his flocks and herds, like those of St Ilya in Slavonic folk-lore, are the cloud-cattle and the fleecy vapours of the heavens.

Ishtar has from an early period been associated with Tammuz as his consort, as she has, indeed, with Merodach and Assur and other deities. Yet she is by no means a mere reflection of the male divinity, but has a distinct individuality of her own, differing in this from all other Babylonian goddesses and betraying her non-Semitic origin. The widespread character of the worship of Ishtar is remarkable. None of the Babylonian or Assyrian deities were adopted into the pantheons of so many alien races. From the Persian Gulf to the pillars of Hercules she was adored as the great mother of all living. She has been identified with Dawkina, wife of Ea, and is therefore mother of Tammuz as well as his consort. This dual relationship may account for that which appears in later myths among the Greeks, where Smyrna, mother of Adonis, is also his sister. Ishtar was regarded sometimes as the daughter of the sky-god Anu, and sometimes as the child of Sin, the lunar deity. Her worship in Babylonia was universal, and in time displaced that of Tammuz himself. The love of Ishtar for Tammuz represents the wooing of the sun-god of spring-time by the goddess of fertility; the god is slain by the relentless heat of summer, and there is little doubt that Ishtar enters Aralu in search of her youthful husband. The poem we are about to consider briefly deals with a part only of the myth—the story of Ishtar's descent into Aralu. It opens thus: "To the land of No-return, the region of darkness, Ishtar, the daughter of Sin, turned her ear, even Ishtar, the daughter of Sin, turned her ear, to the abode of darkness, the dwelling of Irkalla, to the house whose enterer goes not forth, to the road whence the wayfarer never returns, to the house whose inhabitants see no light, to the region where dust is their bread and their food mud; they see no light, they dwell in darkness, they are clothed, like the birds, in a garment of feathers. On the door and the bolt hath the dust fallen." The moral contained in this passage is a gloomy one for mortal man; he who enters the dread precincts of Aralu goes not forth, he is doomed to remain for ever in the enveloping darkness, his sustenance mud and dust. The mention of the dust which lies "on door and bolt" strikes a peculiarly bleak and dreary note; like other primitive races the ancient Babylonians painted the other world not definitely as a place of reward or punishment, but rather as a weak reflection of the earth-world, a region of darkness and passive misery which must have offered a singularly uninviting prospect to a vigorous human being. The garment of feathers is somewhat puzzling. Why should the dead wear a garment of feathers? Unless it be that the sun-god, identified in some of his aspects with the eagle, descends into the underworld in a dress of feathers, and that therefore mortals who follow him must appear in the nether regions in similar guise. The description above quoted of the Babylonian Hades tallies with that given in dream

AT THE GATES OF ARALU

to Eabani by the temple-maiden Ukhut (Gilgamesh epic, tablet VII).

At the Gates of Aralu

Coming to the gate of Aralu, Ishtar assumes a menacing aspect, and threatens to break down the door and shatter its bolts and bars if she be not admitted straightway. The keeper of the gate endeavours to soothe the irate deity, and goes to announce her presence to Eresh-ki-gal (Allatu), the mistress of Hades. From his words it would appear that Ishtar has journeyed thither in search of the waters of life, wherewith to restore her husband Tammuz to life. Allatu receives the news of her sister's advent with a bitter tirade, but nevertheless instructs the keeper to admit her, which he proceeds to do.

Ishtar on entering the sombre domains is obliged to pass through seven gates, at each of which she is relieved of some article of dress or adornment (evidently in accordance with the ancient custom of Aralu), till at last she stands entirely unclad. At the first gate the keeper takes from her " the mighty crown of her head "; at the second her earrings are taken; at the third her necklace; at the fourth the ornaments of her breast; at the fifth her jewelled girdle; at the sixth her bracelets; and at the seventh the cincture of her body. The goddess does not part with these save under protest, but the keeper of the gate answers all her queries with the words : " Enter, O lady, it is the command of Allatu." The divine wayfarer at length appears before the goddess of the underworld, who shows her scant courtesy, bidding the plague-demon, Namtar, smite her from head to foot with disease—in her eyes, side, feet, heart, and head.

During the time that Ishtar is confined within the bounds of Aralu all fertility on the earth is suspended, both in the animal and vegetable kingdoms. Knowledge of this disastrous state of affairs is conveyed to the gods by their messenger, Pap-sukal, who first tells the story to Shamash, the sun-god. Shamash weeps as he bears the matter before Ea and Sin, gods of the earth and the moon respectively; but Ea, to remedy the sterility of the earth, creates a being called Ashushu-namir, whom he dispatches to the underworld to demand the release of Ishtar. Allatu is greatly enraged when the demand is made " in the name of the great gods," and curses Ashushu-namir with a terrible curse, condemning him to dwell in the darkness of a dungeon, with the garbage of the city for his food. Nevertheless she cannot resist the power of the conjuration, wherefore she bids Namtar, the plague-demon, release the Annunaki, or earth-spirits, and place them on a golden throne, and pour the waters of life over Ishtar. Namtar obeys; in the words of the poem he " smote the firmly-built palace, he shattered the threshold which bore up the stones of light, he bade the spirits of earth come forth, on a throne of gold did he seat them, over Ishtar he poured the waters of life and brought her along." Ishtar is then led through the seven gates of Arula, receiving at each the article of attire whereof she had there been deprived. Finally she emerges into the earth-world, which resumes its normal course. Then follow a few lines addressed to Ishtar, perhaps by the plague-demon or by the keeper of the gates. " If she (Allatu) hath not given thee that for which the ransom is paid her, return to her for Tammuz, the bridegroom of thy youth. Pour over him pure waters and precious oil. Put on him a purple robe, and a ring of crystal on his hand. Let Samkhat (the goddess of joy) enter the liver. . . ." These lines indicate with sufficient clearness that Ishtar descended into Hades in order to obtain the waters of life and thus revive her bridegroom Tammuz. The poem does not relate whether or not her errand was successful, but we are left to conjecture that it was. There still remain a few lines of the poem, not, however, continuing the narrative, but forming a sort of epilogue, addressed, it may be, to the hearers of the tale. Mention is made in this portion of mourners, " wailing men and wailing women," of a funeral pyre and the burning of incense, evidently in honour of the god Tammuz.

Ishtar and Persephone

As has been indicated already, the myth of Tammuz and Ishtar furnished the groundwork for certain myths of classic Greece and Rome. The Phœnician Astarte (Ashtoreth), a development of Ishtar, became in time the Aphrodite of the Greeks, a deity who plays a part in the Adonis legend analogous to that of Ishtar in the Tammuz story. The name Adonis itself is derived from *Adoni* (' my lord '), the word with which the Phœnician worshippers of Tammuz hailed the setting sun. The myth of Adonis is perhaps the most nearly related of any to that of Tammuz, since its chief characters are acknowledged counterparts of those in the Babylonian legend, while the tale of Ishtar's descent into Hades may be regarded as a sequel to the Greek story, or rather to an early Babylonian variant thereof. Briefly outlined, the story runs as follows: Adonis was the fruit of an unnatural union between the Syrian king Theias and his daughter Smyrna (Myrrha). Theias pursued the princess, intending to take her life for the crime, but the pity of the gods turned her into a tree from which, at the end of ten months, Adonis was born. It is said that a boar rent open the tree-trunk with its tusk, and thus enabled the divine infant to see the light. Aphrodite, charmed with the beauty of the child, gave him into the care of Persephone, who was so enamoured of her charge that she afterwards refused to give him up. The goddesses appealed to Zeus, who decreed that Adonis should spend six months of each year with Aphrodite and six with Persephone in the underworld; or, according to another version, four months were to be passed with Aphrodite and four with Persephone, while the remaining four were to be at his own disposal. He was afterwards slain by a boar sent against him by Artemis (herself, by the way, a development of Ishtar). It may be remarked that Aphrodite, who figures, like Ishtar, as the goddess of love and beauty, is also closely associated with the nether regions, perhaps because she was identified with the Babylonian goddess in her journey to Hades in search of her spouse.

Akin to Adonis is the god Attis, who likewise, according to one version of his myth, is slain by a boar. After his death he becomes a pine-tree, and from his blood violets spring. He is beloved of Cybele, the mother-goddess, who laments his untimely end.

In the Adonis legend there is evidence of some overlapping. Persephone, or Proserpine, who here corresponds to the Allatu of the Babylonian variant, figures in another well-known myth as the prototype of Tammuz. When she is carried off to the nether-

ISHTAR AND PERSEPHONE

world by Pluto, her mother, Ceres, will not suffer the corn to grow while her daughter remains a prisoner. Like Ishtar in search of her spouse, the mother-goddess seeks her child with weeping and lamentation. Through the eating of a pomegranate seed, Proserpine is finally obliged to pass four (or six) months of every year with her dark captor, as his consort.

Another myth which has affinities with the tale of Tammuz and Ishtar is the Egyptian one which deals with the quest of Isis. The god Osiris is slain through the machinations of his brother Set (who, being identified elsewhere with a black hog, recalls the boar which slew Adonis and Attis), and his body, enclosed in a chest, is cast into the Nile. Afterwards the chest is thrown up by the waves, and round it springs miraculously a tamarisk tree. Meanwhile Isis, wife and sister to Osiris, travels hither and thither in search of his remains, which in due time she finds. However, the chest is stolen from her by Set, who, taking therefrom the body of Osiris, tears the corpse into fourteen pieces, which he scatters broadcast through the land. Isis still pursues her quest, till she has found all the portions and buried them.

These tales were the mythical correlates of certain ritualistic practices designed to bring about the change of seasons, and other natural phenomena, by means of sympathetic magic. The burden of a great duty falls upon the shoulders of primitive man; with his rites and spells and magic arts he must assist the universe in its course. His esoteric plays, typifying the mysterious fact of growth, are necessary to ensure the sprouting of the corn; his charms and incantations are essential even for the rising of the sun; lacking the guarantee of science that one season shall follow another in its proper order, he goes through an elaborate performance symbolizing the decay and revival of vegetation, believing that only thus can the natural order be maintained. Through the force of sympathetic magic he sees his puny efforts related to the mighty results which follow them.

This, then, is the origin of the ritual of the Tammuz festival, which may conceivably have had an existence prior to that of the myth itself. The representation of the death and resurrection of the god, whether in myth or ritual, had undoubtedly a seasonal significance, wherefore the date of his festival varied in the different localities. In Babylonia it was celebrated in June, thus showing that the deity was slain by the fierce heat of the sun, burning up all the springtide vegetation. Ishtar's sojourn in Hades would thus occupy the arid months of summer. In other and more temperate climes winter would be regarded as the enemy of Tammuz. An interesting account of the Tammuz festival is that given by an Arabic author writing in the tenth century, and quoted by Sir James Frazer in his *Golden Bough*. "Tammuz (July). In the middle of this month is the festival of el-Bûgât, that is, of the weeping women, and this is the Ta-uz festival, which is celebrated in honour of the god Ta-uz. The women bewail him, because his lord slew him so cruelly, ground his bones in a mill, and then scattered them to the wind. The women (during this festival) eat nothing which has been ground in a mill, but limit their diet to steeped wheat, sweet vetches, dates, raisins, and the like." The material for this description was furnished by the Syrians of Harran. Of

LAMENTATIONS FOR TAMMUZ

the curious legend attaching to the mourning rites more will be said later.

Lamentations for Tammuz

Characteristic of the Tammuz ritual are the lamentations, of which several series are still extant. In later times it appears that a different cause was assigned for the weeping of the "wailing men and wailing women." They no longer mourned the death of Tammuz, but the departure of Ishtar into the netherworld, and so the legend of her journey to Aralu came to be recited in the temples. Sir James Frazer suggests that the ritualistic counterpart of the Tammuz-Ishtar myth may have included the pouring of water over an effigy of the god, the practice corresponding to the pouring of the water of life over him in order to bring him back to life. If this indeed formed a part of the Tammuz ritual we may take it that it was intended as a rain-charm.

Likewise the Adonia festival of the Greeks symbolized the death and resurrection of Adonis. This feast occupied two days; on the first day, images of Adonis and Aphrodite were made and laid each on a silver couch; on the second day, these images were cast by the women into the sea, together with 'Adonis gardens,' as they were called—pots filled with earth in which cut flowers were stuck. It is believed that this rite was meant to signify the revival of vegetation under the influence of rain. The persons engaged in it indulged in such lamentations as were uttered by the worshippers of Tammuz in Babylonia, tore their hair, and beat their breasts. The festival of Adonis fell in the summer-time at Alexandria and Athens, in the spring at Byblus, while in Phœnicia it occurred in the season when the river Nahr Ibrahim (formerly called Adonis) bore down from the mountains of Lebanon the red earth in which the devout saw the blood of the slain Adonis. Golden boxes of myrrh were employed at the Adonia festival, incense was burned, and pigs were sacrificed. Pigs were sacrificed also to Osiris, whose cult, as has been shown, had much in common with that of Tammuz and Adonis. The Egyptian god was cast by his enemies into the waters of the Nile; and it may be that this myth too had a ritualistic counterpart, designed as a charm to produce rain.

It has been indicated already that the elucidations of the myth of Ishtar's journey to Aralu are many and divergent. The variants above enumerated serve each to cast light on the other, and from a comparison of these we may suceeed in arriving at a satisfactory conclusion. To begin with, however, it must be remembered that when the cult of any deity has reached a fairly advanced stage it is impossible to assign to him any one department of nature, to say that he is a sun-god, a rain-god, a corn-god, for he may possess the attributes of all of these. In giving any god a departmental designation we are striving to express his primitive or predominant characteristics merely.

An Allegorical Interpretation of the Myth

A truly allegorical elucidation of the myth of Ishtar's descent into Hades would depict Ishtar, as the goddess of fertility, seeking in the underworld for her husband, the sun-god, slain by the icy breath of winter. During her sojourn in the nether regions all fertility ceases on the earth, to be resumed only when she returns as the joyful bride of the springtide sun. The surrender of her clothing and jewels

The Mother-goddess Ishtar
Evelyn Paul

AN ALLEGORICAL INTERPRETATION

at the seven gates of Aralu represents the gradual decay of vegetation on the earth, and the resumption of her garments the growing beauty and verdure which mark her return. Another hypothesis identifies Ishtar with Dawkina, goddess of the earth, wife of Ea and therefore mother as well as consort of Tammuz. According to this view Ishtar represents not the fertility of the earth, but the earth itself, deprived of its adornments of flowers and leafage by the approach of winter, or variously, by the burning heat of summer. The waters of life, with which she sprinkles and restores her husband,[1] are the revivifying rains which give to the sun-god his youthful vigour and glory. Against this view it has been urged (*e.g.* by Sir James Frazer) that " there is nothing in the sun's annual course within the temperate and tropical zones to suggest that he is dead for half or a third of the year, and alive for the other half or two-thirds."

Alternatively it is suggested that Tammuz is a god of vegetation, and that Ishtar doubles the rôle. The slaying of Tammuz and the journey of Ishtar would thus represent two distinct myths, each typifying the decay and subsequent revival of vegetation. Other instances may be recalled in which two myths of the same class have become fused into one. This view, then, presents some elements of probability; not only Tammuz but most of his variants appear to possess a vegetable significance, while the Ishtar type is open to interpretation on the same lines. Thus Adonis is associated with the myrrh-tree, from whose trunk he was born, and Osiris with the tamarisk, used in the ritual connected with his cult, while Attis after his

---
[1] Elsewhere Ishtar herself is sprinkled. See p. 130.

death became a pine-tree. Tammuz himself was conceived of as dwelling in the midst of a great world-tree, whose roots extended down to the underworld, while its branches reached to the heavens. This tree appears to have been the cedar, for which the ancient Babylonians had an especial reverence. One feature which leads us to identify the deities of this class, both male and female, with gods of vegetation is their association with the moon. Osiris is regarded, and with much reason, as a moon-god; in one of her aspects Aphrodite is a lunar deity, while a like significance belongs to Proserpine and to the Phœnician Ashtoreth. Ishtar herself, it is true, was never identified with the moon, which in Babylonia was a male divinity; yet she was associated with him as his daughter. Among primitive peoples the moon is believed to exercise a powerful influence on vegetation, and indeed on all manner of growth and productivity. The association of a god with the moon therefore argues for him also a connexion with vegetation and fertility. It may be remarked, in passing, that a lunar significance has been attached by some authorities to the story of Ishtar's descent into Hades, and to kindred myths. It is held that the sojourn of the goddess in Aralu typifies a lunar eclipse, or perhaps the period between the waning of the old moon and the appearance of the new. But, as has been said, the ancient Babylonians saw in the luminary of night a male deity, so that any lunar characteristics pertaining to Ishtar must be regarded as of merely secondary importance.

Ishtar, Tammuz, and Vegetation

If it be granted, then, that Ishtar and Tammuz are deities of vegetation, it is possible still further to

ISHTAR, TAMMUZ, AND VEGETATION

narrow their sphere by associating them particularly with the corn. Adonis and Aphrodite are connected with the growth of the crops. Ceres, who forbids the corn to spring while her daughter is in the realm of Pluto, is undoubtedly a corn-mother, and Proserpine evidently partakes of the same nature. Osiris was the culture-deity who introduced corn into Egypt. A representation of him in the temple of Isis at Philæ depicts corn-stalks growing out of his dead body—the body of Osiris (the grain) is torn to pieces, scattered through the land, and the pieces buried (or planted) in the earth, when the corn sprouts from it. Moreover, Tammuz himself was cruelly disposed of by his lord, who " ground his bones in a mill, and then scattered them to the wind "—plainly a type of the treatment meted out to the corn. An Arabic writer relates that Tammuz was cruelly killed several times, but that he always came to life again, a story which recalls Robert Burns' *John Barleycorn*, itself perhaps based on mythical matter.

May not these examples suggest an elucidation on animistic lines ? Deities of the Tammuz type appear to symbolize the corn-grain and nothing more—cut down, bruised and beaten, buried in the earth, and finally springing to renewed life. Who, then, are the goddesses, likewise identified with the corn, who seek in the underworld for lover or child, endeavouring with tears to ransom the corn from the dark earth ? Are they not the primitive corn-spirits, the indwelling animistic spirits of the standing grain, doomed at the harvest to wander disconsolately through the earth till the sprouting of the corn once more gives them an opportunity to materialize ?

The stories of the mutilation and dispersion of the bodies of Tammuz and Osiris, and of the many

139

deaths of the former god, furnish a basis for yet another explanation of the Tammuz myth. Sir James Frazer brings forward the theory that the 'Lamentations' of the ancient Babylonians were intended not for mourning for the decay of vegetation, but to bewail the cruel treatment of the grain at harvest-time, and cites in this connexion the ballad of *John Barleycorn*, which, we are told, was based on an early English poem, probably itself of mythological origin.

It is, however, most likely that the myth of Tammuz and Ishtar is of a composite nature, as has already been indicated. Possibly a myth of the sun-god and earth-goddess has been superimposed on the early groundwork of the corn-spirit seeking the corn. It would certainly seem that Ishtar in her descent into Aralu typified the earth, shorn of her covering of vegetation. Then in time she might come to symbolize the vegetation itself, or the fertility which produced it, and so would gain new attributes, and new elements would enter into the myths concerning her. Only by regarding her as a composite deity is it possible to reach an understanding of the principles underlying these myths.

Ishtar and Esther

We have already questioned whether the Scripture story of Esther is in some manner connected with the goddess Ishtar. Writing of the Jewish feast of Purim, Sir James Frazer says (*Golden Bough*, vol. iii, p. 153): "From the absence of all notice of Purim in the older books of the Bible, we may fairly conclude that the festival was instituted or imported at a comparatively late date among the Jews. The same conclusion is supported by the

ISHTAR AND ESTHER

Book of Esther itself, which was manifestly written to explain the origin of the feast and to suggest motives for its observance. For, according to the author of the book, the festival was established to commemorate the deliverance of the Jews from a great danger which threatened them in Persia under the reign of King Xerxes. Thus the opinion of modern scholars that the feast of Purim, as celebrated by the Jews, was of late date and Oriental origin, is borne out by the tradition of the Jews themselves. An examination of that tradition and of the mode of celebrating the feast renders it probable that Purim is nothing but a more or less disguised form of the Babylonian festival of the Sacæa or Zakmuk. . . . But further, when we examine the narrative which professes to account for the institution of Purim, we discover in it not only the strongest traces of Babylonian origin, but also certain singular analogies to those very features of the Sacæan festival with which we are here more immediately concerned. The Book of Esther turns upon the fortunes of two men, the vizier Haman and the despised Jew Mordecai, at the court of a Persian king. Mordecai, we are told, had given mortal offence to the vizier, who accordingly prepares a tall gallows on which he hopes to see his enemy hanged, while he himself expects to receive the highest mark of the King's favour by being allowed to wear the royal crown and the royal robes, and thus attired to parade the streets, mounted on the King's own horse and attended by one of the noblest princes, who should proclaim to the multitude his temporary exaltation and glory. But the artful intrigues of the wicked vizier miscarried and resulted in precisely the opposite of what he had hoped and expected;

for the royal honours which he had looked for fell to his rival Mordecai, and he himself was hanged on the gallows which he had made ready for his foe. In this story we seem to detect a reminiscence, more or less confused, of the Zoganes of the Sacæa, in other words, of the custom of investing a private man with the insignia of royalty for a few days, and then putting him to death on the gallows or the cross. . . .

"A strong confirmation of this view is furnished by a philological analysis of the names of the four personages. It seems to be now generally recognised by Biblical scholars that the name Mordecai, which has no meaning in Hebrew, is nothing but a slightly altered form of Marduk or Merodach, the name of the chief god of Babylon, whose great festival was the Zakmuk; and further, it is generally admitted that Esther in like manner is equivalent to Ishtar, the great Babylonian goddess whom the Greeks called Astarte, and who is more familiar to English readers as Ashtaroth. The derivation of the names of Haman and Vashti is less certain, but some high authorities are disposed to accept the view of Jensen that Haman is identical with Humman or Homman, the national god of the Elamites, and that Vashti is in like manner an Elamite deity, probably a goddess whose name appears in inscriptions."

Lang on the Esther Story

Commenting on this theory, Lang in his *Magic and Religion* (p. 161) says: "The name Mordecai resembles Marduk, Esther is like Ishtar, Haman is like Humman, the Elamite god, and there is a divine name in the inscriptions, read as resembling 'Vashti,' and probably the name of an Elamite goddess. Thus the human characters in Esther are in peril of merging in Babylonian and Elamite gods. But, lest that should occur, we ought also to remember that Mordecai was the real name of a real historical Jew of the Captivity, one of the companions of Nehemiah in the return from exile to Jerusalem. Again, Esther appears to me to be the crown-name of the Jewish wife of Xerxes, in the Book of Esther: 'Hadassah, that is Esther.' In the Biblical story she conceals her Jewish descent. Hadassah, says Nöldeke, 'is no mere invention of the writer of Esther.' Hadassah is said to mean 'myrtle bough,' and girls are still called Myrtle. Esther appears to have been an assumed name, after a royal mixed marriage. Now if a real historical Jew might be named Mordecai, which we know to be the case, a Jewess, whether in fact, or in this Book of Esther, which, says Dr. Jastrow, 'has of course some historical basis,' might be styled Esther. . . . But, if Mordecai be, as it is, an historical name of a real Jew of the period, while Esther may be, and probably is, a name which a Jewess might bear, it is not ascertained that Vashti really is the name of an Elamite goddess. Yet Vashti is quite essential as a goddess to Mr. Frazer's argument. 'The derivation,' he says, ' of the names of Haman and Vashti is less certain, but some high authorities are disposed to accept the view of Jensen that Haman is identical with Humman or Homman, the national god of the Elamites, and that Vashti is in like manner an Elamite deity, probably a goddess whose name appears in inscriptions.'"

It is thus seen that the facts regarding these names make such an explanation as is advanced by Sir James Frazer rather a hazardous one. Haman, according to his theory, would represent the dying god, whilst Mordecai would play the part of the re-risen god of vegetation. Lang puts forward a counter-theory, and that is that Haman or Humman was a conquering god of the Elamites, which accounts for him having been whipped and hanged in derision. This Humman was, he thinks, possibly an Elamite god of vegetation.

Nin-Girsu

Girsu was a part of the city of Lagash, and the name Nin-Girsu means 'Lord of Girsu.' Gods frequently had lordship over a city quarter, one of the best-known instances of this being that of Huitzilopochtli, who ruled over that part of the city of Tenochtitlan, called Mexico, which afterwards gave its name to the entire community. Girsu had originally been a city itself and had become merged into Lagash, so its god was probably of ancient origin. Nin-Girsu is frequently alluded to as 'the warrior of Bel'—he who broke through the hostile ranks to aid the worshippers of the great god of the netherworld. Like many combatant deities, however, he presided over local agriculture, and in this connexion he was known as Shul-gur, 'Lord of the corn heaps.' He is even identified with Tammuz.

Bau

In ancient inscriptions, especially those of Gudea, Urbau, and Uru-kagina, the goddess Bau is alluded to as the great mother of mankind, who restores the sick to health. She is called 'chief daughter of Anu,' and seems to play the part of a fate to some extent. She has also an agricultural side to her character. Gudea was especially devoted to her, and has left it on record that she " filled him with eloquence." Her temple was at Uru-Azagga, a quarter of Lagash, and as the goddess of that neighbourhood she would, of course, have come into close contact with Nin-Girsu. Indeed she is spoken of as his consort, and when Uru-Azagga became part of Lagash, Bau was promoted as tutelar goddess of that city and designated 'Mother of Lagash.' She has been identified with the primeval watery depths, the primitive chaos, and this identification has been founded on the similarity between the name Bau and the Hebrew *bohu*, the word for 'chaos,' but proof is wanting to support the conjecture. A closely allied form of her seems to be Ga-tum-dug, a goddess who has probably a common origin with Bau, and who certainly is in some manner connected with water—perhaps with the clouds.

Nannar

Nannar was the moon-god of Ur, the city whence came Abram, and with that place he was connected much as was Shamash with Sippar—that is to say, Ur was his chief but not his only centre of adoration. Why he came to have his principal seat at Ur it would be difficult to say. The name Ur signifies 'light,' so it may be that a shrine dedicated to Nannar existed upon the site of this city and constituted its nucleus. In Babylonian mythology the sun was regarded as the offspring of the moon, and it is easy to see how this conception arose in the minds of a race prone to astronomical study. In all civilizations the lunar method of computing time precedes the solar. The phases of the moon are regarded as more trustworthy and more easily followed than the more obscure changes of the brighter luminary, therefore a greater degree of importance was attached to the moon in very early times than to the sun. The moon is usually represented on Babylonian cylinders as bearing a crescent upon his head and wearing a long, flowing beard described as of the colour of lapis-lazuli—much the same shade as his beams possess in warmer latitudes. Nannar was frequently alluded to as 'the heifer of Anu,' because of the horn which the moon displays at a certain phase. Many monarchs appear to have delighted in the upkeep and restoration of his temple, among them Nur-Ramman and Sin-iddina.

Nannar in Decay

But, as happens to many gods, Nannar became confounded with some earthly hero—was even alluded to as a satrap of Babylonia under the Median monarch Artaios—a personage unknown to history. Ctesias hands down to us a very circumstantial tale concerning him as follows:[1]

"There was a Persian of the name of Parsondes, in the service of the king of the Medes, an eager huntsman, and an active warrior on foot and in the chariot, distinguished in council and in the field, and of influence with the king. Parsondes often urged the king to make him satrap of Babylon in the place of Nannaros, who wore women's clothes and ornaments, but the king always put the petition aside, for it could not be granted without breaking the promise which his ancestor had made to Belesys. Nannaros discovered the intentions of Parsondes, and sought to secure himself against them, and to take vengeance. He promised great rewards to the cooks who were in the train of the king, if they

[1] Translation from Prof. Sayce's *Hibbert Lectures*, p. 157.

succeeded in seizing Parsondes and giving him up. One day, Parsondes in the heat of the chase strayed far from the king. He had already killed many boars and deer, when the pursuit of a wild ass carried him to a great distance. At last he came upon the cooks, who were occupied in preparations for the king's table. Being thirsty, Parsondes asked for wine; they gave it, took care of his horse, and invited him to take food—an invitation agreeable to Parsondes, who had been hunting the whole day. He bade them send the ass which he had captured to the king, and tell his own servants where he was. Then he ate of the various kinds of food set before him, and drank abundantly of the excellent wine, and at last asked for his horse in order to return to the king. But they brought beautiful women to him, and urged him to remain for the night. He agreed, and as soon as, overcome by hunting, wine, and love, he had fallen into a deep sleep, the cooks bound him and brought him to Nannaros. Nannaros reproached Parsondes with calling him an effeminate man, and seeking to obtain his satrapy; he had the king to thank that the satrapy granted to his ancestors had not been taken from him. Parsondes replied that he considered himself more worthy of the office, because he was more manly and more useful to the king. But Nannaros swore by Bel and Mylitta that Parsondes should be softer and whiter than a woman, called for the eunuch who was over the female players, and bade him shave the body of Parsondes and bathe and anoint him every day, put women's clothes on him, plait his hair after the manner of women, paint his face, and place him among the women who played the guitar and sang, that he might learn their arts. This was done, and soon Parsondes played and sang better at the table of Nannaros than any of the women. Meanwhile the king of the Medes had caused search to be made everywhere for Parsondes; and since he could nowhere be found, and nothing could be heard of him, he believed that a lion or some other wild animal had killed him when out hunting, and lamented for his loss. Parsondes had lived for seven years as a woman in Babylon, when Nannaros caused a eunuch to be scourged and grievously maltreated. This eunuch Parsondes induced by large presents to retire to Media and tell the king the misfortune which had come upon him. Then the king sent a message commanding Nannaros to give up Parsondes. Nannaros declared that he had never seen him. But the king sent a second messenger, with orders to put Nannaros to death if he did not surrender Parsondes. Nannaros entertained the messenger of the king; and when the meal was brought, 150 women entered, of whom some played the guitar, while others blew the flute. At the end of the meal, Nannaros asked the king's envoy which of all the women was the most beautiful and had played best. The envoy pointed to Parsondes. Nannaros laughed long and said, 'That is the person whom you seek,' and released Parsondes, who on the next day returned home with the envoy to the king in a chariot. The king was astonished at the sight of him, and asked why he had not avoided such disgrace by death. Parsondes answered, 'In order that I might see you again and by you execute vengeance on Nannaros, which could never have been mine had I taken my life.' The king promised him that his hope should be realized, as soon as he came to Babylon. But when he came there, Nannaros defended himself on the ground that Parsondes,

Assyrian Rock Sculpture
From *The Monuments of Nineveh*, by Sir Henry Layard

though in no way injured by him, had maligned him, and sought to obtain the satrapy over Babylonia. The king pointed out that he had made himself judge in his own cause, and had imposed a punishment of a degrading character; in ten days he would pronounce judgment upon him for his conduct. In terror, Nannaros hastened to Mitraphernes, the eunuch of greatest influence with the king, and promised him the most liberal rewards, 10 talents of gold and 100 talents of silver, 10 golden and 200 silver bowls, if he could induce the king to spare his life and retain him in the satrapy of Babylonia. He was prepared to give the king 100 talents of gold, 1000 talents of silver, 100 golden and 300 silver bowls, and costly robes, with other gifts; Parsondes also should receive 100 talents of silver and costly robes. After many entreaties, Mitraphernes persuaded the king not to order the execution of Nannaros, as he had not killed Parsondes, but to exact from him the compensation which he was prepared to pay Parsondes and the king. Nannaros in gratitude threw himself at the feet of the king; but Parsondes said, 'Cursed be the man who first brought gold among men; for the sake of gold I have been made a mockery to the Babylonians.'"

It is impossible to say what the mythological meaning hidden in this tale may portend. We have the moon-god attempting to feminize an unfortunate enemy. Does this mean that Parsondes came under the influence of the moon-god—that is, that he became a lunatic?

Aralu, or Eres-ki-Gal

The deities of the underworld, of the region of the dead, are usually of later origin than those of the heavens.[1] They are frequently the gods of an older and discredited religion, and are relegated to the 'cold shades of opposition,' dwelling there just as the dead are supposed to 'dwell' in the grave. A legend exists regarding Aralu which was discovered among other texts at Tel-el-Amarna. The story goes that the gods once gave a feast to which they invited Aralu, apologizing at the same time that they were unable to go down to her and regretting that she could not ascend to them. In their dilemma they requested her to send a messenger to bring to her the viands which fell to her share. She complied with the request, and when the messenger arrived all the gods stood up to do him honour for his mistress's sake—all save Nergal. The messenger acquainted Aralu with this slight, and greatly enraged she sent him back to the dwelling of the gods to ask that the delinquent might be delivered into her hands so that she might slay him. The gods after some discussion requested the messenger to take back him who had offended the dark goddess, and in order that the envoy might the more easily discover him, all the gods were gathered together. But Nergal remained in the background. His absence was discovered, however, and he was despatched to the gloomy realm of Aralu. But he had no mind to taste death. Indeed Aralu found the tables turned, for Nergal, seizing her by the hair, dragged her from her throne and prepared to cut off her head. She begged to be allowed to speak, and upon her request being granted, she offered herself as a wife to her conqueror, along with the dominions over which she

---

[1] These deities of the underworld must not be confounded with the gods of the abyss referred to at great length in Chapter II. The first group are gods of the dead, the second gods of the primeval waters.

held sway. Nergal assented to her proposals and they were wed.

Nergal is the sun which passes through the gloomy underworld at night just as does Osiris, and in this character he has to conquer the powers of death and the grave. It is rare, however, to find the sun-hero allying himself by marriage to one of the infernal powers, although in the Central American *Popol Vuh* one of the explorers to the underworld weds the daughter of one of its overlords, and Persephone, the corn-goddess, is forced to become the spouse of the lord of Hades.

Dagon

Dagon, alluded to in the Scriptures, was, like Oannes, a fish-god. Besides being worshipped in Erech and its neighbourhood, he was adored in Palestine and on occasion among the Hebrews themselves. But it was in the extreme south of Palestine that his worship attained its chief importance. He had temples at Ashdod and Gaza, and perhaps his worship travelled westward along with that of Ishtar. Both were worshipped at Erech, and where the cult of the one penetrated it is likely that there would be found the rites of the other.

> Dagon his name; sea-monster, upward man
> And downward fish,

as Milton expresses it, affords one of the most dramatic instances in the Old Testament of the downfall of a usurping idol.

"And the Philistines took the ark of God, and brought it from Eben-ezer unto Ashdod.

"When the Philistines took the ark of God, they brought it into the house of Dagon, and set it by Dagon.

"And when they of Ashdod arose early on the morrow, behold, Dagon was fallen upon his face to the earth before the ark of the Lord. And they took Dagon, and set him in his place again.

" And when they arose early on the morrow morning, behold, Dagon was fallen upon his face to the ground before the ark of the Lord; and the head of Dagon and both the palms of his hands were cut off upon the threshold; only the stump of Dagon was left to him.

" Therefore neither the priests of Dagon, nor any that come into Dagon's house, tread on the threshold of Dagon in Ashdod unto this day.

" But the hand of the Lord was heavy upon them of Ashdod, and he destroyed them, and smote them with emerods, even Ashdod and the coasts thereof.

" And when the men of Ashdod saw that it was so, they said, The ark of the God of Israel shall not abide with us: for his hand is sore upon us and upon Dagon our god."

Thus in the Bible story only the 'stump' or fish's tail of Dagon was left to him. In some of the Ninevite sculptures of this deity, the head of the fish forms a kind of mitre on the head of the man, while the body of the fish appears as a cloak or cape over his shoulders and back. This is a sure sign to the mythological student that a god so adorned is in process of quitting the animal for the human form.[1]

---

[1] In sacrifice, too, the totemic or symbolic animal of the god is often flayed and the skin worn by the priest, who in this manner personates the god. In ancient Mexico the priests of Centeotl wore the skin of a woman sacrificed annually to that goddess.

NIRIG OR ENU-RESTU

Nirig, or Enu-Restu

This deity is alluded to in an inscription as "the eldest of the gods." He was especially favoured by the Kings of Assyria, and we find his name entering into the composition of several of their texts. In a certain poem he is called the "son of Bel," and is described as being made "in the likeness of Anu." He rides, it is said, against the gods of his enemies in a chariot of lapis-lazuli, and his onset is full of the fury of the tempest. Bel, his father, commands him to set forth for the temple of Bel at Nippur. Here Nusku, the messenger of Bel, meets him, bestows a gift upon him, and humbly requests that he will not disturb the god Bel, his father, in his dwelling-place, nor terrify the earth-gods. It would appear from this passage that Nirig was on the point of taking the place of Bel, his father, but that he ever did so is improbable. As a deity of storm he is also a god of war, but he was the seed-scatterer upon the mountains, therefore he had also an agricultural significance. It is strange that in Babylonia tempest-gods possess the same functions and attributes—those of war and agriculture—as do rain or thunder, or rain-thunder, or wind and rain deities elsewhere—a circumstance which is eloquent of the power of climatic conditions in the manufacture of myth. In Mesopotamia fierce sand-storms must have given the people the idea of a savage and intractable deity, destructive rather than beneficent, as many hymns and kindred texts witness.

We have now briefly examined the elder gods of the Babylonian pantheon. Other, and in some cases more imposing, gods were yet to be adopted by the Babylonians, as we shall see in the following chapters.

CHAPTER IV: THE GILGAMESH EPIC

AS it is probable that the materials of the Gilgamesh epic, the great mythological poem of Babylonia, originally belong to the older epoch of Babylonian mythology, it is fitting that it should be described and considered before passing to the later developments of Chaldean religion.

The Gilgamesh epic ranks with the Babylonian myth of creation as one of the greatest literary productions of ancient Babylonia. The main element in its composition is a conglomeration of mythic matter, drawn from various sources, with perhaps a substratum of historic fact, the whole being woven into a continuous narrative around the central figure of Gilgamesh, prince of Erech. It is not possible at present to fix the date when the epic was first written. Our knowledge of it is gleaned chiefly from mutilated fragments belonging to the library of Assur-bani-pal, but from internal and other evidence we gather that some at least of the traditions embodied in the epic are of much greater antiquity than his reign. Thus a tablet dated 2100 B.C. contains a variant of the deluge story inserted in the XIth tablet of the Gilgamesh epic. Probably this and other portions of the epic existed in oral tradition before they were committed to writing—that is, in the remote Sumerian period.

Assur-bani-pal was an enthusiastic and practical patron of literature. In his great library at Nineveh (the nucleus of which had been taken from Calah by Sennacherib) he had gathered a vast collection of volumes, clay tablets, and papyri, most of which had been carried as spoil from conquered lands. He also employed scribes to copy older texts, and this

THE GILGAMESH EPIC

is evidently how the existing edition of the Gilgamesh epic came to be written. From the fragments now in the British Museum it would seem that at least four copies of the poem were made in the time of Assur-bani-pal. They were not long permitted to remain undisturbed. The great Assyrian empire was already declining; ere long Nineveh was captured and its library scattered, while plundering hordes burnt the precious rolls of papyrus, and buried the clay tablets in the debris of the palace which had sheltered them.

There they were destined to lie for over 2000 years, till the excavations of Sir A. H. Layard, George Smith, and others brought them to light. It is true that the twelve tablets of the Gilgamesh epic (or rather, the fragments of them which have so far been discovered) are much defaced; frequently the entire sense of a passage is obscured by a gap in the text, and this, when nice mythological elucidations are in question, is no light matter. Yet to such an extent has the science of comparative religion progressed in recent years that we are probably better able to read the true mythological significance of the epic than were the ancient Babylonians themselves, who saw in it merely an account of the wanderings and exploits of a national hero.

The epic, which centres round the ancient city of Erech, relates the adventures of a half-human, half-divine hero, Gilgamesh by name, who is king over Erech. Two other characters figure prominently in the narrative—Eabani, who evidently typifies primitive man, and Ut-Napishtim, the hero of the Babylonian deluge myth. Each of the three would seem to have been originally the hero of a separate group of traditions which in time became incorporated, more or less naturally, with the other two.

The first and most important of the trio, the hero Gilgamesh, may have been at one time a real personage, though nothing is known of him historically.[1] Possibly the exploits of some ancient king of Erech have furnished a basis for the narrative. His name (for a time provisionally read *Gisdhubar*, or *Izdubar*, but now known to have been pronounced *Gilgamesh* [2]) suggests that he was not Babylonian but Elamite or Kassite in origin, and from indications furnished by the poem itself we learn that he conquered Erech (or relieved the city from a besieging force) at the outset of his adventurous career. It has been suggested also that he was identical with the Biblical Nimrod, like him a hero of ancient Babylon; but there are no other grounds for the suggestion.

So much for the historical aspect of Gilgamesh. His mythological character is more easily established. In this regard he is the personification of the sun. He represents, in fact, the fusion of a great national hero with a mythical being. Throughout the epic there are indications that Gilgamesh is partly divine by nature, though nothing specific is said on that head. His identity with the solar god is veiled in the popular narrative, but it is evident that he has some connexion with the god Shamash, to whom he pays his devotions and who acts as his patron and protector.

The Birth of Gilgamesh

Among the traditions concerning his birth is one related by Ælian (*Historia Animalium*, XII, 21)

---

[1] That is, we have no definite historical notices concerning him, but we may infer from internal evidence in his saga that he possesses a certain amount of historicity.

[2] By the discovery by Mr T. Pinches in a lexicographical tablet that Gisdhubar=Gilgamesh.

THE BIRTH OF GILGAMESH

of Gilgamos (Gilgamesh), the grandson of Sokkaros. Sokkaros, who, according to Berossus, was the first king to reign in Babylonia after the deluge, was warned by means of divination that his daughter should bear a son who would deprive him of his throne. Thinking to frustrate the designs of fate he shut her up in a tower, where she was closely watched. But in time she bore a son, and her attendants, knowing how wroth the King would be to learn of the event, flung the child from the tower. But before he reached the ground an eagle seized him up and bore him off to a certain garden, where he was duly found and cared for by a peasant. And when he grew to manhood he became King of the Babylonians, having, presumably, usurped the throne of his grandfather.

Here we have a myth obviously of solar significance, conforming in every particular to a definite type of sun-legend. It cannot have been by chance that it became attached to the person of Gilgamesh. Everything in the epic, too, is consonant with the belief that Gilgamesh is a sun-god—his connexion with Shamash (who may have been his father in the tradition given by Ælian, as well as the eagle which saved him from death), the fact that no mention is made of his father in the poem, though his mother is brought in more than once, and the assumption throughout the epic that he is more than human.

Given the key to his mythical character it is not hard to perceive in his adventures the daily (or annual) course of the sun, rising to its full strength at noonday (or mid-summer), and sinking at length to the western horizon, to return in due time to the abode of men. Like all solar deities—like the sun itself—his birth and origin are wrapped in mystery. He is, indeed, one of the 'fatal children,' like Sargon, Perseus, or Arthur. When he first appears in the narrative he is already a full-grown hero, the ruler and (it would seem) oppressor of Erech. His mother, Rimat-belit, is a priestess in the temple of Ishtar, and through her he is descended from Ut-Napishtim, a native of Shurippak, and the hero of the Babylonian flood-legend. Early in the narrative he is brought into contact with the wild man Eabani, originally designed for his destruction by the gods, but with whom he eventually concludes a firm friendship. The pair proceed to do battle with the monster Khumbaba, whom they overcome, as they do also the sacred bull sent against them by Anu. Up to the end of the VIth tablet their conquering and triumphant career is without interruption; Gilgamesh increases in strength as does the sun approaching the zenith. At the VIIth tablet, however, his good fortune begins to wane. Eabani dies, slain doubtless by the wrath of Ishtar, whose love Gilgamesh has rejected with scorn; and the hero, mourning the death of his friend, and smitten with fear that he himself will perish in like manner, decides to go in search of his ancestor, Ut-Napishtim (who, as sole survivor of the deluge, has received from the gods deification and immortality), and learn of him the secret of eternal life. His further adventures have not the triumphal character of his earlier exploits. Sunwise he journeys to the Mountain of the Sunset, encounters the scorpion-men, and crosses the Waters of Death. Ut-Napishtim teaches him the lesson that all men must die (he himself being an exception in exceptional circumstances), and though he afterwards gives Gilgamesh an opportunity of eating the plant of life, the opportunity is lost. However, Ut-Napishtim cures Gilgamesh of a disease which he has contracted, apparently while crossing the Waters of Death, and he is finally restored to Erech. In these happenings we see the gradual sinking of the sun into the underworld by way of the Mountain of the Sunset. It is impossible for the sun to attain immortality, to remain for ever in the land of the living; he must traverse the Waters of Death and sojourn in the underworld. Yet the return of Gilgamesh to Erech signifies the fresh dawning of the day. It is the eternal struggle of day and night, summer and winter; darkness may conquer light, but light will emerge again victorious. The contest is unending.

Some authorities have seen in the division of the epic into twelve tablets a connexion with the months of the year or the signs of the zodiac. Such a connexion probably exists, but when we consider that the artificial division of the epic into tablets scarcely tallies with the natural divisions of the poem, it seems likely that the astrological significance of the former was given to the epic by the scribes of Nineveh, who were evidently at some pains to compress the matter into twelve tablets. Of the astro-theological significance of the narrative itself (one of its most important aspects), we shall perhaps be better able to judge when we have considered it in detail.

Eabani

The most important of the various mythological strata underlying the Gilgamesh myth is probably that concerning Eabani, who, as has been said, is a type of primitive man, living among the beasts of the field as one of themselves. But he is also, according to certain authorities, a form of the sun-god, even as Gilgamesh himself. Like the hero of Erech, he rises to the zenith of his powers in a triumphal progress, then descends into the underworld. He is not lost sight of, however, but lives in the memory of his friend Gilgamesh; and in the XIIth tablet he is temporarily brought forth from the underworld (that is, his ghost, or *utukku*), which in a dim and shadowy fashion may typify the daily restoration of the sun.

Another important stratum of myth is that which concerns Ut-Napishtim, the Babylonian Noah; but whereas the myths of Eabani and Gilgamesh, though still distinguishable, have become thoroughly fused, the deluge story of which Ut-Napishtim is the hero has been inserted bodily into the XIth tablet of the epic, being related to Gilgamesh by Ut-Napishtim himself. When he first appears in the narrative he has the attributes and powers of a god, having received these for his fidelity to the gods during the flood, from whose waters he alone of all mankind escaped. The object of his narrative in the Gilgamesh epic seems to be to point out to the hero that only the most exceptional circumstances—unique circumstances, indeed—can save man from his doom.

Other distinct portions of the epic are the battle with the monster Khumbaba, the episode of Ishtar's love for Gilgamesh, the fight with the sacred bull of Anu, and the search for the plant of life. These, whatever their origin, have become naturally incorporated with the story of Gilgamesh. But besides the various historical and mythical elements herein presented, there is also a certain amount of Babylonian religious doctrine, evident to some extent in the XIth tablet (which points the moral that all men must die), but doubly so in the XIIth tablet, wherein the shade of Eabani appears to Gilgamesh, relates the misfortunes of the unburied dead or of those uncared for after death, and inculcates care for the deceased as the only means whereby they may evade the grievous woes which threaten them in the underworld.

Let us examine in detail the Gilgamesh epic as we have it in the broken fragments which remain to us. The Ist and IInd tablets are much mutilated. A number of fragments are extant which belong to one or other of these two, but it is not easy to say where the Ist ends and the IInd begins. One fragment would seem to contain the very beginning of the Ist tablet—a sort of general preface to the epic, comprising a list of the advantages to be derived from reading it. After this comes a fragment whose title to inclusion in the epic is doubtful. It describes a siege of the city of Erech, but makes no mention of Gilgamesh. The woeful condition of Erech under the siege is thus picturesquely detailed: "She asses (tread down) their young, cows (turn upon) their calves. Men cry aloud like beasts, and maidens mourn like doves. The gods of strong-walled Erech are changed to flies, and buzz about the streets. The spirits of strong-walled Erech are changed to serpents, and glide into holes. For three years the enemy besieged Erech, and the doors were barred, and the bolts were shot, and Ishtar did not raise her head against the foe." If this fragment be indeed a portion of the Gilgamesh epic, we have no means of ascertaining whether Gilgamesh was the besieger, or the raiser of the siege, or whether he was concerned in the affair at all.

Gilgamesh as Tyrant

Now we come to the real commencement of the poem, inscribed on a fragment which some authorities assign to the beginning of the IInd tablet, but which more probably forms a part of the Ist. In this portion we find Gilgamesh filling the double role of ruler and oppressor of Erech—the latter evidently not inconsistent with the character of a hero. There is no mention here of a siege, nor is there any record of the coming of Gilgamesh, though, as has been indicated, he probably came as a conqueror. His intolerable tyranny towards the people of Erech lends colour to this view. He presses the young men into his service in the building of a great wall, and carries off the fairest maidens to his court; he "hath not left the son to his father, nor the maid to the hero, nor the wife to her husband." Finally his harshness constrained the people to appeal to the gods, and they prayed the goddess Aruru to create a mighty hero who would champion their cause, and through fear of whom Gilgamesh should be forced to temper his severity. The gods themselves added their prayers to those of the oppressed people, and Aruru at length agreed to create a champion against Gilgamesh. "Upon hearing these words (so runs the narrative), Aruru conceived a man (in the image) of Anu in her mind. Aruru washed her hands, she broke off a piece of clay, she cast it on the ground. Thus she created Eabani, the hero." When the creation of this champion was finished his appearance was that of a wild man of the mountains. "The whole of his body was (covered) with hair, he was clothed with long hair like a woman. His hair was luxuriant, like that of the corn-god. He knew (not) the land and the inhabitants thereof, he was clothed with garments as the god of the field. With the gazelles he ate herbs, with the beasts he slaked his thirst, with the creatures of the water his heart

Assyrian Type of Gilgamesh

Found at Khorsabad

From *Religious Belief and Practice in Babylonia and Assyria*, by Professor Morris Jastrow

By permission of Messrs G. P. Putnam's Sons

rejoiced." In pictorial representations on cylinder-seals and elsewhere Eabani is depicted as a sort of satyr, with the head, arms, and body of a man, and the horns, ears, and legs of a beast. As we have seen, he is a type of beast-man, a sort of Caliban, ranging with the beasts of the field, utterly ignorant of the things of civilization.

The Beguiling of Eabani

The poem goes on to introduce a new character, Tsaidu, the hunter, apparently designed by the gods to bring about the meeting of Gilgamesh and Eabani. How he first encounters Eabani is not quite clear from the mutilated text. One reading has it that the King of Erech, learning the plan of the gods for his overthrow, sent Tsaidu into the mountains in search of Eabani, with instructions to entrap him by whatever means and bring him to Erech. Another reading describes the encounter as purely accidental. However this may be, Tsaidu returned to Erech and related to Gilgamesh the story of his encounter, telling him of the strength and fleetness of the wild man, and his exceeding shyness at the sight of a human being. By this time it is evident that Gilgamesh knows or conjectures the purpose for which Eabani is designed, and intends to frustrate the divine plans by anticipating the meeting between himself and the wild man. Accordingly he bids Tsaidu return to the mountains, taking with him Ukhut, one of the sacred women of the temple of Ishtar. His plan is that Ukhut with her wiles shall persuade Eabani to return with her to Erech. Thus the hunter and the girl set out. "They took the straight road, and on the third day they reached the usual drinking-place of Eabani. Then Tsaidu and the woman placed themselves in hiding. For one day, for two days, they lurked by the drinking-place. With the beasts (Eabani) slaked his thirst, with the creatures of the waters his heart rejoiced. Then Eabani (approached) . . ." The scene which follows is described at some length. Ukhut had no difficulty in enthralling Eabani with the snares of her beauty. For six days and seven nights he remembered nothing because of his love for her. When at length he bethought him of his gazelles, his flocks and herds, he found that they would no longer follow him as before. So he sat at the feet of Ukhut while she told him of Erech and its king. "Thou art handsome, O Eabani, thou art like a god. Why dost thou traverse the plain with the beasts? Come, I will take thee to strong-walled Erech, to the bright palace, the dwelling of Anu and Ishtar, to the palace of Gilgamesh, the perfect in strength, who, like a mountain-bull, wieldeth power over man." Eabani found the prospect delightful. He longed for the friendship of Gilgamesh, and declared himself willing to follow the woman to the city of Erech. And so Ukhut, Eabani, and Tsaidu set out on their journey.

Gilgamesh meets Eabani

The feast of Ishtar was in progress when they reached Erech. Eabani had conceived the idea that he must do battle with Gilgamesh before he could claim that hero as a friend, but being warned (whether in a dream, or by Ukhut, is not clear) that Gilgamesh was stronger than he, and withal a favourite of the gods, he wisely refrained from combat. Meanwhile Gilgamesh also had dreamed a dream, which, interpreted by his mother, Rimat-belit, foretold the coming of Eabani. That part of the poem which deals with

GILGAMESH MEETS EABANI

the meeting of Gilgamesh and Eabani is unfortunately no longer extant, but from the fragments which take up the broken narrative we gather that they met and became friends.

The portions of the epic next in order appear to belong to the IInd tablet. In these we find Eabani lamenting the loss of his former freedom and showering maledictions on the temple-maiden who has lured him thither. However, Shamash, the sun-god, intervenes (perhaps in another dream or vision; these play a prominent part in the narrative), and showing him the benefits he has derived from his sojourn in the haunts of civilization, endeavours with various promises and inducements to make him stay in Erech—" Now Gilgamesh, thy friend and brother, shall give thee a great couch to sleep on, shall give thee a couch carefully prepared, shall give thee a seat at his left hand, and the kings of the earth shall kiss thy feet." With this, apparently, Eabani is satisfied. He ceases to bewail his position at Erech and accepts his destiny with calmness. In the remaining fragments of the tablet we find him concerned about another dream or vision; and before this portion of the epic closes the heroes have planned an expedition against the monster Khumbaba, guardian of the abode of the goddess Irnina (a form of Ishtar), in the Forest of Cedars.

In the very mutilated IIIrd tablet the two heroes go to consult the priestess Rimat-belit, the mother of Gilgamesh, and through her they ask protection from Shamash in the forthcoming expedition. The old priestess advises her son and his friend how to proceed, and after they have gone we see her alone in the temple, her hands raised to the sun-god, invoking his blessing on Gilgamesh: " Why hast thou troubled the heart of my son Gilgamesh? Thou hast laid thy hand upon him, and he goeth away, on a far journey to the dwelling of Khumbaba; he entereth into a combat (whose issue) he knoweth not; he followeth a road unknown to him. Till he arrive and till he return, till he reach the Forest of Cedars, till he hath slain the terrible Khumbaba and rid the land of all the evil that thou hatest, till the day of his return—let Aya, thy betrothed, thy splendour, recall him to thee." With this dignified and beautiful appeal the tablet comes to an end.

The Monster Khumbaba

The IVth tablet is concerned with a description of the monster with whom the heroes are about to do battle. Khumbaba, whom Bel had appointed to guard the cedar (*i.e.*, one particular cedar which appears to be of greater height and sanctity than the others), is a creature of most terrifying aspect, the very presence of whom in the forest makes those who enter it grow weak and impotent. As the heroes draw near Eabani complains that his hands are feeble and his arms without strength, but Gilgamesh speaks words of encouragement to him. It may be noted, in passing, that the word Khumbaba is of Elamite origin, a fact which has led certain authorities to identify the monster with an Elamite dynasty which anciently dominated Erech, and which came to grief about 2250 B.C. It is difficult, if not impossible, to establish the connexion between the mythical encounter and a definite historical event; but it may at least be presumed that the bestowal of an Elamite designation on the monster argues a certain enmity between Elam and Babylon.

The next fragments bring us into the Vth tablet.

ISHTAR'S LOVE FOR GILGAMESH

The heroes, having reached "a verdant mountain," paused to survey the Forest of Cedars. When they entered the forest the death of Khumbaba was foretold to one or other, or both of them, in a dream, and they hastened forward to the combat. Unfortunately the text of the actual encounter has not been preserved, but we learn from the context that the heroes were successful in slaying Khumbaba.

Ishtar's Love for Gilgamesh

In the VIth tablet, which relates the story of Ishtar's love for Gilgamesh, and the slaying of the sacred bull, victory again waits on the arms of the heroes, but here nevertheless we have the key to the misfortunes which later befall them. On his return to Erech after the destruction of Khumbaba, Gilgamesh was loudly acclaimed. Doffing the soiled and bloodstained garments he had worn during the battle, he robed himself as befitted a monarch and a conqueror. Ishtar beheld the King in his regal splendour, the flowers of victory still fresh on his brow, and her heart went out to him in love. In moving and seductive terms she besought him to be her bridegroom, promising that if he would enter her house " in the gloom of the cedar " all manner of good gifts should be his—his flocks and herds would increase, his horses and oxen would be without rival, the river Euphrates would kiss his feet, and kings and princes would bring tribute to him. But Gilgamesh, knowing something of the past history of this capricious goddess, rejected her advances with scorn, and began to revile her. He taunted her, too, with her treatment of former lovers—of Tammuz, the bridegroom of her youth, to whom she clung weepingly year after year; of Alalu the eagle; of a lion perfect in might and a horse glorious in battle; of the shepherd Tabulu and of Isullanu, the gardener of her father. All these she had mocked and ill-treated in cruel fashion, and Gilgamesh perceived that like treatment would be meted out to him should he accept the proffered love of the goddess. The deity was greatly enraged at the repulse, and mounted up to heaven: "Moreover Ishtar went before Anu (her father), before Anu she went and she (said): 'O my father, Gilgamesh has kept watch on me; Gilgamesh has counted my garlands, my garlands and my girdles.'" Underlying the story of Ishtar's love for Gilgamesh there is evidently a nature-myth of some sort, perhaps a spring-tide myth; Gilgamesh, the sun-god, or a hero who has taken over his attributes, is wooed by Ishtar, the goddess of fertility, the great mother-goddess who presides over spring vegetation. In the recital of her former love-affairs we find mention of the Tammuz myth, in which Ishtar slew her consort Tammuz, and other mythological fragments. It is possible also that there is an astrological significance in this part of the narrative.

The Bull of Anu

To resume the tale: In her wrath and humiliation Ishtar appealed to her father and mother, Anu and Anatu, and begged the former to create a mighty bull and send it against Gilgamesh. Anu at first demurred, declaring that if he did so it would result in seven years' sterility on the earth; but finally he consented, and a great bull, Alu, was sent to do battle with Gilgamesh. The portion of the text which deals with the combat is much mutilated, but it appears that the conflict was hot and sustained, the celestial animal finally succumbing to a sword-thrust from

THE BULL OF ANU

Gilgamesh. Ishtar looks on in impotent anger. "Then Ishtar went up on to the wall of strong-walled Erech; she mounted to the top and she uttered a curse, (saying), 'Cursed be Gilgamesh, who has provoked me to anger, and has slain the bull from heaven.'" Then Eabani incurs the anger of the deity —"When Eabani heard these words of Ishtar, he tore out the entrails of the bull, and he cast them before her, saying, 'As for thee, I will conquer thee, and I will do to thee even as I have done to him.'" Ishtar was beside herself with rage. Gilgamesh and his companion dedicated the great horns of the bull to the sun-god, and having washed their hands in the river Euphrates, returned once more to Erech. As the triumphal procession passed through the city the people came out of their houses to do honour to the heroes. The remainder of the tablet is concerned with a great banquet given by Gilgamesh to celebrate his victory over the bull Alu, and with further visions of Eabani.

The VIIth and VIIIth tablets are extremely fragmentary, and so much of the text as is preserved is open to various readings. It is possible that to the VIIth tablet belongs a description of the underworld given to Eabani in a dream by the temple-maiden Ukhut, whom he had cursed in a previous tablet, and who had since died. The description answers to that given in another ancient text—the myth of Ishtar's descent into Hades—and evidently embodies the popular belief concerning the underworld. "Come, descend with me to the house of darkness, the abode of Irkalla, to the house whence the enterer goes not forth, to the path whose way has no return, to the house whose dwellers are deprived of light, where dust is their nourishment and earth their good. They are clothed, like the birds, in a garment of feathers; they see not the light, they dwell in darkness."

The Death of Eabani

This sinister vision appears to have been a presage of Eabani's death. Shortly afterwards he fell ill and died at the end of twelve days. The manner of his death is uncertain. One reading of the mutilated text represents Eabani as being wounded, perhaps in battle, and succumbing to the effects of the wound. But another makes him say to his friend Gilgamesh, " I have been cursed, my friend, I shall not die as one who has been slain in battle." The breaks in the text are responsible for the divergence. The latter reading is probably the correct one; Eabani has grievously offended Ishtar, the all-powerful, and the curse which has smitten him to the earth is probably hers. In modern folk-lore phraseology he died of ju-ju. The death of the hero brings the VIIIth tablet to a close.

In the IXth tablet we find Gilgamesh mourning the loss of his friend.

The Quest of Gilgamesh

On the heart of Gilgamesh, likewise, the fear of death had taken hold, and he determined to go in search of his ancestor, Ut-Napishtim, who might be able to show him a way of escape. Straightway putting his determination into effect, Gilgamesh set out for the abode of Ut-Napishtim. On the way he had to pass through mountain gorges, made terrible by the presence of wild beasts. From the power of these he was delivered by Sin, the moon-god, who enabled him to traverse the mountain passes in safety.

THE QUEST OF GILGAMESH

At length he came to a mountain higher than the rest, the entrance to which was guarded by scorpion-men. This was Mashu, the Mountain of the Sunset, which lies on the western horizon, between the earth and the underworld. " Then he came to the mountain of Mashu, the portals of which are guarded every day by monsters; their backs mount up to the ramparts of heaven, and their foreparts reach down beneath Aralu. Scorpion-men guard the gate (of Mashu); they strike terror into men, and it is death to behold them. Their splendour is great, for it overwhelms the mountains; from sunrise to sunset they guard the sun. Gilgamesh beheld them, and his face grew dark with fear and terror, and the wildness of their aspect robbed him of his senses." On approaching the entrance to the mountain Gilgamesh found his way barred by these scorpion-men, who, perceiving the strain of divinity in him, did not blast him with their glance, but questioned him regarding his purpose in drawing near the mountain of Mashu. When Gilgamesh had replied to their queries, telling them how he wished to reach the abode of his ancestor, Ut-Napishtim, and there learn the secret of perpetual life and youthfulness, the scorpion-men advised him to turn back. Before him, they said, lay the region of thick darkness; for twelve *kasbu* (twenty-four hours) he would have to journey through the thick darkness ere he again emerged into the light of day. And so they refused to let him pass. But Gilgamesh implored, " with tears," says the narrative, and at length the monsters consented to admit him. Having passed the gate of the Mountain of the Sunset (by virtue of his character as a solar deity) Gilgamesh traversed the region of thick darkness during the space of twelve *kasbu.* Toward the end of that period the darkness became ever less pronounced; finally it was broad day, and Gilgamesh found himself in a beautiful garden or park studded with trees, among which was the tree of the gods, thus charmingly depicted in the text—" Precious stones it bore as fruit, branches hung from it which were beautiful to behold. The top of the tree was lapis-lazuli, and it was laden with fruit which dazzled the eye of him that beheld." Having paused to admire the beauty of the scene, Gilgamesh bent his steps shoreward.

The Xth tablet describes the hero's encounter with the sea-goddess Sabitu, who, on the approach of one " who had the appearance of a god, in whose body was grief, and who looked as though he had made a long journey," retired into her palace and fastened the door. But Gilgamesh, knowing that her help was necessary to bring him to the dwelling of Ut-Napishtim, told her of his quest, and in despair threatened to break down the door unless she opened to him. At last Sabitu consented to listen to him whilst he asked the way to Ut-Napishtim. Like the scorpion-men, the sea-goddess perceived that Gilgamesh was not to be turned aside from his quest, so at last she bade him go to Adad-Ea, Ut-Napishtim's ferryman, without whose aid, she said, it would be futile to persist further in his mission. Adad-Ea, likewise, being consulted by Gilgamesh, advised him to desist, but the hero, pursuing his plan of intimidation, began to smash the ferryman's boat with his axe, whereupon Adad-Ea was obliged to yield. He sent his would-be passenger into the forest for a new rudder, and after that the two sailed away.

THE DELUGE MYTH

Gilgamesh and Ut-Napishtim

Ut-Napishtim was indeed surprised when he beheld Gilgamesh approaching the strand. The hero had meanwhile contracted a grievous illness, so that he was unable to leave the boat; but he addressed his queries concerning perpetual life to the deified Ut-Napishtim, who stood on the shore. The hero of the flood was exceeding sorrowful, and explained that death is the common lot of mankind, " nor is it given to man to know the hour when the hand of death will fall upon him—the Annunaki, the great gods, decree fate, and with them Mammetum, the maker of destiny, and they determine death and life, but the days of death are not known."

The narrative is continued without interruption into the XIth tablet. Gilgamesh listened with pardonable scepticism to the platitudes of his ancestor. "'I behold thee, Ut-Napishtim, thy appearance differs not from mine, thou art like unto me, thou art not otherwise than I am; thou art like unto me, thy heart is stout for the battle . . . how hast thou entered the assembly of the gods; how hast thou found life?'"

The Deluge Myth

In reply Ut-Napishtim introduces the story of the Babylonian deluge, which, told as it is without interruption, forms a separate and complete narrative, and is in itself a myth of exceptional interest. Presumably the warning of the deluge came to Ut-Napishtim in a vision. The voice of the god said: 'Thou man of Shurippak, son of Ubara-Tutu, pull down thy house, build a ship, forsake thy possessions, take heed for thy life! Abandon thy goods, save thy life, and bring up living seed of every kind into the ship.' The ship itself was to be carefully planned and built according to Ea's instructions. When the god had spoken Ut-Napishtim promised obedience to the divine command. But he was still perplexed as to how he should answer the people when they asked the reason for his preparations. Ea therefore instructed him how he should make reply, 'Bel hath cast me forth, for he hateth me.' The purpose of this reply seems clear, though the remaining few lines of it are rather broken. Ea intends that Ut-Napishtim shall disarm the suspicions of the people by declaring that the object of his shipbuilding and his subsequent departure is to escape the wrath of Bel, which he is to depict as falling on him alone. He must prophesy the coming of the rain, but must represent it, not as a devastating flood, but rather as a mark of the prosperity which Bel will grant to the people of Shurippak, perhaps by reason of his (Ut-Napishtim's) departure therefrom.

The Babylonian Ark

Ut-Napishtim employed many people in the construction of the ship. During four days he gathered the material and built the ship; on the fifth he laid it down; on the sixth he loaded it; and by the seventh day it was finished. On a hull 120 cubits wide was constructed a great deck-house 120 cubits high, divided into six stories, each of which was divided in turn into nine rooms. The outside of the ship was made water-tight with bitumen, and the inside with pitch. To signalise the completion of his vessel, Ut-Napishtim gave a great feast, like that which was wont to be held on New Year's Day; oxen were slaughtered and great quantities of wine

THE BABYLONIAN ARK

and oil provided. According to the command of Ea, Ut-Napishtim brought into the ship all his possessions, his silver and his gold,[1] living seed of every kind, all his family and household, the cattle and beasts of the field, the handicraftsmen, all that was his.

A heavy rain at eventide was the sign for Ut-Napishtim to enter the ship and fasten the door. All night long it rained, and with the early dawn "there came up from the horizon a black cloud. Ramman in the midst thereof thundered, and Nabu and Marduk went before, they passed like messengers over mountain and plain. Uragal parted the anchor-cable. There went Ninib, and he made the storm to burst. The Annunaki carried flaming torches, and with the brightness thereof they lit up the earth. The whirlwind of Ramman mounted up into the heavens, and all light was turned into darkness." During a whole day darkness and chaos appear to have reigned on the earth. Men could no longer behold each other. The very gods in heaven were afraid and crouched "like hounds," weeping, and lamenting their share in the destruction of mankind. For six days and nights the tempest raged, but on the seventh day the rain ceased and the floods began to abate. Then, says Ut-Napishtim—"I looked upon the sea and cried aloud, for all mankind was turned back into clay. In place of the fields a swamp lay before me. I opened the window and the light fell upon my cheek, I bowed myself down, I sat down, I wept; over my cheek flowed my tears. I looked upon the world, and behold all was sea."

[1] The inconsistency in details is caused by the composite nature of the tale, which is drawn from two different tablets.

The Bird Messengers

At length the ship came to rest on the summit of Mount Nitsir. There are various readings of this portion of the text, thus: "After twelve (days) the land appeared;" or "At the distance of twelve (kasbu) the land appeared;" or "Twelve (cubits) above the water the land appeared." However this may be, the ship remained for six days on the mountain, and on the seventh Ut-Napishtim sent out a dove. But the dove found no resting-place, and so she returned. Then he sent out a swallow, which also returned, having found no spot whereon to rest. Finally a raven was sent forth, and as by this time the waters had begun to abate, the bird drew near to the ship "wading and croaking," but did not enter the vessel. Then Ut-Napishtim brought his household and all his possessions into the open air, and made an offering to the gods of reed, and cedar-wood, and incense. The fragrant odour of the incense came up to the gods, and they gathered, "like flies," says the narrative, around the sacrifice. Among the company was Ishtar, the Lady of the Gods, who lifted up the necklace which Anu had given her, saying: "What gods these are! By the jewels of lapis-lazuli which are upon my neck I will not forget! These days I have set in my memory, never will I forget them! Let the gods come to the offering, but Bel shall not come to the offering since he refused to ask counsel and sent the deluge, and handed over my people unto destruction."

The god Bel was very wroth when he discovered that a mortal man had survived the deluge, and vowed that Ut-Napishtim should perish. But Ea defended his action in having saved his favourite from destruction, pointing out that Bel had refused

Ut-Napishtim makes Offering to the Gods
Allan Stewart
By permission of Messrs Hutchinson and Co.

THE BIRD MESSENGERS

to take counsel when he planned a universal disaster, and advising him in future to visit the sin on the sinner and not to punish the entire human race. Finally Bel was mollified. He approached the ship (into which it would appear that the remnants of the human race had retired during the altercation) and led Ut-Napishtim and his wife into the open, where he bestowed on them his blessing. "Then they took me," says Ut-Napishtim, "and afar off, at the mouth of the rivers, they made me to dwell."

Such is the story of the deluge which Ut-Napishtim told to Gilgamesh. No cause is assigned for the destruction of the human race other than the enmity which seems to have existed between man and the gods—particularly the warrior-god Bel. But it appears from the latter part of the narrative that in the assembly of the gods the majority contemplated only the destruction of the city of Shurippak, and not that of the entire human family. It has been suggested, indeed, that the story as it is here given is compounded of two separate myths, one relating to a universal catastrophe, perhaps a mythological type of a periodic inundation, and the other dealing with a local disaster such as might have been occasioned by a phenomenal overflow of the Euphrates.

The antiquity of the legend and its original character are clearly shown by comparison with another version of the myth, inscribed on a tablet found at Abu-Habbah (the ancient site of Sippar) and dated in the twenty-first century before our era. Notwithstanding the imperfect preservation of this text it is possible to perceive in it many points of resemblance to the Gilgamesh variant. Berossus also quotes a version of the deluge myth in his history, substituting Chronos for Ea, King Xisuthros for

MYTHS OF BABYLONIA AND ASSYRIA

Ut-Napishtim, and the city of Sippar for that of Shurippak. In this version immortality is bestowed not only on the hero and his wife, but also on his daughter and his pilot. One writer ingeniously identifies these latter with Sabitu and Adad-Ea respectively.

To return to the epic: The recital of Ut-Napishtim served its primary purpose in the narrative by proving to Gilgamesh that his case was not that of his deified ancestor. Meanwhile the hero had remained in the boat, too ill to come ashore; now Ut-Napishtim took pity on him and promised to restore him to health, first of all bidding him sleep during six days and seven nights. Gilgamesh listened to his ancestor's advice, and by and by " sleep, like a tempest, breathed upon him." Ut-Napishtim's wife, beholding the sleeping hero, was likewise moved with compassion, and asked her husband to send the traveller safely home. He in turn bade his wife compound a magic preparation, containing seven ingredients, and administer it to Gilgamesh while he slept. This was done, and an enchantment thus put upon the hero. When he awoke (on the seventh day) he renewed his importunate request for the secret of perpetual life. His host sent him to a spring of water where he might bathe his sores and be healed; and having tested the efficacy of the magic waters Gilgamesh returned once more to his ancestor's dwelling, doubtless to persist in his quest for life. Notwithstanding that Ut-Napishtim had already declared it impossible for Gilgamesh to attain immortality, he now directed him (apparently at the instance of his wife) to the place where he would find the plant of life, and instructed Adad-Ea to conduct him thither. The magic plant, which bestowed immortality and eternal

THE BIRD MESSENGERS

youth on him who ate of it, appears to have been a weed, a creeping plant, with thorns which pricked the hands of the gatherer; and, curiously enough, Gilgamesh seems to have sought it at the bottom of the sea. At length the plant was found, and the hero declared his intention of carrying it with him to Erech. And so he set out on the return journey, accompanied by the faithful ferryman not only on the first, and watery, stage of his travels, but also overland to the city of Erech itself. When they had journeyed twenty *kasbu* they left an offering (presumably for the dead), and when they had journeyed thirty *kasbu*, they repeated a funeral chant. The narrative goes on: " Gilgamesh saw a well of fresh water, he went down to it and offered a libation. A serpent smelled the odour of the plant, advanced . . . and carried off the plant. Gilgamesh sat down and wept, the tears ran down his cheeks." He lamented bitterly the loss of the precious plant, seemingly predicted to him when he made his offering at the end of twenty *kasbu*. At length they reached Erech, when Gilgamesh sent Adad-Ea to enquire concerning the building of the city walls, a proceeding which has possibly some mythological significance.

The XIIth tablet opens with the lament of Gilgamesh for his friend Eabani, whose loss he has not ceased to deplore. " Thou canst no longer stretch thy bow upon the earth; and those who were slain with the bow are round about thee. Thou canst no longer bear a sceptre in thy hand; and the spirits of the dead have taken thee captive. Thou canst no longer wear shoes upon thy feet; thou canst no longer raise thy war-cry on the earth. No more dost thou kiss thy wife whom thou didst love; no more dost thou smite thy wife whom thou didst hate. No more dost thou kiss thy daughter whom thou didst love; no more dost thou smite thy daughter whom thou didst hate. The sorrow of the underworld hath taken hold upon thee."[1] Gilgamesh went from temple to temple, making offerings and desiring the gods to restore Eabani to him; to Ninsum he went, to Bel, and to Sin, the moon-god, but they heeded him not. At length he cried to Ea, who took compassion on him and persuaded Nergal to bring the shade of Eabani from the underworld. A hole was opened in the earth and the spirit of the dead man issued therefrom like a breath of wind. Gilgamesh addressed Eabani thus: "Tell me, my friend, tell me, my friend; the law of the earth which thou hast seen, tell me." Eabani answered him: "I cannot tell thee, my friend, I cannot tell thee." But afterwards, having bidden Gilgamesh "sit down and weep," he proceeded to tell him of the conditions which prevailed in the underworld, contrasting the lot of the warrior duly buried with that of a person whose corpse is cast uncared for into the fields. "On a couch he lieth, and drinketh pure water, the man who was slain in battle—thou and I have oft seen such an one—his father and his mother (support) his head, and his wife (kneeleth) at his side. But the man whose corpse is cast upon the field—thou and I have oft seen such an one—his spirit resteth not in the earth. The man whose spirit has none to care for it—thou and I have oft seen such an one—the dregs of the vessel, the leavings of the feast, and that which is cast out upon the streets, are his food." Upon this solemn note the epic closes.

[1] These remarks are perhaps not to be taken literally of Eabani. They represent the entirely formal manner in which any deceased Babylonian was addressed.

THE BIRD MESSENGERS

The doctrine of the necessity for ministering to the dead is here enunciated in no uncertain fashion. Unless their bodies are decently buried and offerings of food and drink made at their graves, their lives in the otherworld must be abjectly miserable. The manner in which they meet their end is likewise taken into account, and warriors who have fallen on the field of battle are pre-eminently fortunate. Eabani is evidently one of the 'happy' spirits; his ghost is designated *utukku*, a name applied not only to the fortunate dead, but likewise to a class of beneficent supernatural beings. The term *edimmu*, on the other hand, designates a species of malevolent being as well as the errant and even vampirish spirits of the unhappy dead. The due observance of funeral and commemorative rites is thus a matter which touches the interests not only of the deceased but also of his relatives and friends.

We have seen from the foregoing that the epic of Gilgamesh is partly historical, partly mythological. Around the figure of a great national hero myths have grown and twined with the passing of the generations, and these have in time become woven into a connected narrative, setting forth a myth which corresponds to the daily or annual course of the sun. Within this may be discerned other myths and fragments of myths—solar, seasonal, and diluvian.

But there is in the epic another important element which has already been referred to—the astro-theological. The zodiacal significance of the division of the epic into twelve tablets may be set aside, since, as has been indicated, the significance is in all probability a superficial one merely, added to the poem by the scribes of Assur-bani-pal, and not forming an integral part of it. At the same time it is not

MYTHS OF BABYLONIA AND ASSYRIA

hard to divide the epic naturally into twelve episodes, thus: (1) Gilgamesh's oppression of Erech; (2) the seduction of Eabani; (3) the slaying of the monster Khumbaba; (4) the wooing of Ishtar; (5) the fight with the sacred bull; (6) Eabani's death; (7) Gilgamesh's journey to the Mountain of the Sunset; (8) his wanderings in the region of thick darkness; (9) the crossing of the waters of death; (10) the deluge-story; (11) the plant of life; (12) the return of Eabani's spirit. Throughout the epic there are indications of a correspondence between the exploits of the hero and the movements of heavenly bodies. It is possible, for instance, that Gilgamesh and his friend Eabani had some relation to the sign Gemini, also associated in ancient Chaldean mythology with two forms of the solar deity, even as were the hero and his friend. The sign Leo recalls the slaying of Khumbaba, the allegorical victory of light over darkness, represented on monuments by the figure of a lion (symbol of fire) fighting with a bull. Following the sign of Leo, the wooing of the hero by the goddess Ishtar falls naturally into the sign of Virgo, the virgin. The sign of Taurus is represented by the slaying of the celestial bull, Alu, by Gilgamesh. The journey of the hero to Mashu and his encounter with the scorpion-men at the gate of the sunset are, of course, mythological representations of the sign of Scorpio, as are also his wanderings in the region of thick darkness. It is noticeable in this respect that Babylonian astrology often doubled the eighth sign (Scorpio) to provide a seventh; it is therefore not unlikely that this sign should correspond with two distinct episodes in the poem. The first of these episodes is associated with Scorpio by virtue of the introduction of scorpion-men; and the second, on

THE BIRD MESSENGERS

the assumption that the scorpion is symbolical of darkness. Perhaps the sea-goddess Sabitu is associated astrologically with the fish-tailed goat which is the conventional representation of Capricornus. Then the placing of the deluge-story in the XIth tablet, corresponding with the eleventh sign of the zodiac, Aquarius, the water-bearer, is evidently in keeping with the astrological aspect of the epic. Chaldean mythology connected the rainy eleventh month with the deluge, just as the first month of spring was associated mythologically with the creation. The healing of Gilgamesh's sickness by Ut-Napishtim may possibly symbolise the revival of the sun after leaving the winter solstice. Lastly, the sign of Pisces, the twelfth sign of the zodiac, corresponding to the return of Eabani from the underworld, and perhaps also to the restoration of Gilgamesh to Erech, is emblematic of life after death, and of the resumption of ordinary conditions after the deluge. It has been suggested, though without any very definite basis, that the epic was first put together before the zodiac was divided into twelve—that is, more than two thousand years before the Christian era. Its antiquity, however, rests on other grounds than these. In later times the Babylonian astrological system became very complicated and important, and so lent its colour to the epic that, whatever the original plan of that work may have been, its astral significance became at length its most popular aspect.

CHAPTER V: THE LATER PANTHEON OF BABYLONIA

THE reign of Khammurabi is a convenient point at which to observe general changes in and later introductions to the pantheon of the Babylonian gods. The political alterations in the kingdom were reflected in the divine circle. Certain gods were relegated to the cold shades of obscurity, whilst new deities were adopted and others, hitherto regarded as negligible quantities, were exalted to the heights of heavenly omnipotence. The worship of Merodach first came into prominence in the days of Khammurabi. But his cult is so outstanding and important that it has been deemed better to deal with it in a separate and later chapter. Meanwhile we shall examine the nature of some of the gods who sprang into importance at or about the era of the great law-maker, and note changes which took place with regard to others.

Nebo

The popularity of Nebo was brought about through his association with Merodach. His chief seat of worship was at Borsippa, opposite to Babylon, and when the latter city became the seat of the imperial power the proximity of Borsippa greatly assisted the cult of Nebo. So close did the association between the deities of the two cities become that at length Nebo was regarded as the son of Merodach—a relationship that often implies that the so-called descendant of the elder god is a serious rival, or that his cult is nearly allied to the elder worship. Nebo had acquired something of a reputation as a god of wisdom, and probably this it was which permitted him to stand

Nebo

Son of Merodach, God of Wisdom, and the inventor of writing

Photo W. A. Mansell and Co.

NEBO

separately from Merodach without becoming absorbed in the cult of the great deity of Babylon. He was credited, like Ea, with the invention of writing, the province of all 'wise' gods, and he presided over that department of knowledge which interpreted the movements of the heavenly bodies. The priests of Nebo were famous as astrologers, and with the bookish king Assur-bani-pal, Nebo and his consort Tashmit were especial favourites as the patrons of writing. By the time that the worship of Merodach had become recognised at Babylon, the cult of Nebo at Borsippa was so securely rooted that even the proximity of the greatest god in the land failed to shake it.

Even after the Persian conquest the temple-school at Borsippa continued to flourish. But although Nebo thus 'outlived' many of the greater gods it is now almost impossible to trace his original significance as a deity. Whether solar or aqueous in his nature—and the latter appears more likely—he was during the period of Merodach's ascendancy regarded as scribe of the gods, much as Thoth was the amanuensis of the Egyptian otherworld—that is to say, he wrote at the dictation of the higher deities. When the gods were assembled in the Chamber of Fates in Merodach's temple at Babylon, he chronicled their speeches and deliberations and put them on record. Indeed he himself had a shrine in this temple of E-Sagila, or 'the lofty house,' which was known as E-Zila, or 'the firm house.' Once during the New Year festival Nebo was carried from Borsippa to Babylon to his father's temple, and in compliment was escorted by Merodach part of the way back to his own shrine in the lesser city. It is strange to see how closely the cults of the two gods were interwoven. The Kings of Babylonia constantly invoke them together, their names and those of their temples are found in close proximity at every turn, and the symbols of the bow and the stylus or pen, respectively typical of the father and the son, are usually discovered in one and the same inscription. Even Merodach's dragon, the symbol of his victory over the dark forces of chaos, is assigned to Nebo!

Nebo as Grain-God

But Nebo seems to have had also an agricultural side to his character. In many texts he is praised as the god " who opens up the subterranean sources in order to irrigate the fields," and the withdrawal of his favour is followed by famine and distress. This seems to favour the idea of his watery nature. His name, 'the proclaimer,' does not assist us much in fixing his mythological significance, unless it was assigned to him in the *rôle* of herald of the gods.

Tashmit

Nebo's consort was Tashmit. It is believed that Khammurabi, unsuccessful in suppressing the cult of Nebo, succeeded with that of his spouse. She seems to have been the same as a goddess Ealur who became amalgamated with Zarpanitum, the wife of Merodach. The name may mean, according to some, ' the hearer,' and to others a ' revelation,' and in view of the character of her wise husband, was perhaps one of the original designations of Merodach himself. Tashmit had therefore but little individuality. None the less she possessed considerable popularity. On a seal-impression dating somewhere between 3500–4500 B.C. there are outlined two figures, male and female, supposed to represent Nebo and Tashmit. The former has a wide-open mouth and the latter ears of extraordinary size. Both are holding wild animals by the horns, and the representation is thought to be typical of the strength or power of speech and silence.

Shamash and Khammurabi

We find that Khammurabi was very devoted to Shamash, the early type of sun-god. His improvements and restorations at Sippar and Larsa were extensive. The later Babylonian monarchs followed his example, and one of them, Mili-Shikhu (*c.* 1450 B.C.) even placed Shamash before Merodach in the pantheon! The early connexion between Merodach and Shamash had probably much to do with the great popularity of the latter. That this was the case, so far at least as Khammurabi was concerned, is obvious from certain of his inscriptions, in which he alludes in the same sentence to Merodach and Shamash and to their close relationship. Khammurabi appears also to have been greatly attached to the cult of a goddess Innana or Ninni ('lady' or 'great lady'), who was evidently the consort of some male deity. He improved her temple at Hallabi and speaks of her as placing the reins of power in his hands. There was another goddess of the same name at Lagash whom Gudea worshipped as 'mistress of the world,' but she does not seem to have been the same as the Innana of Hallabi, near Sippar, as she was a goddess of fertility and generation, of the 'mother goddess' type, and there do not appear to be any grounds for the assertion that the goddess of Hallabi can be equated with her.

Hadad

Ramman or Rimmon, identified with Hadad or Adad, is a deity of later type and introduction.

MYTHS OF BABYLONIA AND ASSYRIA

Indeed Ramman may be merely a variant or subsidiary name, meaning as it does 'the thunderer,' quite a common title for several types of deities. The worship of Hadad was widespread in Syria and Palestine, and he was a god of storms or rains, whose symbol was the thunderbolt or the lightning which he holds in his grasp like a fiery sword. But he bears solar emblems upon his apparel, and seems to wear a solar crown. He does not, however, appear to have had any centre of worship in Babylonia, and was probably a god of the Amorites, and becoming popular with the Babylonians, was later admitted into their pantheon. At Asshur in Assyria he was worshipped along with Anu, with whom he had a temple in common. This building, which was excavated in 1908, contains two shrines having but the one entrance, and the date of its foundation is referred so far back as B.C. 2400. There can be little doubt that the partnership of Hadad with Anu was a late one. Perhaps it was on Assyrian and not Babylonian soil that Hadad first entered from the alien world.

HADAD OR RIMMON
From *Religious Belief and Practice in Babylonia and Assyria*, by Prof. Jastrow: (G. P. Putnam's Sons.)

In many of his characteristics Hadad closely resembled En-lil. Like him he was designated 'the great mountain,' and seems to have been conceived of as almost a counterpart of the older god. It is peculiar that while in Assyria and Babylonia Hadad has many of the characteristics of a sun-god, in his old home in Syria he possessed those of a thunder-god who dwelt among the mountains of northern

HADAD, DÁDA, DAVID, AND DIDO

Palestine and Syria and spoke in thunder and wielded the lightning. But even in Assyria the stormy characteristics of Hadad are not altogether obscured. Hadad's cult in Babylonia is probably not much older than the days of Khammurabi, in whose time the first inscriptional mention of him is made. His worship obtained a stronger hold in the times of the Kassite dynasty, for we find many of its monarchs incorporating his name with their own and altogether affording him a prominent place.

Hadad, Dáda, David, and Dído

In a curious and interesting passage in his *Hibbert Lectures*,[1] Professor Sayce indicates resemblances between the name Hadad, Dáda, the abbreviated form of the name of Abd-Hadad, who reigned at Hierapolis in the fourth century, Queen Dido of Carthage, and that of the Biblical David. Speaking of Hadad he says: "He was, as I have said, the supreme Baal or Sun-god, whose worship extended southward from Carchemish to Edom and Palestine. At Damascus he was adored under the Assyrian name of Rimmon, and Zechariah (xii 11) alludes to the cult of the compound Hadad-Rimmon in the close neighbourhood of the great Canaanitish fortress of Megiddo. Coins bear the name of Abd-Hadad, 'the servant of Hadad,' who reigned in the fourth century at Hierapolis, the later successor of Carchemish, and, under the abbreviated form of Dáda, Shalmaneser speaks of 'the god Dada of Aleppo' (Khalman). The abbreviated form was that current among the nations of the north; in the south it was confounded with the Semite word which appears in Assyrian as *dadu*, 'dear little child.' This

---
[1] Pp. 56 ff.

is the word which we have in Be-Dad or Ben-Dad, 'the son of Dad,' the father of the Edomite Hadad; we have it also in the David of the Old Testament. David, or Dod, as the word ought to be read, which is sometimes written Dodo with the vocalic suffix of the nominative, is the masculine corresponding to a Phœnician goddess whose name means 'the beloved one,' and who was called Dido by the writers of Rome. Dido, in fact, was the consort of the Sun-god, conceived as Tammuz, 'the beloved son,' and was the presiding deity of Carthage, whom legend confounded with Elissa, the foundress of the city. In the article I have alluded to above, I expressed my conviction that the names of Dodo and David pointed to a worship of the Sun-god, under the title of 'the beloved one,' in southern Canaan as well as in Phœnicia. I had little idea at the time how soon my belief would be verified. Within the last year, the squeeze of the Moabite stone, now in the Louvre, has been subjected to a thorough examination by the German Professors Socin and Smend, with the result of correcting some of the received readings and of filling up some of the lacunæ. One of the most important discoveries that have been thus made is that the Israelites of the northern kingdom worshipped a Dodo or Dod by the side of Yahveh, or rather that they adored the supreme God under the name of Dodo as well as under that of Yahveh. Mesha, the Moabite king, in describing the victories which his god Chemosh had enabled him to gain over his Israelitish foes, tells us that he had carried away from Atarath 'the *arel* (or altar) of Dodo and dragged it before Chemosh,' and from Nebo 'the *arels* (or altars) of Yahveh,' which he likewise 'dragged before Chemosh.' Here the *arel* or 'altar' of Dodo is placed in parallelism with the *arels* of Yahveh; and it is quite clear, therefore, that Dodo, like Yahveh, was a name under which the deity was worshipped by the people of the land. I have suggested that Dod or Dodo was an old title of the supreme God in the Jebusite Jerusalem, and that hence Isaiah (v 1), when describing Jerusalem as the tower of the vineyard the Lord had planted in Israel, calls him Dôd-i, 'my beloved.' We can easily understand how a name of the kind, with such a signification, should have been transferred by popular affection from the Deity to the king of whom it is said that 'all Israel and Judah loved him' (I Sam. xviii 16)."

Ea in Later Times

Ea developed with the centuries, and about the epoch of Khammurabi appears to have achieved a high standard of godhead, probably because of the very considerable amount of theological moulding which he had received. In the later Babylonian period we find him described as the protagonist of mankind, the father of Merodach, and, along with Anu and Bel, a member of a great triad. The priests of Babylon were the sole mythographers of these days. This is in sharp contradistinction to the mythographers of Greece, who were nearly always philosophers and never priests. But they were mythographers in a secondary sense only, for they merely rearranged, re-edited, or otherwise altered already existing tales relating to the gods, usually with a view to the exaltation of a certain deity or to enable his story to fit in with those of other gods. It is only after a religion or mythological system has enjoyed a vogue more or less extended that the relationship of the gods towards one another becomes fixed.

The appointment of Merodach to the supreme position in the Babylonian pantheon naturally necessitated a rearrangement so far as the relationship of the other deities to him was concerned. This meant a re-shaping of myth and tradition generally for the purpose of ensuring consistency. The men fitted to accomplish such a task were to hand, for the age of Khammurabi was fertile in writers, scholastic and legal, who would be well equipped to carry out a change of the description indicated. Ea had not in the past enjoyed any very exalted sphere. But as the chief god of the important country in the neighbourhood of the Persian Gulf, the most ancient home of Babylonian culture, Ea would probably have exercised a great influence upon the antiquarian and historic sense of a man like Khammurabi. As the god of wisdom he would strongly appeal to a monarch whose whole career was marked by a love of justice and by sagacity and insight. From a local god of Eridu, Ea became a universal deity of wisdom and beneficence, the strong shield of man, and his benefactor by the gifts of harvest and water. Civilized and softer emotions must have begun to cluster around the cult of this kindly god who, when the angered deities resolved to destroy mankind, interceded for poor humanity and succeeded in preserving it from the divine wrath. As a god of medicine, too, Ea is humane and protective in character, and all the arts fall under his patronage. He is the culture-god of Babylon *par excellence*. He might not transcend Merodach, so he became his father. Thus did pagan theology succeed in merging the cults of deities which might otherwise

THE LEGEND OF ZU

have been serious rivals and mutually destructive.

Zu

Zu was a storm-god symbolized in the form of a bird. He may typify the advancing storm-cloud, which would have seemed to those of old as if hovering like a great bird above the land which it was about to strike. The North-American Indians possess such a mythological conception in the Thunder-bird, and it is probable that the great bird called roc, so well known to readers of the *Arabian Nights*, was a similar monster—perhaps the descendant of the Zu-bird. We remember how this enormous creature descended upon the ship in which Sindbad sailed and carried him off. Certain it is that we can trace the roc or rukh to the Persian simurgh, which is again referable to a more ancient Persian form, the amru or sinamru, the bird of immortality, and we may feel sure that what is found in ancient Persian lore has some foundation in Babylonian belief. The Zu-bird was evidently under the control of the sun, and his attempt to break away from the solar authority is related in the following legend.

The Legend of Zu

It is told of the god Zu that on one occasion ambition awaking in his breast caused him to cast envious eyes on the power and sovereignty of Bel, so that he determined to purloin the Tablets of Destiny, which were the tangible symbols of Bel's greatness.

At this time, it may be recalled, the Tablets of Destiny had already an interesting history behind them. We are told in the creation legend how Apsu, the primeval, and Tiawath, chaos, the first parents of the gods, afterward conceived a hatred for their offspring, and how Tiawath, with her monster-brood of snakes and vipers, dragons and scorpion-men and raging hounds, made war on the hosts of heaven. Her son Kingu she made captain of her hideous army—

> To march before the forces, to lead the host,
> To give the battle-signal, to advance to the attack,
> To direct the battle, to control the fight.

To him she gave the Tablets of Destiny, laying them on his breast with the words: "Thy command shall not be without avail, and the word of thy mouth shall be established." Through his possession of the divine tablets Kingu received the power of Anu, and was able to decree the fate of the gods. After several deities had refused the honour of becoming champion of heaven, Merodach was chosen. He succeeded at length in slaying Tiawath and destroying her evil host; and having vanquished Kingu, her captain, he took from him the Tablets of Destiny, which he sealed and laid on his own breast. It was this Merodach, or Marduk, who afterward became identified with Bel.

Now Zu, in his greed for power and dominion, was eager to obtain the potent symbols. He beheld the honour and majesty of Bel, and from contemplation of these he turned to look upon the Tablets of Destiny, saying within himself:

"Lo, I will possess the tablets of the gods, and all things shall be subject unto me. The spirits of heaven shall bow before me, the oracles of the gods shall be in my hands. I shall wear the crown, symbol of sovereignty, and the robe, symbol of godhead, and then shall I rule over all the hosts of heaven."

THE LEGEND OF ZU

Thus inflamed, he sought the entrance to Bel's hall, where he awaited the dawn of day. The text goes on:

> Now when Bel was pouring out the clear water, (*i.e.* the light of day?)
> And his diadem was taken off and lay upon the throne,
> (Zu) seized the Tablets of Destiny,
> He took Bel's dominion, the power of giving commands.
> Then Zu fled away and hid himself in his mountain.

Bel was greatly enraged at the theft, and all the gods with him. Anu, lord of heaven, summoned about him his divine sons, and asked for a champion to recover the tablets. But though the god Ramman was chosen, and after him several other deities, they all refused to advance against Zu.

The end of the legend is unfortunately missing, but from a passage in another tale, the legend of Etana, we gather that it was the sun-god, Shamash, who eventually stormed the mountain-stronghold of Zu, and with his net succeeded in capturing the presumptuous deity.

This legend is of the Prometheus type, but whereas Prometheus (once a bird-god) steals fire from heaven for the behoof of mankind, Zu steals the Tablets of Destiny for his own. These must, of course, be regained if the sovereignty of heaven is duly to continue, and to make the tale circumstantial the sun-god is provided with a fowler's net with which to capture the recalcitrant Zu-bird. Jastrow believes the myth to have been manufactured for the purpose of showing how the tablets of power were originally lost by the older Bel and gained by Merodach, but he has discounted the reference in the Etana legend relating to their recovery.

MYTHS OF BABYLONIA AND ASSYRIA

Bel

We find a good deal of confusion in later Babylonian religion as to whether the name 'Bel' is intended to designate the old god of that name or is merely a title for Merodach. Khammurabi certainly uses the name occasionally when speaking of Merodach, but at other times he quite as surely employs it for the older divinity, as for example when he couples the name with Anu. One of the Kassite kings, too, speaks of "Bel, the lord of lands," meaning the old Bel, to whom they often gave preference over Merodach. They also preferred the old city of Nippur and its temple to Babylon, and perhaps made an attempt at one time to make Nippur the capital of their Empire.

Some authorities appear to think it strange that Bel should have existed at all as a deity after the elevation of Merodach to the highest rank in the pantheon. It was his association with Anu and Ea as one of a triad presiding over the heavens, the earth, and the deep which kept him in power. Moreover, the very fact that he was a member of such a triad proves that he was regarded as theologically essential to the well-being of the Babylonian religion as a whole. The manufacture or slow evolution of a trinity of this description is by no means brought about through popular processes. It is, indeed, the work of a school, of a college of priests. Strangely enough Khammurabi seems to have associated Anu and Bel together, but to have entirely omitted Ea from their companionship, and it has been thought that the conception of a trinity was subsequent to his epoch. The god of earth and the god of heaven typify respectively that which is above and that which is below, and are reminiscent of the Father-sky

Hall in Assyrian Palace (Restored)
From a drawing made on the spot by Sir Henry Layard

and Mother-earth of many primitive mythologies, and there is much to say for the theory that Ea, god of the deep, although he had existed long prior to any such grouping, was a later inclusion.

The Triad of Earth, Air, and Sea

The habit of invoking the great triad became almost a commonplace in later Babylonia. They nearly always take precedence in religious inscriptions, and we even find some monarchs stating that they hold their regal authority by favour of the trinity. Whenever a powerful curse has to be launched, one may be certain that the names of the gods of the elements will figure in it.

Dawkina

Dawkina was the consort of Ea, and was occasionally invoked along with him. She was a goddess of some antiquity, and, strangely enough for the mate of a water-god, she appears to have originally been connected in some manner with the earth. Therefore she was an elemental deity. In later times her attributes appear to have been inherited by Ishtar. According to some authorities Bel was the son of Ea and Dawkina, Bel in this case meaning Merodach. We find her name frequently alluded to in the Magical Texts, but her cult does not seem to have been very widespread.

Anu

We have already alluded to Anu's position in the triad with Ea and Bel in later Babylonian times. When he stands alone we find him taking a more human guise than as the mere elemental god of earlier days. He is frequently mentioned in the texts apart from Ea and Bel, and is occasionally alluded to along with Ramman, the god of thunder and storms, who of course would naturally stand in close relationship with the sky. We also find him connected with Dagan of Biblical celebrity. But in this case Dagan appears to be the equivalent of Bel.

There is also a host of lesser deities, the majority of whom are no more than mere names. They do not seem to have achieved much popularity, or if they did it was an evanescent one. The names of some are indeed only mentioned once or twice, and so little is known concerning them as almost to leave us entirely in the dark regarding their natures or characteristics.

CHAPTER VI: THE GREAT GOD MERODACH AND HIS CULT

THE entire religious system of Babylonia is overshadowed by Merodach, its great patron deity. We remember how he usurped the place of Ea, and in what manner even the legends of that god were made over to him, so that at last he came to be regarded as not only the national god of Babylonia but the creator of the world and of mankind. He it was who, at the pleading of the other gods, confronted the grisly Tiawath, and having defeated and slain her, formed the earth out of her body and its inhabitants out of his own blood. It is almost certain that this cosmological myth was at one time recounted of Ea, and perhaps even at an earlier date of Bel. The transfer of power from Ea to Merodach, however, was skilfully arranged by the priesthood, for they made Merodach the son of Ea, so that he would naturally inherit his father's attributes. In this transfer we observe the passing of the supremacy of the city of Eridu to that of Babylon. Ea, or Oannes, the fish-tailed god of Eridu, stood for the older and more southerly civilization of the Babylonian race, whilst Merodach, patron god of Babylon, a very different type of deity, represented the newer political power.

Originally Merodach appears to have been a sun-god personifying more especially the sun of the springtime. Thus he was a fitting deity to defeat the chaotic Tiawath, who personified darkness and destruction. But there is another side to him—the agricultural side. Says Jastrow (*Religion in Babylonia and Assyria*, p. 38): " At Nippur, as we shall see, there developed an elaborate lamentation ritual for the occasions when national catastrophes, defeat, failure of crops, destructive storms, and pestilence revealed the displeasure and anger of the gods." At such times earnest endeavours were made, through petitions accompanied by fasting and other symbols of contrition, to bring about a reconciliation with the angered power. This ritual, owing to the religious pre-eminence of Nippur, became the norm and standard throughout the Euphrates Valley, so that when Marduk (Merodach) and Babylonia came practically to replace En-lil and Nippur, the formulas and appeals were transferred to the solar deity of Babylon, who, representing more particularly the sun-god of spring, was well adapted to be viewed as the one to bring blessings and favours after the sorrows and tribulations of the stormy season.

Strange as it will appear, although he was patron god of Babylon he did not originate in that city, but in Eridu, the city of Ea, and probably this is the reason why he was first regarded as the son of Ea. He is also directly associated with Shamash, the chief sun-god of the later pantheon, and is often addressed as the 'god of canals' and 'opener of subterranean fountains.' In appearance he is usually drawn with tongues of fire proceeding from his person, thus indicating his solar character. At other times he is represented as standing above the watery deep, with a horned creature at his feet, which also occasionally serves to symbolize Ea. It is noteworthy, too, that his temple at Babylon bore the same name—E-Sagila, 'the lofty house,'—as did Ea's sanctuary at Eridu.

We find among the cuneiform texts—a copy of an older Babylonian text—an interesting little poem which shows how Merodach attracted the attributes of the other gods to himself.

A NEW-YEAR'S CEREMONY

> Ea is the Marduk (or Merodach) of canals;
> Ninib is the Marduk of strength;
> Nergal is the Marduk of war;
> Zamama is the Marduk of battle;
> Enlil is the Marduk of sovereignty and control;
> Nebo is the Marduk of possession;
> Sin is the Marduk of illumination of the night;
> Shamash is the Marduk of judgments;
> Adad is the Marduk of rain;
> Tishpak is the Marduk of the host;
> Gal is the Marduk of strength;
> Shukamunu is the Marduk of the harvest.

This would seem as if Merodach had absorbed the characteristics of all the other gods of any importance so successfully that he had almost established his position as the sole deity in Babylonia, and that therefore some degree of monotheism had been arrived at.

A New-Year's Ceremony

On the first day of the Babylonian New Year an assembly of the gods was held at Babylon, when all the principal gods were grouped round Merodach in precisely the same manner in which the King was surrounded by the nobility and his officials, for many ancient faiths imagined that the polity of earth merely mirrored that of heaven, that, as Paracelsus would have said, the earth was the microcosm of the heavenly macrocosm—"as above, so below." The ceremony in question consisted in the lesser deities paying homage to Merodach as their liege lord. In this council, too, they decided the political action of Babylonia for the coming year.

It is thought that the Babylonian priests at stated intervals enacted the myth of the slaughter of Tiawath. This is highly probable, as in Greece and Egypt the myths of Persephone and Osiris were represented dramatically before a select audience of initiates. We see that these representations are nearly always made in the case of divinities who represent corn or vegetation as a whole, or the fructifying power of springtime. The name of Merodach's consort Zarpanitum was rendered by the priesthood as 'seed producing,' to mark her connexion with the god who was responsible for the spring revival.

Merodach's ideograph is the sun, and there is abundant evidence that he was first and last a solar god. The name, originally Amaruduk, probably signifies 'the young steer of day,' which seems to be a figure for the morning sun. He was also called Asari, which may be compared with Asar, the Egyptian name of Osiris. Other names given him are Sar-agagam, 'the glorious incantation,' and Meragaga, 'the glorious charm,' both of which refer to the circumstance that he obtained from Ea, his father, certain charms and incantations which restored the sick to health and exercised a beneficial influence upon mankind.

Merodach was supposed to have a court of his own above the sky, where he was attended to by a host of ministering deities. Some superintended his food and drink supply, while others saw to it that water for his hands was always ready. He had also doorkeepers and even attendant hounds, and it is thought that the satellites of Jupiter, the planet which represented him, may have been dimly visible to those among the Chaldean star-gazers who were gifted with good sight. These dogs were called Ukkumu, 'Seizer,' Akkulu, 'Eater,' Iksuda, 'Grasper,' and Iltehu, 'Holder.' It is not known whether these were supposed to assist him in shepherding his flock or in the chase, and their names seem appropriate either for sheep-dogs or hunting hounds.

CHAPTER VII: THE PANTHEON OF ASSYRIA

THE Pantheon of Assyria, as befitted the religious system of a nation of soldiers, was more highly organized than that of the kindred people of Babylonia, the ranks and relationships of the gods who comprised it were more definitely fixed, it was considerably more compact than that of the southern kingdom, and its lesser luminaries were fewer. It has been assumed that the deities of the Assyrians were practically identical in every respect with those of the Babylonians, with the single exception of Asshur, who equated with Merodach. With all due respect to practical Assyriologists the student of Comparative Religion may perhaps be granted leave to take exception to such a statement. Ethnological differences (and these certainly existed between the peoples of the northern and southern culture-groups), climatic conditions, a different political environment—all these as well as other considerations, as important if less obvious, must have effected almost radical changes in the ideas of the gods as conceived by the Assyrians. Exactly what these changes were we shall probably never know. They are scarcely likely to be revealed by inscriptions or sacred writings which undoubtedly conserve for us little more than the purely ecclesiastical view-point, always anxious to embalm with scrupulous care the cherished theological beliefs of an older day. But little of the religious beliefs of a people can survive in priestly inscriptions and the labours of priestly copyists, nor is it safe or scientific to endorse the character of the faith of a race by comparison or analogy with that of a neighbouring folk. If a striking example were required of the danger of such a proceeding it might be found in the vain attempt to discover an exact parallel between the religious systems of ancient Mexico and those of Guatemala and Yucatan. The city-states of the more northerly group of people had evolved a separate system of worship for each pueblo or town, the deities of which, with minor differences, were substantially identical. But when the pantheons of the more southerly region come to be examined it will be found that, although the gods which figure in them spring apparently from the same stock as those of the Mexican people, and even possess names which are mere translations of those of the gods of Mexico, their attributes and characteristics differ profoundly from those of their Mexican congeners. The reason for this dissimilarity is to be found in variations of climate, culture, and politics, three sure factors in the modification of religion. If, then, we are satisfied that such differences existed in the religious systems of two race-groups almost as closely connected as were the peoples of Babylonia and Assyria, may we not be pardoned for the supposition that similar divergences existed between the faiths of the two great races of Chaldea?

We find in the Assyrian pantheon numerous foreign deities whom the Assyrian kings included among the national gods by right of conquest. These we shall deal with later. It will suffice for the present to mention Assur-bani-pal, who speaks of the capture of twenty gods of the Elamites. It was, of course, only upon the rise of a distinct Assyrian empire that the religion of the northern kingdom acquired traits that distinguished it from that of Babylonia.

Having outlined the reasons for the differences which we believe to have existed between the Baby-

THE PANTHEON OF ASSYRIA

lonian and Assyrian faiths, let us briefly consider the variation of type between the two peoples which must have caused this divergence. The languages of the two races were not more distinct than the dialects of northern and southern England—indeed among scholars they are designated by the common name of Assyrian. But the Assyrians had a pure strain of that Semitic blood which has done so much to systematize religions ancient and modern. The Semite cannot content himself with half-truths. It is essential to his very life, that he must feel himself upon sure religious ground. He hates doubt and despises the doubter. At an early time in his ancient career he had so securely systematized religion as to supply the earliest instances of pure dogma. There followed the relentless abjuration of all the troublous circumstances of mistrust. A code founded upon the rock of unquestioning faith was instituted. And in the religious systems of Babylonia and especially of Assyria we observe a portion of the process of evolution which assisted in the upbuilding of a narrow yet highly spiritualized system.

The great gods in Assyria were even more omnipotent than in Babylonia. One cause contributing to this was the absorption of the minor local cults by deities associated with the great centres of Assyrian life. Early religion is extremely sensitive to political change, and as a race evolves from the tribal or local state and bands itself into a nation, so the local gods become national and centralized, probably in the great deity of the most politically active city in the state. Nor is it essential to this process that the deities absorbed should be of a like nature with the absorbing god. Quite often a divinity assumes the name and attributes of one with whom he had little in common.

MYTHS OF BABYLONIA AND ASSYRIA

Asshur

The state religion of Assyria centres in Asshur, nor was any deity ever so closely identified with an empire as he. On the fall of the Assyrian state, Asshur fell with it. Moreover all the gods of Assyria may be said to have been combined in his person.

SYMBOLS OF THE GOD ASSHUR

From *Religious Belief and Practice in Babylonia and Assyria,* by Prof. Jastrow (G. P. Putnam's Sons).

In Babylonia, Merodach was a leader of hosts. In Assyria, Asshur personified these hosts, that is, the other Assyrian gods had become attributes of Asshur, and we can only understand the remaining Assyrian gods if we regard them as lesser Asshurs, so to speak, as broken lights of the great god of battle and conquest.

Asshur originated in the city of his name situated on the west bank of the Tigris, not far from the

ASSHUR

point where the lower Zab flows into that river. It was not of course until the rise of this city to political pre-eminence that its god figured as all-powerful. There are conflicting estimates as regards his original nature, some authorities holding that he was lunar, others that he symbolized fire or water. The facts, however, point to the conclusion that he was solar in character.

Merodach had chiefly been worshipped in Babylon. As other Babylonian territories became subject to that city we do not find them placing the god of Babylon above their own local god. But it was different with Asshur. We find temples to him broadcast over Assyria. Indeed as Assyrian history advances, we see different cities alluded to as the chief centre of his worship, and he resides now at Asshur, now at Calah, now at Nineveh, now at Khorsabad. Wherever the Kings of Assyria took up their official residence there Asshur was adored, and there he was supposed to dwell. He was not symbolized by an idol or any man-like statue which would serve to give the populace an idea of his physical likeness, but was represented by a standard consisting of a pole surrounded by a disc enclosed with two wings. Above the disc was the figure of a warrior with bent bow and arrow on string. This well symbolized the military nature of the Assyrian nation and of its tutelar deity. At the same time indications are not wanting that this pole and its accompanying symbols are the remains of a totem-standard upon which has been superimposed the anthropomorphic figure of a lightning- or tempest-god. The pole is a favourite vehicle for carrying the totem symbols into battle, and it looks here as if the sun had at one time been regarded as a tribal totem. The figure of the archer at the top seems representative of a lightning- or storm-god—a mythic character frequently associated with the sun, that 'strong warrior.' By virtue of his possession of the lightning arrow the storm-god is often accepted as a god of war.

The etymology of the name of Asshur throws little light upon his character as a divinity. The city which took his name was in all probability originally called 'The city of the god Asshur.' To call it by the name of the god alone would not be unnatural. The name is derived from a root meaning 'to be gracious,' and therefore means 'the gracious god,' 'the good god.' But there are indications that an older form of the name had existed, and it has been asserted that the form Anshar has priority. With Kishar, a god Anshar was created as the second pair of deities to see the light, and according to one version it is Anshar who dispatches Anu, Ea, and finally Merodach to destroy the monster Tiawath. This Anshar, then, appears as possessed with authority among the gods. But we find no mention of him in the ancient texts and inscriptions of Babylonia. The version in which Anshar is alluded to may of course have been tampered with, and his inclusion in the creation myth may be regarded as a concession to Assyrian greatness. Indeed in one creation tablet we find Merodach displaced by Asshur as framer of the earth!

The Secret of Assyrian Greatness

Asshur is mentioned in the oldest Assyrian inscription known to us, that of Samsi-Ramman (*c.* 1850 B.C.), the priest-chief of Asshur, who ruled in the days when as yet the offices of king and high priest were undivided. Indeed, when the title of 'king' had come into use some 350 years later, the monarchs

THE SECRET OF ASSYRIAN GREATNESS

of Assyria still retained the right to call themselves 'priests of the god Asshur.' The entire faith in and dependence on their beloved deity on the part of these early Assyrian rulers is touching. They are his children and rely wholly upon him first for protection against their cruel enemies the Kassites and afterwards for the extension of their growing empire. No wonder that with such a faith to stimulate her Assyria became great. Faith in her tutelar god was, indeed, the secret of her greatness. The enemies of Assyria are 'the enemies of Asshur,' her soldiers are 'the warriors of Asshur,' and their weapons are 'the weapons of Asshur.' Before his face the enemies of Assyria tremble and are routed, he is consulted oracularly as to the making and conduct of war, and he is present on the battle-field. But the solitary nature of Asshur was remarkable. Originally he possessed 'neither kith nor kin,' neither wife nor child, and the unnaturalness of his splendid isolation appears to have struck the Assyrian scribes, who in an interesting prayer attempted to connect their divinity with the greater gods of Babylonia, to find him a wife, ministers, a court and messengers.

> A prayer to Asshur, the king of the gods, ruler over heaven and earth,
> the father who has created the gods, the supreme first-born of heaven and earth,
> the supreme muttallu who inclines to counsel,
> the giver of the sceptre and the throne.
> To Nin-lil, the wife of Asshur, the begetter, the creatress of heaven and earth,
> who by command of her mouth . . .
> To Sin, the lord of command, the uplifter of horns, the spectacle of heaven,
> To the Sun-god, the great judge of the gods, who causes the lightning to issue forth,

To Anu, the lord and prince, possessing the life of Asshur, the father of the great gods.
To Rammon, the minister of heaven and earth, the lord of the wind and the lightning of heaven.
To Ishtar, the queen of heaven and the stars, whose seat is exalted.
To Merodach, the prince of the gods, the interpreter of the spirits of heaven and earth.
To Adar, the son of Mul-lil the giant, the first-born . . .
To Nebo, the messenger of Asshur (Ansar) . . .
To Nergal, the lord of might and strength . . .
To the god who marches in front, the first-born . . .
To the seven gods, the warrior deities . . .
the great gods, the lords of heaven and earth.

Asshur as Conqueror

An incident which well illustrated the popularity of the Assyrian belief in the conquering power of the national god is described in an account of the expedition of Sargon against Ashdod stamped on a clay cylinder of that monarch's reign. Sargon states that in his ninth expedition to the land beside the sea, to Philistia and Ashdod, to punish King Azuri of that city for his refusal to send tribute and for his evil deeds against Assyrian subjects, Sargon placed Ahimiti, nephew of Azuri, in his place and fixed the taxes. But the people of Ashdod revolted against the puppet Sargon had placed over them, and by acclamation raised one Yaran to the throne, and fortified their dominions. They and the surrounding peoples sought the aid of Egypt, which could not help them. For the honour of Asshur, Sargon then engaged in an expedition against the Hittites, and turned his attention to the state of affairs in Philistia (c. 711 B.C.), hearing which Yaran, for fear of Asshur, fled to Meroc on the borders of Egypt, where he hid ignominiously. Sargon besieged and

ISHTAR IN ASSYRIA

captured the city of Ashdod, with the gods, wives, children, and treasures of Yaran.

It is plain that this punitive expedition was undertaken for the personal honour of Asshur, that he was believed to accompany the troops in their campaign against the rebellious folk of Ashdod, and that victory was to be ascribed to him and to him alone. All tribute from conquered peoples became the property of Asshur, to whom it was offered by the Kings of Assyria. Even the great and proud monarchs of this warlike kingdom do not hesitate to affirm themselves the creatures of Asshur, by whom they live and breathe and by whose will they hold the royal authority, symbolized by the mighty bow conferred upon them by their divine master. That these haughty rulers were not without an element of affection as well as fear for the god they worshipped is seen from the circumstance that they frequently allude to themselves as the sons of Asshur, whose viceroys on earth they were. Asshur was, indeed, in later times the spirit of conquering Assyria personalized. We do not find him regarded as anything else than a war-god. We do not find him surrounded by any of the gentler attributes which distinguish non-militant deities, nor is it likely that his cult would have developed, had it lasted, into one distinguished for its humanizing influence or its ethical subtlety. It was the cult of a war-god pure and simple, and when Asshur was beaten at his own business of war he disappeared into the limbo of forgotten gods as rapidly as he had arisen.

Ishtar in Assyria

Next to Asshur in the affections of the Assyrian people stood Ishtar. As a goddess in Assyria she was absolutely identical with the Babylonian Ishtar, her favourite shrines in the northern kingdom being Nineveh, Arbela, and the temple of Kidmuru, also in Nineveh. The Assyrians appear to have admitted her Babylonian origin, or at least to have confessed that theirs was originally a Babylonian Ishtar, for Tiglath-pileser I lays emphasis upon the circumstance that a shrine he raised to Ishtar in his capital is dedicated to 'the Assyrian Ishtar.' The date of this monarch is 1010 B.C., or near it, so that the above is a comparatively early allusion to Ishtar in Assyrian history. The Ishtars of Arbela and Kidmuru do not appear in Assyrian texts until the time of Esar-haddon (681 B.C.), thus the Ishtar of Nineveh was much the most venerable of the three. Arbela was evidently a religious centre of importance, and the theory has been advanced that it became the seat of a school of prophets connected with the worship of Ishtar. Jastrow in his *Religion of Babylonia and Assyria* (1898, p. 203), writing on this point, says, "It is quite possible, if not probable, that the three Ishtars are each of independent origin. The 'queen of Kidmuru,' indeed, I venture to think, is the indigenous Ishtar of Nineveh, who is obliged to yield her place to the so-called 'Assyrian Ishtar,' upon the transfer of the capital of Assyria to Nineveh, and henceforth is known by one of her epithets to distinguish her from her more formidable rival. The cult of Ishtar at Arbela is probably, too, of ancient date; but special circumstances that escape us appear to have led to a revival of interest in their cults during the period when Assyria reached the zenith of her power. The important point for us to bear in mind is that no essential distinctions between these three Ishtars were made by the Assyrians. Their traits and

ISHTAR AS A WAR-GODDESS

epithets are similar, and for all practical purposes we have only one Ishtar in the northern empire."

Ishtar as a War-Goddess

Ishtar was frequently placed by the side of Asshur as a war-goddess. Ere she left the plains of Babylonia for the uplands of Assyria she had evinced certain bellicose propensities. In the Gilgamesh epic she appears as a deity of destructive and spiteful character, if not actually of warlike nature. But if the Babylonians regarded her first and foremost as the great mother-goddess, the Assyrians took but little notice of this side of her character. To them she was a veritable Valkyrie, and as the Assyrians grew more and more military so she became more the war-goddess and less the nature-mother of love and agriculture. She appeared in dreams to the war-loving Kings of Assyria, encouraging and heartening them with words of cheer to further military exploits. Fire was her raiment, and, as became a goddess of battle, her appearance was terrific. She consumed the enemies of Assur-bani-pal with flames. Still, strangely enough, in the religious texts, influenced probably by Babylonian sources, she was still to a great extent the mild and bountiful mother of nature. It is in the historical texts which ring with tales of conquest and the grandiloquent boastings of conquering monarchs that she appears as the leader of armies and the martial goddess who has slain her thousands and her tens of thousands. So has it ever been impossible for the priest and the soldier to possess the selfsame idea of godhead, and this is so in the modern no less than in the ancient world. Yet occasionally the stern Assyrian kings unbent, and it was probably in a brief interval of peace that Assur-nazir-pal alluded to Ishtar as the lady who " loves him and his priesthood." Sennacherib also spoke of the goddess in similar terms. It is necessary to state that the name or title of Belit given to Ishtar does not signify that she is the wife or consort of Bel, but merely that she is a 'great lady,' for which the title 'Belit' is a generic term. If she is at times brought into close association with Asshur she is never regarded as his wife. She is not the consort of any god, but an independent goddess in her own right, standing alone, equal with Asshur and the dependant of no other divinity. But it was later only that she ranked with Asshur, and purely because of her military reputation.

Ninib as an Assyrian War-God

Such a deity as Ninib (another name for Ningirsu, the god of Lagash) was certain to find favour among the Assyrians by virtue of those characteristics which would render him a valuable ally in war. We find several kings extolling his prowess as a warrior, notably Tiglath-pileser I, and Assurrishishi, who allude to him as " the courageous one," and " the mighty one of the gods." His old status as a sun-and-wind god, in which he was regarded as overthrowing and levelling with the ground everything which stood in his path, would supply him with the reputation necessary to a god of battles. He is associated with Asshur in this capacity, and Tiglath-pileser brackets them as those " who fulfil his desire." But Ninib's chief votary was Assurnazir-pal (858-60 B.C.), who commenced his annals with a pæan of praise in honour of Ninib, which so abounds in fulsome eulogy that we feel that either he must have felt much beholden to the god, or else

NINIB AS AN ASSYRIAN WAR-GOD

have suffered from religious mania. The epithets he employs in praise of Ninib are those usually lavished upon the greatest of gods only. This proceeding secured immense popularity for Ninib and gave him a social and political vogue which nothing else could have given, and we find Shamsi-ramman, the grandson of Assur-nazir-pal, employing the selfsame titles in honouring him.

The great temple of Ninib was situated in Calah, the official residence of Assur-nazir-pal, and within its walls that monarch placed a tablet recording his deeds, and a great statue of the god. He further endowed his cult so that it might enjoy continuance.

We can readily understand how the especial favour shown to such a god as Ninib by an Assyrian monarch originated. Asshur would be regarded by them as much too popular and national a deity to choose as a personal patron. But more difficult to comprehend are the precise reasons which actuated the Assyrian kings, or indeed the kings of any similar ancient state, in choosing their patrons. Does a polytheistic condition of religion permit of the fine selection of patron deities, or is it not much more probable that the artful offices of ecclesiastical and political wire-pullers had much to do with moulding the preferences of the King before and after he reached the throne? The education of the monarch while yet a prince would almost certainly be entrusted to a high ecclesiastical dignitary, and although many examples to the contrary exist, we are pretty safe in assuming that whatever the complexion of the tutor's mind, that of the pupil would to some extent reflect it. On the other hand there is no resisting the conclusion that the Assyrian kings were very often vulgar parvenus, ostentatious and 'impossible,' as such people usually are, and that, after the manner of their kind, they 'doted' upon everything ancient, and, possibly, everything Babylonian, just as the later Romans praised everything Greek.

Ninib as Hunter-God

But Ninib ministered to the amusement of his royal devotees as well as to their warlike desires. We find Assur-nazir-pal invoking him before commencing a long journey in search of sport, and Tiglath-pileser I, who was a doughty hunter of lions and elephants, ascribes his success to Ninib, who has placed the mighty bow in his hands.

Jensen in his *Kosmologie* points out that Ninib represents the eastern sun and the morning sun. If this is so, it is strange to find a god representing the sun of morning in the status of a war-god. It is usually when the sun-god reaches the zenith of the heavens that he slays his thousands and his tens of thousands. As a variant of Nin-girsu he would of course be identified with Tammuz. His consort was Gula, to whom Assur-nazir-pal erected a sanctuary.

Dagan

Dagan the fish-god, who, we saw, was the same as Oannes or Ea, strangely enough rose to high rank in Assyria. Some authorities consider him of Philistian or Aramean origin, and do not compare him with Ea, who rose from the waters of the Persian Gulf to enlighten his people, and it is evident that the Mesopotamian-Palestinian region contained several versions of the origin of this god, ascribing it to various places. In the Assyrian pantheon he is associated with Anu, who rules the heavens, Dagan supervising the earth. It is strange to observe a

Tiglath-Pileser I directed by Ninib
Evelyn Paul

deity, whose sphere must originally have been the sea, presiding over the terrestrial plane, and this transference it was which cost Dagan his popularity in Assyria, for later he became identified with Bel and disappeared almost entirely from the Assyrian pantheon.

Anu

Anu in Assyria did not differ materially from Anu in Babylon, but he suffered, as did other southern deities, from the all-pervading worship of Asshur. He had a temple in Asshur's own city, which was rebuilt by Tiglath-pileser I 641 years, after its original foundation. He was regarded in Assyria as lord of the Igigi and Anunnaki, or spirits of heaven and earth, probably the old animistic spirits, and to this circumstance, as well as to the fact that he belonged to the old triad along with Bel and Ea, he probably owed the prolongation of his cult. As an elemental and fundamental god opposition could not possibly displace him, and as ruler of the spirits of air and earth he would have a very strong hold upon the popular imagination. Gods who possess such powers often exist in folk-memory long after the other members of the pantheon which contained them are totally forgotten, and one would scarcely be surprised to find Anu lingering in the shadows of post-Assyrian folk-lore, if any record of such lore could be discovered. Anu was frequently associated with Ramman, but more usually with Bel and Eausas in Babylonia.

Ramman

Ramman enjoyed much greater popularity in Assyria than in Babylonia, for there he exercised the functions of a second Asshur, and was regarded as destruction personified. Says an old Assyrian hymn concerning Ramman:

> The mighty mountain, thou hast overwhelmed it.
> At his anger, at his strength,
> At his roaring, at his thundering,
> The gods of heaven ascend to the sky,
> The gods of the earth ascend to the earth,
> Into the horizon of heaven they enter,
> Into the zenith of heaven they make their way.

What a picture have we here in these few simple lines of a pantheon in dread and terror of the wrath and violence of one of its number. We can almost behold the divine fugitives crowding in flight, some into the upper regions of air to outsoar the anger of the destroyer, others seeking the recesses of the earth to hide themselves from the fierceness of his countenance, the roar of his thunderbolts, and the arrows of his lightning. Simple, almost bald, as the lines are they possess marvellous pictorial quality, bringing before us as they do the rout of a whole heaven in a few simple words.

The weapons of Ramman are lightning, deluge, hunger, and death, and woe to the nation upon whom he visits his wrath, for upon it he visits flood and famine. Thus his attributes as a storm-god are brought into play when he figures as a war deity, for just as a weather-god of the lightning wields it as a spear or dart in the fight, so Ramman as storm-god brings to bear the horrors of tempest upon the devoted head of the enemy.

So highly did the Assyrian kings value the assistance of Ramman that they sacrificed to him during the stress and bustle of a campaign in the field. They liken an attack of their troops to his onslaught, and if they wish to depict the stamping out of an adversary,

RAMMAN

his 'eating up,' as Chaka's Zulus were wont to term the process, they declare that their men swept over the enemy as Ramman might have done. Assur-nazir-pal alludes to Ramman as 'the mightiest of the gods,' but as in reality that phrase was employed in connexion with all the principal deities at one time or another by kings or priests who favoured them, there is no reason to suppose that anything more is intended than that Ramman occupied a place of importance in the Assyrian pantheon.

The worship of Ramman in later times came very much into prominence. It was only in the days of Khammurabi that he came into his kingdom, as it were, and even then his worship was not very firmly established in Babylonia. With the rise of the Kassite dynasty, however, we find him coming more into favour, and his name bestowed upon Babylonian kings. He seems to have formed a triad with Sin and Shamash, and in the Hymn of Khammurabi we find him appealed to along with Shamash as 'Divine Lords of Justice.' Nebuchadrezzar I appears to have held him in high esteem, although he was unfriendly to the dynasty which first brought him into prominence, and this monarch couples him with Ishtar as the divinity who has chiefly assisted him in all his great undertakings. Indeed, Nebuchadrezzar evinced much partiality for Ramman, perhaps feeling that he must placate the especial god of those he had cast from power. He speaks of him as the 'lord of the waters beneath the earth,' and of the rains from heaven.

The place of Ramman's origin seems obscure. We have already dealt with his manifestations in more primitive days, but opinions appear to differ regarding the original seat of his worship, some authorities holding that it was Muru in Southern Babylonia, others that it is necessary to turn to Assyria for traces of his first worship. His cult is found in Damascus and extended as far south as the Plain of Jezreel. As Milton says :

> . . . Rimmon, whose delightful seat
> Was fair Damascus, on the fertile banks
> Of Abbana and Pharphar, lucid streams.
> He also 'gainst the house of God was bold
> A leper once he lost, and gained a king,
> Ahaz his sottish conqu'ror, whom he drew
> God's altar to disparage and displace
> For one of Syrian mode, whereon to burn
> His odious offerings, and adore the gods
> Whom he had vanquish'd."

This later theory would make him of Aramaic origin, but his cult appears to have been of very considerable antiquity in Assyria, and it might have been indigenous there. Moreover, the earliest mention of his worship is in the city of Asshur. As has been indicated, he was probably a storm-god or a thunder-and-lightning god, but he was also associated with the sun-god Shamash. But whatever he may have been in Babylonia, in Assyria he was certainly the thunder-deity first and foremost.

A Babylonian text of some antiquity contains a really fine hymn to Ramman, which might be paraphrased as follows, omitting redundancies :—

"O lord Ramman, thy name is the great and glorious Bull, child of heaven, lord of Karkar, lord of plenty, companion of the lord Ea. He that rideth the great lion is thy name. Thy name doth charm the land, and covers it like a garment. Thy thunder shakes even the great mountain, En-lil, and when thou dost rumble the mother Nin-lil trembles. Said the lord En-lil, addressing his son Ramman: 'O son, spirit of wisdom, with all-seeing eyes and high vision, full of knowledge as the Pleiades, may thy sonorous voice give forth its utterance. Go forth, go up, who can strive with thee? The father is with thee against the cunning foe. Thou art cunning in wielding the hail-stones great and small. Oh, with thy right hand destroy the enemy and root him up!' Ramman hearkened to the words of his father and took his way from the dwelling, the youthful lion, the spirit of counsel."

In later times in Babylonia Ramman seems to have typified the rain of heaven in its beneficent as well as its fertilizing aspect. Not only did he irrigate the fields and fill the wells with water, but he was also accountable for the dreadful tempests which sweep over Mesopotamia. Sometimes he was malevolent, causing thorns to grow instead of herbs. The people, if they regarded him in some measure as a fertilizing agent, also seem to have looked upon him as a destructive and lion-like deity quite capable of desolating the country-side and 'eating up the land.' His roar is typical of him, filling all hearts with affright as it does, and signifying famine and destruction. It is not strange that Mesopotamian regions should have had so many deities of a destructive tendency when we think of the furious whirlwinds which frequently rush across the face of the land, raising sand-storms and devastating everything in their track. Ramman was well likened to the roaring lion, seeking what he may devour, and this seems to have symbolized him in the eyes of the peasant population of the land. Indeed, the Assyrians, impressed by his destructive tendencies, made a war-god of him, and considered his presence as essential to victory. No wonder that the great god of storm made a good war-god!

Shamash

The cult of Shamash in Assyria dates from at least 1340 B.C., when Pudilu built a temple to this god in the city of Asshur. He entitled Shamash 'The Protecting Deity,' which name is to be understood as that of the god of justice, whose fiat is unchangeable, and in this manner Shamash differed somewhat from the Babylonian idea concerning him. In the southern kingdom he was certainly regarded as a just god, but not as *the* god of justice—a very different thing. It is interesting as well as edifying to watch the process of evolution of a god of justice. Thus in Ancient Mexico Tezcatlipoca evolved from a tribal deity into a god who was beginning to bear all the marks and signs of a god of justice when the conquering Spaniards put an end to his career. We observe, too, that although the Greeks had a special deity whose department was justice, other divinities, such as Pallas Athene, displayed signs that they in time might possibly become wielders of the balances between man and man. In the Egyptian heavenly hierarchy Maat and Thoth both partook of the attributes of a god of justice, but perhaps Maat was the more directly symbolical of the two. Now in the case of Shamash no favours can be obtained from him by prayer or sacrifice unless those who supplicate him, monarchs though they be, can lay claim to righteousness. Even Tiglath-pileser I, mighty conqueror as he was, recognized Shamash as his judge, and, naturally, as the judge of his enemies, whom he destroys, not because they are fighting against Tiglath,

Assur-nazir-pal attended by a Winged Mythological Being
Bas-relief from the north-western palace at
Nimrûd
Photo W. A. Mansell and Co.

but because of their wickedness. When he set captives free Tiglath took care to perform the gracious act before the face of Shamash, that the god might behold that justice dwelt in the breast of his royal servant. Tiglath, in fact, is the viceroy of Shamash upon earth, and it would seem as if he referred many cases regarding whose procedure he was in doubt to the god before he finally pronounced upon them.

Both Assur-nazir-pal and Shalmaneser II exalted the sun-cult of Shamash, and it has been suggested that the popularity of the worship of Ra in Egypt had reflected upon that of Shamash in Assyria. It must always be extremely difficult to trace such resemblances at an epoch so distant as that of the ninth century B.C. But certainly it looks as if the Ra cult had in some manner influenced that of the old Babylonian sun-god. Sargon pushed the worship of Shamash far to the northern boundaries of Assyria, for he built a sanctuary to the deity beyond the limits of the Assyrian Empire—where, precisely, we do not know. Amongst a nation of warriors a god such as Shamash must have been valued highly, for without his sanction they would hardly be justified in commencing hostilities against any other race.

Sin in the Northern Land

We do not find Sin, the Babylonian moon-god, extensively worshipped in Assyria. Assur-nazir-pal founded a temple to him in Calah, and Sargon raised several sanctuaries to him beyond the Assyrian frontier. It is as a war-god chiefly that we find him depicted in the northern kingdom—why, it would be difficult to say, unless, indeed, it was that the Assyrians turned practically all the deities they borrowed from other peoples into war-gods. So far as is known, no lunar deity in any other pantheon possesses a military significance. Several are not without fear-inspiring attributes, but these are caused chiefly by the manner in which the moon is regarded among primitive peoples as a bringer of plague and blight. But we find Sin in Assyria freed from all the astrological significances which he had for the Babylonians. At the same time he is regarded as a god of wisdom and a framer of decisions, in these respects equating very fully with the Egyptian Thoth. Assur-bani-pal alludes to Sin as 'the firstborn son of Bel,' just as he is alluded to in Babylonian texts, thus affording us a clue to the direct Babylonian origin of Sin.

Nusku of the Brilliant Sceptre

It is strange that although we know that Nusku had been a Babylonian god from early times, and had figured in the pantheon of Khammurabi, it is not until Assyrian times that we gain any very definite information regarding him. The symbols used in his name are a sceptre and a stylus, and he is called by Shalmaneser I 'The Bearer of the Brilliant Sceptre.' This circumstance associates him closely with Nabu, to designate whom the same symbols are employed. It is difficult, however, to believe that the two are one, as some writers appear to think, for Nusku is certainly a solar deity, while Nabu appears to have originally been a water-god. There are, however, not wanting cases where the same deity has evinced both solar and aqueous characteristics, and these are to be found notably among the gods of American races. Thus among the Maya of Central America the god Kukulcan is depicted with both solar and aqueous attributes, and similar instances could be drawn from lesser-known mythologies. Nusku and Nabu are, however, probably connected in some way, but exactly in what manner is obscure. In Babylonian times Nusku had become amalgamated with Gibil, the god of fire, which perhaps accounts for his virtual effacement in the southern kingdom. In Assyria we find him alluded to as the messenger of Bel-Merodach, and Assur-bani-pal addresses him as 'the highly honoured messenger of the gods.' The Assyrians do not seem to have identified him in any way with Gibil, the fire-god.

Bel-Merodach

Even Bel-Merodach was absorbed into the Assyrian pantheon. To the Assyrians, Babylonia was the country of Bel, and they referred to their southern neighbours as the 'subjects of Bel.' This, of course, must be taken not to mean the older Bel, but Bel-Merodach. They even alluded to the governor whom they placed over conquered Babylonia as the governor of Bel, so closely did they identify the god with the country. It is only in the time of Shalmaneser II—the ninth century B.C.—that we find the name Merodach employed for Bel, so general did the use of the latter become. Of course it was impossible that Merodach could take first place in Assyria as he had done in Babylonia, but it was a tribute to the Assyrian belief in his greatness that they ranked him immediately after Asshur in the pantheon.

Prisoner-Gods

The Assyrian rulers were sufficiently politic to award this place to Merodach, for they could not but see that Babylonia, from which they drew their arts and sciences, as well as their religious beliefs, and from which they benefited in many directions, must be worthily represented in the national religion. And just as the Romans in conquering Greece and Egypt adopted many of the deities of these more cultured and less powerful lands, thus seeking to bind the inhabitants of the conquered provinces more closely to themselves, so did the Assyrian rulers believe that, did they incorporate Merodach into their hierarchy, he would become so Assyrian in his outlook as to cease to be wholly Babylonian, and would doubtless work in favour of the stronger kingdom. In no other of the religions of antiquity as in the Assyrian was the idea so powerful that the god of the conquered or subject people should become a virtual prisoner in the land of the conquerors, or should at least be absorbed into their national worship. Some of the Assyrian monarchs went so far as to drag almost every petty idol they encountered on their conquests back to the great temple of Asshur, and it is obvious that they did not do this with any intention of uprooting the worship of these gods in the regions they conquered, but because they desired to make political prisoners of them, and to place them in a temple-prison, where they would be unable to wreak vengeance upon them, or assist their beaten worshippers to war against them in the future.

It may be fitting at this point to emphasize how greatly the Assyrian people, as apart from their rulers, cherished the older beliefs of Babylonia. Both peoples were substantially of the same stock, and any movement which had as its object the destruction of the Babylonian religion would have met with the strongest hostility from the populace of Assyria. Just as the conquering Aztecs seem to have had

THE ASSYRIAN BEL AND BELIT

immense reverence for the worship of the Toltecs, whose land they subdued, so did the less cultivated Assyrians regard everything connected with Babylonia as peculiarly sacred. The Kings of Assyria, in fact, were not a little proud of being the rulers of Babylonia, and were extremely mild in their treatment of their southern subjects—very much more so, in fact, than they were in their behaviour toward the people of Elam or other conquered territories. We even find the kings alluding to themselves as being nominated by the gods to rule over the land of Bel.

The Assyrian monarchs strove hard not to disturb the ancient Babylonian cult, and Shalmaneser II, when he had conquered Babylonia, actually entered Merodach's temple and sacrificed to him.

The Assyrian Bel and Belit

As for Bel, whose place Merodach usurped in the Babylonian pantheon, he was also recognized in Assyria, and Tiglath-pileser I built him a temple in his city of Asshur. Tiglath prefixes the adjective 'old' to the god's name to show that he means Bel, not Bel-Merodach. Sargon, too, who had antiquarian tastes, also reverts to Bel, to whom he alludes as the 'Great Mountain,' the name of the god following immediately after that of Asshur. Bel is also invoked in connexion with Anu as a granter of victory. His consort Belit, although occasionally she is coupled with him, more usually figures as the wife of Asshur, and almost as commonly as a variant of Ishtar. In a temple in the city of Asshur, Tiglath-pileser I made presents to Belit consisting of the images of the gods vanquished by him in his various campaigns. Assur-bani-pal, too, regarded Belit as the wife of Asshur, and himself as their son, alluding to Belit as 'Mother of the Great Gods,' a circumstance which would go to show that, like most of the Assyrian kings, his egoism rather overshadowed his sense of humour. In Assur-bani-pal's pantheon Belit is placed close by her consort Asshur. But there seems to have been a good deal of confusion between Belit and Ishtar because of the general meaning of the word Belit.

Nabu and Merodach

As in Babylonia so in Assyria, Nabu and Merodach were paired together, often as Bel and Nabu. Especially were they invoked when the affairs of Babylonia were being dealt with. In the seventh century B.C. we find the cult of Nabu in high popularity in Assyria, and indeed Ramman-Nirari III appears to have made an attempt to advance Nabu considerably. He erected a temple to the god at Calah, and granted him many resounding titles. But even so, it does not seem that Ramman-Nirari intended to exalt Nabu at the expense of Asshur. Indeed it would have been impossible for him to have done so if he had desired to. Asshur was as much the national god of the Assyrian people as Osiris was of the Egyptians. Nabu was the patron of wisdom, and protector of the arts; he guided the stylus of the scribe; and in these attributes he is very close to the Egyptian Thoth, and almost identical with another Babylonian god, Nusku, alluded to on pages 224, 225. Sargon calls Nabu 'the Seer who guides the gods,' and it would seem from some notices of him that he was also regarded as a leader of heavenly or spiritual forces. Those kings who were fond of erudition paid great devotion to Nabu, and many of the tablets in their literary collections close with thanksgiving to him for having opened their ears to receive wisdom.

Ea

Ea was of course accepted into the Assyrian pantheon because of his membership in the old Assyrian triad, but he was also regarded as a god of wisdom, possibly because of his venerable reputation; and we find him also as patron of the arts, and especially of building and architecture. Threefold was his power of direction in this respect. The great Colossi, the enormous winged bulls and mythological figures which flanked the avenues leading to the royal places, the images of the gods, and, lastly, the greater buildings, were all examples of the architectural art of which he was the patron.

Dibbarra

Another Babylonian deity who was placed in the ranks of the Assyrian pantheon was Dibbarra, the plague-god, who can only be called a god through a species of courtesy, as he partook much more of a demoniac character, and was at one time almost certainly an evil spirit. We have already alluded to the poem in which he lays low people and armies by his violence, and it was probably from one of the texts of this that Assur-bani-pal conceived the idea that those civilians who had perished in his campaigns against Babylonia had been slaughtered by Dibbarra.

Lesser Gods

Some of the lesser Babylonian gods, like Damku and Sharru-Ilu, seem to have attracted a passing interest to themselves, but as little can be found concerning them in Babylonian texts, it is scarcely necessary to take much notice of them in such a chapter as this. Most probably the Assyrians accepted the Babylonian gods on the basis not only of their native reputation, but also of the occurrence of their names in the ancient religious texts, with which their priests were thoroughly acquainted, and though, broadly speaking, they accepted practically the whole of the Babylonian religion and its gods in entirety, there is no doubt that some of these by their very natures and attributes appealed more to them than others, and therefore possessed a somewhat different value in their eyes from that assigned to them by the more peace-loving people of the southern kingdom.

PROCESSION OF GODS

Rock-relief at Malatia (Anti-Taurus range). Order from right to left: Asshur, Ishtar, Sin, En-lil, Shamash, Adad, and Ishtar of Arbela.—From *Religious Belief and Practice in Babylonia and Assyria*, by Prof. Jastrow (G. P. Putnam's Sons).

CHAPTER VIII: BABYLONIAN STAR-WORSHIP

ANCIENT Chaldea was undoubtedly the birthplace of that mysterious science of astrology which was destined to exert such influence upon the European mind during the Middle Ages, and which indeed has not yet ceased to amuse the curious and flatter the hopes of the credulous. Whether any people more primitive than the Akkadians had studied the movements of the stars it would indeed be extremely difficult to say. This the Akkadians or Babylonians were probably the first to attempt. The plain of Mesopotamia is peculiarly suited to the study of the movements of the stars. It is level for the most part, and there are few mountains around which moisture can collect to obscure the sky. Moreover the climate greatly assists such observations.

Like most primitive people the Babylonians originally believed the stars to be pictures drawn on the heavens. At a later epoch they were described as the 'writing of heaven'; the sky was supposed to be a great vault, and the movements observed by these ancient astronomers were thought to be on the part of the stars alone. Of course it would be noticed at an early stage that some of the stars seemed fixed while others moved about. Lines were drawn between the various stars and planets, and the figures which resulted from these were regarded as omens. Again, certain groups or constellations were connected with such lines which led them to be identified with various animals, and in this we may observe the influence of animism. The Babylonian zodiac was, with the exception of the sign of Merodach, identified with the eleven monsters forming the host of Tiawath. Thus it would seem that the zodiacal system as a whole originated in Babylonia. The knowledge of the Chaldean astronomers appears to have been considerable, and it is likely that they were familiar with most of the constellations known to the later Greeks.

Legend of the Origin of Star-Worship and Idolatry

The following legend is told regarding the origin of astrology by Maimonides, the famous Jewish rabbi and friend of Averroes, in his commentary on the *Mischnah*:

"In the days of Enos, the son of Seth, the sons of Adam erred with great error: and the council of the wise men of that age became brutish; and Enos himself was of them that erred. And their error was this: they said,—Forasmuch as God hath *created these stars and spheres to govern the world*, and hath set them on high, and hath imparted honour unto them, and they are ministers that minister before Him, it is meet that men should laud and glorify and give them honour. For this is the will of God that we laud and magnify whomsoever He magnifieth and honoureth, even as a king would honour them that stand before him. And this is the honour of the king himself. When this thing was come up into their hearts they began to build temples unto the stars, and to offer sacrifice unto them, and to laud and magnify them with words, and to worship before them, that they might, in their evil opinion, obtain favour of their Creator. And this was the root of idolatry; for in process of time there stood up false prophets among the sons of Adam, which said, that God had commanded them and said unto them,—

SPECULATIONS OF THE CHALDEANS

Worship such a star, or all the stars, and do sacrifice unto them thus and thus; and build a temple for it, and make an image of it, that all the people, women and children, may worship it. And the false prophet *showed them the image* which he had feigned out of his own heart, and said that *it was the image* of that star which was made known to him by prophecy. And they began after this manner to make images in temples, and under trees, and on the tops of mountains and hills, and assembled together and worshipped them; *and this thing was spread through all the world* to serve images, with services different one from another, and to sacrifice unto and worship them. So, in process of time, the glorious and fearful Name was forgotten out of the mouth of all living, and out of their knowledge, and they acknowledged Him not. And there was found on earth no people that knew aught, save images of wood and stone, and temples of stone which they had been trained up from their childhood to worship and serve, and to swear by their names; and the wise men that were among them, the priests and such like, thought that there was no God save the stars and spheres, for whose sake, and *in whose likeness*, they had made these images; but as for the Rock Everlasting, there was no man that did acknowledge Him or know Him save a few persons in the world, as Enoch, Methusaleh, Noah, Shem, and Heber. And in this way did the world work and converse, till that pillar of the world, Abram our father, was born."

Speculations of the Chaldeans

To arrive at a proper comprehension of Babylonian religious doctrines it is necessary to understand the nature of the astrological speculations of the ancient

Chaldeans. They recognized at an early period that eternal and unchangeable laws underlay planetary motion, and seem to have been able to forecast eclipses. Soon also did they begin to identify the several heavenly bodies with the gods. Thus the path of the sun was known as the 'way of Anu,' and the course of the moon and planets they determined with reference to the sun's ecliptic or pathway. It is strange, too, that they should have employed the same ideograph for the word 'star' and the word 'god,' the only difference being that in the case of a god they repeated the sign three times. If the sun and moon under animistic law are regarded as gods, it stands to reason that the stars and planets must also be looked upon as lesser deities. Indeed, poets still use such an expression regarding them as 'the host of heaven,' and we frequently encounter in classical authors the statement that the stars in their courses fought for such and such a person. This is tantamount to saying that the stars possess volition, and even although omens were looked for out of their movements, it may have been believed that these were the outcome of volition on the part of the stars themselves as deities or deific individuals. Again we can see how the idea that the gods reside in 'heaven' —that is, the sky—arose from early astrological conceptions. The gods were identified in many cases with the stars, therefore it is only natural to suppose that they resided in the sky-region. It is, indeed, one of the most difficult matters for even an intelligent and enlightened man in our enlightened age to dissociate the idea of God from a residence in the sky or 'somewhere up there.'

The idea of space, too, must have assisted in such a conception as the residence of the gods in the upper regions of air. The earth would not be large enough for them, but the boundless vault above would afford them plenty of space in which to dwell. Again, the sun and moon being gods, it would be only natural for the other deities to dwell beside them, that is, in the 'heaven of Anu,' as the Babylonians called the sky. It has been suggested that the conception of a pantheon dwelling in the sky originated in theological processes forwarded by a school or priesthood, but there is no reason to suppose that this was so, and the possibilities are easily covered by the circumstances of the animistic theory.

Planets identified with Gods

Jupiter, the largest of the planets, was identified with Merodach, head of the Babylonian pantheon. We find him exercising control over the other stars in the creation story under the name Nibir. Ishtar was identified with Venus, Saturn with Ninib, Mars with Nergal, Mercury with Nabu. It is more than strange that gods with certain attributes should have become attached to certain planets in more countries than one, and this illustrates the deep and lasting influence which Semitic religious thought exercised over the Hellenic and Roman theological systems. The connexion is too obvious and too exact not to be the result of close association. There are, indeed, hundreds of proofs to support such a theory. Who can suppose, for example, that Aphrodite is any other than Ishtar? The Romans identified their goddess Diana with the patroness of Ephesus. There are, indeed, traces of direct relations of the Greek goddess with the moon, and she was also, like Ishtar, connected with the lower world and the sea. The Greeks had numerous and flourishing colonies in Asia Minor in remote times, and these probably assisted in the dissemination of Asiatic and especially Babylonian lore.

The sun was regarded as the shepherd of the stars, and Nergal, the god of destruction and the underworld, as the 'chief sheep,' probably because the ruddy nature of his light rendered him a most conspicuous object. Anu is the Pole Star of the ecliptic, Bel the Pole Star of the equator, while Ea, in the southern heavens, was identified with a star in the constellation Argo. Fixed stars were probably selected for them because of their permanent and elemental nature. The sun they represented as riding in a chariot drawn by horses, and we frequently notice that the figure representing the luminary on Greek vases and other remains wears the Phrygian cap, a typically Asiatic and non-Hellenic head-dress, thus assisting proof that the idea of the sun as a charioteer possibly originated in Babylonia. Lunar worship, or at least computation of time by the phases of the moon, frequently precedes the solar cult, and we find traces in Babylonian religion of the former high rank of the moon-god. The moon, for example, is not one of the flock of sheep under guidance of the sun. The very fact that the calendar was regulated by her movements was sufficient to prevent this. Like the Red Indians and other primitive folk, the Babylonians possessed agricultural titles for each month, but these periods were also under the direct patronage of some god or gods. Thus the first month, Nizan, is sacred to Anu and Bel; and the second, Iyar, to Ea. Siwan is devoted to Sin, and as we approach the summer season the solar gods are apportioned to various months. The sixth month is sacred to Ishtar, and the seventh to Shamash, great god of the

PLANETS IDENTIFIED WITH GODS

sun. Merodach rules over the eighth, and Nergal over the ninth month. The tenth, curiously enough, is sacred to a variant of Nabu, to Anu, and to Ishtar. The eleventh month, very suitably, to Ramman, the god of storms, and the last month, Adar, falling within the rainy season, is presided over by the seven evil spirits.

None of the goddesses received stellar honours. The names of the months were probably quite popular in origin. Thus we find that the first month was known as the 'month of the Sanctuary,' the third as the 'period of brick-making,' the fifth as the 'fiery month,' the sixth as the 'month of the mission of Ishtar,' referring to her descent into the realms of Allatu. The fourth month was designated 'scattering seed,' the eighth that of the opening of dams, and the ninth was entitled 'copious fertility,' while the eleventh was known as 'destructive rain.'

We find in this early star-worship of the ancient Babylonians the common origin of religion and science. Just as magic partakes in some measure of the nature of real science (for some authorities hold that it is pseudo-scientific in origin) so does religion, or perhaps more correctly speaking, early science is very closely identified with religion. Thus we may believe that the religious interest in their early astronomy spurred the ancient star-gazers of Babylonia to acquire more knowledge concerning the motions of those stars and planets which they believed to be deities. We find the gods so closely connected with ancient Chaldean astronomy as to be absolutely identified with it in every way. A number was assigned to each of the chief gods, which would seem to show that they were connected in some way with mathematical science. Thus Ishtar's number is fifteen; that of Sin, her father, is exactly double that. Anu takes sixty, and Bel and Ea represent fifty and forty. Ramman is identified with ten.

It would be idle in this place to attempt further to outline astrological science in Babylonia, concerning which our knowledge is vague and scanty. Much remains to be done in the way of research before anything more definite can be written about it, and many years may pass before the workers in this sphere are rewarded by the discovery of texts bearing on Chaldean star-lore.

CHAPTER IX: THE PRIESTHOOD, CULT, AND TEMPLES

AT an early period in Babylonian history the priesthood and kingship were blended in one office, and it is not until after several centuries from the beginnings of Babylonian history as we know it that the two offices were separated. Indeed, long afterward the monarchs of Babylonia and Assyria appear to have taken especial pleasure in styling themselves the priests of such and such a deity, and in all likelihood they personally officiated at the altars of the gods on occasions of high religious sanctity. The priesthood in general was called *shangu*, which may mean 'sacrificer,' and there is little doubt that at first, as among other peoples, the Babylonian priest was practically a medicine-man. It was his business to secure people from the attacks of the evil demons who caused disease and the wiles of witches, and to forecast the future and discover the will and intentions of the gods. It is quite clear how such an official as this came to be known as the 'sacrificer,' for it would seem that the best way to find favour with the gods was to make offerings to them through an accredited intermediary. Indeed the early priesthood of Babylonia appears to have been as much magical as religious, and we read of the *makhkhu*, or soothsayer, the *mushelu*, or necromancer, the *asipu*, or sorcerer, and the *mashmashu*, or charmer, whose especial functions are probably outlined in their several titles.

But as civilization proceeded and theological opinion took shape, religious ceremonial began to take the place of what was little better than sorcery. It has been said that magic is an attempt to force the hands of the gods, to overawe them, whereas religion is an appeal to their protective instincts. Now when the feeling began to obtain that there was such a quality as justice in the universe, and when the idea of just gods had an acceptance among the people through the instruction of thinking theologians, the more vulgar practices of the sorcerer-priests fell out of favour with the upper classes, if not with the populace, and a more imposing ceremonial took the place of mere incantation. Besides, being founded on the idea of mercy as opposed to mere power, religion has invariably recommended itself, politically speaking, to the class of mind which makes for immediate and practical progress as apart from that which seeks to encourage mere speculation. As the ritual grew the necessity for new branches of the priesthood was discovered. At the head of the priestly organization was the *shangan-makhu*, and each class of priests had its chief as well. The priests were a caste,—that is, it is probable that the right to enter the priesthood was vested in certain families, but many young men were educated by the priests who did not in after life exercise their functions, but who became scribes or lawyers.

As in the case of most primitive religions, the day of the priest was carefully subdivided. It was made up of three watches, and the night was divided into a similar number of watches. Three relays of priests thus officiated through the day and three through the night.

Priestesses were also known in Babylonia, and many references are made in the texts to the 'sacred women.' Some of these were exorcisers, and others, like the Greek pythonesses, presided at oracular

SACRIFICES

shrines. The cult of Ishtar in especial had many attendant priestesses, and these were of several classes.

Sacrifices

Like the other Semitic peoples the Babylonians attached great importance to the question of sacrifices. Professor Robertson Smith has put it on record in his *Religion of the Semites*, that sacrifice among that race was regarded as a meal shared between the worshipper and the deity. This view of sacrifice is almost world-wide among peoples in the higher stages of barbarism if not in those of savagery.

There is no source from which we can definitely discover the exact manner of Babylonian and Assyrian sacrifices. As civilization advanced what was intended for the god almost invariably went for the use of the temple. Certain parts of the animal which were not fit to eat were burned to the glory of the deity. The blood of the animal may, however, have been regarded as more directly pleasing to the gods, and was probably poured out upon the altar. This practice is distinctly of magical origin. The wizard believes that the dead, demons, and supernatural beings in general have a special desire for blood, and we remember Homer's vivid description of how, when the trench was cut and the blood of the victims poured therein, the shadowy presentments of the dead flocked about it and devoured the steam arising from the sacrifice. In some cults blood alone is offered to the gods, and perhaps the most striking instance of this is afforded by the religion of ancient Mexico, in which blood was regarded as the pabulum or food of the gods, and the body of the victim as the ceremonial corpse of the deity to be eaten by his worshippers.

The Temples of Babylonia and Assyria

The temple-building phase is characteristic of Babylonian religion from an early stage. More than 3000 years before the final extinction of the cult we find places of worship being raised in the Euphrates Valley. Even in later times these Babylonian structures would appear to have been built for practical rather than æsthetic purposes, and in the early part of the temple-building epoch they were of the crudest description, mere rude structures of brick, without an attempt at architectural elaboration. An early ideal was to reproduce in miniature the 'mountain of all lands'—Khursag-kurkura, the birthplace of the gods—and to this end the temple was erected on a mountain-like heap of earth. To the primitive one-storied building other stories came to be added, till in pursuit of a general ideal of height they came to be veritable Towers of Babel, aspiring to reach to heaven. These *zikkurats*, or staged towers, as they have been called, were built of brick, and were quadrangular in form, their four sides facing north, south, east, and west respectively. Their sombre and unlovely appearance was relieved to some extent by the use of brilliant colourings, but in neither form nor colour need we look for any particular artistic interest, nor any especial religious or other symbolism, though attempts have been made both in later Babylonian and in our own times to find astrological interpretations of these. By and by the zikkurat came to be more of a 'high-place' than a temple, the altars and sanctuary proper being disposed about its base.

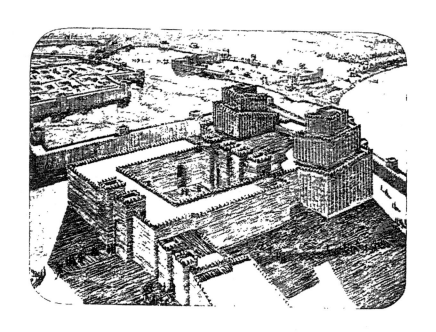

1. Zikkurats of the Anu-Adad at Ashur
2. Stage-tower at Samarra

From *Religious Belief and Practice in Babylonia and Assyria*, by Professor Morris Jastrow

By permission of Messrs G P Putnam's Sons

TEMPLES OF BABYLONIA AND ASSYRIA

With this development of the temple area a new phase was inaugurated. Huge courts were built, supported by brick columns, and enclosing all the various buildings connected with the cult of the deity to whom the temple was dedicated. These courts, which were for the most part open to the sky, covered a large area—as much, perhaps, as ten or twelve acres in some cases. Brick was still the material employed in their structure, though wood was used for gateways and for roofs for the smaller temples. As time went on they became more richly decorated, precious metals and woods were imported for their adornment, and draperies and coloured bricks were employed with more or less æsthetic intent. In some Assyrian temples stone columns were employed. The interior of the temple proper consisted of a central hall, a 'holy of holies,' wherein was set the statue of the god in whose honour the sanctuary was built, and an assembly-room where the gods of the pantheon met.

The temples of Babylonia resemble very closely those of ancient Mexico and Central America, for just as the Chaldean temple was evolved from the idea of the 'holy hill,' so was the Mexican *teocalli*, or 'house of God.' Originating probably in a rude mound of earth, the temple in both countries came through the march of civilization under the influence of architecture proper. In America there are still extant many links in the chain of evolution between the rude earth-mound and the carven teocalli, but in the case of Babylonia we have only inference to support the theory of such a development. This inference is, however, of a very powerful character. Commencing probably with a one-story structure, we find both the Mexican and Babylonian 'high places' developing a second, then a third, fourth, fifth, and even sixth stage in the case of Babylonia, and sometimes a fourth in the case of Mexico.

A sharp distinction must be drawn between the Egyptian pyramid and the temples of Babylonia and Assyria. The pyramid of the Nile country was undoubtedly developed from the grave-mound, the cairn. It is the burial-place of a monarch, and has nothing whatever to do with religious worship. The zikkurats of Babylonia and the teocallis of Mexico, as their names imply, were unquestionably religious in origin, and had nothing whatsoever to do with burial.

But one essential difference there was between them, and that is, that whereas in Mexico the teocallis seldom possessed interiors, this was very frequently the case with the temples of Babylonia. It is true that the Mexican temples had attached to them buildings called *teopan*, but these appear to have been dwelling-places for the various grades of priests. In Babylonia, on the other hand, another description of residence arose. This was the temple proper, apart from the zikkurat or tower. Most Babylonian cities had a definite religious quarter, and excavations have made us familiar to some extent with the plan and appearance of these. Perhaps the best known example is that at Nippur, the extent of which appears to have been about sixteen acres. A large court was lined with brick columns, and when excavated was found to have supported a wooden roof. Close to this was the building in which the temple records were kept. The people gathered for worship in a second court of sixty wooden columns with supports and capitals of metal, and there, in a basin specially built for the purpose, they made their ablutions before offering up sacrifice. At the eastern end of this courtyard was placed a

TEMPLES OF BABYLONIA AND ASSYRIA

tent containing the ark. This kind of courtyard may be said to be characteristic of the Semitic worship, as there was undoubtedly such a structure in most Hebrew temples. This court of columns was surrounded by chambers which probably served the purpose of administrative offices and perhaps dwellings for the priests and attendants, or booths for the sale of sacrificial offerings. The training college for the younger priests was also within the temple area, as were the astronomical observatories, and around these gathered the learned of the district, just as they did in the temple at Jerusalem to dispute concerning religious matters and to split theological hairs. The Babylonian priests were also the lawyers of their period, and the courts of justice were probably hard by the temple.

Many of these religious areas, as, for example, those at Babylon, Nippur, Sippar, and Ur, must have been so extensive as to have constituted what were in reality sacred cities. The whole was enclosed by a containing wall, and even the several divisions of the temple buildings were also surrounded by lesser walls. The material of which these edifices were built was the universal one of brick. In early days sun-dried brick was employed, but as its use resulted in the crumbling and speedy destruction of most of the edifices composed of it, kiln-dried bricks were substituted for it, and as these were often glazed their durability was much enhanced. The cement used to hold these together was common bitumen, found in great quantities in Babylonia, and the roof was usually built of wood, cedars from Lebanon being a favourite material for carpentering.

From the restoration plans with which several explorers have furnished us we can judge how stately and striking the interior of many of the Babylonian temples must have been. The enamelled bricks, the highly-polished woodwork, the brilliant precious stones, the gold and silver inlaid on the walls and ceilings must indeed have dazzled the beholder. The Semites were prone to the use of bright colours, and as it was the aim of the architects to outshine the sun itself in their interiors, we can judge of the effect. Draperies and rugs were probably also lavishly used. The wooden gates were overlaid with bronze in high relief. Passing through them the worshipper must have been deeply affected by the wonderful play of colour and shadow combined in the interior. The vastness of length and height would inspire him with deep awe, and the curtain screening the holy of holies would be for him the boundary betwixt the human and the divine. Behind this curtain was probably the statue of the god, and the chamber which contained this was known as the *papakhu*, which means 'shut off.' In all probability no one had access to it but the king and high religious officials. It was indeed the holy of holies. A stone tablet found at Sippar represents the god Shamash seated in such a chamber. He is sitting on a low throne, and before him is an altar containing a symbol of the sun-god. A monarch and priest stand before him. The decoration of such a chamber was lavish in the extreme, the floors, walls, and ceiling being inlaid with precious stones, and in some cases, as that of Merodach in the temple of Babylon, the statue and the altar in front of it were of solid gold.

The Great Temple-Builders

The history of temple-building in Babylonia begins at an early date. We find Sargon and Naram-sin

THE GREAT TEMPLE-BUILDERS

calling themselves 'Builder of the Temple of En-lil in Nippur.' Gudea was probably the first potentate to achieve great results in temple-building. Khammurabi was also active as a builder of sanctuaries. But besides planning the erection of new temples, the kings of Babylonia and Assyria appear to have been zealous in the restoration and improvement of the older temples in the land. Restoration was frequently necessary because of the fact that many of the older shrines had been built of sun-dried brick, which had not the same lasting power as the glazed brick dried in kilns used in later times.

The Assyrian conquerors of Babylonia considered it their policy as well as their pleasure to restore many of the ancient shrines of the land they had subdued, and in doing so they frequently allude in their records to the age of the temple on which they are at work, sometimes providing us with a clue to the date of its foundation. In this way we can trace the history of some of these ancient buildings over a space of more than 3000 years. Such a sanctuary must have appeared to the Assyrian monarch who rebuilt it, as an edifice erected in the days of Solomon would seem to us. Thus in the times of the later Assyrian kings some of the older temples would have behind them a record as ancient as that of the temple at Jerusalem to-day!

The Assyrian restorers of these ancient fanes refer piously to their original builders. They carefully unearthed the old foundation-stones, which they preserved, and clung tenaciously to the ritual which had been celebrated in the temples of Babylonia from very early times.

There are many long lists of temples in existence, and, assuming that each god possessed his own shrine, hundreds of temples must have been scattered over the length and breadth of the northern and southern lands. These were probably much more numerous in Babylonia, which was older, and whose people exhibited a greater religious feeling.

The Temple of E-Kur

The oldest known temple in Babylonia was that of E-Kur at Nippur, sacred to En-lil. It was probably founded somewhere about 4000 B.C., or even at an earlier date. Before the time of Sargon we find the rulers of Nippur embellishing the temple there. The climate of the place necessitated frequent repairs, and by reason of occasional popular revolutions the fabric received considerable damage. We find Urbau about 2700 B.C. building a zikkurat in the temple area at Nippur, and a few centuries afterward Bur-sin repairing this zikkurat and adding a new shrine. E-Kur saw numerous political changes, and when foreign dynasties ruled the land its importance waned somewhat. But later alien rulers shrewdly saw the advantage of restoring its rather tarnished splendour, and we find several kings of the Kassite dynasty (*c.* 1400 B.C.) so far honouring it as to place within its confines a votive object from Elam, which had originally been placed in the temple of Ishtar at Erech, whence it had been removed by an Elamite conqueror about 900 years before. This was almost as remarkable as if the Stone of Destiny, the Lia Fail, in Westminster Abbey were to be restored to its original seat in Ireland.

The temple at Nippur was at this time dedicated to Bel before that deity was ousted by Merodach. Almost every one of the Kassite rulers made more or less costly additions to the temple at Nippur, and

UR THE MOON-CITY

from their several inscriptions we can follow its history down to Assyrian times. About the twelfth century B.C. E-Kur yielded its supremacy to E-Sagila. It was sacked and partially destroyed, until later restored by Assyrian monarchs, who conscientiously re-decorated it and erected many new buildings within its area. But during the new Babylonian period it was once more sacked by order of southern rulers, and at the end of the seventh century B.C. its history comes to a close. Its site, however, did not lose its sanctity, for it was used as a cemetery and partially inhabited till the twelfth century A.D.

The Brilliant House

This outline of the history of E-Kur will serve for that of many other Babylonian temples. The temple of Shamash at Sippar, which was known as E-babbara, or the 'Brilliant House,' can be traced back as far as the days of Naram-Sin. This was also restored by monarchs of the Kassite dynasty, but the nomadic tribes, who ever threatened the peace of Babylonia, made an inroad, scattered the priesthood, and destroyed the great idol of Shamash. It was nearly 500 years after this that the 'Brilliant House' was restored to its former glory by Nabu-baliddin. Nebuchadrezzar rebuilt portions of the temple, as did the last King of Babylonia, Nabonidus, who scandalized the priests of Babylon by his preference for the worship of Shamash.

Ur, the Moon-City

We shall remember that one of the principal centres of the cult of the moon was at Ur, the city whence came Abram the Patriarch, and it is probable that he was originally a moon-worshipper.

Another such centre of lunar adoration was Harran. These places were regarded as especially sacrosanct, as the moon-cult was more ancient than that of the sun, and was therefore looked upon with a greater degree of veneration. Both of these cities possessed temples to Sin, the moon-god, and in them astrology and stellar observation were enthusiastically carried on. Harran was more than once overrun by the fierce nomadic tribes of the desert, but its prestige survived even their destructive tendencies.

The temple of E-anna at Erech, dedicated to Ishtar, was one of the most famous sanctuaries in Babylonia. It is alluded to in one of the creation legends, as were also the temples at Nippur, as 'The bright house of the gods.'

The Twin Temples

The temple of Merodach at E-Sagila and that of Nabu at E-Zida were inseparably associated, for a visit to one practically necessitated a visit to both. An original rivalry between the gods had ended in a species of amalgamation, and together they may be said to have symbolized the national religion of Babylonia. Indeed so great was their influence that it can scarcely be over-estimated. The theological thought of the country emanated from the schools which clustered around them, and they were the great literary centres of Babylonia, and thus the progenitors of Assyrian culture.

Temples as Banks

It was perhaps typical of the race that its places of worship should gradually become great financial centres and the nuclei of trade and usury. Heavily endowed as they were by the kings of Babylonia

Excavated Ruins of the Temple of E-Sagila

The two walls in the centre mark the entrance to the passage, a quarter of a mile long, which connected the Tower of Babel with this temple

Copyright by Underwood and Underwood, London

FEASTS AND FESTIVALS

and Assyria, and boasting immense wealth in lands, subsidies, and slaves, they also had at their command an army of workmen and labourers. But their directors were also bankers and money-lenders, buyers and barterers of produce and manufactures of every kind, estate-agents and men of commerce generally. Sacred objects of every kind were on sale in the temple precincts, idols, votive offerings, amulets, and so forth. With what object did the priesthood of Babylonia pursue a commercial career? It could scarcely have been one in which personal gain bulked largely, as the impersonal temple swallowed up all the profit. The cost of upkeep of such shrines must have been enormous, and when we think of the gorgeous nature of their interiors, and the costly character of the rich vessels and altars with which they were equipped, we can marvel no longer at what appears a degrading and unnecessary commerce on the part of their priesthood.

Feasts and Festivals

Babylonian religious festivals were, as a rule, periods of jubilation and rejoicing. Each god had his own day of festival in the calendar. The first day of the year, or *Zag-muku*, was sacred to the goddess Bau. Gudea, who had made Nin-girsu his favourite, attempted to 'work him into' this festival by uniting him in marriage with Bau, and he offers her marriage gifts on New Year's Day. But later the *Zag-muku* was transformed into a festival to Merodach. The circumstance that it was celebrated in the first month of the year shows that it did not originally belong to Merodach, whose month was Marcheshuan, the eighth. But it is eloquent of his popularity that the great New Year's feast should have been dedicated to him. It seems to have lasted for at least ten or twelve days. As has already been described, the union of Nabu and Merodach, father and son, was solemnly celebrated, Nabu piously paying a visit to his father's sanctuary. The other gods were supposed to assemble in spirit in Merodach's temple to witness the ceremony, and afterwards the priests of Merodach escorted the idol of Nabu back to its shrine, themselves carrying the image of their deity.

To behold this festival, which was celebrated with all possible magnificence, people flocked from all parts of Babylonia. The king, approaching the statue of the god, seized its hands in token of covenant, and in later times Assyrian monarchs, in order to legitimatize themselves as rulers of Babylonia, went through this ceremony, which came to be recognized as duly fulfilling their claims to sovereignty in the southern land; but whereas they went through the ceremony once only, the kings of Babylonia celebrated it annually with the intensest possible devotion.

The Chamber of Fates

On the eighth day of the festival all the gods were thought to assemble in Merodach's 'Chamber of Fates,' to hearken to Merodach's decree concerning the fates of men for the ensuing year. This remarkable apartment was regarded as the reproduction of the interior of the great mountain wherein the gods met in council, just as the zikkurat was thought to typify that mountain itself. It was situated in a special portion of the 'mountain' known as the *Ubshu-Kenna*, and among its sacred names is one which may be translated 'brilliant chamber,' which shows that it must have been lavishly decorated. Ubshu-Kenna (or Upshukkinaku) must be carefully distinguished from the 'heaven' proper of the Babylonian gods. It is situated in the east, in the Mountain of the Sunrise, not far from the edge of the world, where it was bounded by the waters of the great deep. It is, in fact, the 'brilliant chamber' where the sun takes his rise.

Lamentation Rituals

On the occasion of any national or popular disaster, such as defeat in war, the appearance of a pestilence or an eclipse of the sun or moon, a certain formula of lamentation was gone through, which was thought to have the effect of lessening or averting the malign influence of evil powers, or the punitive measures of an angry god. This formula varied of course with the deity or demon who was considered to have caused the calamity. Many of these ancient lamentations are written in the Sumerian tongue, which witnesses to their great antiquity. From them it would seem that the Babylonians were of the opinion that if the people had in any way sinned, the gods averted their faces from them, and departing from their neighbourhood left them a prey to calamities of all kinds. A definite ritual accompanied these formulas, one of the provisions of which was fasting, and purification ceremonies of a very elaborate nature were also celebrated by the priests, probably in the hope of symbolically washing away the sin which had so offended the gods.

The formula most in use in these propitiatory ceremonies was that which obtained in the sacred city of Nippur, and particularly in the temple of E-Kur. The monotony of these laments is typical of ancient Semitic worship. They describe the disasters that have occurred, and piteously beg that the gods may be appeased. Only now and again in perusing them does a bright line or a picturesque phrase capture the eye and fire the imagination. A paraphrase of one of them may well characterize the whole. The god En-lil, shepherd of the dark-headed people, is implored to return to his city. He is entreated by the various names of his godhead, such as 'lord of lands,' 'lord of the faithful word,' 'lord of self-created vision,' and so forth. Each separate part of the temple area is alluded to in the request that he will return—the great gate, the storehouse, and the other religious departments. A touching domestic picture is drawn of the deserted homes in the city; where the woman could say to her young husband, " My husband," where she could say to the young child, " My child," where the maiden could say, " My brother," where the little girl could say, " My father,"—there the little ones perish, there the great perish. In her banqueting-hall the wind holds revel, her streets are desolate.

From some of the texts it would appear that the suppliants were ignorant of the sin they had committed, and many so-called 'penitential psalms' are extant in which the stricken one appeals fervently to the gods to release him from the burden of his unknown sin. He weeps, and he is unable to restrain himself. He laments earnestly, and begs through the priest for the divine mercy. These appeals always end in the same way—that is, in the pious hope that the heart and liver of the god may be appeased. With the Babylonians, as with the modern Armenians, to whom they are perhaps related, the liver was regarded as the seat of the emotions.

Occasionally a higher intellectual and ethical

THE TERROR OF ECLIPSE

plane is reached by these prayers. "Men," says one of them, "are blind: which of them knows anything? They do not even know good from evil." The god is fervently petitioned not to cast his servant off. He is in a deep morass, and he earnestly prays that the deity may take him by the hand, may change his sin to grace, and permit the wind to carry off his transgressions.

The Terror of Eclipse

The terror of eclipse of the sun or moon was a very real one to the ancient Babylonians. The tablet with the history of the seven evil gods or spirits, though much mutilated, gives us a hint of the attack made by them upon the moon. They dwelt in the lower part of heaven, and were rebellious in heart. Shaped like leopards, serpents, and angry beasts of prey, they went from city to city on the wings of an evil wind, destroying and smiting. And into the heaven of Anu they burst, but Bel and Ea took counsel, and set Sin the moon, Shamash the sun, and Ishtar the planet Venus in the lower part of heaven to govern and control it along with Anu. No sooner had this been accomplished than the seven evil spirits fiercely attacked the moon-god. But Bel saw the peril of Sin, and said to his attendant, the god Nusku, "Carry word of this thing to the ocean, to the god Ea." Ea heard the message, and called his son, the god Merodach. "Go, my son Merodach," quoth he, "enter into the shining Sin, who in heaven is greatly beset, and expel his enemies from heaven." It is impossible to decipher the context from the mutilated remains of the tablets, but we may take it for granted that the pious efforts of Merodach were rewarded with success.

MYTHS OF BABYLONIA AND ASSYRIA

An eclipse to most primitive peoples means that the sun- or moon-god has either met with disaster or has withdrawn his face from his worshippers. The monthly waning of the moon made the ancients believe that it would be entirely blotted out unless the god was pacified. Thus if no eclipse took place it was considered that the efforts of priests and people had prevailed; otherwise they were held to have failed, and panic ruled supreme. In a certain prayer Sin is adjured not to withhold his face from his people. The day of the monthly disappearance of the moon is called a day of distress, but a season of jubilee followed upon the advent of the new moon next day.

CHAPTER X: THE MAGIC AND DEMONOLOGY OF BABYLONIA AND ASSYRIA

LIKE other primitive races the peoples of Chaldea scarcely discriminated at all between religion and magic. One difference between the priest and the sorcerer was that the one employed magic for religious purposes whilst the other used it for his own ends. The literature of Chaldea—especially its religious literature—teems with references to magic, and in its spells and incantations we see the prototypes of those employed by the magicians of mediæval Europe. Indeed so closely do some of the Assyrian incantations and magical practices resemble those of the European sorcerers of the Middle Ages and of primitive peoples of the present day that it is difficult to convince oneself that they are of independent origin.

In Chaldea as in ancient Egypt the crude and vague magical practices of primeval times received form and developed into accepted ritual, just as early religious ideas evolved into dogmas under the stress of theological controversy and opinion. As there were men who would dispute upon religious questions, so were there persons who would discuss matters magical. This is not to say that the terms 'religion' and 'magic' possessed any well-defined boundaries for them. Nor is it at all clear that they do for us in this twentieth century. They overlap; and it has long been the belief of the writer that their relations are but represented by two circles which intersect one another and the areas of which partially coincide.

The writer has outlined his opinions regarding the origin of magic in an earlier volume of this series,[1]

[1] *The Myths of Ancient Egypt.*

and has little to add to what he then wrote, except that he desires to lay stress upon the identification of early religion and magic. It is only when they begin to evolve, to branch out, that the two systems present differences. If there is any one circumstance which accentuates the difference more than another it is that the ethical element does not enter into magic in the same manner as it does into religion.

That Chaldean magic was the precursor of European mediæval magic as apart from popular sorcery and witchcraft is instanced not only by the similarity between the systems but by the introduction into mediæval magic of the names of Babylonian and Assyrian gods and magicians. Again and again is Babylon appealed to even more frequently than Egypt, and we meet constantly with the names of Beelzebub, Ishtar (as Astarte), Baal, and Moloch, whilst the names of demons, obviously of Babylonian origin, are encountered in almost every work on the subject. Frequent allusions are also made to the 'wise men' and necromancers of Babylon, and to the 'star-gazers' of Chaldea. The conclusion is irresistible that ceremonial magic, as practised in the Middle Ages, owed much to that of Babylon.

Our information regarding Chaldean magic is much more complete than that which we possess concerning the magic of ancient Egypt. Hundreds of spells, incantations, and omen-inscriptions have been recovered, and these not only enlighten us regarding the class of priests who practised magic, but they tell us of the several varieties of demons, ghosts, and evil spirits; they minutely describe the Babylonian witch and wizard, and they picture for us many magical ceremonies, besides informing us of the names of scores of plants and flowers possessing magical properties, of

THE ROOTS OF SCIENCE

magical substances, jewels, amulets, and the like. Also they speak of sortilege or the divination of the future, of the drawing of magical circles, of the exorcism of evil spirits, and the casting out of demons.

The Roots of Science

In these Babylonian magical records we have by far the most complete picture of the magic of the ancient world. It is a wondrous story that is told by those bricks and cylinders of stamped clay —the story of civilized man's first gropings for light. For in these venerable writings we must recognize the first attempts at scientific elucidation of the forces by which man is surrounded. Science, like religion, has its roots deep in magic. The primitive man believes implicitly in the efficacy of magical ritual. What it brings about once it can bring about again if the proper conditions be present and recognized. Thus it possesses for the barbarian as much of the element of certainty as the scientific process does for the chemist or the electrician. Given certain causes certain effects *must* follow. Surely, then, in the barbarous mind, magic is pseudo-scientific—of the nature of science.

There appears a deeper gloom, a more ominous spirit of the ancient and the obscure in the magic of old Mesopotamia than in that of any other land. Its mighty sanctuaries, its sky-aspiring towers, seem founded upon this belief in the efficacy of the spoken spell, the reiterated invocation. Thousands of spirits various and grotesque, the parents of the ghosts and goblins of a later day, haunt the purlieus of the temple, battening upon the remains of sacrifice (the leavings of the gorged gods), flit through the night-bound streets, and disturb the rest of the dwellers in houses. Demons with claw and talon, vampires, ghouls—all are there. Spirits blest and unblest, jinn, witch-hags, lemures, sorrowing unburied ghosts. No type of supernatural being appears to have been unknown to the imaginative Semites of old Chaldea. These must all be 'laid,' exorcised, or placated, and it is not to be marvelled at that in such circumstances the trade of the necromancer flourished exceedingly. The witch or wizard, however, the unprofessional and detached practitioner with no priestly status, must beware. He or she was regarded with suspicion, and if one fell sick of a strange wasting or a disease to which he could not attach a name, the nearest sorcerer, male or female, real or imaginary, was in all probability brought to book.

Priestly Wizards

There were at least two classes of priests who dealt in the occult—the *barû*, or seers, and the *asipû*, or wizards. The caste of the barû was a very ancient one, dating at least from the time of Khammurabi. The barû performed divination by consulting the livers of animals and also by observation of the flight of birds. We find many of the kings of Babylonia consulting this class of soothsayer. Sennacherib, for example, sought from the barû the cause of his father's violent death. The asipû, on the other hand, was the remover of taboo and bans of all sorts; he chanted the rites described in the magical texts, and performed the ceremony of atonement. It is

> He that stilleth all to rest, that pacifieth all.
> By whose incantations everything is at peace.

The gods are upon his right hand and his left, they are behind and before him.

PRIESTLY WIZARDS

The wizard and the witch were known as *Kassapu* or *Kassaptu*. These were the sorcerers or magicians proper, and that they were considered dangerous to the community is shown by the manner in which they are treated by the code of Khammurabi, in which it is ordained that he who charges a man with sorcery and can justify the charge shall obtain the sorcerer's house, and the sorcerer shall plunge into the river. But if the sorcerer be not drowned then he who accused him shall be put to death and the wrongly accused man shall have his house.

A series of texts known as 'Maklu' provides us, among other things, with a striking picture of the Babylonian witch. It tells how she prowls the streets, searching for victims, snatching love from handsome men, and withering beauteous women. At another time she is depicted sitting in the shade of the wall making spells and fashioning images. The suppliant prays that her magic may revert upon herself, that the image of her which he has made, and doubtless rendered into the hands of the priest, shall be burnt by the fire-god, that her words may be forced back into her mouth. "May her mouth be fat, may her tongue be salt," continues the prayer. The *haltappen-plant* along with sesame is sent against her. "O, witch, like the circlet of this seal may thy face grow green and yellow!"

An Assyrian text says of a sorceress that her bounds are the whole world, that she can pass over all mountains. The writer states that near his door he has posted a servant, on the right and left of his door has he set Lugalgirra and Allamu, that they might kill the witch.

The library of Assur-bani-pal contains many cuneiform tablets dealing with magic, but there are also extant many magical tablets of the later Babylonian Empire. These were known to the Babylonians by some name or word, indicative perhaps of the special sphere of their activities. Thus we have the Maklu ('burning'), Surpu ('consuming'), Utukki limnûti ('evil spirits'), and Labartu ('witch-hag') series, besides many other texts dealing with magical practices.

The Maklu series deals with spells against witches and wizards, images of whom are to be consumed by fire to the accompaniment of suitable spells and prayers. The Surpu series contains prayers and incantations against taboo. That against evil spirits provides the haunted with spells which will exorcise demons, ghosts, and the powers of the air generally, and place devils under a ban. In other magical tablets the diseases to which poor humanity is prone are guarded against, and instructions are given on the manner in which they may be transferred to the dead bodies of animals, usually swine or goats.

A Toothache Myth

The Assyrian physician had perforce to be something of a demonologist, as possession by devils was held to be the cause of divers diseases, and we find incantations sprinkled among prescriptions. Occasionally, too, we come upon the fag-end of a folk-tale or dip momentarily into myth, as in a prescription for the toothache, compounded of fermented drink, the plant *sakilbir*, and oil—probably as efficacious in the case of that malady as most modern ones are. The story attached to the cure is as follows:

When Anu had created the heavens, the earth created the rivers, the rivers the canals, and the canals the marshes, which in turn created the worm. And the worm came weeping before Ea, saying,

Exorcising Demons of Disease

From *Religious Belief and Practice in Babylonia and Assyria*, by Professor Morris Jastrow

By permission of Messrs G. P. Putnam's Sons

THE WORD OF POWER

"What wilt thou give me for my food, what wilt thou give me for my devouring?" "I will give thee ripe figs," replied the god, "ripe figs and scented wood." "Bah," replied the worm, "what are ripe figs to me, or what is scented wood? Let me drink among the teeth and batten on the gums that I may devour the blood of the teeth and the strength thereof." This tale alludes to a Babylonian superstition that worms consume the teeth.

The Word of Power

As in Egypt, the word of power was held in great reverence by the magicians of Chaldea, who believed that the name, preferably the secret name, of a god possessed sufficient force in its mere syllables to defeat and scatter the hordes of evil things that surrounded and harassed mankind. The names of Ea and Merodach were, perhaps, most frequently used to carry destruction into the ranks of the demon army. It was also necessary to know the name of the devil or person against whom his spells were directed. If to this could be added a piece of hair, or the nail-parings in the case of a human being, then special efficacy was given to the enchantment. But just as hair or nails were part of a man so was his name, and hence the great virtue ascribed to names in art-magic, ancient and modern. The name was, as it were, the vehicle by means of which the magician established a link between himself and his victim, and the Babylonians in exorcising sickness or disease of any kind were wont to recite long catalogues of the names of evil spirits and demons in the hope that by so doing they might chance to light upon that especial individual who was the cause of the malady. Even long lists of names of persons who had died premature deaths were often recited in order to ensure that they would not return to torment the living.

Babylonian Vampires

In all lands and epochs the grisly conception of the vampire has gained a strong hold upon the imagination of the common people, and this was no less the case in Babylonia and Assyria than elsewhere. There have not been wanting those who believed that vampirism was confined to the Slavonic race alone, and that the peoples of Russia, Bohemia, and the Balkan Peninsula were the sole possessors of the vampire legend. Recent research, however, has exposed the fallacy of this theory and has shown that, far from being the property of the Slavs or even of Aryan peoples, this horrible belief is or was the possession of practically every race, savage or civilized, that is known to anthropology. The seven evil spirits of Assyria are, among other things, vampires of no uncertain type. An ancient poem which was chanted by them commences thus:

> Seven are they! Seven are they!
> In the ocean deep, seven are they!
> Battening in heaven, seven are they!
> Bred in the depths of the ocean;
> Not male nor female are they,
> But are as the roaming wind-blast.
> No wife have they, no son can they beget;
> Knowing neither mercy nor pity,
> They hearken not to prayer, to prayer.
> They are as horses reared amid the hills,
> The Evil Ones of Ea;
> Throne-bearers to the gods are they,
> They stand in the highway to befoul the path;
> Evil are they, evil are they!
> Seven are they, seven are they,
> Twice seven are they!

BABYLONIAN VAMPIRES

Destructive storms (and) evil winds are they,
An evil blast that heraldeth the baneful storm,
An evil blast, forerunner of the baleful storm.
They are mighty children, mighty sons,
Heralds of the Pestilence.
Throne-bearers of Ereskigal,
They are the flood which rusheth through the land.
Seven gods of the broad earth,
Seven robber(?)-gods are they,
Seven gods of might,
Seven evil demons,
Seven evil demons of oppression,
Seven in heaven and seven on earth.

Spirits that minish heaven and earth,
That minish the land,
Spirits that minish the land,
Of giant strength,
Of giant strength and giant tread,
Demons (like) raging bulls, great ghosts,
Ghosts that break through all houses,
Demons that have no shame,
Seven are they!
Knowing no care, they grind the land like corn;
Knowing no mercy, they rage against mankind,
They spill their blood like rain,
Devouring their flesh (and) sucking their veins.

. . . .

They are demons full of violence, ceaselessly devouring blood.[1]

This last line clearly indicates their character as vampires. They are akin to the Rakshasas of India or the arch-demons of Zoroastrianism. Such demons are also to be seen in the Polynesian *tii*, the Malayan *hantu penyadin*, a dog-headed water-demon, and the *kephn* of the Karens, which under the form of a wizard's head and stomach devours human souls.

[1] From *Semitic Magic*, by R. Campbell Thompson, p. 47 *ff*. (By permission of Messrs Luzac and Co., London.)

Tylor considers vampires to be "causes conceived in spiritual form to account for specific facts of wasting disease." Afanasief regards them as thunder-gods and spirits of the storm, who during winter slumber in their cloud-coffins to rise again in spring and draw moisture from the clouds. But this theory will scarcely recommend itself to anyone with even a slight knowledge of mythological science. The Abbé Calmet's difficulty in believing in vampires was that he could not understand how a spirit could leave its grave and return thence with ponderable matter in the form of blood, leaving no traces showing that the surface of the earth above the grave had been stirred. But this view might be solved by the occult theory of the 'precipitation of matter'!

The Bible and Magic

The earliest Biblical account of anything supposed to be connected with magic, is to be found in the history of Rachel. When with her sister Leah, and her husband Jacob, she had left the house of her father. "Rachel had stolen the images that were her father's.... Then Laban overtook Jacob ... and Laban said ... yet wherefore hast thou stolen my gods? ... and Jacob answered and said, With whomsoever thou findest thy gods, let him not live: before our brethren discern thou what is thine with me, and take it to thee. For Jacob knew not that Rachel had stolen them. And Laban went into Jacob's tent, and into Leah's tent, and into the two maid-servants' tent, but he found them not. Then went he out of Leah's tent and entered into Rachel's tent. Now Rachel had taken the images, and put them in the camel's furniture and sat upon them. And Laban searched all the tent, but found them not.

THE SPEAKING HEAD

And she said to her father, Let it not displease my lord that I cannot rise up before thee. . . . And he searched, but found not the images." This passage has given no little trouble to commentators; but most of them seem to consider these teraphim or images as something of a magical nature.

The Speaking Head

The targum of Jonathan Ben Uzziel gives the following version: "And Rachel stole the images of her father; for they had murdered a man, who was a first-born son, and, having cut off his head, they embalmed it with salt and spices, and they wrote divinations upon a plate of gold, and put it under his tongue and placed it against the wall, and it conversed with them, and Laban worshipped it. And Jacob stole the science of Laban the Syrian, that he might not discover his departure."

The Persian translation gives us astrolabes instead of teraphim, and implies that they were instruments used for judicial astrology, and that Rachel stole them to prevent her father from discovering their route. At all events the teraphim were means of divination among believers and unbelievers; they were known among the Egyptians and among Syrians. What makes it extremely probable that they were not objects of religious worship is, that it does not appear from any other passage of Scripture that Laban was an idolater; besides which Rachel, who was certainly a worshipper of the true God, took them, it seems, on account of their supposed supernatural powers. It must, however, be observed that some have supposed these teraphim to have been talismans for the cure of diseases; and others, that being really idols, Rachel stole them to put a stop to her father's idolatry. There is a not very dissimilar account related (Judges xviii) of Micah and his teraphim, which seems sufficient to prove that the use of them was not considered inconsistent with the profession of the true religion.

Gods once Demons

Many of the Babylonian gods retained traces of their primitive demoniacal characteristics, and this applies to the great triad, Ea, Anu, and En-lil, who probably evolved into godhead from an animistic group of nature spirits. Each of these gods was accompanied by demon groups. Thus the disease-demons were 'the beloved sons of Bel,' the fates were the seven daughters of Anu, and the seven storm-demons the children of Ea. In a magical incantation describing the primitive monster form of Ea it is said that his head is like a serpent's, the ears are those of a basilisk, his horns are twisted into curls, his body is a sun-fish full of stars, his feet are armed with claws, and the sole of his foot has no heel.

Ea was 'the great magician of the gods'; his sway over the forces of nature was secured by the performance of magical rites, and his services were obtained by human beings who performed requisite ceremonies and repeated appropriate spells. Although he might be worshipped and propitiated in his temple at Eridu, he could also be conjured in mud huts. The latter, indeed, as in Mexico, appear to have been the oldest holy places.

The Legend of Ura

It is told that Ura, the dread demon of disease, once made up his mind to destroy mankind. But

THE LEGEND OF URA

Ishnu, his counsellor, appeased him so that he abandoned his intention, and he gave humanity a chance of escape. Whoever should praise Ura and magnify his name would, he said, rule the four quarters of the world, and should have none to oppose him. He should not die in pestilence, and his speech should bring him into favour with the great ones of the earth. Wherever a tablet with the song of Ura was set up, in that house there should be immunity from the pestilence.

As we read in the closing lines of the Gilgamesh epic, the dead were often left unburied in Babylonia, and the ghosts of those who were thus treated were, as in more modern times and climes, supposed to haunt the living until given proper sepulture. They roamed the streets and byways seeking for sustenance among the garbage in the gutters, and looking for haunted houses in which to dwell, denied as they were the shelter of the grave, which was regarded as the true 'home' of the dead. They frequently terrified children into madness or death, and bitterly mocked those in tribulation. They were, in fact, the outcasts of mortality, spiteful and venomous because they had not been properly treated. The modern race which most nearly approximates to the Babylonian in its treatment of and attitude to the dead seems to be the Burmese, who are extremely circumspect as to how they speak and act towards the inhabitants of the spirit-world, as they believe that disrespect or mockery will bring down upon them misfortune or disease. An infinite number of guardian spirits is included in the Burman demonological system. These dwell in their houses and are the tutelars of village communities, and even of clans. These are duly propitiated, at which ceremonies rice, beer, and tea-salad are offered to them. Women are employed as exorcists for driving out the evil spirits.

Purification

Purification by water entered largely into Babylonian magic. The ceremony known as the 'Incancation of Eridu,' so frequently alluded to in Babylonian magical texts, was probably some form of purification by water, relating as it does to the home of Ea, the sea-god. Another ceremony prescribes the mingling of water from a pool 'that no hand hath touched,' with tamarisk, *mastakal*, ginger, alkali, and mixed wine. Therein must be placed a shining ring, and the mixture is then to be poured upon the patient. A root of saffron is then to be taken and pounded with pure salt and alkali and fat of the *matku*-bird brought from the mountains, and with this strange mixture the body of the patient is to be anointed.

The Chamber of the Priest-Magician

Let us attempt to describe the treatment of a case by a priest-physician-magician of Babylonia. The proceeding is rather a recondite one, but by the aid of imagination as well as the assistance of Babylonian representation we may construct a tolerably clear picture. The chamber of the sage is almost certain to be situated in some nook in one of those vast and imposing fanes which more closely resembled cities than mere temples. We draw the curtain and enter a rather darksome room. The atmosphere is pungent with chemic odours, and ranged on shelves disposed upon the tiled walls are numerous jars, great and small, containing the fearsome compounds

THE CHAMBER OF THE PRIEST-MAGICIAN

which the practitioner applies to the sufferings of Babylonian humanity. The asipu, shaven and austere, asks us what we desire of him, and in the rôle of Babylonian citizens we acquaint him with the fact that our lives are made miserable for us by a witch who sends upon us misfortune after misfortune, now the blight or some equally intractable and horrible disease, now an evil wind, now unspeakable enchantments which torment us unceasingly. In his capacity of physician the asipu examines our bodies, shrunken and exhausted with fever or rheumatism, and having prescribed for us, compounds the mixture with his own hands and enjoins us to its regular application. He mixes various ingredients in a stone mortar, whispering his spells the while, with many a prayer to Ea the beneficent and Merodach the all-powerful that we may be restored to health. Then he promises to visit us at our dwelling and gravely bids us adieu, after expressing the hope that we will graciously contribute to the upkeep of the house of religion to which he is attached.

Leaving the darkened haunt of the asipu for the brilliant sunshine of a Babylonian summer afternoon, we are at first inclined to forget our fears, and to laugh away the horrible superstitions, the relics of barbarian ancestors, which weigh us down. But as night approaches we grow more fearful, we crouch with the children in the darkest corner of our claybrick dwelling, and tremble at every sound. The rushing of the wind overhead is for us the noise of the Labartu, the hag-demon, come hither to tear from us our little ones, or perhaps a rat rustling in the straw may seem to us the Alu-demon. The ghosts of the dead gibber at the threshold, and even pale Uru, lord of disease, himself may glance in at the tiny window with ghastly countenance and eager, red eyes. The pains of rheumatism assail us. Ha, the evil witch is at work, thrusting thorns into the waxen images made in our shape that we may suffer the torment brought about by sympathetic magic, to which we would rather refer our aches than to the circumstance that we dwell hard by the river-swamps.

A loud knocking resounds at the door. We tremble anew and the children scream. At last the dread powers of evil have come to summon us to the final ordeal, or perhaps the witch herself, grown bold by reason of her immunity, has come to wreak fresh vengeance. The flimsy door of boards is thrown open, and to our unspeakable relief the stern face of the asipu appears beneath the flickering light of the taper. We shout with joy, and the children cluster around the priest, clinging to his garments and clasping his knees.

The Witch-Finding

The priest smiles at our fear, and motioning us to sit in a circle produces several waxen figures of demons which he places on the floor. It is noticeable that these figures all appear to be bound with miniature ropes. Taking one of these in the shape of a Labartu or hag-demon, the priest places before it twelve small cakes made from a peculiar kind of meal. He then pours out a libation of water, places the image of a small black dog beside that of the witch, lays a piece of the heart of a young pig on the mouth of the figure and some white bread and a box of ointment beside it. He then chants something like the following: "May a guardian spirit be present at my side when I draw near unto the sick man, when I examine his muscles, when I compose his limbs, when

THE WITCH-FINDING

I sprinkle the water of Ea upon him. Avoid thee whether thou art an evil spirit or an evil demon, an evil ghost or an evil devil, an evil god or an evil fiend, hag-demon, ghoul, sprite, phantom, or wraith, or any disease, fever, headache, shivering, or any sorcery, spell, or enchantment."

Having recited some such words of power the asipu then directs us to keep the figure at the head of our bed for three nights, then to bury it beneath the earthen floor. But alas! no cure results. The witch still torments us by day and night, and once more we have recourse to the priest-doctor; the ceremony is gone through again, but still the family health does not improve. The little ones suffer from fever, and bad luck consistently dogs us. After a stormy scene between husband and wife, who differ regarding the qualifications of the asipu, another practitioner is called in. He is younger and more enterprising than the last, and he has not yet learned that half the business of the physician is to 'nurse' his patients, in the financial sense of the term. Whereas the elderly asipu had gone quietly home to bed after prescribing for us, this young physician, who has his spurs to win, after being consulted goes home to his clay surgery and hunts up a likely exorcism.

Next day, armed with this wordy weapon, he arrives at our dwelling and, placing a waxen image of the witch upon the floor, vents upon it the full force of his rhetoric. As he is on the point of leaving, screams resound from a neighbouring cabin. Bestowing upon us a look of the deepest meaning our asipu darts to the hut opposite and hales forth an ancient crone, whose appearance of age and illness give her a most sinister look. At once we recognize in her a wretch who dared to menace our children when in innocent play they cast hot ashes upon her thatch and introduced hot swamp water into her cistern. In righteous wrath we lay hands on the abandoned being who for so many months has cast a blight upon our lives. She exclaims that the pains of death have seized upon her, and we laugh in triumph, for we know that the superior magic of our asipu has taken effect. On the way to the river we are joined by neighbours, who rejoice with us that we have caught the witch. Great is the satisfaction of the party when at last the devilish crone is cast headlong into the stream.

But ere many seconds pass we begin to look incredulously upon each other, for the wicked one refuses to sink. This means that she is innocent! Then, awful moment, we find every eye directed upon us, we who were so happy and light-hearted but a moment before. We tremble, for we know how severe are the laws against the indiscriminate accusation of those suspected of witchcraft. As the ancient crone continues to float, a loud murmuring arises in the crowd, and with quaking limbs and eyes full of terror we snatch up our children and make a dash for freedom.

Luckily the asipu accompanies us so that the crowd dare not pursue, and indeed, so absurdly changeable is human nature, most of them are busied in rescuing the old woman. In a few minutes we have placed all immediate danger of pursuit behind us. The asipu has departed to his temple, richer in the experience by the lesson of a false 'prescription.'[1] After a hurried consultation we quit the town, skirt the arable land which fringes

[1] He is exempt from the punishment provided by the code of Khammurabi for the false accusation.

THE MAGIC CIRCLE

it, and plunge into the desert. She who was opposed to the employment of a young and inexperienced asipu does not make matters any better by reiterating "I told you so." And he who favoured a 'second opinion,' on paying a night visit to the city, discovers that the 'witch' has succumbed to her harsh treatment; that his house has been made over to her relatives by way of compensation, and that a legal process has been taken out against him. Returning to his wife he acquaints her with the sad news, and hand in hand with their weeping offspring they turn and face the desert.

The Magic Circle

The magic circle, as in use among the Chaldean sorcerers, bears many points of resemblance to that described in mediæval works on magic. The Babylonian magician, when describing the circle, made seven little winged figures, which he set before an image of the god Nergal. After doing so he stated that he had covered them with a dark robe and bound them with a coloured cord, setting beside them tamarisk and the heart of the palm, that he had completed the magic circle and had surrounded them with a sprinkling of lime and flour.

That the magic circle of mediæval times must have been evolved from the Chaldean is plain from the strong resemblance between the two. Directions for the making of a mediæval magic circle are as follows:—

In the first place the magician is supposed to fix upon a spot proper for such a purpose, which must be either in a subterranean vault, hung round with black, and lighted by a magical torch, or else in the centre of some thick wood or desert, or upon some extensive unfrequented plain, where several roads meet, or amidst the ruins of ancient castles, abbeys, or monasteries, or amongst the rocks on the seashore, in some private detached churchyard, or any other melancholy place between the hours of twelve and one in the night, either when the moon shines very bright, or else when the elements are disturbed with storms of thunder, lightning, wind, and rain; for, in these places, times, and seasons, it is contended that spirits can with less difficulty manifest themselves to mortal eyes, and continue visible with the least pain.

When the proper time and place are fixed upon, a magic circle is to be formed within which the master and his associates are carefully to retire. The reason assigned by magicians and others for the institution and use of the circles is, that so much ground being blessed and consecrated by holy words and ceremonies has a secret force to expel all evil spirits from the bounds thereof, and, being sprinkled with sacred water, the ground is purified from all uncleanness; beside the holy names of God being written over every part of it, its force becomes proof against all evil spirits.

Babylonian Demons

Babylonian demons were legion and most of them exceedingly malevolent. The Utukku was an evil spirit that lurked generally in the desert, where it lay in wait for unsuspecting travellers, but it did not confine its haunts to the more barren places, for it was also to be found among the mountains, in graveyards, and even in the sea. An evil fate befel the man upon whom it looked.

The Rabisu is another lurking demon that secretes

BABYLONIAN DEMONS

itself in unfrequented spots to leap upon passers-by. The Labartu, which has already been alluded to, is, strangely enough, spoken of as the daughter of Anu. She was supposed to dwell in the mountains or in marshy places, and was particularly addicted to the destruction of children. Babylonian mothers were wont to hang charms round their children's necks to guard them against this horrible hag.

The Sedu appears to have been in some senses a guardian spirit and in others a being of evil propensities. It is often appealed to at the end of invocations along with the Lamassu, a spirit of a similar type. These malign influences were probably the prototypes of the Arabian jinn, to whom they have many points of resemblance.

Many Assyrian spirits were half-human and half-supernatural, and some of them were supposed to contract unions with human beings, like the Arabian jinn. The offspring of such unions was supposed to be a spirit called Alu, which haunted ruins and deserted buildings and indeed entered the houses of men like a ghost to steal their sleep. Ghosts proper were also common enough, as has already been observed, and those who had not been buried were almost certain to return to harass mankind. It was dangerous even to look upon a corpse, lest the spirit or edimmu of the dead man should seize upon the beholder. The Assyrians seemed to be of the opinion that a ghost like a vampire might drain away the strength of the living, and long formulæ were in existence containing numerous names of haunting spirits, one of which it was hoped would apply to the tormenting ghost, and these were used for the purposes of exorcism. To lay a spirit the following articles were necessary: seven small loaves of roast corn, the hoof of a dark-coloured ox, flour of roast corn, and a little leaven. The ghosts were then asked why they tormented the haunted man, after which the flour and leaven were kneaded into a paste in the horn of an ox and a small libation poured into a hole in the earth. The leaven dough was then placed in the hoof of an ox, and another libation poured out with an incantation to the god Shamash. In another case figures of the dead man and the living person to whom the spirit has appeared are to be made and libations poured out before both of them, then the figure of the dead man is to be buried and that of the living man washed in pure water, the whole ceremony being typical of sympathetic magic, which thus supposed the burial of the body of the ghost and the purification of the living man. In the morning incense was to be offered up before the sun-god at his rising, when sweet woods were to be burned and a libation of sesame wine poured out.

If a human being was troubled by a ghost, it was necessary that he should be anointed with various substances in order that the result of the ghostly contact might be nullified.

An old text says, "When a ghost appeareth in the house of a man there will be a destruction of that house. When it speaketh and hearkeneth for an answer the man will die, and there will be lamentation."

Taboo

The belief in taboo was universal in ancient Chaldea. Amongst the Babylonians it was known as *mamit*. There were taboos on many things, but especially upon corpses and uncleanness of all kinds. We find the taboo generally alluded to in a text " as the barrier that none can pass."

TABOO

Among all barbarous peoples the taboo is usually intended to hedge in the sacred thing from the profane person or the common people, but it may also be employed for sanitary reasons. Thus the flesh of certain animals, such as the pig, may not be eaten in hot countries. Food must not be prepared by those who are in the slightest degree suspected of uncleanness, and these laws are usually of the most rigorous character; but should a man violate the taboo placed upon certain foods, then he himself often became taboo. No one might have any intercourse with him. He was left to his own devices, and, in short, became a sort of pariah. In the Assyrian texts we find many instances of this kind of taboo, and numerous were the supplications that these might be removed. If one drank water from an unclean cup he had violated a taboo. Like the Arab he might not "lick the platter clean." If he were taboo he might not touch another man, he might not converse with him, he might not pray to the gods, he might not even be interceded for by anyone else. In fact he was excommunicate. If a man cast his eye upon water which another person had washed his hands in, or if he came into contact with a person who had not yet performed his ablutions, he became unclean. An entire purification ritual was incumbent on any Assyrian who touched or even looked upon a dead man.

It may be asked, wherefore was this elaborate cleanliness essential to avoid taboo? The answer undoubtedly is—because of the belief in the power of sympathetic magic. Did one come into contact with a person who was in any way unclean, or with a corpse or other unpleasant object, he was supposed to come within the radius of the evil which emanated from it.

MYTHS OF BABYLONIA AND ASSYRIA

Popular Superstitions

The superstition that the evil-eye of a witch or a wizard might bring blight upon an individual or community was as persistent in Chaldea as elsewhere. Incantations frequently allude to it as among the causes of sickness, and exorcisms were duly directed against it. Even to-day, on the site of the ruins of Babylon children are protected against it by fastening small blue objects to their headgear.

Just as mould from a grave was supposed by the witches of the Middle Ages to be particularly efficacious in magic, so was the dust of the temple supposed to possess hidden virtue in Assyria. If one pared one's nails or cut one's hair it was considered necessary to bury them lest a sorcerer should discover them and use them against their late owner; for a sorcery performed upon a part was by the law of sympathetic magic thought to reflect upon the whole. A like superstition attached to the discarded clothing of people, for among barbarian or uncultured folk the apparel is regarded as part and parcel of the man. Even in our own time simple and uneducated people tear a piece from their garments and hang it as an offering on the bushes around any of the numerous healing wells in the country that they may have journeyed to. This is a survival of the custom of sacrificing the part for the whole.

If one desired to get rid of a headache one had to take the hair of a young kid and give it to a wise woman, who would "spin it on the right side and double it on the left," then it was to be bound into fourteen knots and the incantation of Ea pronounced upon it, after which it was to be bound round the head and neck of the sick man. For defects in eyesight the Assyrians wove black and white threads or hairs together, muttering incantations the while, and these were placed upon the eyes. It was thought, too, that the tongues of evil spirits or sorcerers could be 'bound,' and that a net because of its many knots was efficacious in keeping evilly-disposed magicians away.

Omens

Divination as practised by means of augury was a rite of the first importance among the Babylonians and Assyrians. This was absolutely distinct from divination by astrology. The favourite method of augury among the Chaldeans of old was that by examination of the liver of a slaughtered animal. It was thought that when an animal was offered up in sacrifice to a god that the deity identified himself for the time being with that animal, and that the beast thus afforded a means of indicating the wishes of the god. Now among people in a primitive state of culture the soul is almost invariably supposed to reside in the liver instead of in the heart or brain. More blood is secreted by the liver than by any other organ in the body, and upon the opening of a carcase it appears the most striking, the most central, and the most sanguinary of the vital parts. The liver was, in fact, supposed by early peoples to be the fountain of the blood supply and therefore of life itself. Hepatoscopy or divination from the liver was undertaken by the Chaldeans for the purpose of determining what the gods had in mind. The soul of the animal became for the nonce the soul of the god, therefore if the signs of the liver of the sacrificed animal could be read the mind of the god became clear, and his intentions regarding the future were known. The animal usually sacrificed was a sheep, the liver of which animal is most complicated in appearance. The two lower lobes are sharply divided from one another and are separated from the upper by a narrow depression, and the whole surface is covered with markings and fissures, lines and curves which give it much the appearance of a map on which roads and valleys are outlined. This applies to the freshly excised liver only, and these markings are never the same in any two livers.

Certain priests were set apart for the practice of liver-reading, and these were exceedingly expert, being able to decipher the hepatoscopic signs with great skill. They first examined the gall-bladder, which might be reduced or swollen. They inferred various circumstances from the several ducts and the shapes and sizes of the lobes and their appendices. Diseases of the liver, too, particularly common among sheep in all countries, were even more frequent among these animals in the marshy portions of the Euphrates Valley.

The literature connected with this species of augury is very extensive, and Assur-bani-pal's library contained thousands of fragments describing the omens deduced from the practice. These enumerate the chief appearances of the liver, as the shade of the colour of the gall, the length of the ducts, and so forth. The lobes were divided into sections, lower, medial, and higher, and the interpretation varied from the phenomena therein observed. The markings on the liver possessed various names, such as 'palaces,' 'weapons,' 'paths,' and 'feet,' which terms remind us somewhat of the bizarre nomenclature of astrology. Later in the progress of the art the various combinations of signs came to be known so well, and there were so many cuneiform

Clay Object resembling a Sheep's Liver

This is inscribed with magical formulæ; it was probably used for purposes of divination, and was employed by the priests of Babylon in their ceremonies

Photo W. A. Mansell and Co.

THE RITUAL OF HEPATOSCOPY

texts in existence which afforded instruction in them, that a liver could be quickly 'read' by the *barû* or reader, a name which was afterward applied to the astrologists as well and to those who divined through various other natural phenomena.

One of the earliest instances on record of hepatoscopy is that regarding Naram-Sin, who consulted a sheep's liver before declaring war. The great Sargon did likewise, and we find Gudea applying to his 'liver inspectors' when attempting to discover a favourable time for laying the foundations of the temple of Nin-girsu. Throughout the whole history of the Babylonian monarchy in fact, from its early beginnings to its end, we find this system in vogue. Whether it was in force in Sumerian times we have no means of knowing, but there is every likelihood that such was the case.

The Ritual of Hepatoscopy

Quite an elaborate ritual grew up around the readings of the omens by the examination of the liver. The baru who officiated must first of all purify himself and don special apparel for the ceremony. Prayers were then offered up to Shamash and Hadad or Rammon, who were known as the 'lords of divination.' Specific questions were usually put. The sheep selected for sacrifice must be without blemish, and the manner of slaughtering it and the examination of its liver must be made with the most meticulous care. Sometimes the signs were doubtful, and upon such occasions a second sheep was sacrificed.

Nabonidus, the last King of Babylon, on one occasion desired to restore a temple to the moon-god at Harran. He wished to be certain that this step commended itself to Merodach, the chief deity of Babylonia, so he applied to the 'liver inspectors' of his day and found that the omen was favourable. We find him also desirous of making a certain symbol of the sun-god in accordance with an ancient pattern. He placed a model of this before Shamash and consulted the liver of a sheep to ascertain whether the god approved of the offering, but on three separate occasions the signs were unfavourable. Nabonidus then concluded that the model of the symbol could not have been correctly reproduced, and on replacing it by another he found the signs propitious. In order, however, that there should be no mistake he sought among the records of the past for the result of a liver inspection on a similar occasion, and by comparing the omens he became convinced that he was safe in making a symbol.

Peculiar signs, when they were found connected with events of importance, were specially noted in the literature of liver divination, and were handed down from generation to generation of diviners. Thus a number of omens are associated with Gilgamesh, the mythical hero of the Babylonian epic, and a certain condition of the gall-bladder is said to indicate "the omen of Urumush, the king, whom the men of his palace killed."

Bad signs and good signs are enumerated in the literature of the subject. Thus like most peoples the Babylonians considered the right side as lucky and the left as unlucky. Any sign on the right side of the gall-bladder, ducts or lobes, was supposed to refer to the king, the country, or the army, while a similar sign on the sinister side applied to the enemy. Thus a good sign on the right side applied to Babylonia or Assyria in a favourable sense, a bad sign on the right side in an unfavourable sense. A good sign on the left side was an omen favourable to the enemy, whereas a bad sign on the left side was, of course, to the native king or forces.

It would be out of place here to give a more extended description of the liver-reading of the ancient Chaldeans. Suffice it to say that the subject is a very complicated one in its deeper significance, and has little interest for the general reader in its advanced stages. Certain well-marked conditions of the liver could only indicate certain political, religious, or personal events. It will be more interesting if we attempt to visualise the act of divination by liver reading, as it was practised in ancient Babylonia, and if our imaginations break down in the process it is not the fault of the very large material they have to work upon.

The Missing Caravan

The ages roll back as a scroll, and I see myself as one of the great banker-merchants of Babylon, one of those princes of commerce whose contracts and agreements are found stamped upon clay cylinders where once the stately palaces of barter arose from the swarming streets of the city of Merodach. I have that morning been carried in my litter by sweating slaves, from my white house in a leafy suburb lying beneath the shadow of the lofty temple-city of Borsippa. As I reach my place of business I am aware of unrest, for the financial operations in which I engage are so closely watched that I may say without self-praise that I represent the pulse of Babylonian commerce. I enter the cool chamber where I usually transact my business, and where a pair of officious Persian slaves commence to fan me as soon as I take my seat. My head clerk enters and makes obeisance with an expression on his face eloquent of important news. It is as I expected—as I feared. The caravan from the Persian Gulf due to arrive at Babylon more than a week ago has not yet made its appearance, and although I had sent scouting parties as far as Ninnur, these have returned without bringing me the least intelligence regarding it.

I feel convinced that the caravan with my spices, woven fabrics, rare woods, and precious stones will never come tinkling down the great central street to deposit its wealth at the doors of my warehouses; and the thought renders me so irritable that I sharply dismiss the Persian fan-bearers, and curse again and again the black-browed sons of Elam, who have doubtless looted my goods and cut the throats of my guards and servants. I go home at an early hour full of my misfortune. I cannot eat my evening meal. My wife gently asks me what ails me, but with a growl I refuse to enlighten her upon the cause of my annoyance. Still, however, she persists, and succeeds in breaking down my surly opposition.

"Why trouble thy heart concerning this thing when thou mayest know what has happened to thy goods and thy servants? Get thee to-morrow to the Baru, and he will enlighten thee," she says.

I start. After all, women have sense. There can be no harm in seeing the Baru and asking him to divine what has happened to my caravan. But I bethink me that I am wealthy, and that the priests love to pluck a well-feathered pigeon. I mention my suspicions of the priestly caste in no measured terms, to the distress of my devout wife and the amusement of my soldier-son.

THE MISSING CARAVAN

Restlessly I toss upon my couch, and after a sleepless night feel that I cannot resume my business with the fear of loss upon me. So without breathing a word of my intention to my wife, I direct my litter-slaves to carry me to the great temple at Borsippa.

Arrived there, I enquire for the chief Baru. He is one of the friends of my youth, but for years our paths have diverged, and it is with surprise that he now greets me. I acquaint him with the nature of my dilemna, and nodding sympathetically he assures me that he will do his utmost to assist me. Somewhat reassured, I follow him into a tiled court near the far end of which stands a large altar. At a sign from him two priests bring in a live sheep and cut its throat. They then open the carcase and extract the liver. Immediately the chief Baru bends his grey head over it. For a long time he stares at it with the keenest attention. I begin to weary, and my old doubts regarding the sacerdotal caste return. At last the grey head rises from the long inspection, and the Baru turns to me with smiling face.

"The omen is good, my son," he says, with a cheerful intonation. "The compass and the hepatic duct are short. Thy path will be protected by thy Guardian Spirit, as will the path of thy servants. Go, and fear not."

He speaks so definitely and his words are so reassuring that I seize him by the hands, and, thanking him effusively, take my leave. I go down to my warehouses in a new spirit of hopefulness and disregard the disdainful or pitying looks cast in my direction. I sit unperturbed and dictate contracts and letters of credit to my scribe.

Ha! what is that? By Merodach, it is—it is the sound of bells! Up I leap, upsetting the wretched scribe who squats at my feet, and trampling upon his still wet clay tablets, I rush to the door. Down the street slowly advances a travel-worn caravan, and at the head of it there rides my trusty brown-faced captain, Babbar. He tumbles out of the saddle and kneels before me, but I raise him in a close embrace. All my goods, he assures me, are intact, and the cause of delay was a severe sickness which broke out among his followers. But all have recovered and my credit is restored.

As I turn to re-enter my warehouse with Babbar, a detaining hand is placed on my shoulder. It is a messenger from the chief Baru.

"My brother at the temple saw thy caravan coming from afar," he says politely, "and his message to thee, my son, is that, since thou hast so happily recovered thine own, thou shouldst devote a tithe of it to the service of the gods."

CHAPTER XI: THE MYTHOLOGICAL MONSTERS AND ANIMALS OF CHALDEA

TIAWATH was not the only monster known to Babylonian mythology. But she is sometimes likened to or confounded with the serpent of darkness with which she had originally no connexion whatever. This being was, however, like Tiawath, the offspring of the great deep and the enemy of the divine powers. We are told in the second verse of Genesis that " the earth was without form and void, and darkness was upon the face of the deep," and therefore resembling the abyss of Babylonian myth. We are also informed that the serpent was esteemed as " more subtle than other beast of the field," and this, it has been pointed out by Professor Sayce, was probably because it was associated by the author or authors of Genesis with Ea, the god of waters and of wisdom. To Babylonian geographers as to the Greeks, the ocean was a coiling, snake-like thing, which was often alluded to as the great serpent, and this soon came to be considered as the source of all evil and misfortune. The ancients, and especially the ancient Semites, with the exception of the Phœnicians, appear to have regarded it with dread and loathing. The serpent appears to have been called Aibu, 'the enemy.' We can see how the serpent of darkness, the offspring of chaos and confusion, became also the Hebrew symbol for mischief. He was first the source of physical and next the source of moral evil.

Winged Bulls

The winged bulls so closely identified with ancient Chaldean mythology were probably associated with

Merodach. These may have represented the original totemic forms of the gods in question, but we must not confound the bull forms of Merodach and Ea with those winged bulls which guarded the entrances to the temples. These, to perpetrate a double 'bull,' were not bulls at all but divine beings, the gods or genii of the holy places. The human head attached to them indicated that the creature was endowed with humanity and the bull-like body symbolized strength. When the Babylonian translated the word 'bull' from the Akkadian tongue he usually rendered it 'hero' or 'strong one.' It is thought that the bull forms of Ea and Merodach must have originated at Eridu, for both of these deities were connected with the city. The Babylonians regarded the sky-country as a double of the plain in which they dwelt, and they believed that the gods as planets ploughed their way across the azure fields of air. Thus the sun was the 'Bull of Light,' and Jupiter, the nearest of the planets to the ecliptic, was known as the 'Planet of the Bull of Light.'

The Dog in Babylonia

Strangely enough the dog was classed by the Babylonians as a monster animal and one to be despised and avoided. In a prayer against the powers of evil we read, " From the dog, the snake, the scorpion, the reptile, and whatever is baleful . . . may Merodach preserve us." We find that although the Babylonians possessed an excellent breed of dog they were not fond of depicting them either in painting or bas-relief. Dogs are seen illustrated in a bas-relief of Assur-bani-pal, and five clay figures of dogs now in the British Museum represent hounds which belonged to that monarch. The names of these

A DOG LEGEND

animals are very amusing, and appear to indicate that those who bestowed them must have suffered from a complete lack of the humorous sense, or else have been blessed with an overflow of it. Translated, the names are: 'He-ran-and-barked,' 'The-Producer-of-Mischief,' 'The-Biter-of-his-foes,' 'The-Judge-of-his-companions,' and 'The-Seizer-of-enemies.' How well these names would fit certain dogs we all know or have known! Here is good evidence from the buried centuries that dog nature like human nature has not changed a whit.

But why should the dog, fellow-hunter with early man and the companion of civilized humanity, have been regarded as evil? Professor Sayce considers that the four dogs of Merodach "were not always sent on errands of mercy, and that originally they had been devastating winds."

A Dog Legend

The fragment of a legend exists which does not exhibit the dog in any very favourable light.

Once there was a shepherd who was tormented by the constant assaults of dogs upon his flocks. He prayed to Ea for protection, and the great god of wisdom sent his son Merodach to reassure the shepherd.

"Ea has heard thee," said Merodach. "When the great dogs assault thee, then, O shepherd, seize them from behind and lay them down, hold them and overcome them. Strike their heads, pierce their breasts. They are gone; never may they return. With the wind may they go, with the storm above it! Take their road and cut off their going. Seize their mouths, seize their mouths, seize their weapons! Seize their teeth, and make them ascend, by the command of Ea, the lord of wisdom; by the command of Merodach, the lord of revelation."[1]

Gazelle and Goat Gods

The gazelle or antelope was a mythological animal in Babylonia so far as it represented Ea, who is entitled 'the princely gazelle' and 'the gazelle who gives the earth.' But this animal was also appropriated to Mul-lil, the god of Nippur, who was specially called the 'gazelle god.' It is likely, therefore, that this animal had been worshipped totemically at Nippur. Scores of early cylinders represent it being offered in sacrifice to a god, and bas-reliefs and other carvings show it reposing in the arms of various deities. The goat, too, seems to have been peculiarly sacred, and formed one of the signs of the zodiac. A god called Uz has for his name the Akkadian word for goat. Mr Hormuzd Rassam found a sculptured stone tablet in a temple of the sun-god at Sippara on which was an inscription to Sin, Shamash, and Ishtar, as being " set as companions at the approach to the deep in sight of the god Uz." This god Uz is depicted as sitting on a throne watching the revolution of the solar disc, which is placed upon a table and made to revolve by means of a rope or string. He is clad in a robe of goat-skin.

The Goat Cult

This cult of the goat appears to be of very ancient origin, and the strange thing is that it seems to have found its way into mediæval and even into modern magic and pseudo-religion. There is very little

[1] Sayce, *Hibbert Lectures*, p. 288 (by permission of Messrs Williams and Norgate).

THE GOAT CULT

doubt that it is the Baphomet of the knights-templar and the Sabbatic goat of the witchcraft of the Middle Ages. It seems almost certain that when the Crusaders sojourned in Asia-Minor they came into contact with the remains of the old Babylonian cult. When Philip the Fair of France arraigned them on a charge of heresy a great deal of curious evidence was extorted from them regarding the worship of an idol that they kept in their lodges. The real character of this they seemed unable to explain. It was said which the image was made in the likeness of 'Baphomet,' which name was said to be a corruption of Mahomet, the general Christian name at that period for a pagan idol, although others give a Greek derivation for the word. This figure was often described as possessing a goat's head and horns. That, too, the Sabbatic goat of the Middle Ages was of Eastern and probably Babylonian origin is scarcely to be doubted. At the witch orgies in France and elsewhere those who were afterwards brought to book for their sorceries declared that Satan appeared to them in the shape of a goat and that they worshipped him in this form. The Sabbatic meetings during the fifteenth century in the wood of Mofflaines, near Arras, had as their centre a goat-demon with a human countenance, and a like fiend was adored in Germany and in Scotland. From all this it is clear that the Sabbatic goat must have had some connexion with the East. Eliphas Levi drew a picture of the Baphomet or Sabbatic goat to accompany one of his occult works, and strangely enough the symbols that he adorns it with are peculiarly Oriental—moreover the sun-disc figures in the drawing. Now Levi knew nothing of Babylonian mythology, although he was moderately versed in the mythology of modern occultism, and it would seem that if he drew his information from modern or mediæval sources that these must have been in direct line from Babylonian lore.

Adar, the sun-god of Nippur, was in the same manner connected with the pig, which may have been the totem of the city he ruled over; and many other gods had attendant animals or birds, like the sun-god of Kis, whose symbol was the eagle.

Those monsters who had composed the host of Tiawath were supposed, after the defeat and destruction of their commandress, to have been hurled like Satan and his angels into the abyss beneath. We read of their confusion in four tablets of the creation epic. This legend seems to be the original source of the belief that those who rebelled against high heaven were thrust into outer darkness. In the Book of Enoch we read of a 'great abyss' regarding which an angel said to the prophet, "This is a place of the consummation of heaven and earth," and again, in a later chapter, "These are of the stars who have transgressed the command of God, the Highest, and are bound here till 10,000 worlds, the number of the days of their sins, shall have consummated . . . this is the prison of the angels, and here they are held to eternity." Eleven great monsters are spoken of by Babylonian myth as comprising the host of Tiawath, besides many lesser forms having the heads of men and the bodies of birds. Strangely enough we find these monsters figuring in a legend concerning an early Babylonian king.

The Invasion of the Monsters

The tablets upon which this legend was impressed were at first known as 'the Cuthæan legend of

THE INVASION OF THE MONSTERS

creation'—a misnomer, for this legend does not give an account of the creation of the world at all, but deals with the invasion of Babylonia by a race of monsters who were descended from the gods, and who waged war against the legendary king of the period for three years. The King tells the story himself. Unfortunately the first portions of both tablets containing the story are missing, and we plunge right away into a description of the dread beings who came upon the people of Babylonia in their multitudes. We are told that they preferred muddy water to clear water. These creatures, says the King, were without moral sense, glorying in their power, and slaughtering those whom they took captives. They had the bodies of birds and some of them had the faces of ravens. They had evidently been fostered by the gods in some inaccessible region, and, multiplying greatly, they came like a storm-cloud on the land, 360,000 in number. Their king was called Benini, their mother Melili, and their leader Memangab, who had six subordinates. The King, perplexed, knew not what to do. He was afraid that if he gave them battle he might in some way offend the gods, but at last through his priests he addressed the divine beings and made offerings of lambs in sacrifice to them. He received a favourable answer and decided to give battle to the invaders, against whom he sent an army of 120,000 men, but not one of these returned alive. Again he sent 90,000 warriors to meet them, but the same fate overtook these, and in the third year he despatched an army of nearly 70,000 troops, all of whom perished to a man. Then the unfortunate monarch broke down, and, groaning aloud, cried out that he had brought misfortune and destruction upon his realm. Nevertheless, rising from his lethargy of despair, he stated his intention to go forth against the enemy in his own person, saying, "The pride of this people of the night I will curse with death and destruction, with fear, terror, and famine, and with misery of every kind."

Before setting out to meet the foe he made offerings to the gods. The manner in which he overcame the invaders is by no means clear from the text, but it would seem that he annihilated them by means of a deluge. In the last portion of the legend the King exhorts his successors not to lose heart when in great peril but to take courage from his example.

He inscribed a tablet with his advice, which he placed in the shrine of Nergal in the city of Cuthah. "Strengthen thy wall," he said, "fill thy cisterns with water, bring in thy treasure-chests and thy corn and thy silver and all thy possessions." He also advises those of his descendants who are faced by similar conditions not to expose themselves needlessly to the enemy.

It was thought at one time that this legend applied to the circumstances of the creation, and that the speaker was the god Nergal, who was waging war against the brood of Tiawath. It was believed that, according to local conditions at Cuthah, Nergal would have taken the place of Merodach, but it has now been made clear that although the tablet was intended to be placed in the shrine of Nergal, the speaker was in reality an early Babylonian king.

The Eagle

As we have seen, the eagle was perhaps regarded as a symbol of the sun-god. A Babylonian fable tells how he quarrelled with the serpent and incurred

Eagle-headed Mythological Being
In the Louvre
Photo W. A. Mansell and Co.

the reptile's hatred. Feeling hungry he resolved to eat the serpent's young, and communicated his intention to his own family. One of his children advised him not to devour the serpent's brood, because if he did so he would incur the enmity of the god Shamash. But the eagle did not hearken to his offspring, and swooping down from heaven sought out the serpent's nest and devoured his young. On his arrival at home the serpent discovered his loss, and at once repaired in great indignation to Shamash, to whom he appealed for justice. His nest, he told the god, was set in a tree, and the eagle had swooped upon it, destroying it with his mighty wings and devouring the little serpents as they fell from it.

"Help, O Shamash!" cried the serpent. "Thy net is like unto the broad earth, thy snare is like unto the distant heaven in wideness. Who can escape thee?"

Shamash hearkening to his appeal, described to him how he might succeed in obtaining vengeance upon the eagle.

"Take the road," said he, "and go into the mountain and hide thyself in the dead body of a wild ox. Tear open its body, and all the birds of heaven shall swoop down upon it. The eagle shall come with the rest, and when he seeks for the best parts of the carcase, do thou seize him by his wing, tear off his wings, his pinions, and his claws, pull him in pieces and cast him into a pit. There may he die a death from hunger and thirst."

The serpent did as Shamash had bidden him. He soon came upon the body of a wild ox, into which he glided after opening up the carcase. Shortly afterwards he heard the beating of the wings of numberless birds, all of which swooped down and ate of the flesh. But the eagle suspected the purpose of the serpent and did not come with the rest, until greed and hunger prompted him to share in the feast.

"Come," said he to his children, "let us swoop down and let us also eat of the flesh of this wild ox."

Now the young eagle who had before dissuaded his father from devouring the serpent's young, again begged him to desist from his purpose.

"Have a care, O my father," he said, "for I am certain that the serpent lurks in yonder carcase for the purpose of destroying you."

But the eagle did not hearken to the warning of his child, but swooped on to the carcase of the wild ox. He so far obeyed the injunctions of his offspring, however, as closely to examine the dead ox for the purpose of discovering whether any trap lurked near it. Satisfied that all was well he commenced to feed upon it, when suddenly the serpent seized upon him and held him fast. The eagle at once began to plead for mercy, but the enraged reptile told him that an appeal to Shamash was irrevocable, and that if he did not punish the king of birds he himself would be punished by the god, and despite the eagle's further protests he tore off his wings and pinions, pulled him to pieces, and finally cast him into a pit, where he perished miserably as the god had decreed.

CHAPTER XII: TALES OF THE BABY-LONIAN AND ASSYRIAN KINGS

THE tales of the Babylonian and Assyrian kings which we present in this chapter are of value because they are taken at first hand from their own historical accounts of the great events which occurred during their several reigns. On a first examination these tablets appear dry and uninteresting, but when studied more closely and patiently they will be found to contain matter as absorbing as that in the most exciting annals of any country. Let us take for example the wonderful inscriptions of Tiglath-pileser II (950 B.C.) which refer to his various conquests, and which were discovered by George Smith at Nimrud in the temple of Nebo.

Tiglath commences with the usual Oriental flourish of trumpets. He styles himself the powerful warrior who, in the service of Asshur, has trampled upon his haters, swept over them like a flood, and reduced them to shadows. He has marched, he says, from the sea to the land of the rising sun, and from the sea of the setting sun to Egypt. He enumerates the countless lands that he has conquered. The cities Sarrapanu and Malilatu among others he took by storm and captured the inhabitants to the number of 150,000 men, women, and children, all of whom he sent to Assyria. Much tribute he received from the people of the conquered lands—gold, silver, precious stones, rare woods, and cattle. His custom seems to have been to make his successful generals rulers of the cities he conquered, and it is noticeable that upon a victory he invariably sacrificed to the gods. His methods appear to have been drastic in the extreme. Irritated at the defiance of the people of Sarrapanu he reduced it to a heap of earth, and crucified King Nabu-Usabi in front of the gate of his city. Not content with this vengeance, Tiglath carried off his wealth, his furniture, his wife, his son, his daughters, and lastly his gods, so that no trace of the wretched monarch's kingdom should remain. It is noticeable that throughout these campaigns Tiglath invariably sent the prisoners to Assyria, which shows at least that he considered human life as relatively sacred. Probably these captive people were reduced to slavery. The races of the neighbouring desert, too, came and prostrated themselves before the Assyrian hero, kissing his feet and bringing him tribute carried by sailors.

Tiglath then begins to boast about his gorgeous new residence with all the vulgarity of a *nouveau riche*. He says that his house was decorated like a Syrian palace for his glory. He built gates of ivory with planks of cedar, and seems to have had his prisoners, the conquered kings of Syria, on exhibition in the palace precincts. At the gates were gigantic lions and bulls of clever workmanship which he describes as " cunning, beautiful, valuable," and this place he called ' The Palaces of Rejoicing.'

In a fragment which relates the circumstances of his Eastern expeditions he tells how he built a city called Humur, and how he excavated the neighbouring river Patti, which had been filled up in the past, and along its bed led refreshing waters into certain of the cities he had conquered. He complains in one text that Sarduri, the King of Ararat, revolted against him along with others, but Tiglath captured his camp and Sarduri had perforce to escape upon a mare. Into the rugged mountains he rode by night

Capture of Sarrapanu by Tiglath-Pileser II
Evelyn Paul

and sought safety on their peaks. Later he took refuge with his warriors in the city of Turuspa. After a siege Tiglath succeeded in reducing the place. Afterwards he destroyed the land of Ararat, and made it a desert over an area of about 450 miles. Tiglath dedicated Sarduri's couch to Ishtar, and carried off his royal riding carriage, his seal, his necklace, his royal chariot, his mace, and lastly a 'great ship,' though we are not told how he accomplished this last feat.

Poet or Braggart?

It is strange to notice the inflated manner in which Tiglath speaks in these descriptions. He talks about people, races, and rulers 'sinning' against him as if he were a god, but it must be remembered that he, like other Assyrian monarchs, regarded himself as the representative of the gods upon earth. But though his language is at times boastful and absurd, yet on other occasions it is extremely beautiful and even poetic. In speaking of the tribute he received from various monarchs he says that he obtained from them "clothing of wool and linen, violet wool, royal treasures, the skins of sheep with fleece dyed in shining purple, birds of the sky with feathers of shining violet, horses, camels, and she-camels with their young ones."

He appears, too, to have been in conflict with a Queen of Sheba or Saba, one Samsi, whom he sent as a prisoner to Syria with her gods and all her possessions.

The Autobiography of Assur-bani-pal

In a former chapter we outlined the mythical history of Assur-bani-pal or Sardanapalus, and in this place may briefly review the story of his life as told in his inscriptions. He commences by stating that he is the child of Asshur and Beltis, but he evidently intends to convey that he is their son in a spiritual sense only, for he hastens to tell us that he is the "son of the great King of Riduti" (Esar-haddon). He proceeds to tell of his triumphal progress throughout Egypt, whose kings he made tributary to him. "Then," he remarks in a hurt manner, "the good I did to them they despised and their hearts devised evil. Seditious words they spoke and took evil counsel among themselves." In short, the kings of Egypt had entered into an alliance to free themselves from the yoke of Assurbani-pal, but his generals heard of the plot and captured several of the ringleaders in the midst of their work. They seized the royal conspirators and bound them in fetters of iron. The Assyrian generals then fell upon the populations of the revolting cities and cut off their inhabitants to a man, but they brought the rulers of Egypt to Nineveh into the presence of Assur-bani-pal. To do him justice that monarch treated Necho, who is described as 'King of Memphis and Sars,' with the utmost consideration, granting him a new covenant and placing upon him costly garments and ornaments of gold, bracelets of gold, a steel sword with a sheath of gold; with chariots, mules, and horses.

Dream of Gyges

Continuing, Assur-bani-pal recounts how Gyges, King of Lydia, a remote place of which his fathers had not heard the name, was granted a dream concerning the kingdom of Assyria by the god Asshur. Gyges was greatly impressed by the dream and sent to Assur-bani-pal to request his friendship, but having

DREAM OF GYGES

once sent an envoy to the Assyrian court Assur-bani-pal seemed to think that he should continue to do so regularly, and when he failed in this attention the Assyrian king prayed to Asshur to compass his discomfiture. Shortly afterwards the unhappy Gyges was overthrown by the Cimmerians, against whom Assur-bani-pal had often assisted him.

Assur-bani-pal then plaintively recounts how Saulmugina, his younger brother, conspired against him. This brother he had made King of Babylon, and after occupying the throne of that country for some time he set on foot a conspiracy to throw off the Assyrian yoke. A seer told Assur-bani-pal that he had had a dream in which the god Sin spoke to him, saying that he would overthrow and destroy Saulmugina and his fellow-conspirators. Assur-bani-pal marched against his brother, whom he overthrew. The people of Babylon, overtaken by famine, were forced to devour their own children, and in their agony they attacked Saulmugina and burned him to death with his goods, his treasures, and his wives. As we have before pointed out, this tale strangely enough closely resembles the legend concerning Assur-bani-pal himself. Swift was the vengeance of the Assyrian king upon those who remained. He cut out the tongues of some, while others were thrown into pits to be eaten by dogs, bears, and eagles. Then after fixing a tribute and setting governors over them he returned to Assyria. It is noticeable that Assur-bani-pal distinctly states that he 'fixed upon' the Babylonians the gods of Assyria, and this seems to show that Assyrian deities existed in contradistinction to those of Babylonia.

In one expedition into the land of Elam, Assur-bani-pal had a dream, sent by Ishtar to assure him that the crossing of the river Itite, which was in high flood, could be accomplished by his army in perfect safety. The warriors easily negotiated the crossing and inflicted great losses upon the enemy. Among other things they dragged the idol of Susinay from its sacred grove, and he remarks that it had never been beheld by any man in Elam. This with other idols he carried off to Assyria. He broke the winged lions which flanked the gates of the temple, dried up the drinking wells, and for a month and a day swept Elam to its utmost extent, so that neither man nor oxen nor trees could be found in it—nothing but the wild ass, the serpent, and the beast of the desert. The King goes on to say that the goddess Nanâ, who had dwelt in Elam for over 1600 years, had been desecrated by so doing. "That country," he declares, "was a place not suited to her. The return of her divinity she had trusted to me. 'Assur-bani-pal,' she said, 'bring me out from the midst of wicked Elam and cause me to enter the temple of Anna.'" The goddess then took the road to the temple of Anna at Erech, where the King raised to her an enduring sanctuary. Those chiefs who had trusted the Elamites now felt afflicted at heart and began to despair, and one of them, like Saul, begged his own armour-bearer to slay him, master and man killing each other. Assur-bani-pal refused to give his corpse burial, and cutting off its head hung it round the neck of Nabu-Quati-Zabat, one of the followers of Saulmugina, his rebellious brother. In another text Assur-bani-pal recounts in grandiloquent language how he built the temples of Asshur and Merodach.

"The great gods in their assembly my glorious renown have heard, and over the kings who dwell in palaces, the glory of my name they have raised and have exalted my kingdom.

Assur-bani-pal as Architect

"The temples of Assyria and Babylonia which Esar-haddon, King of Assyria, had begun, their foundations he had built, but had not finished their tops; anew I built them: I finished their tops.

"Sadi-rabu-matati (the great mountain of the earth), the temple of the god Assur my lord, completely I finished. Its chamber walls I adorned with gold and silver, great columns in it I fixed, and in its gate the productions of land and sea I placed. The god Assur into Sadi-rabu-matati I brought, and I raised him an everlasting sanctuary.

"Saggal, the temple of Merodach, lord of the gods, I built, I completed its decorations; Bel and Beltis, the divinities of Babylon and Ea, the divine judge from the temple of . . . I brought out, and placed them in the city of Babylon. Its noble sanctuary a great . . . with fifty talents of . . . its brickwork I finished, and raised over it. I caused to make a ceiling of sycamore, durable wood, beautiful as the stars of heaven, adorned with beaten gold. Over Merodach the great lord I rejoiced in heart, I did his will. A noble chariot, the carriage of Merodach, ruler of the gods, lord of lords, in gold, silver, and precious stones, I finished its workmanship. To Merodach, king of the whole of heaven and earth, destroyer of my enemies, as a gift I gave it.

"A couch of sycamore wood, for the sanctuary, covered with precious stones as ornaments, as the resting couch of Bel and Beltis, givers of favour, makers of friendship, skilfully I constructed. In the gate . . . the seat of Zirat-banit, which adorned the wall, I placed.

"Four bulls of silver, powerful, guarding my royal threshold, in the gate of the rising sun, in the greatest gate, in the gate of the temple Sidda, which is in the midst of Borsippa, I set up."[1]

A 'Likeable' Monarch

Esar-haddon, the father of Assur-bani-pal, has been called "the most likeable" of the Assyrian kings. He did not press his military conquests for the mere sake of glory, but in general for the maintenance of his own territory. He is notable as the restorer of Babu and the reviver of its culture. He showed much clemency to political offenders, and his court was the centre of literary activity. Assur-bani-pal, his son, speaks warmly of the sound education he received at his father's court, and to that education and its enlightening influences we now owe the priceless series of cylinders and inscriptions found in his library. He does not seem to have been able to control his rather turbulent neighbours, and he was actually weak enough (from the Assyrian point of view) to return the gods of the kingdom of Aribi after he had led them captive to Assyria. He seems to have been good-natured, enlightened, and easy-going, and if he did not boast so loudly as his son he had probably greater reason to do so.

One of the descendants of Assur-bani-pal, Bel-zakir-iskun, speaks of his restoration of certain temples, especially that of Nebo, and plaintively adds: "In after days, in the time of the kings my sons . . . When this house decays and becomes old who repairs its ruin and restores its decay? May he

[1] George Smith's translation. See his *Assyrian Discoveries*, p. 355 ff.

The Fatal Eclipse
(June 15, 763 B.C.)
M. Dovaston, R.B.A.

who does so see my name written on this inscription. May he enclose it in a receptacle, pour out a libation, and write my name with his own; but whoever defaces the writing of my name may the gods not establish him. May they curse and destroy his seed from the land." This is the last royal inscription of any length written in Assyria, and its almost prophetic terms seem to suggest that he who framed them must have foreseen the downfall of the civilization he represented. Does not the inscription almost foreshadow Shelley's wondrous sonnet on 'Ozymandias'?

> I met a traveller from an antique land
> Who said: Two vast and trunkless legs of stone
> Stand in the desert. Near them, on the sand,
> Half sunk, a shattered visage lies, whose frown,
> And wrinkled lip, and sneer of cold command,
> Tell that its sculptor well those passions read
> Which yet survive, stamped on these lifeless things,
> The hand that mocked them and the heart that fed;
> And on the pedestal these words appear:
> "My name is Ozymandias, king of kings:
> Look on my works, ye mighty, and despair!"
> Nothing beside remains. Round the decay
> Of that colossal wreck, boundless and bare,
> The lone and level sands stretch far away.

The Fatal Eclipse

The reign of Assur-Dan III (773–764 B.C.) supplies us with a picturesque incident. This Assyrian monarch had marched several times into Syria, and had fought the Chaldeans in Babylonia. Numerous were his tributary states and widespread his power. But disaster crept slowly upon him, and although he made repeated efforts to stave it off, these were quite in vain. Insurrection followed insurrection, and it would seem that the priests of

Babylon, considering themselves slighted, joined the malcontent party and assisted to foment discord. At the critical juncture of the fortunes of Assur-Dan there happened an eclipse of the sun, and as the black shadow crept over Nineveh and the King lay upon his couch and watched the gradual blotting out of the sunlight, he felt that his doom was upon him. After this direful portent he appears to have resisted no longer, but to have resigned himself to his fate. Within the year he was slain, and his rebel son, Adad-Narari IV, sat upon his murdered father's throne. But Nemesis followed upon the parricide's footsteps, for he in turn found a rebel in his son, and the land was smitten with a terrible pestilence.

Shalmaneser I (*c.* 1270) was cast in a martial and heroic mould, and an epic might arise from the legends of his conquests and military exploits. In his time Assyria possessed a superabundant population which required an outlet, and this the monarch deemed it his duty to supply. After conquering the provinces of Mitani to the west of the Euphrates, he attacked Babylonia, and so fiercely did he deal with his southern neighbours that we find him actually gathering the dust of their conquered cities and casting it to the four winds of heaven. Surely a more extreme manner of dealing summarily with a conquered enemy has never been recorded!

Although the life of the Babylonian or Assyrian king was lived in the full glare of publicity, he had not to encounter the same criticism as regards his actions that present-day monarchs must face, for the moral code of the peoples of Mesopotamia was fundamentally different from that which obtains at the present time. As the monarch was regarded

Shalmaneser I pouring out the Dust of a Conquered City
Ambrose Dudley
By permission of Messrs Hutchinson and Co.

A ROYAL DAY

as the vicegerent of the gods upon earth; it therefore followed that he could do no wrong. Submission to his will was complete. In the hands of a race of men who wielded this power unwisely it could have been nothing else but disastrous to both prince and people. But on the whole it may be said that the kings of this race bore themselves worthily according to their lights. If their sense of dignity at times amounted to bombast, that was because they were so full of their sense of delegated duty from above. There is every reason to believe that before entering upon their kingly state they had to undergo a most rigorous education, consisting of instruction upon religious subjects, some history, and the inculcation of moral precepts. On the other hand they were by no means mere puppets, for we find them initiating campaigns, presiding over courts of law, and framing the laws themselves and generally guiding the trend of the national policy. As a whole they were a strong and determined race, wise as well as warlike; and by no means unmindful of the requirements of their people. But with them the gods were first, and their reading of the initial duty of a king seems to have been the building of temples and the celebration of religious ceremonies of which a gorgeous and prolonged ritual was the especial feature.

A Royal 'Day'

A sketch of a day in the life of an Assyrian or Babylonian king may assist the reader to visualize the habits of royalty in a distant era. The ceremonies of robing and ablution upon rising would necessitate the attendance of numerous special officials, and, the morning repast over, a private religious ceremony would follow. The business of the court would supervene. Perhaps an embassy from Elam or Egypt would occupy the early hours of the morning, failing which the dictation of letters to the governors of provinces and cities or to distant potentates would be overtaken. As a scholar himself the King would probably carefully scrutinize these productions. A visit might then be paid to a temple in course of construction, where the architect would describe the progress of the building operations, and the King would watch the slow rising of shrine and tower; or, perhaps, the afternoon would be set apart for the pleasures of the chase. Leashes of great dogs, not unlike those of the Danish boarhound breed, would be gathered at a certain point, and setting out in a light but strong chariot, the King would soon arrive at that point where the beaters had assured themselves of the presence of gazelles, wild asses, or even lions. Matters would, of course, be so arranged that the chief glories of the day should be left with royalty. It is not clear whether the King was accompanied by his courtiers in the chase, as was the case in the Middle Ages, or if he was merely attended by professional huntsmen. Be that as it may, when the ceremony of pouring libations over the dead game came to be celebrated, we find no one except the King, the harpers, and professional huntsmen present, for the kings of this virile and warlike race did not disdain to face the lion unattended and armed with nothing but bow and arrows and a short falchion. Unless the inscriptions which they have left on record are altogether mendacious we must believe that many an Assyrian king risked his life in close combat with lions. Great risk attends lion-hunting when the sportsman is

The Marriage Market
From the painting by Edwin Long, R.A.
By permission of the Fine Art Society, Ltd.

A ROYAL DAY

armed with modern weapons of precision, but the risk attending a personal encounter with these savage animals when the hunter is armed with the most rudimentary weapons seems appalling, according to modern civilized ideas.

Or again the afternoon might be occupied by a great ceremonial religious function, the laying of the foundation-stone of a temple, the opening of a religious edifice, or the celebration of a festival. The King, attended by a glittering retinue of courtiers and priests, would be carried in a litter to the place of celebration where hymns to the god in whose honour the function was held were sung to the accompaniment of harps and other instruments, libations to the god were poured out, sacrifices offered up, and prayers made for continued protection.

The private life of an Assyrian or Babylonian king was probably not of a very comfortable order, surrounded as he was by sycophantic officials, spies in the pay of his enemies, schemers and office-seekers of all descriptions. As in most Oriental countries, the harem was the centre of intrigue and political unrest. Its occupants were usually princesses from foreign countries who had probably received injunctions on leaving their native lands to gain as much ascendancy over the monarch as possible for the purpose of swaying him in matters political. Many of these alliances were supposed to be made in the hope of maintaining peaceful relations between Mesopotamia and the surrounding countries, but there is little doubt that the numerous wives of a Mesopotamian king were only too often little better than spies whose office it was to report periodically to their relatives the condition of things in Babylon or Nineveh.

Slaves swarmed in the palaces, and these occupied a rather higher status than in some other countries. A slave who possessed good attainments and who was skilled in weaving, the making of unguents or preserves, was regarded as an asset. The slaves were a caste, but the laws regarding them were exact and not inhumane. They were usually sold by auction in the market-places of the large towns. A strange custom, too, is said by Herodotus to have obtained among the Babylonians in connexion with marriage. Every marriageable woman obtained a husband in the following manner: The most beautiful girls of marriageable age were put up to auction, and the large sums realized by their sale were given to the plainer young women as dowries, who, thus furnished with plentiful means, readily found husbands. The life of a Mesopotamian king was so hedged around by ceremonial as to leave little time for private pleasures. These, as in the case of Assur-bani-pal, sometimes took the form of literary or antiquarian amusements, but the more general form of relaxation seems to have been feasts or banquets at which the tables were well supplied with delicacies obtained from distant as well as neighbouring regions. Dancing and music, both furnished by a professional class, followed the repast, and during the evening the King might consult his soothsayers or astrologers as to some portent that had been related to him, or some dream he had experienced.

The royal lines of Mesopotamia seem to have been composed of men grave, sedate, and conscious of the authority which reposed in them. But few weaklings sat upon the thrones of Babylonia or Assyria, and those who did were not infrequently swept aside to make room for better men.

CHAPTER XIII: THE COMPARATIVE VALUE OF THE BABYLONIAN AND ASSYRIAN RELIGIONS

THE comparative value of the religions of Babylonia and Assyria is very high, as they represent Semitic polytheism in evolution, and in a state of prosperity, though hardly in decay. They are, in fact, typical of Semitic religion as a whole, and as the Semitic race initiated no less than three of the great religious systems of the world—Judaism, Christianity, and Mohammedanism—they are well worth careful study on the part of those who desire to specialize in religious science. It is, however, for a variety of reasons, inevitable that we should compare them most frequently with the religion of Israel, the faith that in general most resembled them, although a wide cleavage existed between the ethics of that system and their moral outlook. That notwithstanding, there was direct contact between the Babylonian and Jewish religions for a prolonged period, and the influence thus absorbed was quickened by racial relationship.

Ere we deal with these purely Semitic and racial resemblances which are so important for the proper comprehension of Biblical history and religious science in general, let us briefly compare the faith of Babylonia and Assyria with some of the great religious systems of the world. It perhaps more closely resembles the composite general Egyptian religious idea (one cannot speak of an Egyptian religion) than any other. But whereas in Egypt the deities had been almost universally evolved from nome or province-patrons, totemic or otherwise, a number often coalesced in one form, the gods of

MYTHS OF BABYLONIA AND ASSYRIA

Chaldea were usually city- or district-gods, showing much less of the nature of the departmental deity in their construction than the divinities of Egypt. The Egyptian god-type was more exact and explicit. We have seldom much difficulty in discovering the nature of an Egyptian god. We have frequently, however, immense trouble in finding out for what a Mesopotamian deity stands. The Babylon-Assyrian idea of godhead appears to have been principally astral, terrestrial, or aquatic—that is, most Babylonian-Assyrian deities are connected either with the heavenly bodies, the earth, or the waters. It is only as an afterthought that they become gods of justice, of letters, of the underworld. This statement must of course be taken as meaning that their connexion with abstract qualities is much more loose than in the case of the Egyptian gods—that their departmental character is secondary to their original character as gods of nature. There is only one exception to this, and that is to be found in the department of war, to which certain of them appear to have been relegated at an early period and later to have become identified with it very closely indeed.

In one circumstance the Babylonian-Assyrian religion closely resembled the Egyptian, and that was the lasting effect wrought upon it by priestly cults and theological schools. Just as the priests of Thebes and Memphis and On moulded the varying cults of Egypt, added to their mythology, and read into them ethical significance, so did the priests of Nippur and Erech mould and form the faith of Babylon. We have plenty of evidence for such a statement, and nowhere perhaps was theological thought so rife in the ancient world as in Babylonia and Egypt.

There are also points of contact with the great

COMPARATIVE VALUE OF RELIGIONS

mythological system of Greece, that system which was so much a mythology that it could scarcely be called a religion. That Greece borrowed largely from Mesopotamia is not to be doubted, but we find the Hellenic departmental deities very explicit indeed in their nature. Pallas, for example, stands for wisdom, Poseidon for the sea, Ares for war, and so forth. One god usually possesses one attribute, and although Zeus has a number of minor attributes we do not find him combining in his one person so many as does Merodach. As has been said, it would seem that the departmental character of many Babylonian gods was purely accidental or fortuitous. The formula seems to run—take a local or city god, probably derived from totemic sources or perhaps of animistic origin, and, having conquered much surrounding territory, exalt him to the position of the god of a large region, which, being incorporated again with a still larger empire, leaves him only a local status. This status he cannot hold in a pantheon where each member must possess a specific attribute, therefore it becomes necessary to impose upon him some quality by which he can be specially recognized. Sometimes that quality is suitable to his character, in fact it may be indicated by it, but at other times it is merely arbitrary. Why, for example, should Ishtar have been made a goddess of war by the Assyrians?

This bestowal of departmental characteristics upon the gods of Babylonia and Assyria was contemporary with the erection of these countries into empires. No pantheon can exist on high without a political reflex in the world below. Like the granting of most departmental offices in religious systems, these changes took place at a comparatively late date in the evolution of Semitic religion. Whenever we find the departmental deities of a religious system more or less sharply outlined as to their duties and status we may premise two things: first, that temporal power has been acquired by the race which conceived them, and secondly that this power is of comparatively recent origin.

Semitic Conservatism

When we speak of departmental deities of a country like Babylonia or Egypt we must bear in mind that these lands knew so many dynasties and had such an extended history that their religious systems must from first to last have experienced the most profound changes. In Egypt, for example, religious phenomena altered slowly and by imperceptible degrees. The changes experienced in the course of fifty centuries of religious evolution must have made the cults of Egypt exhibit very different conditions at the close of their development from, let us say, those seen midway in their evolutionary course. We have seen how the Babylonian and Assyrian faiths altered in the course of generations, but withal there appears to have been something more strongly conservative in the nature of Semitic religion than in any other. Probably in no other land did the same ritual and the same religious practices obtain over so long a period as in Babylonia, where the national life was much stronger and much more centralized than in Egypt, and where, if rival cults did exist, they were all subservient to one, as was by no means the case in the land of the Nile.

Teutonic and Celtic Comparisons

Compared with the great Germanic religion the Babylonian offers few points of resemblance. In the faith of the Teutons departmental deities were the rule rather than the exception; in fact in no mythic system are the gods so associated with departments as in the Teutonic, and this despite the fact that no definite empire was ruled by Teutonic tribes. (Was the Teutonic system the remains of a religious aristocracy which had hived off from some centre of political power?) Nor do the Semitic religions have much in common with the Celtic so far as their basis of polity is concerned, although numerous valiant attempts have been made by antiquarian gentlemen, of the type so common half a century ago and not yet defunct, to prove Babylonian influence upon Celtic faith and story. Thus we have been told that the Celtic Bilé was as certainly allied to the Semitic Bel as the Roman Mars was to the Greek Ares, and this of course through Phœnician influence, the people of Tyre and Sidon having been traced to Ireland as colonists. These 'theories' are, of course, not worth the paper they are printed upon, any more than is the supposition that the Scottish-Celtic festival of Beltane has any connexion with the Babylonian Bel. It was, in fact, presided over by the god Bilé, a Celtic deity who has on other counts been confounded with the Babylonian god.

Babylonian Religion Typically Animistic

We learn, then, from the comparison of the Babylonian religion with that of other ancient races one circumstance of outstanding importance, that is, if the Babylonian gods were so perfunctorily attached to departments expressive of their functions and were so closely bound to the elements that they must have had an elemental origin, that they were indeed originally spirits of the earth, the air, and the water.

This, of course, is no new conclusion, only the circumstance that the Babylonian gods were not strictly departmental, that they have only a slight hold upon their offices, assists in proving the correctness of the theory of their elemental origin. It is also of interest to the student of comparative religion as indicating to him a mythological system in which the majority of the gods are certainly of elemental origin as opposed to totemic or fetishistic origin. Of the spiritistic nature of the Babylonian pantheon small doubt remains. To the Semite, in whom imagination and matter-of-fact are so strongly combined, animistic influences would be sure to appeal most strongly. It stands to primitive reason that if man is gifted with life so is everything else, and this conviction gives imagination full play. We do not discover these animistic influences so strongly entrenched in ancient Egypt. The Osirian cult is certainly animistic to a degree, but the various totemic cults which rivalled it and which it at last embraced held their own for many a day.

A Mother-Goddess Theory

One outstanding feature of Babylonian religion is the worship of the great earth-mother. This is a universal religious phase, but in few systems do we find it so prominent as in Babylonia and indeed in the whole Mesopotamian tract. Efforts have been made to show that in Mesopotamia there encountered one another two streams of people of opposing worship, one worshipping a male, and the other a female deity. With those who worshipped the man-god—hunters and warriors with whom women were considered more as beasts of burden than anything else—man was the superior being.

A Royal Hunt
(See page 310)
Photo W. A. Mansell and Co.

INFLUENCE ON JEWISH RELIGION

The other people who worshipped the woman-god were not necessarily more civilized; the origin of their adoration may have been a scarcity of women in the tribe. Where these two streams fused the worship of an *androgyne*, or man-woman god, is said to have resulted. But were there peoples who specifically and separately worshipped male and female deities? If certainty can be approached in debating such matters, these deities would assuredly be animistic, and a people who worship animistic gods do not worship one god or one sex, but scores of spirit-gods of both sexes. Wherever we find a mother-earth, too, we are almost certain to discover a father-sky. The cult of the great mother-goddess was of rather later origin. All localities and all regions in the Semitic world possessed such a deity and it was the fusion of these in one that produced Ishtar or Astarte, who was probably also the 'Diana of the Ephesians.' Perhaps the best parallel to this Semitic worship of the earth-mother is to be found in the mythology of the ancient Mexican races, where each pueblo, or city-state, possessed its earth-mother, several of whom were finally merged, after the conquest of their worshippers, in the great earth-mother of Mexico.

Babylonian Influence on Jewish Religion

But Babylonian-Assyrian religion is chiefly of interest to the student of comparative religion in that it casts a flood of light upon that wonderful Jewish faith with which the history of our own is so closely identified.

Professor Sayce [1] writes:

"There was one nation at all events which has

---

[1] *Hibbert Lectures*, pp. 38 ff. (by permission of Messrs Williams and Norgate).

exercised, and still exercises, a considerable influence upon our own thought and life, and which had been brought into close contact with the religion and culture of Babylonia at a critical epoch in its history. The influence of Jewish religion upon Christianity, and consequently upon the races that have been moulded by Christianity, has been lasting and profound. Now Jewish religion was intimately bound up with Jewish history, more intimately perhaps than has been the case with any other great religion of the world. It took its colouring from the events that marked the political life of the Hebrew people; it developed in unison with their struggles and successes, their trials and disappointments. Its great devotional utterance, the Book of Psalms, is national, not individual; the individual in it has merged his own aspirations and sufferings into those of the whole community. The course of Jewish prophecy is equally stamped with the impress of the national fortunes. It grows clearer and more catholic as the intercourse of the Jewish people with those around them becomes wider; and the lesson is taught at last that the God of the Jews is the God also of the whole world. Now the chosen instruments for enforcing this lesson, as we are expressly told, were the Assyrian and Babylonian. The Assyrian was the rod of God's anger, while the Babylonish exile was the bitter punishment meted out to Judah for its sins. The captives who returned again to their own land came back with changed hearts and purified minds; from henceforth Jerusalem was to be the unrivalled dwelling-place of 'the righteous nation which keepeth the truth.'

"Apart, therefore, from any influence which the old religious beliefs of Babylonia may have had upon the Greeks, and which, as we shall see, was not so wholly wanting as was formerly imagined, their contact with the religious conceptions of the Jewish exiles must, to say the least, have produced an effect which it is well worth our while to study. Hitherto the traditional view has been that this effect exhibited itself wholly on the antagonistic side; the Jews carried nothing away from the land of their captivity except an intense hatred of idolatry, more especially Babylonian, as well as of the beliefs and practices associated therewith."

Professor Ignatius Goldziher, of Budapest, has enlightened us, in a passage in his *Mythology among the Hebrews*, as to the great influence wielded by Babylonian upon Jewish religion. He says: " The receptive tendency of the Hebrew manifested itself again prominently during the Babylonian Captivity. Here first they gained an opportunity of forming for themselves a complete and harmonious conception of the world. The influence of Canaanitish civilization could not then be particularly powerful on the Hebrews; for that civilization, the highest point of which was attained by the Phœnicians, was quite dwarfed by the mental activity exhibited in the monuments of the Babylonian and Assyrian Empire, which we are now able to admire in all their grandeur. There the Hebrews found more to receive than some few civil, political, and religious institutions. The extensive and manifold literature which they found there could not but act on a receptive mind as a powerful stimulus; for it is not to be imagined that the nation then dragged into captivity lived so long in the Babylonian-Assyrian Empire without gaining any knowledge of its intellectual treasures. Schrader's latest publications on Assyrian poetry have enabled us to establish a striking similarity between both the course of ideas and the poetical form of a considerable portion of the Old Testament, especially of the Psalms, and those of this newly-discovered Assyrian poetry. It would be a great mistake to account for this similarity by reference to a common Semitic origin in primeval times; for we can only resort to that in cases which do not go beyond the most primitive elements of intellectual life and ideas of the world, or designations of things of the external world. Conceptions of a higher and more complicated kind, as well as æsthetic points, can certainly not be carried off into the mists of a prehistoric age. It is much better to keep to more real and tangible ground, and to suppose those points of contact between Hebrew and Assyrian poetry which are revealed by Schrader's, Lenormant's, and George Smith's publications, to form part of the contributions made by the highly civilized Babylonians and Assyrians to the Hebrews in the course of the important period of the Captivity.

"We see from this that the intellect of Babylon and Assyria exerted a more than passing influence on that of the Hebrews, not merely touching it, but entering deep into it and leaving its own impress upon it. The Assyrian poetry of the kind just mentioned stands in the same relation to that of the Hebrews as does the plain narrative texts of the Hebrews, and as does the sacrificial Tablet of Marseilles to the Hebrews' beginnings of a sacerdotal constitution. The Babylonian and Assyrian influence is of course much more extensive, pregnant, and noteworthy."

The Abbé Loisy in a French work, *Les myths babyloniens, et les premiers chapitres de la Genèse*

INFLUENCE ON JEWISH RELIGION

(Paris, 1901), says a few things upon Jewish and Babylonian mythical relations worth translating:

"We can no longer take the first eleven or twelve chapters of Genesis as a whole and treat them as a monotheistic redaction of the Babylonian myths. . . . The Biblical accounts are not mere transcriptions . . . and the gaps between them presuppose much assimilation and transformation, much time, and probably many intermediaries to boot. . . . If the relationship of the Biblical narratives to the Chaldean legends is in many respects less intimate than was thought, it now appears to be more general. The Creation, and the Flood in particular, are still the most obvious points of resemblance; but the story of Adam and Eve, the earthly paradise, the food of life, the explanation of death,—all of which have sometimes been sought where they were not to be found,—are now found where there was no thought of seeking them. . . . The Biblical texts have no literary dependence upon the Babylonian texts; they do not even stand to them in a relation of direct dependence in the case of the special traditions they exhibit: but they rest on a similar—we might say a common—foundation, of Chaldean origin, whose antiquity cannot be even approximately estimated. . . . On the other hand, it appears certain that the period of Assyrian dominance, and the Captivity, quickened the recollection of the old traditions and supplemented them by fresh materials easy to graft on the ancient stem. . . . We may well believe that the metamorphosis was complete in the oral tradition of the people before the legend was embodied in the Biblical narrative."

MYTHS OF BABYLONIA AND ASSYRIA

Babylonian Influence upon the other Semites

The influence of the Babylonian religion upon other Semitic cults is worthy of notice, although its effect upon the Jewish faith was more marked than on any other Semitic form of belief. Yet still through conquest and other causes it undoubtedly exercised a strong influence upon the surrounding peoples, especially those of related stock. We must regard the whole of Asia Minor, or at least its most civilized portion, as peopled by races of diverse origin who yet possessed a general culture in common. Some of those races, if we be permitted to employ rather time-worn ethnological labels, were 'Semitic,' like the Assyrians and Hebrews, others were of the 'Ural-Altaic' or 'Armenoid' type, like the Hittites, whilst still others, like the Philistines, appear to have been of 'Aryan' race, resembling the Greeks and Goths. But all these different races had embraced a common culture, their architecture, pottery, weapons, crafts, and laws seem to have come from a common source, and lastly their religious systems were markedly alike.

The Canaanites

We find a people called the Canaanites as the first historic dwellers in the countries now known as Syria and Palestine. We do not know whether the name Canaan originated with the land or the race, but the name 'Canaanites' is now used as a general designation of the pre-Israelite inhabitants of Palestine. These people were probably neolithic in origin and appeared to have been Semitic. In any case they spoke a language very much akin to Hebrew. They exercised a strong influence upon Egypt about 1400 B.C., and thousands of them settled in that

THE CANAANITES

country as slaves or officials. They invaded Babylonia at an early date under the name of Amorites, and many of the personal names of Babylonian kings during the Hammurabi dynasty seem to be Amorite in origin. From the Egyptian records it seems pretty clear that as early as 2500 B.C. they had invaded Palestine, had exterminated the inhabitants, and that this invasion synchronized with that of Babylonia. Their religion seems to have been markedly Semitic in type but of the earlier variety, that is, animism was just beginning to emerge into polytheism. The gods were not called by their personal names, but rather by their attributes. The general name for 'god' was '*el*,' which was used also by the Hebrews, and which we find in such names as Jezebel, Elkanah, and perhaps in the modern Arabic 'Allah.' But this word was not employed by the Canaanites in a monotheistic sense, it was generic and denoted the particular divinity who dwelt in a certain place. It was indeed the word 'god'—a god, any god, but not *the* God. But such a god having a sanctuary or presiding over a community was known as '*Ba'al*.' This might apply to any supernatural being from fetish to full-fledged deity, and only meant that the spirit or divinity had established a relation with a particular holy place.

We also find amongst the Canaanitish deities Shamash, the sun-god so widely worshipped in Babylonia, Sin the moon-god, Hadad or Rimmon, and Uru, god of light, whose name is found in Uru-Salim or Jerusalem. Dagon, too, is held by some authorities to have been purely an Amorite divinity. The worship of animals was also general, and bulls, horses, and serpents were represented as deities. There were also an immense number of nameless gods or spirits presiding over all sorts of physical objects, and these were known as *ba'alim*. They were the resultants of animistic ideas. The early inhabitants of Canaan were also ancestor-worshippers like many other primitive people, and they seem to have shown a marked preference for the cult of the dead.

But many of their departmental deities were either identical with or strongly resembled the gods of the Babylonians. Ashtart was of course Ishtar. In the mounds of Palestine large numbers of terra cotta plaques bearing her effigy are found. She is often depicted on these with a tall head-dress, necklace, anklets, and girdle quite in the Babylonian style. But other representations of her reveal Egyptian, Cypriote, and Hittite influences, and this goes to show that in all probability the great mother-goddess of Babylon and Asia Minor was compounded of various early types fused into one. To confine ourselves to those deities who are more closely connected with the Babylonian religion, we find the name of Ninib translated by the Canaanites as En-Mashti, and it has been thought that Ninib was a god of the West who had migrated to Babylonia. The name of Nebo, the Babylonian patron of Borsippa, who also acted as scribe to the gods, appears in that of the town of Nebo in Moab in Judea, and that Canaanites were conversant with the name of Nergal, the war-god, is proved by a sealed cylinder of Canaanitish workmanship which bears the inscription, "Atanaheli, son of Habsi servant of Nergal." Resheph also appears to have been known to the Canaanites.

The Gods of the Phœnicians

The Phœnicians who were the lineal descendants of the Canaanites adopted many of the deities of

Elijah prevailing over the Priests of Baal
Evelyn Paul

THE GODS OF THE PHŒNICIANS

Babylonia. Like the early deities of that great empire, the Phœnician gods were associated either with the earth, the waters, or the air. Some of these in later times held sway over more than one element. Thus the god Melkarth of Tyre had both a celestial and a marine aspect, and Baal and Ashtart assumed celestial attributes in addition to their earthly one. The Phœnicians described their gods in general as *alônim*, much as the Israelites in early times must have described theirs, for we find in the first chapters of Genesis the word *elohim* employed. Both then went back to the singular form *el*, the common Semitic name for 'god,' adding to it the Semitic plural ending *im*. The god of a locality or shrine was known as its '*ba'al*,' and, as in early times, this did not apply to any particular deity. Although their gods all had names, yet still they were merely the *ba-alim* of Tyre, the chief of whom was Melkarth, whose name signifies merely 'king' or patron of the city. Perhaps one of their most venerated gods was Ba'al-Hamman, who was also worshipped in Carthage, a Phœnician colony. One of the most strongly marked characteristics of the Phœnician religion was the unvarying addition of a female to every male god. Ashtart or Ishtar was quite as popular in modern Phœnicia as she has been in ancient Canaan. It must be borne in mind that Tyre and Sidon were closely in touch with Assyria, and that their ships probably carried Assyrian commerce far and wide throughout the Mediterranean, exchanging Syrian goods for Egyptian, Cyprian, and Hellenic. Ashtart or Ishtar had temples at Sidon and Askelon, and Phœnician mariners seem to have carried her worship as far as Cyprus and even Sicily. Indeed it was probably through their agency that she was introduced into the Greek world, but there were Greek colonies on the shores of Asia Minor at an early date, and these may have transferred her cult to the people of their own race in the Greek motherland. Another goddess specially honoured at Carthage was Tanith, who was also called the 'Countenance of Ba'al.' Eshmun, the god of vital force and healing, seems to have been worshipped especially at Sidon but also at Carthage. Melkarth, the patron deity of Tyre, the Greeks equated with their Heracles; Reshef, the lightning god, was of Syrian origin, and was identified by the Greeks with Apollo. The Phœnicians were also prone to fuse their gods one with another, so that we have such combinations as Eshmun-Melkarth, Melkarth-Reshef, and so forth. Phœnician religion was also strongly influenced by Egyptian ideas, and Plutarch has put it on record that when Isis journeyed to Byblus she was called Astarte. Certain Phœnician settlers at Piræus, the port of Athens, worshipped the Assyrian god Nergal, and many of their proper names are compounded of the names of Babylon deities. The worship of Moloch was also popular in Phœnicia, where he was called Melk ('King'), and to him, as to the Moloch of the other Semitic peoples, infants were offered up in sacrifice. The Phœnicians likewise adopted the custom of burning the chief god of the city in effigy or in the person of a human representative at Tyre and Carthage. (See remarks on Hamman, pages 142-144; and on Sardanapalus, pages 31-34.)

We know very little concerning Phœnician myth. We cannot credit what is written by Philo of Byblus concerning it, as he professed that he had used as his authority the writings of one Sanchuniathon, an

THE CARTHAGINIAN RELIGION

ancient Phœnician sage, who, he says, derived his information from inscribed stones in Phœnician temples. All of Philo that remains (and thus all of Sanchuniathon) is preserved in the works of Eusebius. It would seem, however, to be unfair to regard Eusebius as the inventor of Sanchuniathon. As we have already remarked in the paragraphs dealing with the legend of Oannes or Ea, several of the myths he quotes as coming from the Phœnician sage are manifestly of Babylonian origin.

Like all Semites the Phœnicians closely identified themselves with their gods, in whom, if inscriptions can be believed, they seemed to find a great deal of comfort. They were assiduous devotees of their several cults, and as prone to sacrifice as were their cousins of Babylonia. Probably, too, their voyages and mercantile ventures made them firm believers in the efficacy of divination, and it cannot be doubted that the trade of the seer in ancient Tyre or Sidon must have been a flourishing one indeed.

The Carthaginian Religion

Very little is known concerning the religion of the Semites of Carthage, those colonists from Phœnicia who settled on the north-western shores of Africa at an early date, and this is probably owing to the circumstance that the jealousy of their Roman conquerors ordained that all records pertaining to them should so far as possible be blotted out. In Virgil's *Æneid* we find Queen Dido of Carthage worshipping and sacrificing to the gods of Rome, but whether this error is due to Roman lack of imagination or otherwise it would be difficult to say. Carthaginian religion was strongly influenced by Assyrian belief. The chief gods worshipped in

Carthage were Baal-ammon or Moloch, Tanit, goddess of the heavens and the moon, Ashtart or Ishtar, and Eshmun, the patron deity of the city. The cult of Tammuz-Adonis was also greatly in vogue, as was that of the god Patechus, a repulsive monster who may have been of Eygptian origin. The Tyrian Melkarth, too, was widely worshipped. We also encounter in inscriptions the names of deities concerning whom we know nothing, such as Rabbat Umma, 'the Great Mother,' Illat, Sakon, and Tsaphon.

About the beginning of the third century B.C. the intimate relations between the Carthaginians and the Greeks of Sicily favoured the introduction of a Hellenic element into the Punic religion, and there was reciprocal borrowing on the part of the Greeks. In the forum of Carthage was a temple to Apollo containing a colossal statue which was later removed to Rome, and on one occasion the Carthaginian worshippers of Apollo actually sent offerings to Delphi. We also find their goddess Tanit compared with the Greek Demeter. Her symbol is a crescent moon, and in her temple at Carthage was preserved a famous veil which was regarded as the palladium or 'mascot' of the city, its luck-bringer. Inscriptions to Tanit and Baal-ammon abound, and as these are usually found in conjunction it is only reasonable to suppose that these two deities are worshipped together. Tanit was, in fact, frequently alluded to as 'The Countenance of Baal,' whose name we find in those of the Carthaginian heroes, Hannibal and Hasdrubal. The Carthaginian Baal-ammon is represented as an old man with ram's horns on his forehead, and that animal was frequently portrayed along with him.

THE CARTHAGINIAN RELIGION

He also holds a scythe. At Carthage children were sacrificed to him, and their bodies were placed in the arms of a colossal bronze statue which represented him. When they grew tired they slipped through the embrace of the god into a furnace below amid the excited cries of the fanatical worshippers. Even Roman severity could not put an end to these horrors, which persisted in secret until a relatively late date.

It is strange to think that after the fall of Carthage the goddess Tanit became identified with Dido by the new Roman colonists of the city. Virgil had celebrated her misfortunes, and a public Dido cult grew up, the colonists even claiming to have discovered the very house from which she had watched the departure of Æneas.

It is not unlikely that through the agency of the Phœnicians some fragments of the Babylonian religion may have penetrated even to our own shores. We know that they traded for tin with the ancient inhabitants of Cornwall and the Scilly Isles, and some writers believe they have philology on their side when they try to show that several Cornish names are of Phœnician origin. For example, the name Marazion appears to mean in Semitic 'Hill by the Sea,' and Polgarth, say some, owes its second syllable to the Phœnician word for 'city.' But it will not do to be dogmatic regarding these names, which may after all be explicable from Cornish or other sources.

We see then that the Semitic religion travelled over a considerably wide area, that beginning in all probability in Arabia it spread itself through Mesopotamia northward as far as Lake Van, and southward through the Sinaitic peninsula into Egypt and the north of Africa. It is strange to observe that the later Semitic religion of Mohammed followed almost precisely the same course, and that its early progress westward halted almost on the very site of ancient Carthage; that when it overflowed into Spain its disciples were acting precisely as Carthaginian Hannibal had done long before, and that it was beaten back by European effort in almost exactly the same way

Robertson Smith in his valuable work, *The Religion of the Semites*, mentions that in his view Semitic religion does not differ so fundamentally from the other types of world religion as many writers on the subject appear to think. But the longer one considers it the greater do the barriers between Semitic and other religions appear and the more clearly marked their lines of demarcation. The prolonged isolation to which the Semitic peoples seem to have been subjected appears to have greatly affected their manner of religious thought. They are in truth a 'peculiar people,' practical yet mystical, strongly of the world yet finding their chief solace in those things which are not of the world.

The materials for a complete inquiry into the history of Semitic religion are lacking, and we must perforce fill up the gaps which are many by comparative methods. But in this we are greatly assisted by the numerous manifestations of Semitic faith which, including as it does Babylonian, Assyrian, Canaanitish, Phœnician, Arabian, and Mohammedan cults, provides us with rich comparative material.

The Religion of Zoroaster

The faith which immediately supplanted that of ancient Babylonia and Assyria could not fail to draw considerably from it. This was the Zoroastrian

THE RELIGION OF ZOROASTER

faith, the religion of the Persians introduced by the reformer Zarathustra, the earliest form of Zoroaster's name as given in the *Avesta*. Uncertainty hangs over the date and place of his birth. The Greeks spoke of him as belonging to a remote age, but modern scholars assign the period of his life to the latter half of the seventh and early sixth century B.C. It seems certain that he was not a Persian, but a Mede or a Bactrian, either supposition being supported by indications of one kind or another. From the whole tenor of the Gathas, the most ancient part of the *Avesta*, we are led, says Dr. Haug, their translator, to feel that he was a man of extraordinary stamp acting a grand part on the stage of his country's history. Zarathustra speaks of himself as a messenger from God sent to bring the people the blessing of civilization and to destroy idolatry. Many legends grew up around his memory, of miraculous signs at his birth, of his precocious wisdom, whereby even as a child he confounded the Magi, of his being borne up to the highest heaven and there receiving the word of life from Deity itself, together with the revelation of all secrets of the future. He retired as a young man from the world to spend long years of contemplation before he began his teaching at thirty, and he lived to the age of seventy-seven. The religion he taught was the national religion of the Persians from the time of the Achæmenidæ, who dethroned Cyaxares' son, 558 B.C., to the middle of the seventh century A.D. It declined after Alexander's conquest under the Seleucidæ and the succeeding dynasty of the Arsacidæ, but was revived by the Sassanian rulers and flourished for the four centuries A.D. 226-651. Then followed the Mohammedan conquest, accompanied by persecution, before which the faithful followers of Zarathustra fled to India, where they are now represented by their descendants, the Parsis of Bombay.

The religious belief taught by Zarathustra is based on the dual conception of a good principle, Ahura Mazda, and an evil principle, Anra Mainyu, and the leading idea of his teaching is the constant conflict between the two, which must continue until the end of the period ordained by Ahura Mazda for the duration of the world, when evil will be finally overcome; until then the god's power is to some degree limited, as evil still withstands him. Zarathustra's doctrine was essentially practical and ethical; it was not in abstract contemplation, or in separation from the world, that man was to look for spiritual deliverance, but in active charity, in deeds of usefulness, in kindness to animals, in everything that could help to make the world a well-ordered place to live in, in courage and all uprightness. To build a bridge or dig a canal was to help to lessen the power of evil. As Reinach has concisely expressed it, "a life thoroughly occupied was a perpetual exorcism."

The two figures of Ahura Mazda and Anra Mainyu, the one with his attendant archangels and angels, and the other with his arch-demons and demons, or Divs, compose the Zarathustrian celestial hierarchy, as represented in the earlier sacred writings; in the later ones other figures are introduced into the pantheon. The sacred writings that have been preserved are of different periods, and outside the range of Zarathustra's moral system of religion there are traces in them of revivals of an older primitive nature worship, and of the beliefs of an early nomadic shepherd life, as, for instance, the sacredness in which cow and dog are held, as well as reminiscences of general Indo-Germanic myths.

THE RELIGION OF ZOROASTER

Ahura Mazda was the creator of the universe for the duration of which he fixed a certain term. It seems uncertain whether the Persians pictured the world as round or flat, but according to their idea it was divided into seven zones, of which the central one was the actual habitable earth. Between these zones and enveloping the whole was the great abyss of waters. Between earth and heaven rose the celestial mountain whence all the rivers upon earth had their source, and on which was deposited the Haoma.

The central feature of Zoroastrian ritual was the worship of fire, an old-established worship which had existed before Zoroaster's time. In the oldest period images were forbidden, and holy rites could be performed without temples, portable fire-altars being in use. Temples were, however, built in quite early times, and within these was the sanctuary from which all light was excluded, and where the sacred fire was kept alight, which could only be approached by the priest with covered hands and mouth. The Persians carried the fear of defilement to an extreme, and had even more elaborate regulations than most Easterns concerning methods of purification and avoidance of defilement, both as regards personal contamination or that of the sacred elements of earth, fire, and water. Even hair and nails could not be cut without special directions as to how to deal with the separated portions. But this perpetual and exhausting state of caution and protective effort against contact with defiling objects and rigorous system of purification had an ultimate concern with the great struggle going on between good and evil. Death and everything that partook of death, or had any power of injury, were works of the arch-enemy.

MYTHS OF BABYLONIA AND ASSYRIA

It was owing to the fear of contaminating the three elements named above that the Persians neither buried nor cremated their dead, and looked upon it as a criminal act to throw a corpse into the water. The old mode of disposing of the dead was similar to that now practised by the Parsis of Bombay, who carry the body to one of the Towers of Silence. So the Persians exposed the corpse, till one or other devouring agent, birds of prey or the elements, had reduced it to a skeleton. As regards man himself he was thought to be a reasonable being of free will with conscience, soul, and a guardian spirit or prototype of himself who dwelt above, called a Fravashi—his own character, indeed, put into a spiritual body, almost identical with the *amei-malghen* or spiritual nymphs of the Araucanian Indians of Chile. He had the choice of good and evil, and consequently suffered the due punishment of sin. For the first three days after death the soul of the dead was supposed to hover about its earthly abode.

During this time friends and relatives performed their funerary rites, their prayers and offerings becoming more earnest and abundant as the hour drew nigh when the soul was bound to start on its journey to the beyond. This was at the beginning of the fourth day, when Sraosha carried it aloft, assailed on the way by demons desirous of obtaining possession of his burden. On earth everything was being done to keep the evil spirits in check, fires lighted as particularly effective against the powers of darkness. And, thus assisted, Sraosha arrived safely with his charge at the bridge that spanned the space between earth and heaven. Here at the entrance to the 'accountants' bridge' the soul's account was cast up by Mithra and Rashnu; the latter weighed its good and evil deeds, and even if the good deeds turned the scale, the soul had still to undergo immediate penance for its transgression, so strict was the justice meted out to each. Now the bridge may be crossed, and a further automatic kind of verdict is given, for to those fit for heaven the bridge appears a wide and easy way; to the unfortunate ones doomed to destruction it seems but of a hair's breadth, and stepping on to it they straightway fall into the yawning gulf beneath. The blessed ones are met at heaven's gate by a radiant figure, who leads them through the antechambers that finally open into the everlasting light of the celestial abode. This is the triumph of the individual soul; but there is 'a far-off divine event' awaiting, which will be heralded by signs and wonders. For 3000 years previous to it there are alternate intervals of overpowering evil and conquering peace. At last the great dragon is let loose and the evil time comes, but Mazda sends a man to slay it. Then the saviour Saoshyant is born of a virgin. The dead arise, the sheep and goats are divided, and there is lamentation on the earth. The mountains dissolve and flood the earth with molten metal, a devouring agent of destruction to the wicked, but from which the good take no hurt. The spiritual powers have now to battle it out. Mazda and Sraosha overcome Ahriman and the dragon, and "then age, decay, and death are done away, and in their place are everlasting growth and life."

Babylonian Ethics

And, lastly, what of the ethics of ancient Babylon and Assyria? On the whole the moral standard of these countries was not by any means so exalted as our own, although the religious outlook was not a low one. To begin with, the character of Babylonian myth was a great deal purer than that of Hellenic or Scandinavian myth. The gods of Babylonia appear to be more dignified than those of the Greeks or Norsemen, for example. They do not descend to the same puerilities, and their record is immeasurably cleaner. This may have something to do with the very great body of ritual connected with the Babylonian religion, for when a people is so hedged in by religious custom as were the ancient Chaldeans, so threatened on every side by taboo, the mere thought of wrongdoing and the consequence thereof is sufficient to deter them from acting otherwise than reasonably. In course of time sin becomes so ugly and repulsive in the light of punishment that the moral code receives a tremendous impulse.

There is no doubt that the Babylonians devoutly believed that their gods demanded rigid adherence to the moral code. It was generally thought that misfortune and illness were the consequences of moral transgression. But the Babylonians did not believe that the cardinal sins alone were heinous, for they included in transgression such misdemeanours as maliciousness, fraud, unworthy ambitions, and injurious teaching.

CHAPTER XIV: MODERN EXCAVATION IN BABYLONIA AND ASSYRIA

IN no land has excavation assisted history so greatly as in Mesopotamia. In Egypt, although spade-work has widened our knowledge of life and religion in the Nile country, most of what we know of these subjects has been gleaned from temples and pyramids, rock-tombs and mastabas, for the proper examination of which little or no digging was necessary, and generally speaking it may be said that excavation in Egypt has furnished us with a greater insight into the earlier periods of Egyptian progress, its 'prehistoric' life. But in the Babylonian-Assyrian region, practically every discovery has been due to strenuous labour with pick and spade; our knowledge of Chaldea in its hey-day has literally been dug up piece by piece.

The honour of beginning the great task of unearthing the buried cities of Mesopotamia belongs to M. Botta, who was French consul at Mosul in 1842. Moved by the belief that many of the great sand-covered mounds which are so conspicuous a feature of the Mesopotamian landscape probably concealed ruins of a vanished civilization, Botta commenced to excavate the large mound of Kouyunjik, which is situated close to the village where he resided. But he found little to reward his labours, and he does not seem to have gone about the business of excavation in a very workmanlike manner. His attention was called by an intelligent native to the mounds of Khorsabad, the site of ancient Nineveh, and he dispatched a party of workmen to the spot. Soon his perseverance was rewarded by the discovery of some sculptures, and recognizing the superior importance of Khorsabad for archæological purposes, he transferred his establishment to that village and resolved to devote himself to a thorough investigation of the site.

Soon a well-planned sinking operation came upon one of the palace walls, and subsequent digging was rewarded by the discovery of many chambers and halls faced with slabs of gypsum covered with mythological figures, battle scenes, processions, and similar subjects. He had, in fact, unearthed a palace built at Nineveh by Sargon, King of Assyria, who reigned 722–705 B.C., one of the finest examples of Assyrian palatial architecture. He continued his excavations at Khorsabad until 1845, and was successful in bringing to light a temple and a grand porch decorated by three pairs of wings, under which passed the road from the city to the palace. Many of the fruits of his labours were removed to Paris and deposited in the Louvre. His successor, Victor Place, continued Botta's work at Khorsabad, and discovered a city gate guarded by winged bulls, the backs of which supported the arch of the entrance.

Sir Henry Layard

Meanwhile Mr, afterward Sir Henry, Layard had visited the country in 1840, and was greatly impressed by Botta's work and its results. Five years later, through the assistance of Sir Stratford Canning, he was enabled himself to commence excavations at Nimrûd. He soon unearthed the remains of extensive buildings—in fact he discovered two Assyrian palaces on the very first day of his excavations! At the outset he had only eleven men in his employ, and being anxious to push on the work in fear that the

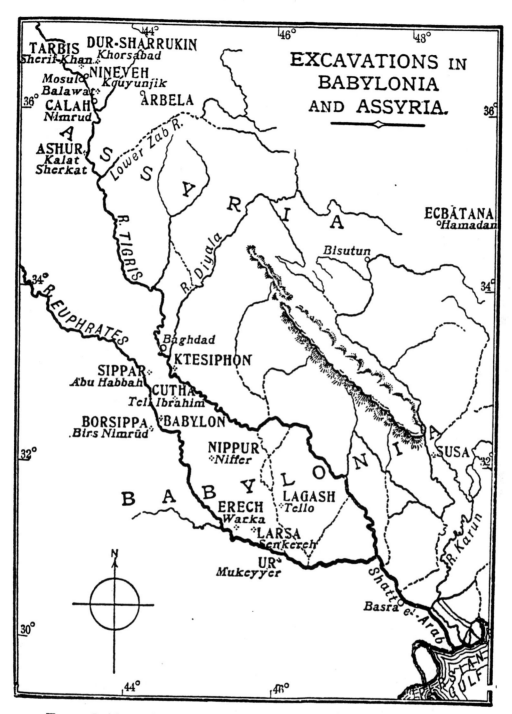

From *Guide to the Babylonian and Assyrian Antiquities*, by permission of the Director of the British Museum.

local Turkish governor or the approach of the winter season would put an end to his operations, he increased his staff to thirty men. The peasants laboured enthusiastically, but to the excavator's disgust the Turkish authorities forbade him to proceed. Layard, nevertheless, hoodwinked the authorities, and succeeded in uncovering several large figures of winged bulls and lions.

Soon after this Layard spent Christmas with Sir Henry Rawlinson of the British Museum, with whom he cemented a warm friendship, and together they were able to overcome the unfriendliness of the Turkish officials. Hormuzd Rassam, an intelligent native Christian, came to Layard's assistance, and operations were once more commenced at Nimrûd. Rassam's labours were quickly crowned by success, for he came upon a large hall in a fine state of preservation. The serious work of excavation was not without its humorous side, for if they chanced to unearth a carven monster with the body of a bull and the head of a bearded man, the native labourers threw down their tools and ran. The Turkish Governor, too, hearing from a native source that 'Nimrod' had been found, sent a message to the effect that "his remains should be treated with respect and be no further disturbed."

Layard had now unearthed many valuable sculptures, and he resolved to attempt their dispatch to England. Rawlinson sent a small steamer, the *Nitocris*, to Nimrûd, but it was found impossible to ship the massive pieces on this frail craft, and even the smaller sculptures had perforce to be floated down the Tigris on rafts. Layard's health was by this time in no very robust state, but a two months' mountain holiday in Kurdistan refreshed him, and

The 'Black Obelisk' of Shalmaneser II
Photo W. A. Mansell and Co.

SIR HENRY LAYARD

once more he recommenced his labours at Nimrûd, heartened by the news that the British Government had awarded a grant for the continuation of his researches. The grant, however, was distressingly small, and its inadequacy compelled him to limit his excavations in the most unsatisfactory way. Despite this, the new operations were rich in results, especially those in the building known as the 'south-west palace.' This palace, he ascertained from bricks unearthed, had been built by Esar-haddon, King of Assyria. Sculptures glorifying King Assur-nazir-pal (885–860 B.C.) were also discovered at the north-west palace, some of them of a most spirited character, representing the King in battle, crossing a river full of turtles and fishes, or leading his army.

It was in the central building, however, that one of his most important discoveries awaited him. This was the obelisk of Shalmaneser II (860–825 B.C.), nearly seven feet high, and in admirable preservation. The monarch had erected this in his palace to commemorate the leading military events of his career. It contains twenty small bas-reliefs and 210 lines of cuneiform inscription, alluding among other things to the receipt of the tribute of "Jehu, son of Omri."[1] This priceless relic is one of the treasures in the keeping of the British Museum.

Layard devoted the first four months of 1847 to the exploration of the north-west palace, and disclosed painted chambers on which were represented hunting-scenes and various religious ceremonies, each design separated by a conventional representation of the sacred tree. Many of the lesser objects found here exhibited Egyptian influence. Here he

---
[1] But *cf.* 1 Kings xix 16, *ff.*; 2 Kings ix and x.

also came upon the oldest Assyrian arch ever discovered.

He had now collected a large number of important sculptures, and of these he succeeded in sending three by raft to Basra, whence they were later shipped to England. By the middle of May 1847 he had finished his work at Nimrûd, and had commenced his search for the ruins of Nineveh in the mound of Kouyunjik, near Mosul, where Botta had laboured before him. He dug for the platform of sun-dried bricks which he knew by experience formed the foundation of all large Assyrian edifices, and came upon it, as he had expected, at a depth of twenty feet, shortly afterward discovering the entrance, flanked by the inevitable winged bulls. But the building itself had been so damaged by fire as to present little more than crumbling heaps of lime.

Layard returned to England in June 1847, and was appointed attaché to the Embassy at Constantinople. Meanwhile his published works had created an extraordinary impression throughout Europe, and the pressure of public opinion so wrought upon the Government that he was requested to lead a second expedition to Nineveh.

Where Rawlinson Slept

Better equipped, Layard left Constantinople in August 1849 and arrived at Kouyunjik in October. Employing about a hundred men, he set strenuously to work, removing only as much earth as was necessary to show the sculptured walls. Having fairly started the work at Kouyunjik, Layard, accompanied by Rassam, returned to Nimrûd, and recommenced work there. One morning he was inspecting the trenches when he found Rawlinson asleep on the floor of an excavated chamber, wrapped in his travelling cloak, " wearied out by a long and harassing night's ride." He was on his way home to England, which he had not seen for twenty-two years.

The rich finds in the painted palace of Sennacherib at Kouyunjik consisted chiefly of mural paintings and bas-reliefs. Of these Professor Hilprecht says:[1] " Hundreds of figures cover the face of the slabs from top to bottom. We become acquainted with the peculiarities, in type and dress, of foreign nations, and the characteristic features and products of their lands; we are introduced into the very life and occupations of the persons represented. The sculptor shows us the Babylonian swamps with their jungles of tall reeds, frequented by wild boars, and barbarous tribes skimming over the waters in their light boats of wicker-work, exactly such as are used to-day by the inhabitants of the same marshes; or he takes us into the high mountains of Kurdistan, covered with trees and crowned with castles, endeavouring even to convey the idea of a valley by reversing the trees and mountains on one side of the stream, which is filled with fishes and crabs and turtles. He indicates the different head-gear worn by female musicians, or by captive women carried with their husbands and children to Nineveh. Some wear their hair in long ringlets, some plaited or braided, some confined in a net; others are characterized by hoods fitting close to their heads, others by a kind of turban; Elamite ladies with their hair in curls falling on their shoulders, bound above the temples by a band or fillet, while those from Syria wear a high conical head-dress, similar to that which is frequently found to-day in those regions."

[1] *Explorations in Bible Lands* (T. and T. Clark, 1903).

MYTHS OF BABYLONIA AND ASSYRIA

The excavation of Sennacherib's palace with its seventy rooms, halls, and galleries was indeed one of the most striking results of Layard's second expedition to Nineveh. But even more remarkable was the find of Assur-bani-pal's famous royal library at Nineveh, which has already been described. Results at Nimrûd, too, had been favourable, perhaps the most interesting being the discovery of the tower of Calah, regarded at first as the tomb of Sardanapalus. Now for the second time Layard began to feel the effects of overwork and exposure, and in April 1851, accompanied by Rassam, he turned from the ruins of Nineveh "with a heavy heart." Twenty-four years later he was to become Ambassador at Constantinople, in which capacity he loyally assisted the zealous Rassam, his worthy subordinate.

In 1851 Rawlinson was entrusted by the British Government with the excavations in Assyria and Babylonia. He had the invaluable assistance of Rassam as 'chief practical excavator.' Stationing his workmen at as many sites as possible, he unearthed the annals of Tiglath-pileser I at Qal'at Sherqat, discovered E-zide, the temple of Nebo at Nimrûd, and a 'stele' of Samsi-Adad IV (825–812 B.C.). At Kouyunjik he came upon the palace of Assur-bani-pal. A beautiful bas-relief was recovered representing Assur-bani-pal in his chariot on a hunting expedition. The 'lion-room,' the walls of which represented a lion-hunt, was also unearthed, and was shown to have been used both as a library and a picture-gallery, many thousands of clay book-tablets being found therein.

Abandoning excavation for a political appointment, Mr Rassam was followed by William Kennet Loftus,

Outline of the Mounds at Nimrûd
From a drawing made on the spot by Sir Henry Layard

GEORGE SMITH

who did good work at the ruins of Warkâ in Babylonia. Meanwhile the French expedition under Fresnel, Oppert, and Thomes was excavating at Babylon, coming upon the remains of the Nebuchadrezzar period and excavating the mound of Bâbil.

George Smith

One who was to perform yeoman service for Assyriology now entered the field. This was George Smith, whose name is so unalterably associated with the romantic side of that science he loved so well. Writing of himself he says: "Everyone has some bent or inclination which, if fostered by favourable circumstances, will colour the rest of his life. My own taste has always been for Oriental studies, and from my youth I have taken a great interest in Eastern explorations and discoveries, particularly in the great work in which Layard and Rawlinson were engaged. For some years I did little or nothing, but in 1866, seeing the unsatisfactory state of our knowledge of those parts of Assyrian history which bore upon the history of the Bible, I felt anxious to do something towards settling the questions involved."[1] Smith found the Deluge tablets among the scores of fragments sent to the British Museum by Layard and Loftus, and this and other discoveries whetted his desire to go to Mesopotamia and unearth its treasures with his own hands. In consequence of the wide interest taken at the time in these discoveries the proprietors of *The Daily Telegraph* came forward with the offer of a thousand guineas for fresh researches at Nineveh, with the proviso that Smith should head the expedition and supply the journal with accounts of his discoveries. The

[1] *Assyrian Discoveries*, p. 9 (London, 1875).

offer was accepted, and Smith, now a member of the staff of the British Museum, received leave of absence for six months.

Arrived at Nimrûd, Smith settled down to excavation there, commencing operations at the temple of Nebo; but he found little to justify his labour, as the structure was in a ruinous condition and had latterly been used as a granary. On each side of the entrance stood a colossal figure of the god with crossed arms in an attitude of meditation, and lesser images of him were found inside the ruined building. Smith's reason for digging here was that he suspected the presence of inscriptions which might cast light upon the reign of Tiglath-pileser II (745 B.C.) and therefore upon Bible history. His industry was rewarded by the discovery of the upper portion of a tablet of this monarch, but further finds of importance were not forthcoming.

The Palace of Nimrûd

Smith then instituted systematic excavations in the south-east palace, and made some interesting discoveries. On examining this part of the mound he saw a considerable tunnel in the south face, commencing on the sloping part of the mound. This tunnel appeared to go along the middle of a chamber, the floor having been cut through and appearing in a line on each side of the tunnel. Further on, the tunnel reached the wall at the end of the chamber, and the face of this had been cleared for some little distance; then, descending below the foundation of this wall, the passage ran for some distance into the base of the mound. He commenced on the two sides of this cutting, and cleared away to the level of the pavement, soon coming to

The Palaces of Nimrûd (Restored)
From a sketch by James Ferguson for Sir Henry Layard

THE PALACE OF NIMRÛD

the wall on each side. The southern wall of the chamber had fallen over into the plain, as it was here close to the edge of the platform, and the chamber commenced with two parallel walls running north and south. The right-hand wall, in a place near the edge where it was much broken down, showed three steps of an ascent which had gone apparently to some upper chambers. Further on it showed two recesses, each ornamented on both sides with three square pilasters. The left hand showed an entrance into a second chamber running east to west, and from this turned a third, running parallel with the first. Altogether in this place he opened six chambers, all of the same character, the entrances ornamented by clusters of square pilasters and recesses in the rooms in the same style. The walls were coloured in horizontal bands of red, green, and yellow on plaster; and where the lower parts of the chambers were panelled with small stone slabs, the plaster and colours were continued over these. In one of these rooms there appeared a brick receptacle let into the floor, and on lifting the brick which covered this Smith found six terra-cotta winged figures, closely packed in the receptacle. Each figure was full-faced, having a head like a lion, four wings, with one hand across the breast, holding a basket in the other, and clothed in a long dress to the feet. These figures were probably intended to preserve the building against the power of evil spirits.

All the eastern and southern portions of the mound of Nimrûd had been destroyed by being turned into a burial-place. The ruins had been excavated after the fall of the Assyrian empire, walls had been dug through, and chambers broken into, and the openings filled with coffins.

MYTHS OF BABYLONIA AND ASSYRIA

Mr Smith then turned his attention to the ruins of Nineveh at Kouyunjik and Nebbi Yunas. Layard and even the Turkish Government had both been before him here. He commenced operations by cutting trenches at the south-eastern corner of Assurbani-pal's palace. But at first nothing of great interest resulted, and he diverted operations to the palace of Sennacherib hard by. Here he came upon a number of inscriptions which compensated him for his labour. At length the excavations in Assurbani-pal's palace bore fruit, for there were unearthed the greater portion of seventeen lines of inscription belonging to the first column of the Deluge narrative, and fitting into the only place where there was a serious blank in the story.

The palace of Sennacherib also steadily produced its tribute of objects, including a small tablet of Esar-haddon, King of Assyria, some new fragments of one of the historical cylinders of Assur-bani-pal, and a curious fragment of the history of Sargon, King of Assyria, relating to his expedition against Ashdod, which is mentioned in the twentieth chapter of the Book of Isaiah. On the same fragment was also part of the list of Median chiefs who paid tribute to Sargon.

The proprietors of *The Daily Telegraph* considered that with the finding of the Deluge fragment the purpose of the expedition had been served, and that further excavation in Mesopotamia should be carried on under national auspices. Mr Smith was therefore forced to return to England, but not before he had discovered further a valuable syllabary, and two portions of the sixth tablet of the Deluge story, as well as other minor objects of interest.

About the end of 1873, however, the British

THE PALACE OF NIMRÛD

Museum authorities dispatched Mr Smith once more to Mesopotamia, where he recommenced operations at Kouyunjik, and unearthed on this occasion an inscription of Shalmaneser I, King of Assyria (1300 B.C.), recording that he founded the palace of Nineveh, and alluding to his restoration of the temple of Ishtar. Inscriptions of his son Tukulti-ninip were also found at this place, as were dedications of Assur-nazir-pal (885 B.C.) and Shalmaneser II (860 B.C.). Some very curious pottery, too, came from this spot, ornamentations being laid on the clay, as in many examples of the pottery of the Maya of Central America. At the same time fragments of sculptured walls representing marching warriors were brought to light, and some tablets of great importance giving the names of six new Babylonian kings, a sixth tablet of the Deluge series, and a bilingual tablet in fine preservation.

In the south-west palace Smith excavated at the grand entrance to see if any records remained under the pavement, but there were none. This part of the pavement had been broken through, and anything under it had long ago been carried away. He sank some trenches in the grand hall and found a fragment of inscription, and further on in the palace several other fragments. His principal excavation was, however, carried on over what Layard called the library chamber of this palace. Layard, who discovered the library chamber, describes it as full of fragments of tablets, up to a foot or more from the floor. This chamber Layard had cleared out and he had brought its treasures to England, but Smith thought on examining the collection at the British Museum that not one-half of the library had been removed, and steadily adhered to the belief that the rest of the tablets must be in the palace of Sennacherib. On excavating he found nearly three thousand fragments of tablets in the chambers round Layard's library chamber, and from the position of these fragments he was led to the opinion that the library was not originally situated in these chambers but in an upper story of the palace, and that on the collapse of the building they fell into the chambers below. Some of the chambers in which he found inscribed tablets had no communication with each other, while fragments of the same tablets were in them; and looking at this fact, and the positions and distribution of the fragments, he was convinced that the tablets were scattered over a wide area and resolved to excavate over an extensive section of the palace.

"In the long gallery, which contained scenes representing the moving of winged figures," says Smith, "I found a great number of tablets, mostly along the floor; they included syllabaries, bilingual lists, mythological and historical tablets. Among these tablets I discovered a beautiful bronze Assyrian fork, having two prongs joined by ornamental shoulder to shaft of spiral work, the shaft ending in the head of an ass. This is a beautiful and unique specimen of Assyrian work, and shows the advances the people had made in the refinements of life. South of this there were numerous tablets round Layard's old library chamber, and here I found part of a curious astrolabe, and fragments of the history of Sargon, King of Assyria, 722 B.C. In one place, below the level of the floor, I discovered a fine fragment of the history of Assurbanipal, containing new and curious matter relating to his Egyptian wars, and to the affairs of Gyges, King of Lydia.

THE PALACE OF NIMRUD

From this part of the palace I gained also the shoulder of a colossal statue, with an inscription of Assurbanipal. In another spot I obtained a bone spoon, and a fragment of the tablet with the history of the seven evil spirits. Near this I discovered a bronze style, with which I believe the cuneiform tablets were impressed. In another part of the excavation I found part of a monument with the representation of a fortification. In the western part of the palace, near the edge of the mound, I excavated and found remains of crystal and alabaster vases, and specimens of the royal seal. Two of these are very curious; one is a paste seal, the earliest example of its kind, and the other is a clay impression of the seal of Sargon, King of Assyria. Near where the principal seals were discovered I found part of a sculpture with a good figure of a dead buffalo in a stream. Among these sculptures and inscriptions were numerous small objects, including beads, rings, stone seals, etc."[1]

By January 1, 1874, Smith had no less than six hundred men employed. But he had to encounter tremendous local difficulties, especially demands that he should pay immense sums to the proprietors of the land which he excavated. Soon afterward, the season being unpropitious, he returned to England. A third visit to Mesopotamia proved his last, as he became ill and passed away at Aleppo in 1876, to the universal regret not only of those who were privileged to have his friendship, but to all who had perused his works and were aware of his strenuous life and studies. From the position of a bank-note engraver he had raised himself to that of an esteemed scholar, and his kindness of

[1] *Assyrian Discoveries*, p. 148 (London, 1875).

heart and honesty of purpose, no less than his outstanding abilities, make him one of the most gracious figures in the history of a science to which many men of high endeavour have devoted their lives.

Hormuzd Rassam

The lamented death of Smith caused the British authorities to request Mr Hormuzd Rassam, who had retired into private life in England, to take up the vacant post. Mr Rassam at once accepted the trust, and started for Constantinople in November 1876. At first there was serious trouble with the Turkish Government, but in January 1878 Rassam was enabled to commence excavations, which he carried on almost continuously for five years. Layard, as ambassador at Constantinople, stood him in good stead. He took much advantage of native talent, which, if not up to the standard of European efficiency, he found in no wise despicable. But too many excavations were being carried on at one and the same time. Again, Rassam was prone to attempt sensational finds rather than to keep steadily at the more solid and less showy work of excavation. Guided by certain indications of the presence of objects of the Shalmaneser period at Kouyunjik, he dug there once more and succeeded in unearthing the bronze plaques which had covered the cedar gates of a large Assyrian building at least 2500 years old, and built by Shalmaneser II. They represented warriors and equestrian figures, and it was found that the site on which they were discovered had been the city of Imgur-Bel. Rassam also recovered further clay tablets from the library of Assur-bani-pal at Kouyunjik. With his return to England in 1882 it may be said that the Assyrian

Work of the Excavators in Babylon

One hundred workmen laboured in digging this cut, which is 40 feet deep

Copyright by Underwood and Underwood, London

excavations of the nineteenth century, in contradistinction to those carried out on Babylonian soil, came to an end.

De Sarzec

With the excavations of the Frenchman de Sarzec at Tellô the second great period of Chaldean archæological research may be said to have commenced. Ernest de Sarzec was French Vice-consul at Basra, but by his private efforts he succeeded in making Tellô 'the Pompeii of early Babylonian antiquity.' The two principal mounds excavated by him are known to Assyriologists as 'Mound A' and 'Mound B.' Digging in the former he soon collected sufficient evidence to convince him that he stood on a site of great antiquity. He found indeed that Mound A consisted of a platform of unbaked bricks crowned by an edifice of considerable size and extent. He unearthed part of a great statue, on the shoulder of which was engraved the name of Gudea (2700 B.C.), patesi, or ruler, of Lagash, with which city Mound A proved to be identical, and later exposed numerous large columns of bricks of the time of Gudea, the 'stele of vultures' erected by King E-anna-tum, and two large terra-cotta cylinders of Gudea, each inscribed with about 2000 lines of early cuneiform writing.

On a later visit, at the end of 1880 and beginning of 1881, he further developed excavation in Mound A, and discovered nine large dolerite statues, fragments of precious bas-reliefs, and numerous inscriptions. He also came upon layers of more ancient remains beneath the building he had unearthed in Mound A.

The collection of early Babylonian sculptures regained by de Sarzec was hailed with acclamation in Paris. An Oriental section was instituted in the Louvre, and Léon Heuzy commenced the publication of a monumental work, *Découvertes en Chaldée par Ernest de Sarzec* (Paris, 1884, *seq.*), which laid the foundation for a methodical treatment of ancient Chaldean art. The subsequent excavation of de Sarzec in Tellô and its neighbourhood carried the history of the city back to at least 4000 B.C., and a collection of more than 30,000 tablets of the time of Gudea was gradually unearthed.

In 1886–1887 a German expedition under Dr Koldewey explored the cemetery of El Hibba to the South of Tellô, and succeeded in throwing much light upon the burial customs of ancient Babylonia. A second German expedition under Dr Andrae, working at Babylon in 1889, laid bare the palace of Nebuchadrezzar and the great processional road, and subsequently conducted excavations at Qal'at Sherqat, the site of Asshur.

The American Expedition of 1889

There had been keen interest in Babylonian archæology in America almost from the inception of the series of excavations dealt with in this sketch, and this was in all likelihood due to the popularity of Biblical studies in the great republic of the West. The Babylonian Exploration Fund was instituted on November 30, 1887. Excavatory labours were commenced at Nippur in 1889, and on first beholding the immense mass of the mounds which concealed the ruins of the temple-city the members of the expedition were not a little disturbed. "Even at a distance I began to realize that not twenty, not fifty years would suffice to excavate this important

THE AMERICAN EXPEDITION OF 1889

site thoroughly," writes Professor Hilprecht.[1] The ruins resembled "a picturesque mountain range" rather than "the last impressive remains of human

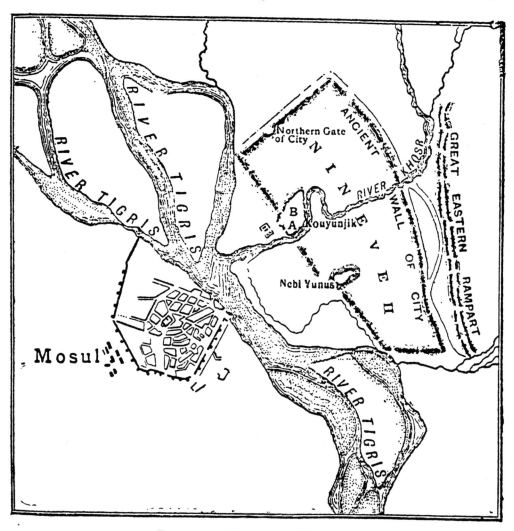

PLAN OF NINEVEH (NIPPUR)
A. Palace of Sennacherib.   B. Palace of Assur-bani-pal.
By permission of the Director of the British Museum.

constructions." But the Americans 'sat down' before the mass with the courage of their race, resolved to probe into its innermost secrets. At first they speculated as to the character of the

[1] *Explorations in Bible Lands* (T. and T. Clark, 1903).

buildings hidden from their view. The director, Dr Peters, was rapidly exhausting his fund of $15,000 without coming upon anything of value, and recognizing the necessity for the prompt discovery of important objects if opinion at home was to be placated, Hilprecht pointed out to him the desirability of attacking an isolated mound which in his judgment contained the residences of the priests and the temple library. Peters agreed to the proposal, and almost at once an important series of tablets was discovered. The mound seemed, indeed, inexhaustible, and most of its contents were of a date about 2000 B.C., but there were also later tablets belonging to the reign of Nabopolasser, Nebuchadrezzar, Nabonidus, and even Cyrus, Cambyses, and Darius. Shortly after this the first expedition was brought to a close.

In the second expedition, also undertaken at Nippur, Dr Peters decided to dispense with the services of Messrs Hilprecht and Field, the expert Assyriologists who had been dispatched to advise him professionally. Himself not an Assyriologist, he laboured at a disadvantage without the assistance of these experts. The work of the first expedition had concentrated at three conspicuous points—the temple, the 'tablet' hill which had yielded such good results, and the 'Court of Columns.' The principal objective was now the conical hill of Bint-el-Amir, containing the zikkurat and temple of Bel. Peters regarded the temple as having been built by a king "not far removed from Nebuchadrezzar in time," but many of his inferences have been traversed by Hilprecht. "In his endeavour to reach the older remains before the more recent strata had been investigated in the least adequately, Peters

THE BUSINESS QUARTER OF NIPPUR

broke through the outer casing of the zikkurat, built of 'immense blocks of adobe,' in a cavity of which he discovered a well-preserved goose egg, and perceived that there was an older stage-tower of quite a different form and much smaller dimensions enclosed within the other. By means of a diagonal trench cut through its centre, he ascertained its height and characteristic features down to the level of Ur-Gur, and came to the conclusion (which, however, did not prove correct) that the zikkurat of this ancient monarch was the earliest erected at Nippur. 'Wells and similar shafts were sunk at other points of the temple,' especially at the northern and western corners, where he reached original constructions of Ashurbanapal (668–626 B.C.) and Ur-Gur (about 2700 B.C.), and discovered scattered bricks . . . 'showing that many kings of many ages had honoured the temple of Bel at Nippur.' "[1]

The Business Quarter of Nippur

The excavators soon concluded that they had hit upon the business quarter of Nippur, basing their belief upon the commercial character of the tablets found, the large number of day labels pierced for attachment to sacks and jars, books of entry in clay, and weights and measures. So much damage had been done to the buildings while excavating, however that the appearance and plan of any of the Babylonian business houses and warehouses could not be arrived at.

In August 1893 Haynes commenced a search for the original bed and embankment of the river Chebar, which he came upon at a depth of twenty

---

[1] Hilprecht, *Explorations in Bible Lands*, p. 232 (T. and T. Clark, 1903).

feet from the surface. In the dried-up bed of the river or canal he found a round terra-cotta fountain in three fragments, decorated with birds from whose mouths the water passed.

The Fourth Campaign

The fourth campaign covered the years 1898–1900, and was under the direct control of the University of Pennsylvania. Excavations were commenced at the extreme south-eastern end of the west ridge. Spring and summer were spent by Haynes in a 'nervous search' for tablets, although a strictly scientific examination of Nippur had been asked for. Late tablets and coffins resulted from this search; finds of old Babylonian character were meagre. The director did not see eye to eye with his architects, and one of them, Mr Fisher, resigned, returning, however, in the autumn of 1899. The Committee in America requested Haynes to confine his efforts to the exploration of the eastern half of the temple court, and to this task he addressed himself with zeal if only with partial success. Tablets, according to the director, sufficient to institute " a distinct library by itself," continued to pour out of 'Tablet Hill.' But technical and expert advice was lacking. The architects desired to remove a Parthian round tower, Haynes reluctantly consented, and upon its removal the gate of an ancient temple was unearthed.

Hilprecht Returns

Professor Hilprecht now reappeared, and his coming put a new complexion on affairs. A trained and efficient archæologist, he saw at once that 'Tablet Hill' represented the site of the temple library, so resolved to leave its excavation to a later expedition, and meantime to settle "the more essential topographical questions." He saw that these once answered, "it would be a comparatively easy task for the Committee to have the single mounds excavated one after another by somebody else, if necessity arose, who was less familiar with the ruins and the history of their exploration. Every trench cut henceforth—and there were a great many—was cut for the sole purpose of excavating structures systematically and of gathering necessary data for the history and topography of ancient Nippur. If these trenches yielded tangible museum results at the same time, so much the better; if they did not," he says, "I was not troubled by their absence." However, "antiquities were found so abundantly in the pursuit of the plan described, that the principle was established anew that a strictly scientific method of excavating is at the same time the most profitable."

Summarizing his 'explanations' of the ruins at Bint-el-Amir, Hilprecht writes: "1. A stage-tower of smaller dimensions existed at Nippur before Sargon I (about 3800 B.C.). 2. In pre-Sargonic times the ground around the sacred enclosure was a vast graveyard, a regular fire necropolis. 3. One of the names of the stage-tower of Nippur suggested the idea of a tomb to the early inhabitants of the country. In the course of time certain zikkurats were directly designated by the Babylonians as tombs of the gods. 4. The stage-tower of Bel did not occupy the centre of the enclosed platform, but the south-west section of it, while the north-east part was reserved for 'the house of Bel,' his principal sanctuary, which stood at the side of the stage-tower.

5. The temple of Bel consisted of two large courts adjoining each other, the north-west court with the zikkurat and 'the house of Bel' representing the most holy place or the inner court, while the south-east (outer) court seems to have been studded with the shrines of all the different gods and goddesses worshipped at Nippur, including one for Bel himself. 6. Imgur-Marduk and Nimit-Marduk, mentioned in the cuneiform inscriptions as the two walls of Nippur (dûru and Shalkhû), cannot have surrounded the whole city. According to the results of the excavations conducted under my own supervision, only the temple was enclosed by a double wall, while in all probability the city itself remained unprotected. 7. The large complex of buildings covering the top of Bint-el-Amir has nothing to do with the ancient temple below, but represents a huge fortified Parthian palace grouped around and upon the remains of the stage-tower then visible."[1]

By means of careful tunnelling Hilprecht also unearthed the south-east side of a pre-Sargonic temple-tower, but the nature of the excavation, risking as it did a sudden collapse of soil and bricks, was too dangerous to permit of further labours upon it.

The House of the Dead

A building-record of Assur-bani-pal was brought to light which described the temple-tower of Nippur as E-gigunnû, 'House of the Tomb.' Before this other titles of it had been recovered which alluded to it as 'Mountain of the Wind,' and it was understood to have been a local representation of the great mythological 'mountain of the world,' Kharsag-

[1] *Explorations in Bible Lands* (T. and T. Clark, 1903).

A BABYLONIAN MUSEUM

kurkura. This was puzzling until Hilprecht found that the tower penetrated so far into the earth as to descend to the 'city of the dead' which, according to Babylonian belief, was directly below and within the earth.

The Temple Library

Hilprecht now turned his attention to the temple library in 'Tablet Hill,' with results most important for the science of Assyriology. This building, contemporary with the time of Abram, now yielded large quantities of ancient tablets, occurring in strata of from one to four feet in thickness, as if they had once been disposed upon wooden shelves.

A Babylonian Museum

An important find was made of a jar containing about twenty inscribed objects, mostly clay tablets, which constituted a veritable small Babylonian museum, evidently collected by a late Babylonian priest or someone connected with the temple library. Archæology was probably fashionable about the time of Nabonidus (556–539 B.C.), himself a monarch of antiquarian tastes. The collector of this 'museum' had actually taken a 'squeeze' or impression of an inscription of Sargon I (3800 B.C.), in his time about 3340 years old, and had even placed upon it a label stating that the object was a 'squeeze' or 'mould' of an inscribed stone " which Nabûzêrlîshir, the scribe, saw in the palace of King Naram-Sin at Agade."

Says Hilprecht concerning this remarkable collection, "The owner, or curator, of the little museum of Babylonian originals must have obtained his specimens by purchase or through personal excavations carried out in the ruined buildings of Bel's city. He doubtless lived in the sixth century, about the time of King Nabonidos, and was a man well versed in the ancient literature of his nation and deeply interested in the past history of Nippur. This follows from the fact that his vase was found in the Neo-Babylonian stratum of 'Tablet Hill,' and from the circumstance that the latest antiquity of his collection is dated in the government of Sin-sharishkun, the last representative of the Assyrian dynasty (about 615 B.C.)."

In the second year of this campaign Peters contented himself with 'sounding' as many places as possible rather than settling down to the steady work of excavation, in which preference he resembled Rassam. But his labours were crowned with no little success, for he came upon a large number of Kassite votive objects, the first great collection of antiquities of this dynasty ever found, and a shrine of King Bur-Sin I dedicated to Bel about 2600 B.C. The excavation of the large and important building remains grouped around the temple tower of Bel was, however, Peters' principal task during his second campaign. But his hope of discovering many inscribed tablets while excavating these ruins was not to be realized. He was more fortunate, however, in the triangular mound (that known as 'Mound IV') to the south of the temple, which yielded some 2000 tablets, scientific, literary, and financial manuscripts, and even school exercises being turned up by the spade. About the same time excavations in the south-eastern wing of the large mounds disclosed the presence of thousands of tablets and many figures of Bel and his consort Beltis. Most of the tablets here were commercial, and of date about 2600 to 2000 B.C. In May the labours of the second campaign came to a close.

Haynes' Work at Nippur

The third campaign (1893–1896) Peters delegated to Haynes, who commenced operations at Nippur in the great ridge which stretches along the southward bank of the Shatt-en-Nîl, where numerous tablets had already been unearthed. In about four months he had collected some 8000 tablets, and when the supply of these began to fail he transferred his attention to the temple mound which had been worked at before, and which he continued to explore until April 1894. With the help of Joseph A. Meyer, a young American architect, Haynes concentrated his work on the zikkurat at Nippur. Unfortunately Meyer died in December, but not until he had rendered priceless service to Haynes in his capacity as advisory architect. Haynes, unable to continue the exploration of the temple-mound without expert advice, undertook to unearth a sufficient quantity of tablets to meet Peters' demand for inscribed material. Later he pursued excavations at the Bint-el-Amir, where Peters had worked before him, cleared the zikkurat of Assur-bani-pal there and excavated the court of that building down to the water level. The excavation of the immense façade of this great erection was a work of enormous labour, hundreds of thousands of cubic feet of rubbish having to be removed before a partial clearance was effected.

The excavation of the south-west court of the zikkurat of Assur-bani-pal was the most interesting part of Haynes' work on the temple of Bel. First he had to clear away the Parthian ruins superimposed upon the site, until he came to the brick pavement of Assur-bani-pal. He then came upon a pavement of the Sargonic period which extended through a considerable part of the mound as a dividing line. The rubbish which lay beneath this was about sixteen feet in depth, and had been accumulated within a period of more than three thousand years (3800–350 B.C.). The most important of the many strata of this rubbish-heap is that which lies between the pavement of King Ur-Ninib and that immediately below it. Over 600 fragments of vases, statues, and slabs were gathered here, all seemingly deliberately broken, "by somebody who lived between the reigns of Ur-Gur of Ur and Ur-Ninib of Nisin"—perhaps the leader of an Elamite raid. The famous text of Lugalzuggisi, King of Erech, with its 132 lines of writing, was found here and restored by Hilprecht from sixty-four fragments.

Digging elsewhere, Haynes unearthed the oldest arch in the world at a considerable depth, drain-pipes of the date about 4500 B.C., and pre-Sargonic cellars containing large wine- or oil-jars. In one chamber twenty feet below the surface were found the business archives of a great Babylonian firm, Murashu and Sons, bankers and brokers at Nippur (*c.* 464–424 B.C.).

Recent Research

Recent research in Mesopotamia has centred around the site of Babylon, where results of a most interesting and encouraging description have been achieved. The German Oriental Society commenced work upon the site in the spring of 1899, and after twelve years of incessant labour under the direction

Ruins of Babylon

Uncovered after twelve years' labour by German archæologists, who began excavating in 1900

Copyright by Underwood and Underwood, London

THE OUTER WALL

of Dr Robert Koldewey, published the report of their labours in 1911.

The Babylon of Nebuchadrezzar II

The portion of the city laid bare in these twelve years of digging was contemporary with the reigns of Nebuchadrezzar II and Nabonidus, the last native King of Babylon, but certain parts of the ruins unearthed had been built in the much more ancient era of Khammurabi, the great law-maker, and even during the First Dynasty. The later Babylon is known to us from the pages of Herodotus and Ctesias, and the explorers speedily found that the accounts of these writers in nowise squared with the actual topographical conditions of the ruins unearthed and surveyed. Herodotus speaks of a Babylon 53 miles in circumference, and Ctesias is not much more modest in his estimate of over 40 miles. The city wall to the north-east side may still be traced in its entirety, and remains to prove that the city on this side measured not more than $2\frac{3}{4}$ miles, and judging from this, we obtain an approximate circumference of 11 miles—a figure far short of the estimate of the 'Father of History.'

The Outer Wall

The walls themselves are of considerable interest. The outer wall was nearly twenty feet in thickness, and was built of burnt bricks impressed with the royal stamp of Nebuchadrezzar. Here and there its length was broken by towers for outlook or defensive purposes. Herodotus states that so broad was the top of the wall that a four-horse chariot could easily turn upon its surface, and that two of these vehicles had a sufficiency of room to pass one another without risk to horses or driver. Companies of men could be moved along this mural highway in time of siege, so that a supply of defenders could be brought with dispatch to guard any portion of the defences that was imminently threatened.

Bâbil as a Citadel

The mound of Bâbil, to which we have frequently referred in this account of Babylonian excavation, was recognized by the German expedition as a citadel built for defensive purposes by Nebuchadrezzar—a place of refuge to which the King and court could repair in case of the capture of the city itself. It contained the royal stores and treasury, a large armoury and arsenal, and there is reason to believe that the monarch resided there even in times of peace. It was, indeed, a miniature city, a lesser Babylon, containing everything necessary for the royal support and pleasure.

Babylon's Water-Supply

The question of a suitable water-supply agitated municipal Babylon just as keenly as it does any of our own great centres of population, and recent excavations have illustrated the manner in which the Euphrates was utilized for this purpose. Nabopolasser has left inscriptions to show how he rebuilt the walls of a channel called the Arakhtu to lead the river Euphrates past the city boundaries. Nebuchadrezzar built a massive fortification with walls of from fifty to sixty feet in thickness into the bed of the Euphrates to prevent the formation of sandbanks in the river which possibly caused the flooding of the left bank above the temple of E-Sagila. This left a narrow channel between the

THE GREAT THRONE ROOM

new wall and the old quay, and it is probable that this huge construction caused a subsequent change in the course of the Euphrates.

Nebuchadrezzar's Palace

Nebuchadrezzar's palace was situated in the southern citadel on the mound known as the Kasr. On this building he lavished both time and treasure. When he came to the throne he found the site occupied by the residence of his father Nabopolasser, but when he returned from his triumphant Egyptian campaigns he despised the plain old place and, like some modern potentates, resolved to build himself a royal edifice which would symbolize the power and majesty of the empire he had won for himself. He turned his father's palace into a mere platform upon which to rear his own more flamboyant structure, and filled in its rooms, courts, and spaces with rubble.

The Palace without Windows

For the most part the palace was built round open courts, much in the Spanish fashion, and there is no trace of windows, a phenomenon which constantly recurs in ancient buildings in the East, in Egypt, and in Central America. But when we consider the extremes of heat encountered in these latitudes we can appreciate the desire for a cool semi-gloom which called for the windowless chamber. The flat roofs, too, were used for sleeping purposes, so that the inhabitants did not wholly dispense with fresh air.

The Great Throne Room

But by far the most interesting apartment in the palace is the great Throne Room of Nebuchadrezzar, the apartment upon which he lavished so much personal care and consideration. It stands immediately south of the Great Court, and is much the most spacious room in the palace. In the wall opposite the grand entrance from the court is a deep recess or niche, where it is thought the royal throne must have stood, so that not only the courtiers in the Throne Room but the lesser dignitaries thronging the courtyard without could have had sight of the monarch of the Eastern World seated in all his splendour upon his imperial throne. Strangely enough the walls of this great apartment of state were merely plastered with white gypsum, while the brickwork of the outer façade which faced the court was decorated with brightly coloured enamels displaying the most involved designs, floral and geometrical, in blue, yellow, black, and white. Such ornamentation would probaby be banned from the Throne Room because of the high reflections from a brightly polished enamelled surface, and as we have seen heat and light were taboo in Babylonian interiors.

The Drainage System
  Doors in the throne-room wall communicated with what were probably the King's private apartments. The harem and other purely private suites were placed further to the west, over the earlier residence of Nabopolasser, the official portion of the palace being situated towards the east. There was a most elaborate drainage system which not only carried rain-water from the flat roofs but from the courts and walls as well. The larger drains had corbel-shaped roofs, but the smaller ones were formed of bricks set together in the shape of a 'V'

The Hanging Gardens of Babylon
M. Dovaston, R.B.A.
By permission of Messrs Hutchinson and Co.

and closed in at the top with other bricks laid flat. Vertical shafts and gutters were also in use, and these were conducted down the sides of towers and fortifications.

The Hanging Gardens

Another structure has been indicated as perhaps the foundation of the famous Hanging Gardens of Babylon. It consists of a number of barrel-vaulted cells, seven on each side of a central passage. These cells are roofed over with semi-circular arches, and are flanked on the north by the palace wall. It is known that hewn stone was employed in the construction of this 'wonder of the world,' and only in three other places in the palace demesne (the Sacred Road, the bridge over the Euphrates, and the Kasr Wall) is stone employed. This points to the identification of the site in question as being that of the Hanging Gardens, on which layers of earth were laid and the shrubs, trees, and arbours which decorated it planted thereon. Berossus distinctly states that these gardens were within the buildings by which Nebuchadrezzar enlarged his father's palace. But the dimensions of this structure do not tally with those given by Strabo and Diodorus, and the imagination revolts at the conception of these famous and romantic gardens having for their foundation this obscure and prosaic cellarage. Archæology must leave us something. By all means let us have truth and enlightenment—unless where truth is itself uglier than falsehood! It has been shrewdly conjectured by Professor King[1] that these cellars formed the palace granary, and we must be grateful to him for the suggestion.

[1] *History of Babylon*, p. 50 (1915).

MYTHS OF BABYLONIA AND ASSYRIA

The Great Gate of Ishtar

It was in the spring of 1902 that Dr. Koldewey made the important discovery of the Great Gate of the goddess Ishtar which spanned the Sacred Way of the imperial city. This turreted erection, ornamented in relief by the figures of mythical animals in coloured brick, has been excavated clean out of the superincumbent earth, and constitutes a double monument to its ancient builders and to the patient archæologists who recovered it from the sands of antiquity. It was the main gate in the north citadel wall, and had been reconstructed by the zealous Nebuchadrezzar. It is double (for the fortification line in which it stood was twofold), and in front consists of two high towers with gate-houses behind. The figures of the animals are so arranged that to the eye of one approaching the city they would seem advancing to meet him. At least 575 of these creatures were depicted on the gate, the favourite subjects being bulls and dragons, beautifully and realistically modelled in relief.

The Street of Processions

A portion of the Street of Processions upon which this gateway opened has also been excavated. This highway was of imposing breadth, and ran its course from north to south directly across the city. It was a species of Via Sacra, for over its stones was carried the image of Merodach upon his day of high festival. Its use was restricted to foot-passengers, and no chariots or other horse-drawn vehicles were permitted to make use of it. Its foundation is of burnt brick upon which is overlaid an upper pavement of breccia (conglomerate rock) in slabs.

THE TEMPLES OF BABYLON

The Temples of Babylon

Interest has naturally centred around the excavation of the five great temples of Babylon, the ground-plans of four of which have been laid bare. The temple of E-Makh, dedicated to the goddess Nin-Makh was the first to be excavated. It contains one of the only two altars found in Babylon, a structure of plain, crude brick, simple and unadorned, which stands outside its main entrance. As the only other example in the city occupies an exactly similar position, we must conclude that custom or ritual dictated an exterior site for the sacrificial altar. The temple of Nin-Makh was a simple shrine of mere mud-brick, decorated with black and white designs superimposed upon a scanty coating of whitewash. Nin-Makh (the great lady) was one of the titles of Ishtar. The temple appears to have been built round a large court, and to have been entered by a gateway flanked by a series of square, solid towers, three on either side. There is a long, narrow passage behind the shrine, which probably gave access to a concealed opening in the back wall of the temple behind the image of the goddess, who could thus have been made to give forth oracular utterances. In the courtyard was a well from which water was drawn for the purpose of performing lustral rites.

We are ignorant of the precise form of the upper part of Babylonian temples (apart from the *zikkurats* or towers), as only the lower portions of their walls in most cases remain to us. But from certain plaques and seals on which temples are represented we can glean that they were probably turreted or castellated in front and perhaps at the sides as well, and that the entrance was arched, the frontage presenting a picture not very unlike that of a heavily constructed castle of the Norman epoch. Indeed one unidentified temple bears resemblance to a prison, so forbidding is it in its almost unbroken line of turret and retaining wall. We must remember, however, that colour lent embellishment to these buildings, the otherwise heavy façades of which would have been dreary indeed.

E-Sagila

The temple of E-Sagila, which was dedicated to Merodach, patron deity of Babylon, is of course by far the most important within the city bounds. It has not been wholly excavated from the mound of Tell Amran, but the main western portion of it has been brought to light, and has been shown, like other Babylonian shrines, to have consisted of a series of chambers built round an open court. In the centre of each side was an open gateway where once stood the famous eight bronze serpents, two to each entrance. The especial shrine of Merodach, which has not yet been unearthed, lay on the western side, and had a towered entrance and decorated façade which Nebuchadrezzar stated he caused 'to shine like the sun.' He coated the walls of the shrine with gold and roofed it with the choicest cedars from Lebanon, ' the noble forest.' Here, says Herodotus, the mighty figure of the god rested, which, with the throne, dais, and table before it was fashioned of pure gold, of 800 talents in weight. To the north of Merodach's temple rose its *zikkurat* or tower. So far excavation upon it has in a measure disproved the account of Herodotus that it consisted of a stepped tower in eight stages with the ascent to the summit encircling the outside. The first stage, now uncovered, has a triple stairway built against one side of the tower, but we shall never know what the upper stories were like, for they have long since crumbled into desert dust. Dr. Koldewey considers that the great tower was built in one stage, decorated with coloured bands, and surmounted by a shrine.

The Great Tower of Nabu (E-Zida)

The foundations of the great tower of Nabu at Borsippa, a suburb of Babylon, still awaits excavation, but as it stands it rises to a height of over 100 feet above the desert. The clearing of its base will necessitate a colossal amount of labour, but when effected, our knowledge of these temple-towers will be considerably enhanced.

The Euphrates Bridge

The bridge over the river Euphrates is worthy of mention, since it represents the oldest bridge known to the science of archæology. It possessed stone piers, built in the shape of boats, thus showing that it had been evolved from an earlier bridge of boats. The bows of these piers point up-stream, and thus break the force of the current. The river at the point where it was crossed by the bridge was at least sixty feet broad, and the passage-way of wood was laid across the boat-piers, and must have been rather narrow. The structure was the work of Nabopolasser.

The Elder Babylon

During the first years of their labours the excavators were under the impression that the destruction of the older portions of the city by Sennacherib had been so complete that but few of its remains were to be looked for in the course of excavation. But as time progressed it was found that the relics

MYTHS OF BABYLONIA AND ASSYRIA

of the older quarters lay mostly beneath the present water-level. In the Menkes Mound a quarter of the ancient city has been unearthed at a depth of some thirty feet, and the outline of its streets clearly shown. Still lower were found houses dating from the period of Merodach-baladan I (1201–1189 B.C.) and Meli-shipok II (1216–1202 B.C.). A thick layer of ashes showed that a still earlier portion of the city had been destroyed by fire, and this archaic quarter has been identified as the city of Khammurabi, the princely law-maker (2123–2081 B.C.), and his immediate successors, according to dated tablets found among the burnt debris—mute witnesses of the disaster which overtook Babylon's First Dynasty.

Town-Planning

It is noticeable that the later streets follow closely the trend and plan of the older thoroughfares, which, generally speaking, ran north and south, parallel to the course of the Sacred Way. Professor King[1] gives it as his opinion that here we have a deliberate attempt at town-planning on a scientific basis! He credits this to the Semitic element in the population, as in Sumerian towns there is no trace of town-planning. And yet Babylon was strangely conservative. As she commenced, so she continued, and her early efforts were only superseded in magnitude, not in quality of purpose.

[1] *History of Babylon*, p. 85.

CHAPTER XV: THE TWILIGHT OF THE GODS

WITH the fall of the Assyrian empire in 606 B.C., Babylonia once more regained her national status. This meant that her national god Merodach was no longer subservient to the Assyrian Asshur in a political sense, and regained his place as sole head of the Babylonian pantheon.

Great must have been the satisfaction of the people of Babylon when, this comparatively mild tyranny removed, they could worship their own gods in their own way, free from the humiliating remembrance that their northern neighbours regarded all Babylonian sacred things as appanages of the Assyrian empire. Nabopolasser and Nebuchadrezzar, his successor, gave effect to these changes, and the latter king placed Nabu on a footing of equality with Merodach. Was this the cause of his punishment? Was it because he had offended in a religious sense that he had to undergo the terrible infliction of which we read in the Scriptures? The priesthood of Merodach must have possessed immense and practically unlimited power in Babylon, and we may feel sure that any such interference with their new-found privilege, as is here suggested, would have met with speedy punishment. Was the wretched monarch led to believe that an enchantment had been cast upon him, and that he had been transformed into animal shape at the command of an outraged deity? We cannot say. The cause of his misfortune must for ever remain one of the mysteries of the ancient world.

The unfortunate Nabonidus, too, attempted to replace the cults of Merodach and Nabu by that of Shamash. And that hastened his doom, for the priests became his bitter enemies, and when the Persian Cyrus entered the gates of Babylon as a conqueror he was hailed as the saviour of Merodach's honour.

The last native kings of Babylonia were great temple-builders, and this policy they continued until the end. Indeed in the time of Nebuchadrezzar there was a revival of ancient and half-forgotten cults, and many local gods were exalted to a pitch of popularity hitherto unknown.

The Conquering Cyrus

Then in 539 B.C. came the conquering Cyrus, and the period of the decay of the Babylonian religion began. The victor merely upheld the cults of Merodach and Nabu for reasons of policy, and when in turn the Greeks ruled over Babylonia they followed the Persian lead in this respect. By the defeat of the Persian Darius at the battle of Arbela (331 B.C.) the way to Babylon was left open to the mighty Alexander the Great. This was the beginning of the end. The old religion dragged out a broken existence until about the beginning of the Christian era, then slowly but surely vanished beneath the attacks of Hellenic scepticism, Christian propaganda, and pagan caprice.

That a faith so virile, so ancient, so entrenched in the love of a people as that of Babylonia should fall into an oblivion so profound as to be totally forgotten for nearly nineteen centuries is a solemn and impressive reminder of the evanescent character of human affairs. They were men of their hands, these ancient Mesopotamians, great theologians, great builders, great soldiers. Yet their mighty

A GREAT LESSON

works, their living faith left 'not a wrack behind' save mounds of rubbish which, when excavated by the modern antiquary, were found to contain a few poor vestiges of the splendour that was Babylon and the pomps of the city of Asshur. Does there not reside in this a great lesson for modernity? Must our civilization, our faith, all that is ours and that we have raised—must these things, too, fade into the shadows of unremembrance as did the civilization of Mesopotamia?

A Great Lesson

The answer to such a question depends upon ourselves—upon each and every one of us. If we quit ourselves as civilized men, striving and ever striving to refine and purify our lives, our conduct, our intellectual outlook, to spiritualize our faith, then though the things of our hands may be dust, the works of our minds, of our souls shall not vanish, but shall remain in the consciousness of our descendants so long as human memory lasts. The faith of ancient Babylon went under because it was built rather on the worship of frail and bestial gods than the love of truth,—gods many of whom were devils in disguise, but devils no whit worse than our fiends of ambition, of greed, of pugnacity, of unsympathy. Through the worship of such gods Babylon came to oblivion. Let us contemplate the colossal wreck of that mighty work of man, and as we gaze over the gulf of a score of centuries to where its "cloud-capp'd towers and gorgeous palaces" glitter in the mirage of legend, let us brace ourselves for the struggle which humanity has yet to wage with darkness, with disease, with superstition. But while we remember her fall with sadness, let us think generously and kindly of her dead mightiness, of the ancient effort she made, striving after her lights, of her picturesque and many-coloured life, and, not least, of her achievements—the invention of those symbols by which the words of man can be transferred to his brother across the silent ocean of time.

GLOSSARY AND INDEX

THE PRONUNCIATION OF ASSYRIAN

ASSYRIAN differs in many respects from the other Semitic languages. There are few gutturals, these having been mostly smoothed out. Thus 'Ba'l' became 'Bel,' and 'Hadad,' 'Adad.' On the other hand it is thought that the cuneiform inscriptions may have omitted guttural sounds. The cuneiform system of writing is so imperfect and complicated that we must make certain reservations in our acceptance of the transcriptions of contemporary Assyriologists, and it must therefore be understood that Assyrian names and words as we know them and as found in the present work and index may be yet greatly modified by future researches. Assyrian names as known to-day are pronounced according to analogy gleaned from the pronunciation of the other Semitic languages. Thus 'Shin'ar' is spelt with the Hebrew *'ain*, (guttural *a*) in the Scriptures, and we are unaware whether the Scriptural author interpolated the guttural or not. Analogy in this instance is not nearly so valuable a guide as in the case of Egyptian, where we have in Coptic the modern form of the Egyptian language to guide us, nor is it at all likely that we shall ever know much more than we do concerning the pronunciation of a language the written symbols of which are so uncertain as regards their precise alphabetic values.

GLOSSARY AND INDEX

A

AA or Â. Consort of Shamash, 110

ABED'NEGO. One of Daniel's companions, 38

AB'RAM. Ur, city of, 15, 145, 249; Nimrod and, 51-56; Jewish legends *re*, 51, 52; Persian traditions *re*, 52, 53; another tradition *re*, preserved in the East, 53-56; star Venus and, 55

AB'U-HABB'AH. The ancient site of Sippar, 177

ABYDENUS. Statement of, *re* Ea, 112

ABYSS, THE. Paradise and, 82

ACCA'D. Part of Nimrod's kingdom, 49

ACHÆMENIDÆ: Cyaxares' son dethroned by, 333

A'DAD. Equivalent, Hadad, 187-191

A'DAD-EA. Ut-Napishtim's ferryman, 172; Gilgamesh consults, 172; Ut-Napishtim, Gilgamesh and, 178

A'DAD-NARARI IV. Son of Assur-Dan III, 308

ADAM. The sons of, 232

AD'APA. The South Wind and, story of, 116-121

AD'AR. Sun-god of Nippur; Hymn to, 68; connected with the pig, 93, 294

AD'NA. Wife of Azar; according to an Eastern tradition the parents of Abram, 54

AD-ÔNIS. Smyrna, mother of, reference to, 127; myth of related to that of Tammuz, 131

AEDORACHUS. Of Pantibiblon, reference to, 112

ÆLIAN. Of Gilgamos (Gilgamesh); grandson of Sokkaros, 157

AF-AN-AS-I'EF. On vampires, 266

AFRICA, 329; Semitic religion in, 331

A'HAB. King of Israel, overthrown by Shalmaneser II, 24

A'HI-MI-TI. Sargon displaces Azuri by, 210

AH'RI-MAN. Mazda and Sraosha overcome, 337

AHURA MAZDA. Good principle of Zarathustra's religion, 334; creator of the universe, 335

A-I'BU. The serpent, 289

AKK'AD. Kingdom founded by Semites, 16; King Sargon of, founds first great Semitic empire in Babylonia, 16

AKK-AD'IANS. Description of, 13-16; language, 13, 14; Babylonian Semites receive germs of culture from the, 14; modern equivalent for the older, is the expression 'Sumerian,' 15; stars studied by, 231

AKK'U-LU (Eater). Attendant hound of Merodach, 202

A-LAL'U. The eagle; Ishtar and, 167

ALEXANDER THE GREAT, 378

'ALL'AH.' Modern Arabic name, 325

ALL-A-TU. Equivalent, Eresh-kigal, mistress of Hades, 129; realms of, 237

Al-ô-nim. Descriptive term of Phœnicians for their gods, 327

ALTAR-S. Of Dodo, and of Yahveh, 190, 191

A'LU. Bull, sent by Anu against Gilgamesh, 168, 169

AL'U-DEMON. The, 271, 277

A-MAR'UDUK. The name Merodach, originally, 202

AM'EN-HET'EP IV. King of Egypt; letters to, unearthed at Tel-el-Amarna, 22

AMORITE-S. Hadad, a god of the, 188; deity; Dagon an, 352

AN'A-TU. The consort of Anu, 123; mother of Ishtar, 168

ANCESTOR-WORSHIP. The Canaanites and, 326

383

ANDRAE, DR. A German explorer, 356
ANIMALS. Babylonian gods having form of, 92, 93; mythological monsters and, of Chaldea, 289–298; the dog, 290–292; the pig, 294
ANIMISTIC. Babylonian religion typically, 317, 319
AN-NE-DA'TUS. Appears from Eruthrean Sea, 112
Ann'-u-na-ki, THE. Generic name for the gods of the earth, 82, 130; spirits of earth, 90; decree fate, 173; torches carried by, 175
AN'SAR. God; birth of, 71; Tiawath and, 76
AN'SHAR. Variant of Asshur; created with Kishar, 208; Anu, Ea, and Merodach sent to destroy Tiawath, 208
AN'U. God of the sky; son of Ansar and Kisar, 72; Ansar and, 76; Merodach and, 79; most ancient of Babylonian deities, 90; held sway over Erech and Der, 94; temple of, 102; South Wind and, 117–121; En-lil, Ea and, the universal triad, 121; significance, 121–123; Anatu, the consort of, 123; Bau and, 144; sacred bull sent against Gilgamesh by, 158; father of Ishtar, 168; Hadad worshipped with, at Asshur, 188; the Tablets of Destiny and, 195; in a triad with Ea and Bel, but more frequently in the texts apart from them, 197, 198; Dagan and, 198; in Assyria—in Babylon, 217; invoked with Bel, 227; the Pole Star, 236; eclipses and, 255
ANU'NIT. Lesser goddess, merged in conception of Ishtar, 124
APH-RO-DI'TÉ. Ishtar and cult, of, 124; Ishtar and, connected, 235
APOCRYPHA. Legend of Bel and the Dragon in, 97

APOLLO. Temple to, at Carthage, 330
APOLLODORUS. Statement of, *re* Ea, 112
Ap'su. The deep, or 'house of knowledge,' 72; alternative, Zigarun; mother of Ea, 72, 73, 74; the primeval, 193
AQUARIUS, SIGN OF. The deluge story and, 183
ARABIA. Semites believed to have come from, 15, 16; Naram-Sin penetrates, 17; Semitic religion in, 331
AR-AKH'TU. Nabopolasser and the channel called the, 368
AR-A-LÛ. 1. The underworld, 125; 128–131, 171. 2. Goddess; variant, Eres-ki-gal; Nergal and, 150
AR-BE'LA. Ishtar's shrine in, 212; battle of, 378
ARCHÆOLOGY. Babylonian, 46, 47; Chaldean, 339–366; American interest in Babylonian, 356–366; fashionable about the time of Nabonidus (556–539 B.C.), 363
ARES. Greek god, 315
AR'GO. Ea identified with a star in the constellation, 236
ARK. The Babylonian, 174–178
AR-TA'IOS. Median monarch; Nannar confounded with, 146
ARTEMIS. Reference to, 132
ART-S. Babylonian; gem-cutting, etc., 17; Babylonian literature and, under Khammurabi the Great, 20; all the, under Ea's patronage, 192
A-RU'-RU. Goddess who aided the formation of man, 82, 86, 123; creates a champion against Gilgamesh, 162
AR'Y-AN. Race; the Philistines of, 324
AS-A'RI. Appellation of Merodach, 202; may be compared with Asar (Osiris), 202
ASH'DOD. Temple of Dagon at, 151; Sargon's expedition against, 210, 211, 350

GLOSSARY AND INDEX

ASH'TART or ISH'TAR. Worshipped in Carthage, 327, 330

ASH'TER-OTH or AS-TAR'TE. Ishtar known to Canaanites, Phœnicians, and Greeks as, 124, 319, 326; the Aphrodite of the Greeks, 131; Phœnician god, 328

ASHURBAN'APAL. See Assur-banipal.

A-SHU'SHU-NA'MIR. Created by Ea, 130

ASIA. Submitted to Ninus, 25; Tiglath-pileser III invested with sovereignty of, 30; Belit and Asshur in pantheon of, 228

ASIA MINOR. Greek colonies in, 235, 236; peopled by diverse races, 324; worship of Ashtart in, 328

A'si-pû. The wizards, 260; 273, 274

AS'KE-LON. Temple of Ashtart (Ishtar) at, 327

ASSH'UR. 1. City; site of, explored by the German expedition of 1899, 47; residence of god Asshur, 207; Bel's temple in, 227. 2. God; identified with Merodach, 94; Ishtar, consort of, 125; religion of Assyria centres in, 206–211; etymology of name, 208; variant, Anshar, 208; mentioned in inscription of Samsi-Ramman, 208; Sargon and the conquering power of, 210, 211; Ishtar and, 214; Bel-Merodach placed after, in the Assyrian Pantheon, 225, 377; prisoner-gods and, 226; Belit and, 227

ASSUR-BAN'I-PAL. King of Assyria; Greek equivalent, Sardanapalus, 32; historic reality, 33; death of, 33; succeeded Esar-haddon, 34; Samus-sumyukin, brother of, 34; his death, 35; his library at Nineveh, 35, 46, 71, 261, 282, 346; patron of literature, 154; Sin and, 224; Belit and, 227, 228; capture of twenty gods of the Elamites by, 204; tablets dealing with magic in library of, 261; the five hounds of, 290, 291; autobiography of, 301–306; palace of, discovered by Rawlinson, 346; fragment of history of, discovered by George Smith, 352; tablets of, 354; zikkurat of, 365

ASS'UR-DAN III. The fatal eclipse and, 307–309

ASSUR-NAZ'IR-PAL. Son of Tuk-ul-ti-in-Aristi, 23; places Hadad-nadin-akhi on throne of Babylon, 23; Ishtar and, 214; Ninib, and, 214, 216; Calah residence of, 215; Shamash and, 223; Sin and, 223; sculptures glorifying, 343; dedications of, unearthed, 351

ASSUR-NAZ'IR-PAL III. King of Assyria, reference to his reign, 23

ASS'UR-RI-SHI'-SHI'. Ninib and, 214

ASS'UR-YU-BALL'IDH. The Kassite king of Babylonia marries daughter of, 22

ASSYRIA-NS. Race origin, 12; Hittite and Amorite elements intermingled with, 12, 13; land boundaries, the Tigris and Euphrates, 12; the Akkadians and, 13; Tiglath-pileser, King of, 23; Semiramis the Great, Queen of, 24–29; Assur-banipal desired to make the centre of religious influence of the empire, 35; Scythians penetrate into, 36; Sin-sar-iskin, last King of, 36; cuneiform writing of, 60–66; religion, Semitic influence on, 91, 92; the Pantheon of, 203–230; religion of, centres in Asshur, 206; greatness; secret of, 208, 209; Ishtar in, 211–214; worship of Ramman in, 220; Shammash's cult in, 222, 223; Bel-Merodach and, 225; cult of Nabu in, 228; temples of, 242–251; culture; progenitors of, 250; magic and demonology, 257–288; belief in taboo, 278;

religions of Babylonia and, comparative value of, 313-337; religion of Zoroaster supplanted that of ancient, 332; ethics, 337, 338; modern excavations in, 339-366; empire, fall of, in 606 B.C., 377

ASTROLOGY. Birthplace of, 231

ATARATH. The *arel* (or altar) of Dodo carried from, 190

ATARGA'TUS. God; Dagon worshipped as, 27

ATARYAT'IS. Alternative, Derketo. Fish-goddess, legendary mother of Semiramis, 25

ATHENAG'ORAS. Refers to worship of Semiramis, 27

ATHENS. Piræus, port of, 328

AT'TIS. A god akin to Adonis, 132

AU'RA MA-I-NYU. Evil principle of Zarathustra's religion, 334

A-VERR'-O-ES. Friend of Maimonides, 232

AVESTA. Earliest form of Zoroaster's name in the, 333

A'YA. The betrothed of Shamash, 166

AZ'AR. One of Nimrod's guards; traditional father of Abram, 54

AZ'TECS. Reverence of, for worship of Toltecs, 226, 227

AZ-U-RI, KING. Sargon displaces, by Ahimiti, 210

B

BAAL. Sun-god; Hadad the supreme, 189; magic and, 258; Phœnician god, 327; Tanit alluded to as 'The Countenance of —,' 330

'BA'AL.' Canaanitish god, 325; term applied by Phœnicians, 327

BAAL-AMM'ON or MO'LOCH. See Moloch

BA'AL-HAMM'AN. Phœnician god worshipped in Carthage, 327

Ba'alim. Presiding spirits, 326; of Tyre, the Phœnicians and, 327

BA'BEL. The Tower of, 48; Hebrew verb *babal* confused with word *babel*, 48; story of Tower of, suggested by one of the towers of Babylon; the beginning of Nimrod's kingdom was, 49

BÂBIL. Mound and enclosure of 103, 347; as a citadel, 368

BA'BU. Esar-haddon, restorer of, 306

BABYLON-IA-N. Racial origin, 12; mother of astrology and magic, 12; land boundaries, the Tigris and Euphrates, 12; the Akkadians and, 13; Semites—receive germs of culture from Akkadians, 14; language, 14; civilization, 14; offshoot of culture of Eridu, 15; first founders, 15; Semite conquerors enter, 15, 16; first great Semitic empire in, founded by Sargon of Akkad, 16; Syria and Palestine welded with, by Sargon, 17; kings, vicegerents of the gods, 17; art; gem-cutting, etc., 17; communication between island of Cyprus and, 18; fall of 'First Dynasty of —' 21; Burna-buryas, King of, 22; Tukulti-in-Aristi takes, and slays King Bitilyasu, 22; built by Semiramis, 26; finally conquered by Tiglath-pileser III, 30; surrender of, through starvation, 34; literature; Assur-bani-pal and, 35; Nebuchadrezzar leads Jews into captivity in, 37; Kings; Nabonidus, last of, 40; independence of, recovered after death of Darius, 41; Persians conquer, 41; destruction of, 41; Seleucia built out of ruins of, 42; archæology, 46, 47; legend of confusion of tongues and towers of, 47; E-Sagila, tower of, 47; built by Nimrod, 50; cuneiform writing of, 60-66; cosmogony, 70-87; religion, early, 88-153; spirits and gods in ancient, 89-153; religion, Semitic influence on,

GLOSSARY AND INDEX

91, 92; religion, signs of totemism in, 92; the Pantheon—Early, 94, 95: Later, 184–198; Nippur preferred to, 196; the country of Bel, 225; star-worship in, 231–238; temples of, 242–251; magic and demonology, 257–288; belief in taboo, 278; conquered by Shalmaneser I, 308; religions of Assyria and, comparative value, 313–336, etc.; captivity, 321; religion, penetrated to Britain, 331; the religion of Zoroaster supplanted that of ancient, 332; ethics, 337, 338; myth, compared with Hellenic and Scandinavian, 338; moral code, 338; modern excavations in, 339–366; the, of Nebuchadrezzar II, 367; water supply of, 368; hanging gardens of, 371; the elder, 375, 376; national status of, regained, 377; religion, decay of, 378, 379

Bab-y-lon'ic-a. A work by Iamblichus, containing fragments of Babylonian history, 56; reference to an epitome of the, by Photius, 56

BANKS. Temples as, 250, 251

BAPHOMET. Name of pagan idol, 293

BARBARO, JOSAPHAT. Cuneiform writing and, 61

BAR-SA'NES. King of Armenia, 25

Barû. The seers, 260

BAS'RA. Layard sends sculptures to, 344; Ernest de Sarzec, French vice-consul at, 355

BAS-RELIEF-S. Found in palace of Sennacherib at Kouyunjik, 345; found in palace of Assur-bani-pal, 346

BAU. Goddess; mother of mankind, 'chief daughter of Anu,' 144, 145; *Zag-muku* and, 251

BE-DAD or BEN-DAD. The father of the Edomite Hadad, 190

BE-EL'ZE-BUB. Magic and, 258

BE-HIS-TÛN. Persian text at, 65

BEL. Babylonian sun-god, 41; the Dragon and 71; Merodach and, 79, 194; at Nippur, looked on as creator of man, 86; ruled at Nippur (Niffur), 94; earlier variant, En-lil; description of, 95–97; legend of the Dragon and, in the Apocrypha, 97; worship of, at Babylon, 98; King Cyrus and worship of, 98–101; the temple of, 101–105; discovery of Mr George Smith *re* temple of, 101; Nebo, son of, 102; father of Nirig, 153; Ut-Napishtim and, 174, 176; Gilgamesh resorts to, 180; Tablets of Destiny and, 193–195; Dagan and, 198, 216; the Assyrians and the country of, 225; Merodach usurped place of, 227; the Pole Star (of equator), 236; eclipses and, 255; Bilé allied with, 317; shrine to, of King Bur-Sin I, 364

Bel, The Observations of. In library founded by Sargon, 18; translated into Greek by Berossus, 18

BEL'IT. A generic term given to Ishtar, 214, 227; Anu's consort, 227; figures as wife of Asshur, 227; Tiglath-pileser I and, 227; Assur-bani-pal and, 227

BEL-KU'DUR-U'ZUR. The last of the old Assyrian line, killed by Hadad-nadin-akhi, 23

BEL-MER'O-DACH. Babylonian god; avenged by Cyrus, 41; son of Ea and Dawkina, 73; absorbed into the Assyrian pantheon, 225

BE'LOS. *See* variant, Bel-Merodach, 73

BEL-TE-SHAZZ'AR. Babylonian appellation for Daniel, 37

BEL'TIS. Variant, Nin-lil; the wife of En-lil, 101; sanctuary of, at Girsu, 101; name signified 'lady,' 101; tablets and figures of, found by Dr Peters, 364

BEL'US. Temple of; mound of Bâbil identified with, 103; delineations of animals preserved in temple of, 114; variant, Dis, 114
BEL-ZAK'IR-ISK'UN. Descendant of Assur-bani-pal, 306, 307
BE-NA'NI. God; husband of Melili, 82
BE-NI'NI. King of the monsters, 295, 296
BER-OSS'US. 1. Babylonian historian; translates *The Observations of Bel* into Greek, 18; narrative of, *re* creation of man, 81; his statement *re* Ea copied by Alexander Polyhistor, etc., 112, 113; quotes version of the deluge myth, 177, 178; the hanging gardens of Babylon and, 371. 2. A priest of Bel at Babylon, 42; 'history' by, 42–45; extracts from history of, preserved by Josephus and Eusebius, 42; Sisuthrus and, 42; his legend of Oannes, 42; his account of the deluge, 42–44; Daonus and, 127
BILÉ. A Celtic deity, 317
BINT-EL-AMIR. Hill of, 358, 361, 362, 365
BIRD MESSENGERS. Ut-Napishtim sends out, 176
BIRS NIMRŪD. Ruins of, 103
Bit-ili, THE. Sacred stones, 19
BIT-IL-YA'SU. King of Babylon, slain by Tukulti-in-Aristi, 22
BOMBAY. The Parsis of, 336
BOR-SIP'PA. Site of Nebo's temple at, 103; 'The Stages of the Seven Spheres,' the wonder of, 104; chief seat of Nebo's worship, 184
BOTTA, M. Archæological researches at Nineveh, 46; French Consul at Mosul; his excavations in Mesopotamia, 339, 340
BRITISH MUSEUM. Bricks in, containing Assur-bani-pal's researches, 35, 71, 154, 155, 290; obelisc of Shalmaneser II in, 343

BULL. Sacred, slain by Gilgamesh and Eabani, 158; Ramman's name the great, 220; forms of Ea and Merodach, 290
BULL, WINGED. Symbol of and En-lil, 97; associated with Merodach, 289, 290
BURMESE. Attitude of, to the dead, 269
BUR'NA-BUR'YAS. King of Babylonia, 22
BURNOUF. Cuneiform writing and, 63
BUR-SIN. Repairs Urbau's zikkurat, 248; shrine to Bel dedicated by, 364
BYB'LUS. Journey of Isis to, 328; Philo of, 328

C

CA'LAH. Sennacherib takes nucleus of Assur-bani-pal's library from, 154; residence of Asshur, 207; Ninib's temple at, 215; residence of Assur-nazir-pal, 215; Sin's temple of, 223; tower of, discovered by Layard, 346
CALMET, ABBÉ. Disbelief of, in vampires, 266
CAL'NEH. Part of Nimrod's kingdom, 49
CAM-BY'SES. Son of Cyrus, 41
CANAANITES, THE. First historic dwellers in Syria and Palestine, 324–326; gods of, 325, 326; ancestor-worship and, 326
CANNING, SIR STRATFORD. Sir Henry Layard assisted by, in his excavations at Nimrûd, 340
CAPRICORNUS, SIGN OF. Sea-goddess Sabitu and, 183
CAPTIVITY, THE BABYLONIAN, 321–323
CARAVAN. The story of the missing, 285–288
CAR-CHE'MISH. Worship of Hadad extended from, to Edom, 189
CARTHAGE. Dido, the presiding deity of, 190; Ba'al-Hamman

GLOSSARY AND INDEX

worshipped in, 327; Tanith honoured at, 328; Eshmun worshipped at, 328; religion of Semites of, 329; Dido, Queen of, 329; Apollo's temple at, 330; Mohammedanism at, 332

CELTIC. Teutonic religion and, compared, 317; deity; Bilé a, 317

CE'RES. Reference to, 133

CHAL'CHIS. Iamblichus a native of, 56

CHALDEAN MYTHOLOGY. The sign Gemini, associated with the two forms of the solar deity in, 182

CHAL-DE'A-N-S. Birthplace of Abram, 52; Nimrod, King of, 52; star-gazers, 202; difference between the faiths of the two great races of, 204; astrologers, 231, 232; speculations, 233–235; magic, 258, 259; belief in taboo, 278; belief in superstitions, 280; divination, 281; excavations in, 339

CHA'OS. Tiawath, 193

CHARDIN, JOHN. Cuneiform writing and, 61

CHE'MOSH. God of the Moabite king, Mesha, 190

CHRISTIANITY. Initiated by Semitic race, 313; Jewish influence upon, 320

CHRO'NOS. Berossus substitutes for Ea in the version of the deluge myth quoted in his history, 177

CHUS. The Æthiop; equivalents, Cush, or Cash (a coloured race), 49; father of Nimrod, 49

CIRCLE, THE MAGIC. Chaldean sorcerers and, 275, 276

CODE, MORAL. Of the Babylonians, 338

COLOSSI. Gate of, 101; example of art of which Ea was patron, 229

COR-CY'RE-AN MOUNTAINS. Reference to, by Berossus, 44

CORN-SPIRITS. The primitive, 139

CORNWALL. Phœnicians in, 331

COSMOGONY. Babylonian, 70–87; Jastrow's opinion, 84; type of, 84–87

CREATION. Babylonian myth of, 70–87; story of, in Genesis; myths found in Egyptian papyri; and that in the *Popol Vuh*, 70; Seven Tablets of, 71; of man, by Merodach, 80, 81; legend; Apsu and Tiawath in, 193; 'Cuthæan legend of—,' 294–296; common origin of Biblical and Babylonian accounts of, 323

CTES'I-AS. His tale *re* Parsondes, 146–149; reference to, 367

CUNE-I-FORM TEXTS. Merodach and, 200

CUNEIFORM WRITING. *See* Writing

CUSH, or CASH. *See* equivalent, Chus

CU'THAH. Temple of Nergal at, 82, 94, 105; 296

CU-THÆ'AN LEGEND, THE. Of creation, 294–296

CYAXARES. Scythian king of Ecbatana, 36; son of, dethroned by Achæmenidæ, 333

CYBE'LÉ. The mother-goddess, 132

CYPRUS. Among the conquest of Sargon, 18; communication between Babylonia and island of, 19; worship of Ashtart at, 327

CYRUS, KING. The worship of Bel and, 98–101

CYRUS THE PERSIAN. Invasion of Babylonia by, 41; the pretended avenger of Bel-Merodach, 41; Cambyses, son of, 41; conqueror of Babylon and saviour of Merodach's honour, 378

D

DA'DA. Abbreviated form of Abd-Hadad; resemblances between Hadad, Dido, Davad, and, 189–191; Shalmaneser (II) speaks of, 189

DAG'AN. Palestinian form of Dagon; a fish-god, same as Oannes or Ea, 216, 217; associated with Bel, 217; Anu and, 198

DAG'ON. God Atargatus worshipped under the name of, 27; a fish-god, 151, 152; an Amorite deity, 325

DAM'AS. One of the two eunuchs appointed to watch Rhodanes and Sinonis, 57

DAM-AS'CI-US. The last of the Neoplatonists, 72; author of *Doubts and Solutions of the First Principles*, 73

DAM-AS'CUS. Worship of Hadad at, under name of Rimmon, 189; worship of Ramman in, 220

DAM'KU. One of the lesser Babylonian gods, 229

DAN'I-EL. Babylonian appellation, Belteshazzar, 37; Nebuchadrezzar and, 37-40; Shadrach, Meshach, and Abednego companions of, 38; reference to a corrupted story of the deliverance of the three Hebrew princes recorded by, 53; Book of, 97; the worship of Bel and, 98-101

DA'ON. The shepherd king of Pantibiblon, 112

DA-O'NUS or DAOS. King of Babylonia, *vide* Berossus, 127.

DAR-I'US. Babylonia independence recovered after death of, 41; defeated at Arbela, 378

DA'VID. Resemblances between Hadad, Dáda, Dido, and, 189-191; variants, Dod, Dodo, 190

DAW-KI'NA. Belos (Bel-Merodach), the son of Ea, and, 73; saved from the deluge, 115; Ishtar identified with, 127, 137; consort of Ea, 197

DE MORGAN. Unearths monument of Naran-Sin at Susa, 17; copy of Khammurabi's code found by, 21

DE SAR'ZEC, ERNEST. French vice-consul at Basra; diorite statues of Gudea (2700 B.C.) found by, 47; excavations of, at Tellô, 355, 356; *Découvertes en Chaldée par*, reference to, 356

DEAD. The doctrine of ministering to, 181; often left unburied in Babylonia, 269; attitude of Burmese to, 269; Canaanites and cult of the, 326; Persians and their, 336; Parsis and their, 336; 'House of the —,' at Nippur, 362

DELLA VALLE, PIETRO. Cuneiform writing and, 61

DELPHI. Worshippers of Apollo send offerings to, 330

DELUGE, THE. Berossus' account of, 42-45; reference to account of, in *Gilgamesh Epic*, 42; analogies with Flood Myth, 45, 46; Babylonian and Hebrew story of, have a common origin, 45, 323; myth of, 112, 173-178; refugees saved from—Ea, etc., 115

DEMETER. Tanit compared with, 330

DEMONOLOGY. Of Babylonia and Assyria, 257-288

DEMONS. Many Babylonian gods evolved from, 268; Babylonian, described, 276-278

DESTINY. Mammetum, the maker of, 173; Zu and the Tablets of, 193-195; the Lia Fail, the Stone of, reference to, 248

DEVIL-S. Possession by, 262

DI-A'NA. Goddess, 235, 319

DI-BARR'A. A variant of Nergal, 106; a Babylonian deity placed in the Assyrian pantheon, 229

DI'DO. Resemblances between Hadad, Dáda, David, and, 189-191; Queen of Carthage, 329; Tanit identified with, 331

DIS. Variant of Belus, 114

DIVINATION. Practice of, by Babylonians and Assyrians, 281-288; Shamash, Hadad, and Rimmon, ' lords of —,' 283; Phœnicians' belief in, 329

DIVINITIES, TRIBAL. The most outstanding, 94

DIVS. Arch-demons and demons, 334

GLOSSARY AND INDEX

Dod or Dodo. *See* David; worship of, by the side of Yahveh, 190

Dog-s. The, in Babylonia; five hounds of Assur-bani-pal, 290, 291; legend of a, 291, 292

Dragon, The. Bel and, 71; China and, 80; in Egypt, it is the serpent Apep, 80; in India, the serpent Vritra (Ahi), 80; in Australia and in parts of N. America a great frog, 80; Beowulf and, 80; Faffnir and, 80; legend of Bel and, in the Apocrypha, 97; Merodach's, 186; the, in Zoroaster's religion, 337

Dream-s. Nebuchadrezzar's, and Daniel, 37–40; of Gyges, King of Lydia, 302, 303

Du-mu-zi. A contraction of Dumu-zi-apsu; name of Tammuz derived from, 126

Dun'gi. Gudea vassal of the throne of, 19

Dynasty. 'The First, of Babylon,' 21; a Kassite, founded by Kandis, 21; the First, of Ur, 101; Khumbaba, and an Elamite, 166; reference to Kassite, 248; the Hammurabi, 325; the Seleucidæ and the Arsacidæ, 333

E

E'a, or O'an-nes. The Babylonian god of light and wisdom, 14; held sway at Eridu, 14; legendary father of Semiramis, 25; source of all things and, 72; Apsu (Zigarun), mother of, 72; variant, Nudimmud, 73; Tiawath and, 76; Merodach and, 79; displaced politically by Merodach, 86, 199; name of Jonah may be compared with that of, 87; fish-form of, 93; the god of the deep, 93; Eridu, city of, 94; temple of, 102; the god of the waters and of the abyss, 111–116; father of Merodach, 111, 191; Greek name, Oannes, 111; instructions tending to humanize mankind, 112, 113; writings of, 113–116; myth *re* creation of world and, 115; variant, Nina-gal, 116; variant, En-ki, 116; Adapa, son of, 116; Dagon (Dagan) same as, 151, 152, 216, 217; Ut-Napishtim instructed by, 174, 176; in later times, 191–193; Dawkina, consort of, 197; identified with a star in the constellation Argo, 236; eclipses and, 255; demons and name of, 263; gazelles and, 292

Ea-ba'ni. Goddess Aruru and, 86; temple maiden Ukhut and, 129, 163; typifies primitive man in Gilgamesh epic, 155, 159, 160; the monster Khumbaba and, 158; slain by wrath of Ishtar, 158; shade of, appears to Gilgamesh, 160; a sort of satyr, 163; the beguiling of, 163, 164; Gilgamesh meets, 164–166; death of, 170; Gilgamesh laments, 179; ghost of, designated *utukku*, 181

Eagle. Symbol of Kis, 294, 296; Babylonian fable *re* the, 296–298

Ea-lur. Goddess; amalgamated with Zarpanitum, 186

E-anna. Temple of, at Erech, 250

E-anna-tum. Shamash first mentioned in reign of, 109; 'stele of vultures' erected by, discovered by de Sarzec, 355

Earth. The *Annunaki*, the spirits of, 90; -mother, worship of, 318, 319

E-babb'ara. 'The shining house'; name of Shamash's sanctuary, 109, 249

Ec-ba-ta'na. Cyaxares, the Scythian king of, 36

Eclipse. Terror of, to Babylonians, 255, 256; the fatal, in case of Assur-Dan III, 307–309

391

E'DOM. Worship of Hadad extended from Carchemish to, 189

E-GIG-UN-NÛ. 'House of the Tomb'; the temple-tower of Nippur, 362

EGYPT. Semitic immigrants in, 15; conquered by Semiramis, 26; Esar-haddon wars with, 31; Nebuchadrezzar invades, 37; cult of Ishtar in, 124; Semitic religion in, 331; excavations in, 339

E-KUR. The temple of, 248, 253; temples of E-Sagila and, 249

E'LAM-ITES. Northern Mesopotamia and, overcome by Sargon, 17; yoke of, thrown off by Khammurabi, 20; name of Khumbaba argues enmity between Babylon and, 166; Assur-bani-pal and gods of the, 204; votive object from, 248

EL-BUGÂT. Feast of, 134

EL-IS'SA. Dido confounded with, 190

Elôhim. Term employed in Genesis, 327

EN-KI. Variant of Ea, 116

EN-LIL. The god, 14; temple of, unearthed, 47; Merodach and, 84; earlier name of Bel, 95–97; a god of vegetation, 96; symbol of winged bull represents, 97; word *lil* signifies a 'demon,' 97; Beltis (Nin-lil), wife of, 101; Hadad resembled, 188; Ramman, son of, 221; temple of E-Kur sacred to, 248

EN-MASH'TI. Name of Ninib translated by Canaanites as, 326

E'NOCH, BOOK OF. Quoted, 294

E'NOS. Son of Seth, 232

EPH'ES-US. Patroness of, and Diana, 235

EP-I-PHA'NI-US. His allegations *re* Nimrod, 49

ER'ECH. Part of Nimrod's kingdom, 49; temple of, 82; Dibarra plunders, 106–109; centre of Ishtar's cult, 124; Gilgamesh, prince of, 154; temple of Ishtar at, 248

ER'ESH-KI-GAL (Allatu). The mistress of Hades, 129

ER-I-DU. Babylonian civilization grouped round, 14; the home of Ea, or Oannes, the god of light and wisdom, 14; Ur a near neighbour of, 15; culture of, and Babylon, 15; 'magical' hymns emanated from, 68; worshippers of Ea at, 72; temple of Ea at, 111; the deluge and, 116; supremacy of, passes to Babylon, 199; Merodach originated at, 200

E-SAG-I'LA. Nabonidus and the priests of, 41; Nebo's shrine, E-Zila, in temple of, 185; name of Merodach's temple at Babylon, 200; temples of E-Kur and, 249; temple of, 250, 368, 374, 375

E-SAGILA. Tower in Babylon, 47, 374, 375

E'SAR-HAD'DON. Son of Sennacherib, 31; Assur-bani-pal succeeded, as King of Assyria, 34; Ishtar and, 212; 'the most likeable' of the Assyrian kings, 306, 307; palace built by, unearthed by Layard, 343

ESHMÛN. The god of force and healing, 328, 330

ESHMUN-MEL'KARTH. Phœnician combination, 328

ES'THER. Ishtar and, 124, 140–144; Book of, why written, 141; equivalent, Ishtar, 142; Lang, on story of, 142, 143; Xerxes and, 143; variant, Hadassah, 143; Dr Jastrow on Book of, 143

ET-A'NA. The legend of, 195

ETHICS. Babylonian and Assyrian, 337, 338

ETHNOLOGICAL DIFFERENCES. Between the peoples of the northern and southern culture-groups, 203

EUPHRATES. 1. River, 177, 368, 369; 2. Bridge, 375

EUPH-RA'TES - TIG'RIS. Valley; civilization of, influenced Semitic field, 92

GLOSSARY AND INDEX

Eu-se'bi-us. Sanchuniathon, Philo, and, 329

Excavation-s. Modern, in Babylonia and Assyria, 339–366; in Egypt, 339; map relating to, in Babylonia and Assyria, 341; at Nineveh by George Smith, 347–354; at Kouyunjik by Rassam, 354, 355; of de Sarzec at Tellô, 355, 356; Babylonian Exploration Fund instituted in America, 356–366; under control of the University of Pennsylvania, 360–366; recent, by German Oriental Society, 367–377

E-Zi'da. 1. Temple of Nabu at, 250; discovered by Rawlinson 346; 2. Great tower of Nabu, 375

E-Zila. 'The firm house'; Nebo's shrine in temple of E-Sagila, 185

F

Fable. A Babylonian, re the eagle, 296–298

Fate-s. The great gods Annunaki decree, 173; the Chamber of, 185, 252, 253

Father-sky. Of primitive mythologies, 196

Feast-s. The Jewish, of Purim, 140; Babylonian, 251, 252

Festival-s. Of Adonis, 135; of the Sacæa or Zakmuk, 141; New Year; Nebo and, 185; Babylonian; *Zag-muku*, sacred to Bau, 251, 252; Scottish-Celtic, of Beltane, 317.

Field. An expert Assyriologist, 358

Fire-god. Gibil, the, 225

Fire-worship. The central feature of Zoroastrian ritual, 335

Fisher, Mr. Architect in American exploration campaign, 360

Flood. See Deluge.

Fra-vash'i. Guardian spirit of the Persians, 336

Frazer, Sir James. On the Greek way of representing Ashurbanapal (*i.e.* Sardanapalus), 32; on the real and the mock Sardanapalus, 34; Tammuz, and his *Golden Bough*, 134; Ishtar and, 137; feast of Purim and, 140; on Vashti, 143

Fresnel. French exploration expedition and, 347

G

Gardens, Hanging. Of Babylon, 371

Gar'mus. King of Babylon; romance of Sinonis and, 56–60; Rhodanes and, 56–60

Gathas. The most ancient part of the Avesta, 333

Ga-tum-dug. Goddess; allied form of Bau, 145

Ga'za. Temple of Dagon at, 151

Gazelle. Goat and, gods, 292–294

Gem'i-ni, Sign. Gilgamesh and Eabani some relation to the, 182

Genesis, Book of. Reference to, re Nimrod, 49; creation story in, 70, 289; Abbé Loisy and, 322, 323; term *elohim* in, 327

Germany. Goat-demon adored in, 293

Ghosts. Assyrian, 277, 278

Gi'bi. Prayer and the god, 68

Gib'il. The god of fire; Nusku and, 225

Gilgamesh. Hero; Nimrod identified with, 50, 156; epic; goddess Aruru figures in, 86; prince of Erech, 154–183; provisional name *Gisdhubar*, or *Izdubar*, 156; Shamash and, 156; birth of, related by Ælian, 156; Rimatbelit, mother of, 158; shade of Eabani appears to, 160; Ishtar's love for, 167, 168; mourning the loss of Eabani, 170; his quest for the secret of perpetual life, 170–173; his ancestor, Ut-Napishtim, 170; Sin delivers, 170; seeks from Ut-Napishtim the secret of

393

perpetual life, 173–180; Adad-Ea and, 178, 179
GIL-GA′MESH EPIC, THE. Account of deluge in, reference to, 42; one of the greatest literary productions of ancient Babylonia, 154–183; Ishtar in, 213
GIR′SU. Beltis' sanctuary at, 101
GIS-DHU′BAR or IZDU′BAR. Gilgamesh's provisional name, 156
GISH-ZI′DA. One of the guardians of the gates of heaven, 118
GOATS. Gazelle and, gods, 292–294
GOD-s. Ea, or Oannes, 14, 25, 72, 73, 76, 79, 86, 87, 93, 94, 102, 111–116, 216, 229; En-lil, 14, 47, 84, 95–97, 101; Babylonian kings the direct vicegerents of the, on earth, 17; Babylonian, Merodach, 41, 47, 50, 68, 76–82, 81, 84, 86, 93, 94, 103, 106, 184–198, 199–202; Bel, Babylonian sun-, 41, 196, 197; the birth of the, 71–87; Tiawath, Apsu, and Mummu, a trinity of, 74; Horus, reference to, 75; Kingu; Tiawath and, 75; Merodach, the creator of the, 82; Semites and, 89; spirits and, in ancient Babylonia, 89–91; Anu, most ancient of Babylonian, 90, 121–123, 197, 198, 217; invoked by Assyrian kings, 90; Kis, the sun-, 93, 294; under animal forms, 92, 93; the great, 93–153; Sin, moon-, 94, 109, 128, 170, 325; tribal divinities, 94; pantheon that held sway prior to Khammurabi, 94, 95; description of Bel, 96; a trinity of (Bel, Ea, and Anu), 97; Sibi, 108; Shamash, the sun-, 41, 94, 109, 187, 222, 223, 325; Nergal, 82, 94, 105, 106, 151, 180, 235, 326, 328, 329; Adapa, 116–121; Ishtar, 123–144; Tammuz, sun-god of Eridu, 126–144; Ishtar and Persephone, 131–135; Nin-Girsu, 144; Bau, 144; Pap-sukal, messenger of the, 130; Gatum-dug, 145; Nannar, the moon-god of Ur, 145–149; Dagon, a fish-, 151, 152, 216, 217, 325; Nirig, or Enu-Restu, 153; Gilgamesh, a sun-, 157; Eabani, a sun-, 159; Later Pantheon of Babylonia, 184–198; Nebo, 184–186, 326; Ramman, 187–189, 195, 217–222, 325; Hadad or Adad, 187–191, 325; Baal, a sun-, 189, 327, 328; Dáda, Dido, Dodo, 189–191; Zu, a storm-, 193–195; Merodach originally a sun-, 199; the great, of Assyria, 205–229; Asshur, 94, 124, 206–211; Nin-ib, war-god and hunter-, 214–216, 326; the moon-, 94, 109, 128, 170, 180, 223, 224; Nusku, 224, 225; Gibil, the fire-, 225; Bel-Merodach, 225; prisoner-, 225, 226; Belit alluded to as 'Mother of the Great—', 228; procession of—*see* illustration, 230; ideograph the same for 'star' and, 234; planets identified with, 235; Nabu and Merodach, 228; Dibbarra, 229; Damku and Sharru-Ilu, 229; many Babylonian, evolved from demons, 268; gazelle- and goat-, 292–294; Hellenic departmental, 315; departmental characteristics of the, of Babylonia and Assyria, 315, 316; general equivalent, 'el,' used by Canaanites and Hebrews, 325, 326; of light —Uru, 325; of the Phœnicians, 327–329; Resheph, a Canaanite, 326, 328; Melkarth of Tyre, 327; Ashtart, 326, 327, 330; Eshmun, god of vital force, 328; Moloch, 328; Carthaginian Moloch, 330; Patechus, a monster, 330; Illat, 330; Sakon, 330; Tsaphon, 330; of Babylon more dignified than those of the Greeks or Norsemen, 338; the Twilight of the, 377–380
GODDESS-ES. Ishtar, 28, 94, 101, 106, 107, 111, 123–144, 158, 165–168, 176, 211–214, 326; 'Ishtar' a generic designation for,

GLOSSARY AND INDEX

124; Nanâ and Anunit, 124; Samkhat—of joy, 131; Cybele, the mother-, 132; Bau, 'mother of Lagash,' 144, 145; Ga-tum-dug, allied form of Bau, 145; Azalu, 149–151; Sabitu, a sea-, 172; Ealur, amalgamated with Zarpanitum, 186; Innana or Ninni, 187; Dawkina, 197; worship of great mother, 318, 319; Tanith, 328; Ashtart, 326, 327, 328; Isis (Astarte), 328; Tanit, the moon, 330; Rabbat Umma, 330; Tanit, 330

GRAIN-GOD. Nebo as, 186
GREECE. Cult of Ishtar in, 124
GREEKS. Babylonia ruled over by, 378
GROTEFEND, GEORG. Cuneiform writing and, 62–64
GU-BARR'A. Prayer and god, 68
GU-DE'A. A vassal of the throne of Dungi, 19; high-priest of Lagash, 19; his building and architectural ability, 19, 247; diorite statues of, found by de Sarzec, 47; Bau alluded to in ancient inscriptions of, 144; worship of Innana by, 187; Nin-girsu favourite of, 251; hepatoscopy and, 283; de Sarzec and, 355
GU'LA. Consort of Ninib, 216
GY'GES. King of Lydia; Assurbani-pal and, 302, 303; George Smith's discoveries *re*, 352

H

HABB'AC-UC. A prophet; sent to feed Daniel, 100
HA'DAD or ADAD. Ramman or Rimmon identified with, 187–191; resemblances between Dáda, Dido, David and, 189–191; the supreme Baal, 189; a Canaanitish god, 325
HA'DAD-NA'DIN-AKHI. Placed on throne of Babylon by Assur-nazir-pal, 23; kills the Assyrian monarch, Bel-kudur-uzur, 23

HAD-ASS'AH. Variant of Esther, 143
HA'DES. Descent of Ishtar into, 125, 126, 128–131; Erish-ki-gal (Allatu), mistress of, 129
HAL'LA-BI. Innana's temple at, 187
HAM'AN. The Book of Esther and, 141; accepted identity with Humman or Homman, 142
HAMMURABI. Dynasty, 325
HAN'NI-BAL. Carthaginian hero, 330, 332; Baal's name in, 330
HA-O'MA. Deposited on the celestial mountain, 335
HAR-AN'. Abram's youngest brother, 52
HAR'RAN. A centre of lunar adoration, 250, 283
HAS'DRU-BAL. Carthaginian hero; Baal's name in, 330
HAUG, DR. Translator of the Gāthăs, 333
HAYNES. Excavations of, at Nippur, 360–366
HAYNES, MR J. H. Sent in 1889 to excavate at Nippur, 47
HEAVEN. The *Igigi* the spirits of, 90
HEBREW-S. 1. Symbol; the serpent the, for mischief, 285; 2. Religion; Babylonian influence upon, 321, 322
HE-PAT-OS'CO-PY. Ritual and practice of, 282–288
HER'AC-LES. Melkarth equated with, 328
HER'CU-LES. Reference to, 87
HER-O'DOT-US. Statements of, *re* Semiramis, 28; account of, *re* temple of Bel, 101, 103; marriage customs in Babylonia described by, 312; reference to, 367, 374
HEZ-EK-I'AH. King of Judah, 30, 37; Sennacherib's campaign against, 30; praise of, sung by Byron in his *Hebrew Melodies*, 30
HI-ER-A'POL-IS. Memorials of Semiramis preserved at, 27
HILPRECHT, PROFESSOR. An expert Assyriologist, 345, 357, 360–363

HINKS, REV. EDWARD. Language found at Persepolis deciphered by, 65
HO'RUS. The Egyptian god of light; Tiawath reminds of, 75
'HOUSE OF NO RETURN.' Equivalent, Hades, 126
HUITZILOPOCHTLI (pron. *Hweetzil-o-potch-tlee*). Reference to, 144
HUR-AK-ÂN. The storm-god alluded to in the *Popol Vuh*, 97
HYMN-S. To Adar, 68; to Nebo, 69; to Nusku, 69; 'magical,' emanated from Eridu, 68; Akkadian, in which Tammuz is addressed, 126; of Khammurabi, 219; to Ramman, 220

I

I-AM'BLI-CHUS. Author of a *Babylonica*, 56
IDOLATRY. Legend *re* origin of, 232; Laban's images, 266–268
IG'I-GI, THE. Spirits of heaven, 90
IK-SU'DA (Grasper). Attendant hound of Merodach, 202
IL-A-BRAT. Minister of Anu, 117
ILL'AT. Carthaginian deity, 330
IL-TE'HU (Holder). Attendant hound of Merodach, 202
IMAGE-S. Stars and, 233
IM-GÛR-BEL. City of, 354
'INCANTATION OF ERIDU.' The ceremony of the, 270
INDIA-NS. Semiramis makes war on Strabrobates, King of, 26, 27; followers of Zarathustra fled to; descendants, the Parsis of, 334; Araucanian, of Chile, 336
IN'ESH. The pilot of Eridu, 115
IN'MAR-MA'ON. City of, 108
INSCRIPTION-S. Of Shalmaneser I, 351; of Tukulti-ninip, 351
IR'KAL-LA. The abode of; the house of darkness, 128, 169
IR'NI-NA. A form of Ishtar, 165
IS-AI'AH. Jerusalem described by, 191; reference to Sargon's expedition against Ashdod mentioned by, 350
ISH'NU. Ura's counsellor, 269

ISH'TAR. Goddess; fame of Semiramis mingled with that of the, 28; goddess of Nineveh, 94, 212; court of Zamama and, 101; witnesses plunder of Erech by Dibarra, 106, 107; both male and female, 111; significance, 123–144; generic designation for goddess, 124; equivalents, Ashteroth or Astarte, 124, 327; cult of Aphrodite began in that of, 124; Esther and, 124, 140–144; identified with Venus, 124, 235; identified with Nin-lil, 124; the consort of Asshur, 125; descent into Hades of, 125–126; wargoddess, 127, 213, 214; consort of Tammuz, 127; consort of Merodach and Assur, 127; identified wih Dawkina, 137; a goddess of vegetation, 137, 138; slays Eabani, 158; Irnina a form of, 165; love of, for Gilgamesh, 167, 168; Anu father of, 168; Anatu mother of, 168; Lady of 'the Gods,' 176; Assyrians and, 211–214; Assur-nazir-pal and, 214; confusion between Belit and, 228; Aphrodite and, connected, 235; sixth month sacred to, 236; temple of E-anna dedicated to, 250; magic and, 258; variant, Ashtart, 326, 327, 330; great gate of, discovered by Dr Koldewey, 372
ISH'UM. Attendant of Dibarra, 106–108
I'SIS. Osiris and, 133; journey to, as Astarte, 328
ISRAELITES. Worship of Dodo, or Dod, by the side of Yahveh, by the, 190
I'YAR. The second month, sacred to Ea, 236
IZ-DU'BAR or GISDHUBAR. Provisional name of Gilgamesh, 156

J

JA'COB. Laban and, 267
JE-HO'IA-KIM. King of Jerusa-

GLOSSARY AND INDEX

lem; Nebuchadrezzar puts to death, 37

JE'HU. Son of Omri (sic); obelisk of Shalmaneser and, 343

JEN'SEN. View of, re Hamon, 142, 143; explanation of, re Ninib, 216

JERUSALEM. Reference to deliverance of, from Sennacherib, 30; King Nebuchadrezzar wars against, 37; Isaiah describes, 191

JEW-S. Nebuchadrezzar leads into captivity, 37; feast of Purim and, 140; Mordecai name of a real, 143

JEWISH. Religion; Babylonian influence on, 319-329

JO'NAH. Story of, and supposed allusion to Babylonian cosmology, 86; Tiawath and the 'fish' of, 87

JOP'PA. Place, 86

JUDAISM. Initiated by the Semitic race, 313

JU'PIT-ER. The planet; represented Merodach, 202, 235; controlled stars under name Nibir, 235; the 'Planet of the Bull of Light,' 290

K

KAA'BA (Temple). The celebrated, at Mecca, 52

KAN'DIS. A Kassite dynasty founded by, 21

Kas'sa-pu or *Kas'sap-tu*. Names by which the wizard and the witch were known, 261

KASS'ITE. Dynasty; founded by Kandis, 21; King of Babylonia marries daughter of Assur-yuballidh of Assyria, 22; dynasty, reference to, 248; rulers and temple at Nippur, 248; votive objects found by Dr Peters, 358, 359, 364, 365

KHAM-MUR-A'BI THE GREAT. Most famous name in Babylonian history, 20; art and literature blossomed under care of, 20; is to be regarded as the Babylonian Alfred, 21; pantheon that held sway prior to, 94; worship of Merodach and, 184; Nebo, Tashmit, and, 186; Shamash and, 187; goddess Innana or Ninni and, 187; age of, fertile in writers, 192; Hymn of—Ramman and Shamash appealed to in, 219; builder of sanctuaries, 247; city of, discovered, 376

KHARSAG-KURKURA. 'Mountain of the World,' 362

KHI-KHI. Mountain of, 108

KHOR'SA-BAD. City; residence of Asshur, 207; M. Botta and mounds of, 339; Victor Place's work at, 340

KHUM'BA-BA. Monster, overcome by Gilgamesh and Eabani, 158, 160, 166, 167

KHUR'SAG KUR'KUR-A. The birthplace of the gods, 242

KID'MU-RU. Ishtar's shrine in, 212

KING, PROFESSOR, 371, 376

KING-S. Of Babylonia and Assyria—Sargon of Akkad, 16-21, 47, 210, 211, 340, 350, 352; 'of the Four Zones'—Naram-Sin, 17; of Ur—Dungi, 19; of Lagash—Gudea, 19; of Babylonia—Khammurabi the Great, 20, 21, 109; of Babylonia (Kassite dynasty)—Kandis, 21; of Egypt—Amenhetep IV, 22; of Babylonia—Burna-buryas, 22; of Assyria—Shalmaneser I, 22, 351; of Assyria—Tukulti-in-Aristi, 22; of Babylon—Bitilyasu, 22; of Babylon — Hadad-nadin-akhi, 23; of Assyria—Bel-kudur-uzur, 23; of Assyria—Tiglath-pileser I, 23, 346; of Assyria—Assur-nazir-pal III, 23, 214-216, 223, 343, 351; of Assyria—Shalmaneser II, 24, 343, 351; of Israel—Ahab, 24; of Assyria—Samsi-Rammon, 24; of Assyria'—Ninus, 25; of Armenia—Barsanes, 25; of India—Strabrobates, 26; 'of the World, etc., etc.'—Semiramis, 29; of Assyria—Tiglath-pileser III, 29; of Assyria—Shalmaneser IV, 30; of Judah—Hezekiah, 30, 37; of Assyria—Sennacherib, 30; of Assyria—Esar-haddon, 31, 306, 307, 343, 350; of Assyria—Assur-bani-pal (Sardanapalus), 31, 32, 301-306, 346; of Assyria—Ashurbanapal, 33; of Assyria—Sin-sar-iskin, 36; of Ecbatana—Cyaxares, 36; of Babylonia—Nebuchadrezzar II, 36-40, 47, 104; of Babylonia—Nabonidus, 40, 249; Cyrus the Persian, 41; of Babylon—Cambyses, 41; Alexander the Great, 42; of Chaldea—Nimrod, 52; Rammannirari I, 90; of Persia—Cyrus, 98; Daon, the shepherd, of Pantibiblon, 112; of Persia—Xerxes, 141; of Babylonia—Sokkaros, 157; of Babylonia—Mili-Shikhu, 187; the Moabite—Mesha, 190; of Ashdod—Azuri, 210, 211; of Babylonia, and soothsayers, 260; tales of Babylonian and Assyrian, 299-312; Nabu-Usabi, King of Sarrapanu, 300; Gyges, King of Lydia, 302; Tiglath-pileser II, 299-301; of Assyria—Assur-Dan III, 308; of Assyria—Adad-Narari IV, 308; a royal 'day,' 309-312; of Assyria—Ur-Gur, 359, 366; of Assyria—Ur-Ninib, 366

KIN'GU. God; 'only husband' of Tiawath, 75; bound by Merodach, 78; son of Tiawath, 194

KIS. The Babylonian sun-god, 93, 294

KI'SAR. God; birth of, 71

KOLDEWEY, DR. German explorer, 356, 367; great gate of Ishtar discovered by, 372; temple of E-Sagila and, 374, 375

Kosmologie. Jensen's, 216

KOU-YUN-JIK. M. Botta and mound of, 339; Layard's searches in mound of, 344, 345; George Smith's excavations at, 351; Rassam's excavations at, 354, 355

KUK-UL-CAN. Reference to the god, 224

L

LAB'AN. Jacob and, 267
LAB'AR-TU. The hag-demon, 271, 277
LADY OF THE GODS. Ishtar the, 176
LAG'ASH. The modern Tel-lo, earliest Semite monuments come from, 16; the priests of became kings, 16; Gudea high-priest of, 19, 355; Bau 'mother of,' 145
LA'HA-MÉ. God; birth of, 71
LAH'MU. God; birth of, 71
LAM-AS'SU. A spirit of similar type to the Sedu, 277
LAMENTATION-S. For Tammuz, 135, 136, 140; Rituals, 253-255
LANGUAGE. The Akkadian, 13, 14; Babylonian priesthood preserved old Akkadian tongue as a sacred, 14; Sumerians borrowed from rich Semitic tongue, 15; cunciform writing, 60-66, *see* Writing; Median, 65; Susian, 65; Assyrian, 65; Longpérier's translation of Assyrian, 66; of Babylonia and Assyria, compared, 205
LAR'SA. Shamash worshipped at, 109; Khammurabi's improvements at, 187
LA'YARD, Sir HENRY. Assur-bani-pal's library at Nineveh and, 35, 46; archæological researches at Nineveh, 46, 155, 344, 346; researches of, at Nimrûd, 340, 342-344, 346
LEGEND-S. Jewish, *re* Abram and Nimrod, 51; Persian, *re* Abram and Nimrod, 52, 53; the creation, 193-195; of Etana, 195; of the origin of star-worship, 232-3; the, of Ura, 268-270; of a dog, 291, 292; 'Cuthæan, of creation,' 294-296

GLOSSARY AND INDEX

LENORMANT. Hebrew and Assyrian poetry and, 322

LEO, SIGN OF. Recalls the slaying of Khumbaba, 182

LETTER-S. Franked by clay seals bearing name of Sargon, 18

LEVI, ELIPHAS. The Baphomet goat and, 293

LIA FAIL, THE. The Stone of Destiny; reference to, 248

LIBRARY. Assur-bani-pal's, 35, 46, 71, 261, 282, 346; the temple in 'Tablet Hill,' 363

LIGHT. Merodach and Tiawath, and the primal strife between darkness and, 79

LITERATURE. Babylonian art and, under Khammurabi the Great, 20; Assur-bani-pal and Babylonian, 35; sacred, of Babylonia, 67–69

LIVER-READING. By priests, 281–283

LOFTUS, WILLIAM KENNET. Successor of Mr Hormuzd Rassam, 346, 347

LO'KI. God of fire; Nergal not unlike, 106

LU'GAL-BAN'DA. Storm-bird god; like Prometheus, 93

LU'GAL-ZUG-GI'SI. King of Erech; famous text of, found by Hilprecht, 366

M

MAAT. Reference to, 222

MAGI. Confounded by Zoroaster, 333

MAGICAL TEXTS. Dawkina alluded to in the, 197; Anu mentioned in, 198; of Babylonia and Assyria, 257, 288; alluded to in Bible, 266, 267; circle, the, 275, 276

MAGICIAN-S. The word of power and, 263; Ea, the great, of the gods, 268

MAHOMET-AN. 'Baphomet' a corruption of, 293; conquest, 333

MAI-MON'I-DES. Jewish rabbi, friend of Averroes; his commentary on the *Mischnah*, 232

'MAK'LU.' A series of texts known as, 261

Mam'it. Equivalent for taboo, 278

MAM-MET'UM. The maker of destiny, 173

MAN-KIND. Creation of, by Merodach, 80, 81; goddess Aruru assists in the creation of, 82, 86; humanizing of, 112, 113

MARAZION. Signifies in Semitic, 'Hill by the Sea,' 331

MAR-CHESH-UAN. Merodach's month, 251

MAR'DUK. See Merodach, 175, 200

MARRIAGE. Customs in Babylonia, 312

MARS. Identified with Nergal, 235

MAS'HU. The Mountain of Sunset, 171

MAZ'DA. One of the spiritual powers in Zoroaster's religion, 337

MEC'CA. Reference to the celebrated Kaaba (temple) at, 52

MEDE. Zoroaster a, 333

ME'DI-A. Subdued by Ninus, 25

MEDICINE. Ea, a god of, 192

MEG-ID'DO. The Canaanitish fortress of, 189

ME-LI'LI. 1. Queen; wife of Benani, 82; 2. Mother of the monsters, 295, 296

MEL'I-SHIP'OK II. Houses found dating from period of, 376

MELK ('KING'). Variant of Moloch, 328

MEL'KARTH. Phœnician god of Tyre, 327, 328; worship of, in Carthage, 330

MEL'KARTH-RESH'EF. Phœnician combination, 328

MEM-AN-GAB. Leader of the monsters, 295, 296

MEM'PHIS. Assyrians enter, 31

MEN'KES MOUND, 376

MER-AG-A'GA. Variant of Merodach, 202

MER'CURY. Identified with Nabu, 235

MER'OC. Yaran flees to, 210, 211

MER'O-DACH. Babylonian god, 41; temple of, 47, 374; Nimrod identified with, 50; prayer and god, 68; Tiawath and, 76–82; creates man, 81; the central figure of a popular myth, 84; god Ea displaced by, 86, 199; may have been a bull-god, 93; worshipped at Babylon, 94; Asshur identified with, 94; Nebuchadrezzar and, 104; Diabarra and, 106; the name Mordecai a form of, 142; great festival of, the Zakmuk, 141; worship of, first prominent in days of Khammurabi, 184–198; association with Nebo, 184–186; the Chamber of Fates in temple of, 185; Zarpanitum, wife of, 186, 202; supremacy of, 192; variant Marduk, 194, 200; Shamash and, 200; variants, Amaruduk, Asari, Saragagam, and Mer-agaga, 202; attendant hounds of, 202; usurped place of Bel, 227; Bel paired with, 228; Jupiter, identified with, 235; eighth month ruled over by, 237; month Marcheshuan belonged to, 251; eclipses and, 256; demons and the name of, 263; four dogs of, 291; head of the Babylonian Pantheon, 377; Nabonidus, 377

MER'O-DACH-BAL-A-DAN I. Houses found dating from period of, 376

MESH'A. The Moabite king; Chemosh, god of, 190

MESH'ACH. One of Daniel's companions, 38

MES-O-POT-A'MI-A. Elam and Northern —, overcome by Sargon, 17; Semitic religion in, 331; excavations in, 339, ff.; George Smith dispatched to, 351; recent research in, 366–376

MEXICO. Reference to religious system of ancient, 204; reference to temples, on, 243

MIC'AH. Reference to his teraphim, 268

MIDDLE AGES. The Sabbatic goat of the witchcraft of the, 293

MI-LI-SHIK'HU. Babylonian monarch; Shamash and, 187

Misch'nah. Commentary on the, 232

MITANI. Provinces of, conquered by Shalmaneser I, 308

MITH'RA. Rashnu and, 337

MIT-RA-PHER'NES. Artaios' eunuch, 149

MOFFLAINES. Wood of, 293

MOHAMMEDANISM. Initiated by the Semitic race, 313, 332

MO'LOCH. Magic and, 258; worship of, in Phœnicia, 328; worship of, in Carthage, as Baalammon, 330; children sacrificed to, 331

MOMMU TI-A-WATH. The primeval ocean, 71. *See* Moumis

MONSTER-S. Mythological animals and, of Chaldea, 289–298; the dog, 290, 291; invasion of the, 294–296; Patechus, 330

MONTH-S. Titles of, by Babylonians, 236–238

MOON. Babylonian religion and, 236; city; Ur, the, 249, 250; Abram, probably a moon-worshipper, 249; eclipses and the, 256

MOON-DEITIES. Osiris, 138; Aphrodite, 138; Proserpine, 138; Phœnician Ashtoreth, 138; Nannar, moon-god of Ur, 145–149; Sin, 94, 109, 128, 170, 223, 224, 250; Tanit, 330

MOR'DE-CA-I. The Book of Esther and, 141; a form of Marduk or Merodach, 142

MOSÛL. M. Botta French Consul at, 339; Layard's researches at, 340–344

MOTHER-EARTH. Of primitive mythologies, 197

MOTHER-GODDESS. Theory, 318, 319; compounded of various types, 326

GLOSSARY AND INDEX

MOTHER OF THE GREAT GODS,' Belit alluded to as, 228

MOU'MIS or MUM'MU. Son of Tiawath and Apsu, 73; name at one time given to Tiawath, 73

MOUNTAIN. Of the Sunset, Gilgamesh journeys to, 158, 159, 171; of the Sunrise, 253; of the Earth, 305; of the Wind, 362; of the World, 362

MUL-LIL. The 'gazelle god' of Nippur, 292

MU-RASH'U AND SONS. Bankers and brokers at Nippur, 366

MU'RO. Worship of Ramman originated at, 220

MEYER, JOSEPH A. An American architect who assisted Haynes at Nippur, 365

MYRRH. Used at the Adonia festival, 136; -tree and Adonis, 137

MYTH-S. Of Sardanapalus, reference to, 32; analogies with Flood-, 45; North American Indian, reference to, 46, 122; Algonquin, reference to, 46; Babylonian, of creation, 70–87; confusing, connected with Ea, 112; of deluge, 111, 173–178; of Merodach and Tiawath, reference to, 78, 114, 199; Mexican, reference to, 115; Greek, reference to, 122, 315; of Tammuz, 126–129; Tammuz and Ishtar, groundwork of those of Greece and Rome, 131; of Adonis, 131–133; Egyptian, re quest of Isis, 133; Tammuz-Ishtar, 135; various strata underlying the Gilgamesh, 159, 160; of the slaughter of Tiawath, 201; of Persephone and of Osiris, 201; a toothache-, 262, 263; Phœnician, little known re, 328; Indo-Germanic, reminiscences in Zarathustra's religion, 334; character of Babylonian, compared with that of Hellenic and Scandinavian, 338

N

NA-BO-NI'DES. Archæology fashionable in time of, 363

NABONIDOS. See Nabonidus, 364

NA-BO-NI'DUS. The last of the Babylonian kings, 40, 110, 283; displaced by Cyrus, 41; cults of Merodach, Nabu, and Shamash, and, 377

NAB'O-POL-AS'SER. Reference to inscriptions of, 368; father of Nebuchadrezzar, 369, 370; Euphrates bridge, work of, 375; god Merodach and, 377

NAB'U, 175; Nusku and, connected, 225; Merodach and, paired, 228; Bel paired with, 228; Ramman-Nirari and, 228; called by Sargon 'the Seer who guides the gods,' 228; Mercury and, 235; tenth month sacred to, 237; tower of, 375; Nebuchadrezzar and, 377; Nabonidus and, 377

NAB'U-BALIDDIN. Shamash's temple restored by, 249

NABU-QUA'TI-ZA'BAT. Assur-bani-pal and, 304

NAB'U-USA'BI, KING. Crucified by Tiglath-pileser II, 300

NA-BÛ-ZÊR-LÎ-SHIR. Scribe, 363

NAM'TAR. The plague-demon, 129

NANÂ. Merged in conception of Ishtar, 124; Assur-bani-pal and, 304

NAN'NAR. The moon-god of Ur, 145–149

NANN'AR-OS. Satrap of Babylon, 146–149

NANN'A-RU. The new moon, established by Merodach, 79

NA'RAM-SIN. Son of Sargon; title, 'King of the Four Zones,' 17, 19; Nabonidus and, 41; bricks discovered with name of, on, 47; 'Builder of the Temple of En-lil,' 247; omens and, 283; 'mould' of an inscribed stone belonging to Sargon I in palace of, 363

NE'BO. Hymn to, 69; son of Bel, 102; shrine sacred to,

102; Tashnit, wife of, 102, 185, 186; association with Merodach, 184–186; chief seat, Borsippa, 184, 326; as grain-god, 186; the altars of Yahveh dragged from, 190; temple of, 306, 346, 348

NEB'ROD. *See* Nimrod

NE-BUCH-AD-REZ'ZAR I. Ramman and, 219

NEBUCHADREZZAR II (or NEBUCHADNEZZAR). King of Babylonia, reign of, 36–40; invades Egypt 37; wars against Jerusalem, 37; puts Jehoiakim to death, 37; sets up Zedekiah as King of Jerusalem, 37; Daniel and, 37–40; his dreams, 37–40; Shadrach, Meshach, and Abednego, and, 38; ruins of palace of, explored in 1899, 47; Sir H. C. Rawlinson's discovery *re*, 104; Shamash's temple restored by, 249; Dr Andrae's discovery *re*, 356; Merodach and, 377

NEBUCHADREZZAR III. King of Babylonia, 41

NEM'ART. *See* Nimrod

NER'GAL. Temple of, at Cuthah, 82, 296; of Cuthah, 94; patron god of Cuthah, 105; not unlike Loki, 106; Dibarra, variant of, 106; Aralu and, 150, 151; shade of Eabani, and, 180; Mars and, 235; Canaanitish war-god, 326; worshipped by Phœnicians, 328

NEW YEAR. Assembly of gods at Babylon on first day of, 201; Merodach and, 201; Bau and, 251; Gudea and, 251

NI-BI'RU. Merodach's star, 79

NIM'ROD. The mighty hunter, 49–56; son of Chus, the Æthiop, 49; a reputed descendant of Ham, 49; figures in Biblical and Babylonian tradition, 49; built Babylon, 50; Greek named Nebrod or Nebros, 50; identified with Merodach, Gilgamesh, and Orion, 50; name found in Egyptian documents of XXII Dynasty as 'Nemart,' 50; derivation of name may mean 'rebel,' 50; legends of, related by Philo in his *De Gigantibus*, 50; Abram and, 51–56; King of Chaldea, 52; suggested identity with Gilgamesh, 156

NIM'RÛD. Sir Henry Layard's excavations at, 340, 342–344; Rassam's searches at, 344; George Smith's searches at, 348–354

NIN-A-GAL. Variant of Ea, 116

NIN'EV-EH. Built by Sennacherib, 31; Assur-bani-pal's library at, 35, 71, 154, 346; archæological researches of Layard and Botta at, 46; George Smith's labours at, 46; Mr Hormuzd Rassam's work at, 47; built by Asshur, 49; tablet written for temple of Nergal discovered at, 82; residence of Asshur, 207; Ishtar's shrine in, 212; M. Botta and site of, 339, 340; Layard and, 344; plan of, 357

NIN-GIR'SU. Name means 'Lord of Girsu,' 144; known as Shulgur ('Lord of the corn heaps'), 144; identified with Tammuz, 144; variant, Ninib, 214, 216; favourite of Gudea, 251; temple of, 283

NIN'IB, 84, 175; a war-god, 214; variant of, Nin-girsu, 214, 216; Tiglath-pileser I, Assur-rishishi, Assur-nazir-pal, and, 214; as hunter-god, 216; extolled by Tiglath-pileser I, 216; invoked by Assur-nazir-pal, 216; Gula, consort of, 216; Saturn and, 235; translated as En-Mashti by Canaanites, 326

NIN-IGI-NAG'IR-SIR. Saved with Ea, etc., from deluge, 115

NIN-LIL. Variant of Beltis, 101; consort of En-lil; Ishtar and, 124

NIN'NI. Variant of Innana, 187

NIN'SUM. Gilgamesh resorts to, 180

NI'NUS. King of Assyria, 25;

GLOSSARY AND INDEX

Semiramis, wife of, 25; Ninyas, son of, 26

NIN'YAS. Son of Ninus; during minority of, Semiramis assumed the regency, 26

NIPPUR. Babylonian civilization grouped round, 14; god En-lil and, 14; city of Ur colonized by, 15; Mr Haynes' excavations at, 47, 359, 360, 365, 366; temple of, 82; cosmological tales at, 84; of Sumerian origin, 96; preferred to Babylon, 196; lamentation ritual at, 199, 200; temple of E-Kur at, 248; business quarter of, unearthed, 359, 360; stage-tower of, 361; temple-tower of, 362

NIR'IG. God; variant, Enu-Restu; Bel, father of, 153

NIZ'AN. First month; sacred to Anu and Bel, 236

NO'AH. Patriarch, reference to, 45; legend of deluge and Ea, 115; variant, Ut-Napishtim, 116

NO-RETURN. Land of, 128

NU-DIM-MUD. Variant of name of Ea, 73; Tiawath and, 76

NUMBERS. Assigned to each of the gods, 237, 238

NUS'KU. The messenger of Mullil, 68; hymn to, 69; temple of, 102; 'of the "Brilliant Sceptre,' 224, 225; Nabu and, connected, 225; eclipses and, 255

O

O-AN'NES. See Ea, 14

OBELISK. Of Shalmaneser II, 343

O-DA'CON. Appears from sea of Eruthra, 112

OMEN-S. Library of Sargon contained book dealing with, 18; divination by, 281, 282

O-MOR'CA. Chaldaic equivalent, Thalath; Greek, *thalassa*, 114

ON'NES. One of Ninus' generals, husband of Semiramis, 25

OPPERT. French exploration expedition and, 347

O-RI'ON. Nimrod identified with, 50

O-SI'RIS. Isis and, reference to, 133; reference to, 201, 228

'O-ZY-MAN'DI-AS.' Shelley's sonnet on, 307

P

PAINTINGS. Discovered in Sennacherib's palace at Kouyunjik, 345

PALACE-S. Built at Nineveh by Sargon; M. Botta unearths, 340; Assyrian, two discovered at Nimrûd, 340; built by Esarhaddon, unearthed by Layard, 343; of Sennacherib, found by Layard, 345; Assur-bani-pal's, discovered by Rawlinson, 346; of Nimrûd, George Smith's excavations in, 348, 349; Nebuchadrezzar's, excavated, 369–371

PALESTINE. Syria and, invaded by Sargon, 17; worship of Hadad in, 188; the Canaanites first dwellers in, 324

PALL'AS A-THÊ-NÉ. Reference to, 222, 315

PAN'THE-ON, ASSUR-BANI-PAL'S. Belit and Asshur in, 228

PANTHEON OF ASSYRIA, 203–230; differences between the Babylonian and, 203, 204; Dagon in, associated with Anu, 216, 217; Bel-Merodach absorbed in the, 225; Ea in the, 229; Dibbarra, in the, 229

PANTHEON OF BABYLONIA. 1. Early. Prior to Khammurabi, 94, 95. 2. Later. General changes in and additions to, 184–198; Bel's place usurped in the, by Merodach, 227; spiritistic nature of, 318

PAP-SUK'AL. The messenger of the gods, 130

PARADISE. The Abyss and, 82

PAR'SÎS. Of Bombay, 334

PAR-SON'DES. Ctesias' tale *re*, 146–149

PAT-E'CHUS. God; a repulsive monster, 330
PATRIARCH, THE. See Abram
PER-SEPH'O-NÉ or PROS'ER-PINE. Reference to, 132, 201; corresponds to Allatu, 132
PER-SE'POLIS. Reference to, 61; language found at, deciphered by Löwenstern and Hinks, 65; Longpérier translated language found at, 66
PER'SE-US. Reference to, 87
PERSIAN-S. Signs in connexion with cuneiform writing, 60-66; religion of (Zoroaster's), 332-336, etc.; fear of defilement, 335
PETERS, DR. Director of American expeditions, 358, 359, 364, 365
PHIL-IS'T'I-A. Sargon's expedition against, 210, 211
PHŒ-NIC'I-A. Worship of Moloch in, 328
PHŒNICIAN-S. The Gods of the, 326-329; religion; Egyptian influence, 328
PICTURE-WRITING. Cuneiform and, 66. See Writing
PIR-Æ'US. Port of Athens, 328
PIS'CES, SIGN OF. Eabani and, 183
PLACE, VICTOR. Botta's work at Khorsabad, continued by, 340
PLANET-S. Identified with gods, 235
PLUTARCH. Isis (Astarte) and, 328
PLU'TO. Reference to, 133
POETRY. Assyrian, 321, 322
POLGARTH. Phœnician word 'city' and, 331
POL-Y-HIS'TOR, ALEXANDER. God Ea and, 112, 113
POLYTHEISM. Semitic, 313
Pop'ol Vuh. Reference to, 97, 151
POS-EI'DON. Greek god, 315
PRAYER-S. To the sun-god, etc., 67, 68
PRIEST-S. Akkadian tongue preserved by Babylonian, 14; those of Lagash became kings, 16; high, of Asshur, took title of king, 21, 208; sole mythographers, 191; -hood, cult and temples, 239-241; wizards and, 260; -magician; the chamber of the, 270-275; liver-reading by, 282; of Thebes, Memphis, and On, 314; of Nippur and Erech, 314
PRIESTESSES. In Babylonia, 240, 241
PRIEST-HOOD. See Priests
PRISONER-GODS. Assyrian rulers and, 225, 226
PRO-ME'THE-US. Lugalbanda and, 93; Zu and, 195
PSALMS, BOOK OF THE. National, not individual, 320; poetical form of, 322
PU'NIC. Religion, 330
PURIFICATION, 270; by water, in connexion with Babylonian magic, 270
PÛRIM. Feast of, 140, 141

Q

QAL'AT SHER'QAT. Annals of Tiglath-pileser I discovered by Rawlinson, 346; Dr Andrae's excavations at, 356

R

RA. Worship of, in Egypt, 223
RAB'BAT UM'MA. 'The Great Mother,' 330
RAB-I'SU. A lurking demon, 276, 277
RACES. Asia Minor peopled with diverse, 324
RACHEL. The stolen images and, 266-268
RACH'MET. Reference to, 61
RAM'MAN, 175; equivalent, Rimmon; identified with Hadad or Adad, 187-189; the Tablets of Destiny and, 195; popularity and functions, 217-222; weapons of, 218; worship of, in days of Khammurabi and Nebuchadrezzar I, 219; Assur-

GLOSSARY AND INDEX

nazir-pal and, 219; attributes and signification, 218–222; eleventh month sacred to, 237

RAM'MAN-NIR-A'RI I. The *Annunaki* and *Igigi* and, 90

RAM'MAN-NI-RA'RI III. Nabu exalted at expense of Asshur by, 228

RASH'NU. Mithra and, 337

RASS'AM, MR HOR'MUZD. Assurbani-pal's library at Nineveh and, 35; his archæological researches at Nineveh and at Abu-habba, 47; stone tablet found at Sippard by, 292; researches at Nimrûd, 342, 344, 346, 354, 355

RAWLINSON, MAJOR (SIR) HENRY. Cuneiform writing and, 64–66; his discovery *re* Nebuchadrezzar, 104; Layard and, 342, 344, 345, 346

RED INDIANS. Titles of months and, 236

REINACH. Reference to, 334

RELIGION-S. Akkadian tongue used as a sacred language by Babylonian priesthood, 14; early Babylonian, 88–153; Jewish, 88; of ancient Mexico, 88; Vedic, of India, 88; Semitic influence on Babylonian, 91, 92; official system of Babylonian and Assyrian, 92; Semitic, Euphrates-Tigris influence on, 92; totemism in Babylonian, 92; system of, in Babylonia, overshadowed by Merodach, 199; Jastrow's *Religion in Babylonia and Assyria* quoted, 199, 212; star-worship, the origin of, 237; *of the Semites* quoted, 91, 241, 332; cult of the gods, 292; comparative value of the, of Babylonia and Assyria, 313–336 and on; Teutonic and Celtic, comparisons, 316; Babylonian, typically animistic, 317, 318; worship of great earth-mother, 318, 319; Jewish, 319–329; Canaanite, 324–326; Carthaginian, 329; Semitic, 329, 331; Punic, 330; Mohammedanism, 313, 332; of the Persians (Zoroaster), 332–337; of Babylonians, 338; decay of Babylonian, 378, 379

RESH'EPH. Known to the Canaanites, 326; the lightning god; origin; identified with Apollo, 328

RHO-DA'NES. Romance of Sinonis and, 56–60

RIM'AT-BEL'IT. Mother of Gilgamesh, 158; interprets Gilgamesh's dream, 164

RIM'MON. *See* Rammon

RITUAL. Lamentation at Nippur, 199, 200; of hepatoscopy, 283–288; Zoroastrian fire worship central feature of, 335

S

SABBATIC GOAT. Witchcraft of Middle Ages and the, 293

SAB-I'TU. The sea-goddess; Gilgamesh and, 172; sign Capricornus and, 183

SAC'A. One of the two eunuchs appointed to watch Rhodanes and Sinonis, 57

SAC-Æ'A. The Asiatic equivalent of the Saturnalia, 33; festival of Zakmuk, or, 141

SACRIFICE-S. Babylonian, 241, 242

SADI-RAB'U-MA-TA'TI. The great mountain of the earth, 305

SAG'GAL. Temple of Merodach, 305

SAK'ON. Carthaginian deity, 330

SAM-AS-SUM-YU'KIN. Viceroy of Babylonia, 34; raises revolt in Assyrian empire, 34; his death, 34

SAM'KHAT. Goddess of joy, 131

SAM-MUR'A-MUT. Assyrian title of Semiramis. *See* Semiramis

SAM'SI - A'DAD IV. Rawlinson discovers stele of, 346

SAM'SI-RAM'MON. Son of Shalmaneser II; succeeds his father

as King of Assyria, 24; Sammuramat favourite of, 24; Asshur mentioned in inscription of, 208

SANCH-UN-I-A'THON. Philo and, preserved in works of Eusebius, 329

SAOSHYANT. The saviour, in Zoroaster's religion, 337

SAR-AG-AG'AM. Variants of Merodach, 202

SAR-A'KOS. Greek equivalent for Sin-sarkin, 36

SAR-DA-NA-PAL'US THE SPLENDID. Assur-bani-pal known to Greek legend as, 31; King of Assyria, 31; reference to, in *The Golden Bough*, 32; Sir James Frazer on, 32, 34; prominent features in legends of, 33; weaving of legend of, 34

SAR'GON. I. Of Akkad, founds first great Semitic empire in Babylonia, 16; a Babylonian Arthur, 16, 21; the legend of his birth, 16, 17; invasions of Syria and Palestine, 17; Elam and N. Mesopotamia overcome by, 17; Naram-Sin son of, 17, 19; letters franked by clay seals bearing name of Sargon, 18; first founder of Babylonian library, 18; bricks discovered with name of, on, 47; Asshur's conquering power and, 210, 211; King Azuri and, 210; Ahimiti and, 210; Yaran and, 210; Sin and, 223; Bel and, 227; Nabu termed 'that Seer who guides the gods,' 228; 'Builder of the Temple of En-lil,' 247; hepatoscopy and, 283; palace built by, unearthed at Nineveh, 340; George Smith finds fragments of history of, 352. II. Usurping general, claimed descent from Sargon the Great, 30; father of Sennacherib, 30

SAR'RA-PAN-U. Tiglath-pileser II captures, 299

SASS-AN'I-AN. Rulers, 333

SAT'URN. Identified with Ninib, 235

SAUL-MU-GI'NA. Rebellious brother of Assur-bani-pal, 304

SCHRADER. Assyrian poetry and, 321, 322

SCIENCE. Star-worship the origin of, 237; the roots of, 259

SCILLY ISLANDS. Phœnicians in, 331

SCOR'PIO, SIGN OF. Gilgamesh and, 182

SCOTLAND. Goat-demon adored in, 293

SCULPTURE-S. Discovery of, glorifying Assur-nazir-pal, 343; Babylonian, discovered by de Sarzec, 355

SCYTHIAN-S. Penetrate into Assyria, 36

SED'U. A guardian (sometimes an evil) spirit invoked with the Lamassu, 277

SEL-EU'CI-A. City, built out of ruins of Babylon, 42

SEM-IR'A-MIS THE GREAT. Assyrian Queen, 24–29; legendary origin, 25; wife of Onnes, and later of Ninus, 26; Ninyas son of, 26; engages in battle Strabrobates, King of India, 27; fame of, 28, 29; Sammuramat, her Assyrian title, 29; wife of Samsi-Rammon, 29; mythical connexion with Ishtar, 29; worshipped by the Syrians, 27; esteemed as the daughter of Dercatus, 27; district round Lake Van called after, Shamiramagerd, 28

SEMITES. Germs of culture received from Akkadians by Babylonian, 13; their love of wisdom, 14, 15; Babylon entered by, 15, 16; believed to have come from Arabia, 15, 16; made by the code of Khammurabi, 21; ancient, and gods, 89; serpent loathed by, 289; animistic influences; appeal of, to, 318

SEMITIC. Empire, first great, founded in Babylonia by Sar-

GLOSSARY AND INDEX

gon of Akkad, 16; religious thought, 235; worship and, lamentations, 253; polytheism 313; conservatism, 316; cults; Babylonian influence upon, 324; religion, 329, 331; peoples; a 'peculiar people,' 332; faith, includes various manifestations, 332

SEN-NACH'E-RIB. Son of usurping general Sargon, 30; campaign of, against Hezekiah, 30; Nineveh built by, 30; Esar-haddon son of, 31; takes nucleus of Assur-bani-pal's library from Calah, 154; soothsayers and his death, 260; Layard's discoveries in palace of, 345

SERPENT. The ancients and the, 289; equivalent, Aibu ('the enemy'), 289

SET. Osiris and, reference to, 133

SET-A'PO. A wealthy Babylonian who harbours Sinonis, 59

'SEVEN SPHERES, THE STAGES OF.' A building, the wonder of Borsippa, 104

SEVEN TABLETS. Of creation; primary object of, 71

SHAD'RACH. One of Daniel's companions, 38

SHAL-MA-NE'SER I. King of Assyria, 22, 308; Tukulti-in-Aristi, son of, 22; Nusku and, 224; inscription of, unearthed by George Smith, 351

SHAL-MA-NE'SER II. King of Assyria in succession to Assur-nazir-pal III, 24; overthrows Ahab, King of Israel, 24; Samsi-Rammon son of, 24; the god Dáda and, 189; Merodach (Bel) and, 225, 227; discovery of obelisk of, 343; dedications of, unearthed, 351

SHAL-MA-NE'SER IV. Successor of Tiglath-pileser III, 30

SHAM'ASH. 1. Temple of, at Sippar, restored by Nabonidus, 41; adored at Sippar, 94; the sun-god, 109–111; son of Sin, 109; Aa, consort of, 110; Ishtar and, 130; Gilgamesh and, 156, 165; Khammurati and, 187; Zu captured by, 195; Merodach and, 200; cult of, in Assyria, 222, 223; seventh month sacred to, 236; a Canaanitish god, 325; Nabonidus and, 377. 2. The great idol of, 249

SHAR'RU-ILU. One of the lesser Babylonian gods, 229

SHATT-EN-NÎL. Excavations along bank of, by Haynes, 365

SHE'BA, QUEEN OF. Tiglath-pileser II quarrels with, 301

SHEPHERD. The sun the, of the stars, 236; En-lil, of the dark-headed people, 254

SHEPHERD KING, THE. Daon, of Pantibiblon, 112

SHI'NAR, PLAIN OF. Babylon built on, 52

SHUL-GUR. Variant of Nin-Girsu, 144

SHU-RIPP'AK. 1. Son of Ubara-Tutu, 173. 2. City of, 177, 178

SHU'TU. Variant of South Wind, 117

SI'BI. The god, 108

SICILY. Worship of Ashtart (Ishtar) at, 327

SID'DA. The temple, 306

SI'DON. Tyre and, in touch with Assyria, 327; Ashtart or Ishtar, temple of, in, 327; Eshmun worshipped at, 328

SIGN-S. Gemini, Leo, Virgo, Taurus, Scorpio, 182; Capricornus, Aquarius, Pisces, 183

SILENCE, TOWERS OF. Parsis' dead and the, 336

SIN (perhaps pron. *Sin*). The moon-god, 94, 223, 224; ruled at Ur, 94; Shamash son of, 109; Ishtar daughter of, 128; Gilgamesh delivered by, 170; Gilgamesh resorts to, 180; eclipses and god, 256; a Canaanitish god, 325

SIN-A-IT'IC PENINSULA. Semitic religion in, 331

SI-NO'NIS. Romance of Garmus and, 56–60

407

SIN-SAR-IS'KIN. Last King of Assyria, 36; the Sarakos of the Greeks, 36
SIN-SHAR-ISH'KUN. The last representative of the Assyrian dynasty, 364
SIP'PAR. Shamash worshipped at, 109; Aa worshipped at, 110; Abu-Habbab, the ancient site of, 177; Berossus substitutes, for Shurippak, 178; Khammurabi's improvements at, 187; Shamash's temple at, 249
SIP'PA-RA. Temple of sun-god, Mr Rassam discovers, 47, 292
SIS-U'THRUS. The Flood Myth and, 45
SI'WAN. Month sacred to Sin, 236
SMITH, GEORGE. Reference to archæological labours, 46, 155, 347–354; discovery of, re Bel, 101; discovery of, re Tiglath-pileser II, 299; Babylonian and Assyrian poetry and, 322
SMYR'NA. Mother of Adonis, reference to, 127
SOUL. Supposed to reside in the liver, 281
SPAIN. Mohammedanism in, 332
SPEAKING HEAD, THE. Laban and, 267
SPIRIT-S. Assyrian, 277, 278
SOKK-A'ROS. First king to reign in Babylonia after the deluge, 157; Ælian the grandson of, 157
SOOTHSAYERS. Sennacherib and, 260
SOR-ACCH'US. Magistrate, who sends Sinonis to Babylon, 58
SORCERERS. Chaldean, and the magic circle, 275, 276
SRA-O'SHA. Soul carried by, to the beyond, 336, 337
STAR-S. Formed by Belus, 115; Babylonian worship of, 231–238; ideograph the same for 'god' and, 234; the sun the shepherd of the, 236; Anu the Pole, 236; Bel the Pole (equator), 236; Ea and star in constellation Argo, 236; -gazers of Chaldea, 258

ST IL'YA. Tammuz compared with, 127
STONE. The Moabite, 190; examined by Professors Socin and Smend, 190
STRA-BRO-BA'TES. King of India; Semiramis makes war on, 26, 27
'SU-ME'RI-AN.' Modern equivalent for the old expression 'Akkadian,' 15
SUN. Merodach's ideograph is the, 202; known as the 'Way of Anu,' 234; the 'Bull of Light,' 290
SUN-GOD. See Gods.
SUPERSTITION-S. In Chaldea, 280, 281
SU'SA. Monument of Naram-Sin unearthed by de Morgan at, 17; copy of Khammurabi's code found at, by J. de Morgan, 21
SUS'I-AN. Language; alternative, Median, 65
SUS'IN-AY. Idol of, 304
SYRIA. Palestine and, invaded by Sargon, 17; worship of Hadad in, 188; the Canaanites first dwellers in, 324
SYSTEM-S. Official, of religion in Babylonia and Assyria, 92; of religion in Babylonia, 199; religious, of ancient Mexico, Guatemala, and Yucatan; reference to, 204; Hellenic and Roman, 235; religions—Judaism, Christianity, Mohammedanism, 313; of religious races in Asia Minor, 324; Zarathustra's moral, 334

T

'TABLET HILL.' Haynes' discoveries at, 360; the temple library in, 363; King Nabonidos' (Nabonidus) vase found at, 364
TABLETS. Twelve, of the Gilgamesh epic, 155, 158, 159; detailed examination of, 161–180; of Destiny, 193–195; cuneiform, dealing with magic,

GLOSSARY AND INDEX

261, 262; Surpu and Maklu, series of, 262; the deluge, discovered by Smith, 347, 351, 352; discovered by Rassam, 354; of Nabopolasser, Nebuchadrezzar, Nabonidus, Cyrus, Cambyses, and Darius, 358

TAB'OO. Prayers, etc., against, 262; belief in, in Chaldea, 278; known in Babylonia as *mamit*, 278

TAM'MUZ. One of the guardians of the gates of heaven, 118; Ishtar's search for, 126; myth of, 126–129; name derived from Dumu-zi, 126; Professor Sayce and, 126; addressed as 'shepherd and lord' in Akkadian hymn, 126; Ishtar, consort of, 127; Adonis myth related to that of, 131; Sir James Frazer's *Golden Bough* and, 134; lamentations for, 135, 136, 140; a god of vegetation, 137, 138; Nin-Girsu (Shulgur) identified with, 144; the bridegroom of Ishtar's youth, 167; Dido and, 190; Ninib and, 216

TAM'MUZ-A-DO'NIS. Worshipped in Carthage, 330

TAM'TU. Assyrian term signifying 'the deep sea,' 72

TA'NIT. Goddess of the heavens and the moon; compared with Demeter, 330; inscriptions to, 330; identified with Dido, 331

TA'NITH. Goddess, honoured at Carthage, 328

TASH'MIT. Nebo's consort, 102, 185, 186; patron of writing, 185

TAU'RUS, SIGN OF. Represented by the slaying of the celestial bull, Alu, 182

TELL AM'RAN. Mound of, 374

TEL-LÔ. Ernest de Sarzec's researches at, 355, 356

TEMPLE-S. Of Bel, 101–105, 227; of Nebo and Tashmit, 102; of Ea and Nusku, 102; of Bel and Anu, 102; of Belus, reference to, 103; of Ea, 111; of Belus, reference to, 114; of Dagon, at Ashdod and Gaza, 151; of Merodach, at Babylon, 185, 374; of Asshur, 207; of Sin, at Calah, 223; priesthood, cult and, 239–241; of Babylonia and Assyria, 242–251; oldest, in Babylonia, was E-Kur, 248; as banks, 250; begun by Esarhaddon, 305; Saggal, of Merodach, 305; Sidda, 306; of Ashtart or Ishtar, at Sidon and Askelon, 327; to Apollo, 330; Zoroastrian, 335; of Nebo, 348; of Babylon, 373–375

TE'RAH. Father of Abraham, 51, 52

TESTAMENT, OLD. Nergal mentioned in, 105; Dagon in, 151, 152; David of the, 190; poetical form of, 322

TEUTONIC. Celtic religion and, compared, 316, 317

TEXTS, CUNEIFORM. *See* Cuneiform

TEXTS, MAGICAL. Dawkina alluded to in, 197; Anu mentioned in, 197, 198; a series known as 'Maklu,' 261, 262

TEZ-CAT-LI-PO'CA. Reference to, 222

THAL-ATH. Chaldaic equivalent for Omorca, 114

THEIAS, KING. Reference to, 132

T'hom or 'DEEP.' Tiawath a parallel to the Old Testament expression, 72

THOMES. French exploration expedition and, 347

THOTH. Reference to, 185, 222, 224, 228

THUNDER-BIRD. North-American Indian conception, 193

THUNDER-GOD. Hadada, 188, 189

TI'A-MAT. Variant of Tiawath, 71

TI'AWATH. Variant, Tiamat, 71; a parallel to Old Testament expression *T'hom* (or 'deep'), 72, 73; her ill-will toward the gods of heaven, 76–78; her death by Merodach, 78, 199; the 'fish' of Jonah and, 87;

chaos, 193; slaughter of, enacted, 201; the host of, 232; not the only Babylonian monster, 289
TIG'LATH-PIL-E'SER I. Alternative, Tukulit-pal-E-saria, King of Assyria, 23; god Bel (En-lil) and, 95; Ishtar and, 212; Ninib and, 214, 216; Shamash and, 222; Merodach and, 227; Rawlinson discovers annals of, 346
TIG'LATH-PIL-E'SER II. Tales of, 299–301
TIG'LATH-PIL-E'SER III. Second Assyrian Empire commenced with, 29; conquers Babylon and is invested with the sovereignty of 'Asia,' 36
TIGRIS. The river, 206, 342
TOL'TECS. Reference to Aztecs, and, 226, 227
TONGUES. Babylonian towers and legend of confusion of, 47; legend of confusion of, found in Central America, 48; among African tribes some such myth found, 49; certain Australian and Mongolian peoples possess a similar tradition, 49
TOOTHACHE MYTH, A, 262
TOTEMISM. Signs of, in Babylonian religion, 92
TOWER OF BABEL. Legend of confusion of tongues and, 47. See Babel
TREE-S. Adonis and myrrh-, 137; Osiris and tamarisk-, 137; Attis and pine-, 137, 138; Tammuz and cedar, 138
TRIAD. See Trinity
TRIBAL DIVINITIES. The most outstanding, 94
TRINITY, A. Tiawath, Apsu, and Mummu, 74; Bel, Ea, and Anu, 97, 111, 191, 196–198; En-lil, Ea, and Anu, 121; of earth, air, and sea, 197; Ramman, Sin, and Shamash, 219; Ea, Anu, and Enlil evolved from demons, 268
TSAI'DU. The hunter; Gilgamesh, Eabani, and, 163–166

TSA'PHON. Carthaginian deity, 330
TUK-UL'TI-IN-AR-IS'TI. Son of Shalmaneser I; takes Babylon and slays its king, Bitilyasu, 22
TUK-UL'TI-NIN'IP. Son of Shalmaneser I; inscriptions of, 351
TYRE. Sidon and, in touch with Assyria, 327

U

U-BA'RA-TU-TU. Shurippak son of, 173
UB'SHU-KEN'NA (or Upshukkinaku). The 'brilliant chamber' where the sun takes his rise, 252, 253
UK'HUT. Eabani and, 129, 163; one of the sacred women of the temple of Ishtar, 163
UKK'U-MU (Seizer). Attendant hound of Merodach, 202
UNDERWORLD, THE, 125, 128–132, 136; Eabani descends into, 160; description of, in VIIth of Gilgamesh tablets, 169
UR. City from whence Abram came, a near neighbour of Eridu, colonized by Nippur, 15; fall of the dynasty, 20; Nannar, the moon-god, of, 145–149; the moon-city, 249, 251
U'RA. The legend of, 268–270
UR-A-GAL, 175
UR'BAU. Bau alluded to in inscriptions of, 144; Zikkurat built by, at Nippur, 248
UR'GA. A town in Mesopotamia; equivalents, Caramit and Diarbekr, 52
UR-GUR. King of Assyria, 359, 366
UR-NIN'IB. Reference to pavement of, 366
U'RU. Canaanitish god of light; name found in Uru-Salim, 325
URU-AZ-AG'GA. Bau's temple at, 145
UR'UK. Place, 84
URU-KAG-I'NA. Bau alluded to in inscriptions of, 144

GLOSSARY AND INDEX

UT-NAP-ISH'TIM. Variant of Noah, 116, 160; hero of Babylonian deluge myth, figures in Gilgamesh epic, 155, 158, 160; Gilgamesh's ancestor, 170–173; Gilgamesh seeks secret of perpetual life from, 173–178; the deluge myth and, 173–178

UT-UKKU. Ghost of Eabani designated, 181; an evil spirit, 276

Uz. God; worshipped under form of a goat, 93, 292

UZZ'I-EL, JONATHAN, BEN. The targum of, 267

V

VAMPIRES. Babylonian, 264–266

VAN. Lake, 331

VASH'TI. Reference to, 142; Frazer on, 143

VED'IC GODS. Reference to, 77

VEGETATION. En-lil (Bel), a god of, 96; Ishtar, 'great mother' of, 123, 137, 138, 168; seven gates of Aralu and the decay of, 137; Tammuz, a god of, 137, 138, 140; Adonis and Aphrodite connected with, 139; Ceres, a corn-mother, 139; Proserpine, same nature, 139; Osiris introduced corn into Egypt, 139; Mordecai as god of, 144; Humman an Elamite god of, 144

VE'NUS. Star; Abram and, 55; temple of, 58; Ishtar and, 124, 235

VIR'GO, SIGN OF. Ishtar and the, 182

W

WAR. Ishtar, goddess of, 127, 213, 214; -god, Ninib a, 214; -god, Ramman a, 221

WAR-KÂ. Work of Loftus at, 346, 347

WATER. Purification by, 270

WATERS OF DEATH. Gilgamesh crosses, 158, 159

WESTERGAARD. Median language and, 65

WIND, SOUTH. Adapa and the, story of, 116–121; variant, Shutu, 117

WINDOWS. None in Nebuchadrezzar's palace at Babylon, 369

WITCH. Known as *Kassaptu*, 261; -finding, 272–275; -orgies in France, 293

WIZARDS. Priestly, 260–262; known as *Kassapu*, 261

WORD OF POWER, THE. The magicians of Chaldea and, 263

WORSHIP. Of gods by gods, 77; of gods under animal forms, 92, 93; of Bel, 98–101; of Shamash, 109; of Aa, 110; of Ishtar, 124; of Dagon, 151; of Merodach, 184, 185; of Nebo, 184, 185; of Hadad, in Syria, 188; of the Sun-god in Canaan and Phœnicia, 190; of Dodo or Dod, by the side of Yahveh, 190; of Ramman, 219, 220; of Aztecs and Toltecs, 226, 227; of stars, Babylonian, 231–238; lunar, 236; moon-, 249; Semitic, and lamentations, 253; of the gazelle and goat, 292–294; of great earth-mother, 318, 319; of ancestors; Canaanites, 326; of Moloch, 328; Carthaginian, 329–332; Zoroastrian, 332–336; of fire, 335, etc.

WRITING, CUNEIFORM. Restoration of 60–67; Josaphat Barbaro and, 61; Pietro della Valle and, 61; Sir John Chardin and, 61; Niebuhr and, 61; Tychsen and, 61; Münter and, 61; Georg Grotefend, and, 62; Professor Lassen and, 63; Burnouf and, 63; Major Henry Rawlinson and, 64–66; Westergaard and, 65; Morris and, 65; Löwenstern and, 65; Hinks and, 65; Longpérier and, 66; origin of, 66, 67; on obelisk of Shalmaneser II, 343

WRITING-S. Religions, of Babylonia, 67 ; of Oannes, 113–116 ; Nebo credited, like Ea, with the invention of, 185 ; Tashmit patron of, 185 ; stars, the, of heaven, 231 ; Zarathustrian sacred, 334

X

XER'XES, KING. Reference to, 141 ; Esther, the crown-name of Jewish wife of, 143

Y

YAH'WEH. The Hebrew name of God, 49 ; worship of, by the side of Dodo, by the Israelites, 190
YAR'AN. Sargon and, 210, 211
YEAR, NEW. *See* New

Z

ZAB. The river, 207
ZAG-MU'KU (*Zak-muk*). Festival of Sacæa or, 141 ; goddess Bau and, 251
ZAK-MUK. *See* Zag-muku.
ZA'MAMA. Court of Ishtar and, 101
ZA-RA-THUS'TRA. *See* Zoroaster
ZAR-PA-NI'TUM. Goddess, wife of Merodach, 186, 202 ; Ealur amalgamated with, 186
ZECH-A-RI'AH. Allusion of, to Hadad-Rimmon, 189
ZED-EK-I'AH. King of Jerusalem ; Nebuchadrezzar and, 37
ZEUS. Reference to, 132, 315
ZIG-A-RUN. Variant of Apsu, 72
ZIK-KU-RAT-S. Staged towers ; described, 242, 246 ; of Assurbani-pal, 365
ZI'RAT-BA'NIT. The seat of, 306
ZIS-U'THROS, KING. Berossus substitutes, for Ut-Napishtim, 177, 178
ZO'DIAC. Signs of the, in the Babylonian astrological system, 183, 231, 232 ; the goat, one of the signs of the, 292
ZOG-A'NES. The, of the Sacæa, 142
ZOR-O-AS'TER. The religion of, 332– ; earliest form of name Zarathustra, 333 ; a Mede, 333 ; good and evil principles of religion of, 334
ZU. The storm-god ; retained a bird-like form, 93, 193–195 ; legend of, 193–195
ZU-BIRD. The bird roc, in *Arabian Nights*, a possible descendant of, 193